Life-Span Development and Behavior

VOLUME 2

Edited by

Paul B. Baltes

College of Human Development
The Pennsylvania State University
University Park, Pennsylvania

and

Orville G. Brim, Jr.

Foundation for Child Development
New York, New York

Academic Press

New York   San Francisco   London   1979

A Subsidiary of Harcourt Brace Jovanovich, Publishers

ACADEMIC PRESS, INC.
111 Fifth Avenue, New York, New York 10003

United Kingdom Edition published by
ACADEMIC PRESS, INC. (LONDON) LTD.
24/28 Oval Road, London NW1 7DX

LIBRARY OF CONGRESS CATALOG CARD NUMBER: 77–0531

ISBN 0–12–431802–9

PRINTED IN THE UNITED STATES OF AMERICA

79 80 81 82   9 8 7 6 5 4 3 2 1

Contents

Historical Change in Life Patterns and Personality

Glen H. Elder, Jr.

Family Development Theory and Life-Span Development

Reuben Hill and Paul Mattessich

**Dialectics, History, and Development: The Historical Roots of the
Individual–Society Dialectic**

Allan R. Buss

List of Contributors

Numbers in parentheses indicate the pages on which the authors' contributions begin.

Paul B. Baltes (255),* College of Human Development, The Pennsylvania State University, University Park, Pennsylvania 16802

Allan R. Buss (313), Department of Psychology, The University of Calgary, Calgary, T2N IN4 Canada

Nancy W. Denney (37), Department of Psychology, University of Kansas, Lawrence, Kansas 66044

Glen H. Elder, Jr. (117), Center for the Study of Youth Development, Boys Town, Omaha, Nebraska 68010

Reuben Hill (161), Department of Sociology and Family Study Center, University of Minnesota, Minneapolis, Minnesota 55455

David F. Hultsch (1), College of Human Development, Pennsylvania State University, University Park, Pennsylvania 16802

Paul Mattessich (161), Family Study Center, University of Minnesota, Minneapolis, Minnesota 55455

Judy K. Plemons (1), College of Human Development, The Pennsylvania State University, University Park, Pennsylvania 16802

Guenther Reinert (205), Department of Psychology, University of Trier, Trier, West Germany

K. Warner Schaie (67), Andrus Gerontology Center and Department of Psychology, University of Southern California, Los Angeles, California 90007

Hans Thomae (281), Psychologisches Institut, University of Bonn, Bonn, West Germany

* Present address: Center for Advanced Study in the Behavioral Sciences, Stanford, California 94305.

Preface

This is the second volume of a new annual serial publication. *Life-Span Development and Behavior* is aimed at reviewing life-span research and theory in the behavioral and social sciences, with a particular focus on contributions by psychologists and sociologists. In order to permit a multidisciplinary and pluralistic approach to the study of development and behavior, we will emphasize no specific theoretical view or paradigm. In fact, the contents of this volume provide a clear illustration of the wide scope of interests that life-span researchers display. It is also becoming increasingly evident that the life-span approach is not a specific theory or collection of specific theories, but a general orientation to the study of behavior. The orientation expressed in a life-span, life-course, or life-cycle framework is a fairly simple one. It suggests that behavior develops throughout life (from conception to death) and, moreover, that developmental processes, whatever their age location, can be better understood if they are seen in the context of the entire lifetime of individuals. A life-span orientation easily points to another perspective that characterizes much current work in the field. Because life-span development occurs over extended periods of time, life-span research gives much attention to the interplay between biocultural (social) change and individual–ontogenetic development.

The editors are making little attempt to organize each volume around a particular topic or theme. Rather, they solicit manuscripts from investigators who are either conducting programmatic research on current problems or are interested in refining particular theoretical positions. Occasionally, authors are invited to identify new areas of concern worthy of theoretical articulation or exploration. At present, there are also some immediate guidelines for selecting prospective contributors. As editors, we are committed to introducing a stronger dose of empirical work into the life-span arena than has been true for the germination period of the field. In addition, we are interested in strengthening the connections between neighboring disciplines. For example, a life-span view is being explored and elucidated in a number of disciplines outside psychology and sociology, such as in anthropology, biology, economics, and history. We are persuaded that it is worthwhile to capitalize on this conjoint development in several disciplines and to offer the present series as a forum for such interdisciplinary explorations and dialogues. We hope that forthcoming publications of the series will reflect these editorial perspectives with more clarity than might be true of the first two volumes.

The editors wish to acknowledge with gratitude and respect the contribution of several colleagues who assisted in making the volume what it is. They deserve much of the credit and none of the blame. In addition to the wise counsel of our advisory editors, a number of ad hoc reviewers (Peter M. Bentler, Carlfred B. Broderick, Steven W. Cornelius, Bruce Dohrenwend, Kenneth J. Gergen, Irene M. Hulicka, David F. Hultsch, Lloyd G. Humphreys, Douglas Kimmel, Roy Lachman, Richard M. Lerner, John A. Meacham, Vincent Morello, Marion Perlmutter, Leon Rappoport, Hayne W. Reese, David F. Ricks, Carol D. Ryff, Ellen Skinner, Graham Spanier, and Read D. Tuddenham) provided valuable comments to the contributors before final chapters were prepared. In her dual role as reviewer and bibliographic taskmaster, Ellen Skinner, our chief editorial assistant, was particularly helpful. We also thank Jackie Unch and Diane Bernd for their able secretarial assistance. Finally, Paul B. Baltes would like to express his gratitude both to his home institution, The Pennsylvania State University, and to the Center for Advanced Study in the Behavioral Sciences, Stanford, California. Both institutions have been generous in their administrative and collegial support for this publication.

PAUL B. BALTES
ORVILLE G. BRIM, JR.

Contents of Volume 1

Life Events and Life-Span Development

David F. Hultsch and Judy K. Plemons

COLLEGE OF HUMAN DEVELOPMENT
THE PENNSYLVANIA STATE UNIVERSITY
UNIVERSITY PARK, PENNSYLVANIA

Abstract

It is argued in this chapter that examination of life events must consider the basic metamodels within which theory and research are articulated. In our view, most research on life events has been rooted in two distinct metamodels—the organismic and the mechanistic. Current life event approaches are examined in light of the metamodel from which they are derived. It is concluded that developmental perspectives on life events have typically been rooted in the organismic metamodel. Thus, an attempt is made in the present chapter to delineate a life-span developmental perspective on life events consistent with the mechanistic approach. The primary goal in developing this explanatory model is to provide a general framework within which a broad range of life events, mediating variables, and developmental outcomes can be viewed.

I. Introduction

The concepts of stress and adaptation have been approached from a variety of perspectives (Coelho, Hamburg, & Adams, 1974; Datan &

1

Ginsberg, 1975; Dodge & Martin, 1970; Dohrenwend & Dohrenwend, 1974b; Holmes & Rahe, 1967; Janis, 1958; Lazarus, 1966; Levine & Scotch, 1970; Lowenthal, Thurnher, & Chiriboga, 1975; Selye, 1956). Within the context of this broad literature, some writers (Datan & Ginsberg, 1975; Dohrenwend & Dohrenwend, 1974b; Holmes & Rahe, 1967; Lowenthal, Thurnher, & Chiriboga, 1975) have focused specifically on a set of stimuli which have been labeled "life events," and include such experiences as marriage, birth of a child, divorce, and death of a family member. Generally, life events are viewed as stressful and disruptive of customary behavior patterns. As such, they are hypothesized to be related to the adaptation of the individual in various ways. However, beyond such generic points of agreement, there is considerable diversity in approach to the construct of life events. For example, some researchers define life events as objective, external occurrences, while others define them as subjective, internal transitions.

Historically, such diversity is apparent even in early investigations of life events. On the one hand, Meyer (1951) encouraged a tradition of focusing on objective events, such as changes of habitat, entrance into or graduation from school, births or deaths in the family, and "other fundamentally important environmental incidents" (p. 53). He recorded such life events and incidents of physical illness on a life chart and examined these data for relationships between the two sets of variables. Based on this research, Meyer (1951) argued that life events may be important in the etiology of various physical disorders. On the other hand, Bühler (1951, 1953, 1962) encouraged a tradition of focusing on life transitions which involve complex inner states. Based on the life histories of elderly persons, she divided the life span into five periods and identified two broad sets of events—the biological and the biographical—which wax and wane over the life span. At a later date, Bühler defined a set of life tendencies including need satisfaction, adaptive self-limitation, creative expansion, establishment of inner order, and self-fulfillment. In a paper published in 1962, Bühler combined these concepts and proposed a set of 10 phases or transitions which occur over the course of the life cycle.

Developing from such diverse antecedents, research on life events has grown exponentially. Investigators have examined the relationship of life events to physical illness in general (Hinkle, 1974; Holmes & Masuda, 1974; Rahe, McKean, & Arthur, 1967; Thurlow, 1971), to specific types of physical illness (Antonovsky & Kats, 1967; Theorell, 1974), to psychiatric disorders (Brown & Birley, 1968; Hudgens, Morrison, & Barchha, 1967), to psychological symptoms (Dohrenwend, 1973b; Myers, Lindenthal, & Pepper, 1974), to self-assessed status (Antonovsky, 1974), and to life transitions (Lowenthal & Chiriboga, 1973; Lowenthal, Thurnher, &

Chiriboga, 1975). Researchers have also focused on specific events, such as combat (Grinker & Spiegel, 1963; Star, 1949), natural disasters (Fritz & Marks, 1954), entrance into school (Kellam & Schiff, 1967; Kellam, Branch, Agrawal, & Ensminger, 1975; Lindemann & Ross, 1955), marriage (Raush, Goodrich, & Campbell, 1963), parenthood (Gutmann, 1975), widowhood (Lopata, 1975), personal death (Kastenbaum, 1975), migration (Levine, 1966), and institutionalization (Lieberman, 1975).

Given this diversity, the use of the term "life events" is somewhat hazardous. The confusion is due, in part, to a lack of examination of the basic metamodels underlying the various approaches. As Reese and Overton (1970) have pointed out, such models are representations of reality which are not empirically testable. Nevertheless, they define the basic parameters of theory and research, such as the nature of the questions to be asked and the truth criteria to be applied.

In our view, most research on life events has been rooted in two distinct metamodels—the organismic and the mechanistic. On the one hand, the bulk of the research focusing on subjective, internal events and their role in life transitions has been rooted in the organismic metamodel. Typically, this research has been developmental in nature. On the other hand, the bulk of the research focusing on objective, external events and their role in specific outcomes has been rooted in the mechanistic metamodel. Typically, this research has been nondevelopmental in nature. Since the differences between metamodels cannot be reconciled (Kuhn, 1962; Pepper, 1942; Reese & Overton, 1970), the failure to specify these different roots has led to considerable confusion.

The purpose of this chapter is to summarize these two perspectives on life events and to propose a life-span developmental approach which is rooted in the mechanistic metamodel. As such, the emphasis will be on objective, external events and the identification of these events as antecedents to specific outcomes. The development of such a perspective leads quite logically to the examination of a series of issues: (a) a summary of the organismic and mechanistic metamodels of development; (b) a review of current approaches to life events derived from these two metamodels; and (c) an outline of a life-span developmental approach to life events.

II. Metamodels of Development

A model is a representation of reality rather than a description of reality (Lachman, 1963; Overton & Reese, 1973; Reese & Overton, 1970). As such, it functions as a metaphor. In addition, there are several levels of models arranged along a continuum from the highly specific to the highly general. The latter are of particular importance to our present discussion since they determine the basic parameters of theory and research. This determinism extends from the metaphysical and epistemological levels, through theoretical constructs (Pepper, 1942; Reese & Overton, 1970), to the manner in which we draw inferences from empirical data (Hultsch & Hickey, 1978; Overton & Reese, 1973).

There is only a small number of basic metaphysical and epistemological models which define the essence of human beings and their encompassing world. As summarized by Reese and Overton (1970), these models have been "variously designated as 'paradigms' (Kuhn, 1962), 'presuppositions' (Pap, 1949), 'world-views' (Kuhn, 1962; Seeger, 1954), and 'world hypotheses' (Pepper, 1942)" (p. 117). Such models are independent and mutually exclusive, and they denote a certain logical rigor in their approaches to the formulation of theory and method. The value of models is specifically found in their usefulness rather than in the extent to which they can be found to be "true."

Detailed discussions of the metamodels salient for the study of human development have been presented elsewhere (Cassirer, 1951; Matson, 1964; Overton & Reese, 1973; Pepper, 1942; Reese & Overton, 1970; Schon, 1963). The following constitutes a brief summary of these metamodels, designed to illustrate central themes. Wherever clarification or supporting argument is needed, the reader is referred to the references noted above.

A. MECHANISM

The mechanistic model derives its constructs from the concept of a machine. Within this model, the world is defined as a universal machine composed of many discrete parts which move through time and space according to basic laws. As Pepper (1942) has noted, there are different kinds of mechanistic models analogous to machines of varying levels and degrees of sophistication; however, the basic principles and theoretical constructs are the same. Within the mechanistic view, the human organism is reactive from a basic state of rest. Activity is a result of external stimulation. Although changes in the organism may appear to be qualitative, all changes are truly quantitative. Complex activities, such as problem solving and affect, are viewed as ultimately reducible to simple phenomena governed by efficient causes (Overton & Reese, 1973). A mechanistic model of development, then, is reducible to an analysis of various elements within a context of reaction to explicit causes.

B. ORGANICISM

The organismic model, on the other hand, is living and active, deriving its meaning from its organic wholeness. Moreover, the components of the model assume additional significance from their connotations as parts of an organized total. Within the organismic view, the human organism is an active totality. Determining principles of organization, rather than studying component parts, becomes the fundamental inquiry; and synthesis replaces analysis as the general level of methodology. Moreover, qualitative change becomes possible in an active organism model, where the component parts as well as their organizational structure change both qualitatively and quantitatively. Although efficient causes may have some effect on various qualitative and quantitative changes in the organism, fundamental causation is teleological in nature (Overton & Reese, 1973).

Thus, the mechanistic model stresses the analysis of elements and the discovery of antecedent–consequent relations. As a result, development is seen as consisting of behavior change and is continuous in that later behaviors are reducible to or predictable from previous antecedents. On the other hand, the organismic model stresses the synthesis of organized complexities and the construction of structure–function relations. As a result, development is seen as consisting of structural change and is discontinuous in that later states are not reducible to or predictable from previous states.

It should also be noted that additional metamodels or potential classifications of metamodels (Pepper, 1942; Riegel, 1972) are possible. For example, Pepper (1942) posits a world hypothesis labeled "contextualism" in which the root metaphor is the historic event. In the present context, however, the mechanistic–organismic distinction seems to be particularly useful, since there appear to be two separate traditions of research on life events rooted in these metamodels. In the next section we briefly summarize these traditions.

III. Current Approaches to Life Events

A. ORGANISMIC PERSPECTIVES

One set of perspectives on life events is consistent with the organismic metamodel. Typically, these approaches describe a sequence of psychosocial stages occurring over the life cycle. Historically, as we have noted, this tradition is consistent with Bühler's (1951, 1953, 1962) work.

Probably the most widely know examples of the approach are Erikson's (1950, 1963) eight stages of man and Havighurst's (1952, 1972) developmental tasks. More recently, Levinson, Darrow, Klein, Levinson, and McKee (1974) have proposed a sequence of five eras and related periods which span the adult life cycle. Other approaches consistent with the organismic metamodel according to Looft (1973) include those of Kohlberg (1969), Loevinger (1969), and Neugarten (1969). In this section, we summarize Levinson's theory to illustrate the organismic perspective on life events.

Levinson and his colleagues have proposed a developmental theory of psychosocial periods during adulthood based on a biographical, longitudinal study of 40 men (Levinson, 1977a, 1977b; Levinson, Darrow, Klein, Levinson, & McKee, 1974, 1976). Levinson has focused on constructing universal sequences which underlie the unique and diverse individual biographies of the subjects. Based on this research, Levinson has identified five eras within the life span, each of roughly 20 years' duration. These are not stages of biological, psychological, or social development but represent a life cycle macrostructure. The eras are (1) preadulthood, age 0–20; (2) early adulthood, age 20–40; (3) middle adulthood, age 40–60; (4) late adulthood, age 60–80; and (5) late late adulthood, age 80+. The evolution of these eras is structured by a series of developmental periods and transitions. The primary task of the stable periods is to build a life structure. This involves making certain crucial choices and striving to attain particular goals. Stable periods ordinarily last 6–8 years. The primary task of the transition periods is to terminate the existing life structure and initiate a new one. This involves a reappraisal of the current structure, exploration of new possibilities for change, and a movement toward crucial choices that will provide the basis for a new life structure. Transition periods ordinarily last 4–5 years.

To date, Levinson's research has focused on the periods within early adulthood (20–40) and middle adulthood (40–60). Within these eras, Levinson *et al.* (1974, 1976) have identified the following periods.

Early Adult Transition.   This transition ordinarily begins at age 17–18 and extends until age 22–23. The early adult transition represents a developmental link between preadulthood and early adulthood. It involves modifying relationships with the family and other persons, groups, and institutions significant to the preadult era. At the same time, it involves making initial explorations and choices within the adult world. Events within this transition may include graduation from high school, entrance into college, and moving out of the family home.

Getting into the Adult World.   This period ordinarily begins in the early 20s and extends until the late 20s. The focus of the period is on exploration and provisional commitment to adult roles and responsibilities. Examples of events which are often crucial during this period are marriage and occupational choice. According to Levinson *et al.* (1976), many men develop this initial structure within the context of a "dream." This consists of a vision of the future, usually involving a major achievement and articulated within an occupational context.

Age 30 Transition. The age range 28–33 represents a transition period between getting into the adult world and the next period. This transition provides an opportunity to modify the provisional adult life structure created earlier. According to Levinson *et al.* (1976), it "may occasion considerable turmoil, confusion, and struggle with the environment and within oneself; or it may involve a more quiet reassessment and intensification of effort. But it is marked by important changes in life structure and internal commitments" (p. 23). Levinson notes that events such as divorce and occupational changes peak at this point.

Settling Down. This period ordinarily begins in the early 30s and extends until the late 30s. As implied in the name, this period emphasizes stability and security. The individual makes deeper commitments to his occupation, family, or whatever enterprises are significant to him. In addition, there is an emphasis on what Levinson calls "making it." This involves long range planning toward specific goals within the context of a timetable for their achievement—an effort which Levinson labels a personal enterprise.

During the last years of the settling down period there is a distinctive phase which Levinson has designated becoming one's own man. This phase ordinarily occurs at age 35–39. The major developmental task of this phase is to achieve a greater measure of independence and authority in connection with the goals of the various personal enterprises. As Levinson *et al.* (1976) note, "a key element in this period is the man's feeling that, no matter what he has accomplished to date, he is not sufficiently his own man. He feels overly dependent upon and constrained by persons or groups who have authority over him or who, for various reasons, exert great influence on him" (p. 23). During this phase there is an emphasis on affirmation by society. Levinson reports that most of his subjects fix on a key event such as a promotion or new job as representative of ultimate affirmation or devaluation by society.

Midlife Transition. This transition spans a period of from 4 to 6 years, reaching a peak in the early 40s. The midlife transition represents a developmental link between two eras of the life cycle—early adulthood and middle adulthood. It represents a beginning and ending, a meeting of past and future. The transition may be relatively smooth or involve considerable turmoil. However, this outcome is not dependent on a man's previous success or failure in achieving goals. "The issue, rather, is what to do with the experience of disparity between what he has gained in an inner sense from living with a particular structure and what he wants for himself" (Levinson *et al.*, 1974, p. 24). According to Levinson (1977a, 1977b), the transition is not prompted by any one event or series of events. Rather, multiple processes are involved, including the reality and experience of bodily decline, changing relations among the various generations, and the evolution of career and other enterprises. As the midlife transition ends, there is a new period of stability. A new life structure emerges which provides the basis for living in middle adulthood.

The midlife transition is the last specific period which Levinson identifies since the men in his longitudinal sample are currently 35–45 years of age. However, other periods would be expected to characterize middle, late, and late late adulthood.

In our view, Levinson's theory is rooted in the organismic metamodel. In considering these roots we will briefly review five emphases characteristic of the organismic model in relation to the theory: the emphasis on holism, structure–function relations, structural change, discontinuity of development, and universality. For additional discussion of these issues see Overton and Reese (1973) and Reese and Overton (1970).

First, Levinson's theory sees development as consisting of an organized totality rather than discrete elements. The focus is on parts in reciprocal interaction with one another such that the parts derive their meaning from the whole. Levinson's concept of the life structure refers to "self-in-world" and requires consideration of both these elements and the transactions between them. More specifically, the organized totality involves three aspects (Levinson, 1977a): (a) the sociocultural world, including structures (class, family, occupational, political) and historical events (war, economic depression—prosperity); (b) participation in this world, including roles (husband, friend, worker, parent) and events related to these roles (marriage, birth of a child, promotion, retirement); and (c) aspects of the self that are expressed or suppressed.

Second, Levinson's theory emphasizes structure–function relationships rather than antecedent–consequent relationships. The major explanatory task is to define functions or goals and the structures which serve them. In Levinson's framework, the various developmental tasks of the periods constitute a set of functions, and these are served by the various life structures. The concept of structure–function leads to a deemphasis on the discovery of "causes" except in the most generic sense. Indeed, once the structure–function relations are described the explanatory task is completed. Thus, Levinson does not perceive historical or life events as causes but as integral components of the organized complexity.

Third, Levinson's theory focuses on structural change rather than response change. While the behavior of an individual changes over time, it is the change in life structure which provides the explanation of development. For Levinson, examination of events, such as marriage, divorce, birth of a child, and retirement, or characteristics, such as anxiety, introversion, or ego strength, can only yield diverse biographies. Structural change, or "life as it evolves," must be examined. Within the context of structural change, the organismic model assumes change is goal directed. This is clearly a teleological concept in that it attributes purpose to the organism. While Levinson does not explicitly clarify the goal aspect of his theory, purpose is implied. He suggests that there is at least the potential for an optimum developmental sequence and notes that failure to make certain transitions results in developmental dysfunctions. For example, Levinson hypothesizes that if a man does not make significant progress toward settling down by age 34, the chances of developing a satisfying life structure are small. He also notes that many men who do not have a significant midlife crisis are unable to continue developing in later adulthood.

Fourth, Levinson's theory emphasizes the discontinuity of development rather than the continuity of development. Changes in the life structure represent qualitative change. The new properties are emergent in the sense that they are not reducible to previous events. Thus, there is a basic discontinuity between the various periods, although they are clearly linked. It is this discontinuity which makes the periods or stages theoretically powerful rather than trivial (Reese & Overton, 1970). Unlike some organismic theories, Levinson does emphasize periods of transition as well as periods of stability.

Finally, Levinson's theory emphasizes universality rather than relativity. He does note that the sequence of periods is descriptive of males, and that a different sequence may be descriptive of females. He also notes that the sequence may change over historical time. However, the emphasis on universality is clearly there. Levinson (1977b) suggests the sequence is grounded in the nature of humanity and human society and has characterized the male life cycle for the past several thousand years.

B. MECHANISTIC PERSPECTIVES

A second set of perspectives on life events is consistent with the mechanistic metamodel. These approaches typically focus on the role of events as antecedents to various response outcomes. Historically, as we have noted, this tradition is consistent with Meyer's (1951) research on life events and physical illness. More recently, the work of Antonovsky

(Antonovsky, 1974; Antonovsky & Kats, 1967), Brown (Brown, 1974; Brown & Birley, 1968; Brown, Sklair, Harris, & Birley, 1973), Dohrenwend and Dohrenwend (B. P. Dohrenwend, 1961, 1974; B. S. Dohrenwend, 1973a, 1973b; Dohrenwend & Dohrenwend, 1977), Hinkle (Hinkle, 1974), and Holmes (Holmes & Masuda, 1974; Holmes & Rahe, 1967) is reflective of this metamodel. To date, most of this research has been nondevelopmental in nature. In this section, we summarize a portion of the Dohrenwends' research in order to illustrate a mechanistic perspective on life events.

Dohrenwend (1961) presents a model for the conceptualization of life events based on Selye's (1956) general paradigm of the stress response. The model contains four main elements: a set of antecedent stressors, a set of mediating factors, a social-psychological adaptation syndrome, and consequent adaptive or maladaptive responses.

Within the context of this model, life events, including both those that are typically positive (e.g., marriage) and those that are typically negative (e.g., divorce), are seen as potential stressors. Mediating factors include both inner resources (e.g., intellectual abilities, physical health) and external resources (e.g., income, social support from others). Social-psychological adaptation involves changes in affect (e.g., fear, anger), changes in orientation (e.g., beliefs), and change in activity (e.g., increasing, decreasing, adding, abandoning). These processes may lead to either functional or dysfunctional outcomes.

The Dohrenwends have attempted to articulate this model in an extensive research program (B. P. Dohrenwend, 1961, 1974; B. S. Dohrenwend, 1970, 1973a, 1973b, 1977; Dohrenwend & Dohrenwend, 1972, 1974a, 1977). The reader is directed to these references for a more complete description of their work. The following constitutes only a brief summary of an empirical study to illustrate application of the model. Dohrenwend (1973b) examined the relationship of life events to social status and psychological symptoms. In particular, she hypothesized that women, disadvantaged ethnic groups, and members of the lower class are exposed to more stressful life events than men, advantaged ethnic groups, or members of higher classes. Further, it was hypothesized that the exposure of lower status persons to stressful life events explains, in part, their relatively higher levels of psychological distress.

A total of 257 men and women of varying class and ethnic background responded to an open-ended question and a checklist on life events. These data were used to compute indices of the magnitude of life change involved in the events and the levels of responsibility for the event (e.g., controlled, influenced, or not controlled by the respondent). The respondents also completed a measure of psychological symptoms.

Dohrenwend (1973b) reports that life change scores and psychological symptom scores were positively correlated (+ .35). However, a major issue is whether such a relationship is obtained because stressful life events produce psychological symptoms, or because persons with psychological problems tend to create stressful life events. In order to examine this issue, Dohrenwend computed separately the correlation for life events not controlled by the respondents. According to Dohrenwend (1973b), if persons with psychological problems tend to create stressful life events, this correlation should be lower than the correlation for all life events. However, in the present instance, the correlations were of the same magnitude, suggesting that stressful life events are antecedent to psychological symptoms. Using this approach, Dohrenwend (1973b) concluded that women and members of the lower class are exposed to a higher rate of life change than men or members of the upper classes. Further, in both cases, the evidence suggested that this instability was a factor in producing the relatively high levels of psychological distress reported by the lower status individuals. In contrast to women and members of the lower class, disadvantaged ethnic groups did not experience a higher rate of life change than advantaged ethnic groups.

In our view, the Dohrenwends' research is rooted in a mechanistic metamodel. We will briefly review five characteristics of the mechanistic model in relation to the research: the emphasis on elementarism, antecedent–consequent relations, behavior change, continuity of development, and relativism.

First, Dohrenwend's model sees behavior as consisting of discrete elements rather than an organized complexity. The focus is on parts and their combination, such that the whole derives its meaning from the parts. Life events and mediating factors are seen as elements which combine in additive and linear fashion to produce outcomes. Within this framework, complete prediction is possible, in principle, given knowledge of the elements and the way in which they combine.

Second, Dohrenwend's model emphasizes antecedent–consequent relationships rather than structure–function relationships. The major explanatory task is to isolate causes which produce certain effects. In this approach, life events are seen as potential antecedents or causes. The goal of research is to articulate the role that such events play as antecedents to particular outcomes, such as physical illness or psychopathology. Intervening between antecedent and consequence is a process. This hypothetical construct provides an explanatory framework. In Dohrenwend's model, the hypothetical construct is the social-psychological adaptation process. No inherent functions or goals are assumed as in the organismic model.

Third, Dohrenwend's model focuses on behavioral change rather than structural change. The emphasis is on specific, observable behaviors. As we have noted, changes in behavior are determined by specific antecedents. This means that response changes, whether within the context of several hours or several years, occur as a result of specific internal or external physical causes. In this context, Dohrenwend's research has focused largely on concurrent antecedents and, thus, is essentially nondevelopmental.

Fourth, Dohrenwend's model emphasizes the continuity of behavior change rather than the discontinuity of behavior change. Changes are seen as strictly continuous in the sense of being reducible to or predictable from earlier states. Apparent novel behaviors are actually a result of antecedent events. As we have noted, Dohrenwend's model is essentially nondevelopmental in nature, focusing on concurrent events and making no distinctions as a function of age or any other developmental variable. However, a developmental extension of the model would emphasize the concept of continuous rather than discontinuous development.

Finally, Dohrenwend's model emphasizes the relativity of behavior rather than the universality of behavior. There is no concept of a universal response to life events. Rather, responses vary depending on a variety of mediating variables. As a result, there is considerable emphasis on individual differences within the model.

C. SUMMARY

Within the organismic model, development is seen as consisting of an organized complexity. The major task of research is the explication of structure–function relations. Development involves structural change and is discontinuous in that it is, in principle, not completely reducible to or predictable from previous structures. Thus, development is goal directed. Generally, there is an emphasis on universal sequences rather than on individual differences. From this perspective, life events are seen as components of the organized complexity rather than as specific causes. Events are important, but examination of them as such will not explain development. One must focus on the underlying structure to which life events contribute.

Within the mechanistic model, development is seen as consisting of discrete elements. The major task of research is the explication of antecedent–consequent relations. Development involves behavior change and is continuous in that it is, in principle, completely reducible to or predictable from previous antecedents. Generally, there is an emphasis on individual differences rather than on universal sequences. From this perspective, life events are seen as specific causes of specific outcomes. The task is to identify these cause–effect relations and the variables which mediate or interact with them.

As we have noted, there are additional metamodels from which other approaches to life events may be derived. For example, Riegel (1975) has presented a dialectical approach to life crises which may be viewed as rooted in contextualism (Pepper, 1942). Beyond this, some writers have attempted to develop eclectic positions which combine elements of the various metamodels. For example, Lowenthal (1971) indicates that her approach falls midway between what she refers to as the "jigsaw puzzle" and "developmental stage" models. However, as Reese and Overton (1970) have noted, such eclecticism is suspect since the various metamodels are irreconcilable. Different metamodels involve different criteria for determining the truth of propositions. Therefore, an eclectic view leads to confusion (Kuhn, 1962; Pepper, 1942; Reese & Overton, 1970).

If the various models represent mutually incompatible belief systems, then which one should be chosen? A corollary of the incompatibility argument is that one position will eventually prove to be more useful and will be retained while the others are discarded. Kuhn (1962) describes this as a process of scientific revolution. On this point, Lerner and Ryff (1978) have argued that the multiple and interdependent change processes characteristic of human ontogenetic and historical development can be described only through conceptual and empirical pluralism. Such pluralism is seen as a hallmark of the life-span developmental perspective. Thus, we suggest that while the different metamodels lead to different interpretations of life events, both should be retained and applied. The contrasting perspectives obtained from the use of multiple approaches will provide a more comprehensive understanding of human development than the use of any single approach. Indeed, it is this conviction which has led us to focus on the mechanistic perspective in the present chapter. As we have noted previously, developmentally oriented treatments of the life event construct have most often been rooted in the organismic model (Bühler, 1951, 1953, 1962; Erikson, 1950, 1963; Havighurst, 1952, 1972; Levinson *et al.*, 1974, 1976) or the contextualistic model (Riegel, 1975). These approaches have been extremely useful to our understanding of human development. However, in our view, a life-span developmental perspective rooted in the mechanistic model will provide a useful contrast to these perspectives. Present conceptualizations on life events rooted in this perspective either have been nondevelopmental (Dohrenwend & Dohrenwend, 1977) or have focused on a particular event (Ahammer, 1973) or segment of the life span (Lieberman, 1975).

IV.   Life Events: A Life-Span Developmental Perspective

Three major antecedent systems that influence behavioral development are specified by Baltes, Cornelius, and Nesselroade (1979, and this volume)—ontogenetic age-graded influences, evolutionary history-graded influences, and nonnormative influences. This latter set of influences, which are graded by neither age nor history in any systematic fashion, consist of various period-specific or "significant" life events.

In this section, we outline a life-span developmental perspective on life events consistent with the mechanistic metamodel. This section is organized into a review of a generic developmental orientation and the construction of a conceptual framework for the study of life events across the life span.

A.   A LIFE-SPAN DEVELOPMENTAL ORIENTATION

As we have noted, the focus of the mechanistic metamodel is behavior change. Such behavior change is assumed to be continuous in that new behavior is reducible to or predictable from previous states. Thus, the explanatory task of this perspective is the specification of antecedent–consequent relations. Baltes and his colleagues (Baltes, 1973; Baltes & Schaie, 1973; Baltes & Willis, 1977) have proposed a generic developmental orientation consistent with these basic assumptions. Their approach is reproduced in Fig. 1. This model suggests that antecedent–consequent relations are organized around three elements: stimulus variables (S), organismic variables (O), and response variables (R). It is proposed that each of these elements (S, O, R) may function as antecedents. However, consistent with the mechanistic metamodel, the consequent is always a behavior (R).

In terms of a developmental time sequence, such antecedent–consequent relations may be either concurrent or historical in time. On the one hand, concurrent explanations focus on antecedents or combinations of antecedents which are proximal in time to the phenomenon to be explained. On the other hand, historical explanations focus on antecedents or combinations of antecedents which are distal in time to the phenomenon to be explained. Of course, this distinction is arbitrary, and definitions of proximal and distal may vary. Nevertheless, the distinction is useful. If developmental phenomena are accounted for solely by concurrent antecedents, then a life-span orientation is not particularly exciting (Baltes & Schaie, 1973).

Within this framework, the model sees change as a function of time-related interactions between stimulus, organismic, and response vari-

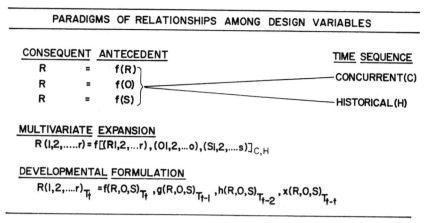

PARADIGMS OF RELATIONSHIPS AMONG DESIGN VARIABLES

CONSEQUENT   ANTECEDENT   TIME SEQUENCE

$R \quad = \quad f(R)$

$R \quad = \quad f(O)$ ———————————— CONCURRENT(C)

$R \quad = \quad f(S)$ ———————————— HISTORICAL(H)

MULTIVARIATE EXPANSION

$R(1,2,.....r) = f[(R1,2,...r),(O1,2,...o),(S1,2,....s)]_{C,H}$

DEVELOPMENTAL FORMULATION

$R(1,2,....r)_{T_t} = f(R,O,S)_{T_t}, g(R,O,S)_{T_{t-1}}, h(R,O,S)_{T_{t-2}}, x(R,O,S)_{T_{t-t}}$

Fig. 1. Prototypical paradigms and relationships among design variables in psychological and development research. See text for explanation of symbols. (From "Handbook of the Psychology of Aging," edited by James E. Birren and K. Warner Schaie. © 1977 by Litton Educational Publishing, Inc. Reprinted by permission of Van Nostrand Reinhold Company.)

ables. Such interactions define the behavior of individuals and interindividual differences at any given point in time. Further, the model emphasizes change in both the antecedent and the consequent side of the paradigm. Thus, either the same or a different set of antecedents, or causal functions, may exist at different points in time. First, different antecedents (S, O, R) may operate at different points in the behavior change process. Second, the nature of the functional relationships (f, g, h) between antecedents and consequents may vary at different points in the behavior change process.

Thus, the focus of Baltes' model is on the explanation of time-ordered but potentially changing systems of antecedent–consequent relations. It is this patterned accumulation of effects which produces intraindividual change and interindividual differences in intraindividual change.

B. AN EXPLANATORY MODEL OF LIFE EVENTS

In the following section the developmental orientation outlined above is translated into an explanatory model focused on life events over the life span. Figure 2 provides an overview of the framework. The primary goal in delineating this model is to provide a general framework within which a broad range of life events, mediating variables, and developmental outcomes can be viewed. To accomplish this goal, it is necessary to em-

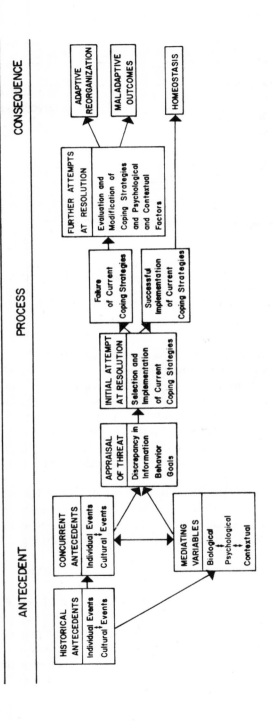

Fig. 2. An explanatory model of life events.

phasize a macrolevel, sociological perspective as well as a more molecular, psychological perspective. The utility of such an overall framework lies in drawing attention to the general areas upon which we need to focus regardless of the particular event with which we are concerned. Within these general areas, the examination of specific variables will depend primarily on the particular event or events selected for study.

An additional goal is to suggest how the general areas delineated within this explanatory model of life events may interact with the other two major antecedent systems that influence development, namely, ontogenetic, age-graded influences and evolutionary, history-graded influences. Thus, the present model, while focusing on life events, recognizes the importance of viewing them within a multitheoretical context.

1. Life Event Antecedents

a. Definition of Life Events. In the broadest sense, an event is a noteworthy occurrence. Attempts at more specific definition have led to a focus on the "stressful, critical, or significant" aspects of life events. For example, Holmes and Rahe (1967) define stressful life events as those "whose advent is either indicative or requires a significant change in the ongoing life pattern of the individual" (p. 217). Myers, Lindenthal, Pepper, and Ostrander (1972) focus on "experiences involving a role transformation, changes in status or environment, or impositions of pain" (p. 399). Antonovsky and Kats (1967) refer to "life crises" as "objective situations which on the face of it would seem to be universally stressful" involving "an experience which either imposed pain or necessitated a role transformation" (p. 16). These definitions have in common the fact that a life event involves a change in the individual's usual activities. However, beyond this general characteristic, there is little consistency.

Typically, these definitions have been operationalized by requesting subjects to respond to lists of life events constructed by the researcher (Antonovsky & Kats, 1967; Brown & Birley, 1968; Holmes & Rahe, 1967; Lowenthal & Chiriboga, 1973). Two main arguments have been used to support the construct validity of such event lists (Dohrenwend & Dohrenwend, 1977). The first consists of agreement among various types of judges that the events involved are indeed stressful (Antonovsky & Kats, 1967; Brown & Birley, 1968). The second consists of a correlation between researcher constructed lists and events reported in retrospect by patients admitted to hospitals or clinics with physical and/or psychiatric illnesses (Cochrane & Robertson, 1973; Holmes & Rahe, 1967). In one instance, life event nominations have been obtained from a nonpatient population (Dohrenwend, 1974).

Although the lists compiled by the different investigators overlap—for example, marriage, birth of a first child, and death of a family member are common to most—they are by no means identical. They vary in number of items and in content. With respect to content, for example, Antonovsky and Kats (1967) included events relevant to concentration camps in research done in Israel; Lowenthal and Chiriboga (1973) included events applicable to adolescents and the elderly in their research on four stages of life. Some of these differences undoubtedly reflect the unique experiences of the particular subject samples involved. However, at a more basic level, the differences reflect inadequate preoperational explication of the life event construct.

In spite of surface differences among the lists, it appears that most attempts to operationalize the life event construct are based on the implicit assumption that there is only one population of events, or if not, that there is considerable overlap as far as the most common events are concerned (Dohrenwend & Dohrenwend, 1977). For example, the widely used Social Readjustment Rating Scale (Holmes & Rahe, 1967) combines events which may be characterized as subjective and objective, voluntary and involuntary, positive and negative, and so forth.

One approach to this lack of differentiation is to narrow the definition of life events in an attempt to reduce the possibility of surplus construct irrelevancies. Such a strategy is implicit, for example, in Hudgens' (1974) restriction of events to "personal catastrophies" such as life threatening illnesses. Another approach to the problem is to attempt more adequate dimensionalization of the domain of life events (Dohrenwend, 1974; Dohrenwend & Dohrenwend, 1974a, 1977; Lowenthal & Chiriboga, 1973). In this regard, distinctions have been drawn among subjective and objective events (Brown, 1974; Hinkle, 1974; Lowenthal & Chiriboga, 1973; Thurlow, 1971), gain and loss events (Dohrenwend, 1973a; Lowenthal & Chiriboga, 1973), and events that the individual is responsible for bringing about and events over which he or she has no control (Brown, Sklair, Harris, & Birley, 1973; Dohrenwend, 1973b; Lowenthal & Chiriboga, 1973), to name a few.

In our view, adequate explication of the life event construct requires that this type of dimensionalization be examined systematically. Such a process is likely to involve both the categorization of events into broad groupings and the delineation of event attributes.

b. Event Categories.   Two broad categories of events which are crucial to the present framework are "individual" and "cultural" events. Individual events are defined here as events which are experienced as a part of the usual life course. Such events (e.g., marriage, birth of a child, illness, death of a loved one), while they give shape to the life cycle and its transitions, cannot be considered to be strictly age graded. The occurrence of some of these events is based, in part, on biological capacity and social norms. Their effect is primarily evident with respect to the individual who is experiencing the event and, secondarily, with respect to the individual's significant others.

In the case of individual events, one would expect to find age changes or differences in the frequency of exposure to and nature of life events. For example, Lowenthal, Thurnher, and Chiriboga (1975) note differences in the frequency of stressful life events reported by younger and older subjects for the 10 years preceding the interview. Generally, young persons reported exposure to more stressful events than older persons. Indeed, more than 25% of the older respondents reported no stressful events at all during the previous 10 years. In addition, the young tended to report more positive stresses, while the old tended to report more negative stresses. The exception to this rule were the older male subjects who reported more positive than negative events. Finally, age differences in the nature of the stressful events were also apparent. Related to this work, Rosow (1973) indicates that the type of events experienced by older adults are more likely to involve loss and a decrease and restriction of the social context. In the absence of sequential data, it is difficult to say whether these cross-sectional differences reflect ontogenetic changes or cohort differences in life event experiences.

Cultural events are events which are not experienced as part of the usual life course and which affect a large number of individuals. Such events (e.g., wars, natural catastrophes, economic depression) are likely to be major social events which not only have an immediate effect on the individuals present but also continue to exert their influence to the extent that they are related to historical change within the culture. Thus, events of this type play a primary role in determining the cultural context of a particular birth cohort.

In addition to the above general categories, it is crucial for the present framework that events be distinguished with respect to whether they are concurrent or distal in time. With the exception of Lowenthal and Chiriboga (1973), little attention has been directed toward categorization of this type. From a developmental perspective, such distinctions are crucial (Baltes, 1973; Bortner & Hultsch, 1974).

Drawing the latter distinction between concurrent and distal antecedents leads to an issue of particular importance—namely how events which are distal in time may be considered antecedents to present developmental phenomena. The simplest manner in which both individual and cultural events may operate as distal antecedents to development is through having altered, at the time of their occurrence, the intrapersonal context of the individual. This change, depending upon its nature and extensiveness, continues to serve as an influence on later development to the extent that the individual affects his or her own development through interpretation of and interaction with his or her environment.

In addition, major cultural events may continue to influence development, even for individuals not in existence at the time of the occurrence of the event, by affecting evolutionary, history-graded (cohort-related) determinants of development. In other words, a major social event may be the antecedent of historical change within the culture, thus altering the manner in which patterns relating to different aspects of the proximal interpersonal environment change with historical time.

The proximal interpersonal environment can be differentiated into four general contexts: the family, the social and community context, the occupation and career context, and primary friendship networks. The key assumption is that in order for a cultural event to continue to affect developmental phenomena, it must be linked in some manner to the individual's proximal interpersonal environment (Elder, 1973, 1975; Jessor & Jessor, 1973).

It is proposed that a major cultural event can directly affect change in (a) the social and community context (e.g., by altering the availability of social and community resources), (b) the career context (e.g., by increasing or decreasing available jobs and career life options), and (c) cohort size and composition (Elder, 1975; Waring, 1975). This latter effect is brought about by changes in fertility rate, mortality rate, migration, and sex ratios (Baltes, Cornelius, & Nesselroade, 1978; Neugarten & Hagestad, 1976; Waring, 1975). Change in cohort size and composition can directly affect (a) family structure (e.g., size, age at marriage, spacing of children, family stability and divorce rates, joint career patterns), (b) friendship networks (e.g., identity, number, and type of friends), and (c) cohort flow (Riley, 1976; Waring, 1975). Cohort flow refers to the fit between the cohort and the extant role system. Altering this fit (e.g., too many people and too few jobs, or vice versa) results in "disordered cohort flow" (Waring, 1975). Disordered cohort flow can directly affect (a) the social and community context, through an altered balance in the availability of health and educational resources; (b) the career and employment context, through affecting job opportunities and options; and (c) the timing and sequencing of individual life events (Clausen, 1972; Elder, 1975). This latter element, the timing and sequencing of individual life events, is considered in greater detail in a later section.

　　c. Event Attributes.　As stated previously, adequate dimensionalization of the life event construct relates, in part, to the determination of attributes or dimensions of life events. Explication of event attributes is essential as such attributes relate to the impactfulness of the event and, thus, the degree to which the event is assessed as stressful.

Few event attributes have been examined systematically. A first step toward doing so would be to study the degree to which various dimensions are related to the characteristics of the event versus the characteristics of the individuals experiencing the event. For example, Dohrenwend (1977) examined the degree to which the anticipation and control of life events was related to the characteristics of the individuals experiencing the event or the characteristics of the event situation. She found that anticipation of the event was largely determined by the former, while control of the event was largely determined by the latter. Thus, certain variables, such as control over events, appear to be primarily a function of the nature of the events themselves, while other dimensions, such as anticipation, are not.

Other dimensions, such as gain versus loss (Lowenthal & Chiriboga, 1973), may characterize events as well and should be examined systematically. Once such attributes have been established, it is necessary to determine the extent to which different life events vary on these dimensions and the relationship of the attributes to the impactfulness of life events.

One aspect of life events which has received little attention and which would seem to be particularly important is the degree to which different events require change in the proximal interpersonal contexts of the individual and the types of changes required in different contexts (Parkes, 1971). It is proposed that the more change required in these various contexts, the greater the impactfulness of the event.

    d. Timing and Sequencing of Life Events. Particularly crucial to a life-span developmental perspective on life events are timing and sequencing. The life-span developmental orientation outlined previously emphasizes patterned change. This implies a sensitivity to the timing of events over the life span and the historical context in which they occur. Thus, from this perspective, events do not have uniform meaning. When an event occurs is perhaps as important as whether it occurs at all. One might expect that the birth of an illegitimate child to a woman 16 years of age is a different event than the birth of an illegitimate child to a woman 26 years of age. As a specific example, consider Elder's (1974) work on the impact of the Great Depression on the work careers of men who experienced this event at different points in the life cycle. In the case of middle-class men, Elder reports that younger men were more negatively affected by the Depression than older men. Individuals who experienced the event as young men were just beginning their work careers, while the older men had already established them. At a later date, men who had experienced the Depression at an early age showed a much higher rate of career instability and disadvantage than men who had experienced the Depression at a later age. Elder notes that this pattern was reversed in the case of lower-class men, reflecting a historical pattern of age discrimination in unskilled occupations. In the case of this group, then, the Depression had a more negative impact on men who were older at the onset of the event than on men who were younger.

In part, the timing of some individual events is defined by normative factors. According to theory, age norms specify appropriate times for certain life events, such as leaving the family home, achieving economic independence, marriage, bearing children, and retirement (Neugarten & Datan, 1973). As individuals move through the life cycle, they are made aware of whether they are early, on time, or late with respect to these norms through an informal system of positive and negative sanctions. Again, from a life-span developmental perspective it is not only the presence or absence of an event but its timing which is crucial. For example, Lowenthal, Thurnher, and Chiriboga (1975) indicate that middle-aged men reported that being off-time with respect to promotions or salary increases was a major reason for a reduction in their life satisfaction. Similarly, Bourque and Back (1977) note that such events as the departure of children and retirement are perceived by respondents as most disruptive if they occur at a nonnormative age. In this regard, however, it is important to note that there is little empirical evidence on age expectations and sanctions over the life span (Elder, 1977). In particular, attention has not been directed to inevitable differences in such norms and sanctions as a function of sex, race, community size, region, and the like. Further, as Neugarten and Moore (1968) have noted, norms and sanctions will also differ for various cohorts over historical time.

Another consideration with respect to patterning and timing of events concerns the event context as it is affected by the clustering and duration of other concurrent and recent distal events. Other recently occurring events affect the individual's resource–deficit balance, a notion which will be discussed in greater detail shortly. It is proposed that the greater the disruption of the event context by other concurrent and recent distal events, the greater the likelihood that the final event outcome will involve some aspects which are dysfunctional. This hypothesis does receive support from empirical research. To illustrate generally, for example, Holmes and Masuda (1974) report that 93% of the major health changes reported by a group of physicians were preceded during a 2-year period by a clustering of life events whose Life Change Scores summed to at least 150 units per year.

It is important to note that the issue of the pattern of events extends beyond a single individual. That is, it is not just the pattern of events within a single life cycle that is important, but how these events interact with events in the life cycles of significant others. Elder (1977) stresses this point in relation to the family. In this context, for example, scheduling problems often arise. The events of early career establishment may conflict with the events of child bearing and rearing. Lowenthal, Thurnher, and Chiriboga (1975) report that the events which happen to significant others may be particularly important for females.

Finally, let us return to our earlier discussion concerning distal, cultural life event antecedents and their effect on the timing and sequencing of individual, normative life events. As described previously, disordered cohort flow may result from the occurrence of a major cultural event. Disordered cohort flow can affect the timing and sequencing of individual life events by means of one or both of two mechanisms: (a) through society's attempts to correct the imbalance of disordered cohort flow by changing the social constraints and incentives associated with various individual events, i.e., by modifying extant age norms and expectations (Neugarten & Hagestad, 1976; Rosow, 1976), or (b) through the decision processes of the individual (Waring, 1975). In either case, the individual can be affected either through experiencing the phenomenon of being "off-time" versus "on-time" (Neugarten & Datan, 1973) or through changes in the timing and sequencing of any of the four proximal interpersonal environments compared with previous cohorts of a different composition (for example, in this latter case, the prolongation of educational requirements, resulting in occupying first job at a later age than previous cohorts).

2. Mediating Variables

The effects of both individual and cultural events are contingent on a variety of mediating variables defined by various biological, psychological, and contextual resources and deficits. It is clear that individuals tend to react very differently to any given life event. A circumstance which is stressful for one person may be challenging for another (Dohrenwend & Dohrenwend, 1974a; Lazarus, 1966; Lowenthal & Chiriboga, 1973; Moss, 1973). The stress and coping literature suggests a variety of possible variables which may function as mediators of life event antecedents. As indicated in Fig. 2, these variables can be viewed as falling into the following categories: biological, psychological, and contextual. It can be expected that large interindividual differences will exist with respect to all of these mediating variables. Further, these variables may be considered as creating a balance of resources and deficits which determine the individual's current state of functioning. Finally, these three categories of mediating variables play important roles at different points in the process described by the model. In the following discussion, these variables are delineated further and evidence is presented concerning how these variables may differ in their impact depending upon the individual's position in the life cycle.

Within the category of contextual variables, examples of elements which enter into determining the resource–deficit balance include the state of the individual's supportive frameworks and interpersonal relationships, socioeconomic status, and income level. High status and income tend to result in an individual's having greater access to external resources and greater freedom in terms of manipulating his or her environment. Supportive frameworks and interpersonal relationships may serve as resources for the individual to the degree to which they operate to maintain the individual's self-esteem and sense of self-worth (Adams & Lindemann, 1974; Hamburg, Coelho, & Adams, 1974). The impact of these resources and deficits is likely to vary over the life cycle. For example, supportive frameworks and interpersonal relationships frequently decrease with increasing age. Older individuals tend to belong to fewer groups, have fewer friends, and see them less (Rosow, 1973). However, there is also evidence to suggest that the relationships among older adults are more likely to be complex and subtle (Lowenthal, Thurnher, & Chiriboga, 1975). Further, among men, interpersonal resources increasingly served as buffers against stressful events.

Biological resources and deficits may be viewed as creating a floor effect. That is, biological deficits predict an impairment of the individual's adaptive capacity (Lieberman, 1975). Of equal importance, however, the reverse is not true. Inadequate biological resources predict maladaptation, but adequate resources do not necessarily predict successful adaptation. Beyond this base, other psychological and contextual variables become critical (Lieberman, 1975). These observations tend to suggest the likelihood of increasing maladaptation with increasing age.

Examples of psychological variables which may enter into determining the balance of resources to deficits include cognitive abilities, accumulated knowledge, anticipatory socialization, time perspective, attitudes toward the self and one's ability to deal with the environment, and general personality factors which influence cognitive style and behavioral tendencies. Similar to biological variables, certain cognitive abilities appear to create a floor effect (Lieberman, 1975). In order for the individual to realistically appraise his or her environmental context and personal resources, a certain level of cognitive functioning would appear to be essential. This aspect of cognitive functioning will be discussed again at a later point with respect to the appraisal process.

Accumulated knowledge functions as a resource in the sense that it provides the individual with a broader perspective within which to evaluate the life event. One might expect that older individuals would have a greater accumulation of knowledge than younger individuals and, thus, be able to utilize this resource to a greater extent. There is some evidence that a broader perspective does indeed appear to be utilized by older adults and may underlie, at least partially, the empirical finding that older subjects tend to report fewer stresses than younger subjects (Lowenthal, Thurnher, & Chiriboga, 1975).

Anticipatory socialization for the event concerned would serve as a resource for the individual to the extent that it acts to decrease the ambiguity of the situation and increase the responses available to the individual (Albrecht & Gift, 1975; Hamburg, Coelho, & Adams, 1974). There appears to be less anticipatory socialization for events which are seen as involving defeats or losses. In addition, with respect to different points in the life span, there is evidence that there is generally less anticipatory socialization for events associated with aging than for events at other points in the life span (Rosow, 1973).

Time perspective, defined as the assessment of personal status in reference to the past and future, shows important shifts over the adult life span (Bortner & Hultsch, 1972). Generally, indices of both gains made in the past and gains anticipated in the future decline with age. These patterns interact with a variety of other variables, particularly social class (Bortner & Hultsch, 1974), although they appear to be relatively consistent over historical time (Hultsch & Bortner, 1974). A positive assessment of the future as well as the ability to introspect appear to be significant resources for older adults (Lieberman, 1975; Lowenthal, Thurnher, & Chiriboga, 1975).

Motivational factors may be considered to be a particularly important class of psychological mediating variables due to the important role they play in the appraisal process. Motivational factors include the values and goals which provide the individual with a framework for organizing the course of his or her life. Empirical evidence indicates that values and goals tend to shift across the life span (Lowenthal, Thurnher, & Chiriboga, 1975; Ryff & Baltes, 1976). For example, younger age groups tend to have more expansive goals and higher expectations, whereas older age groups are more likely to caution against setting goals and expectations high. In the present model, the explication of this shift in values involves an examination of the previous pattern and sequencing of life events encountered by the individual.

Coping strategies represent a final class of psychological mediating variables. In the present context, these refer to behavioral and psychological processes designed to mitigate or eliminate threat (Lazarus, 1966). The range of possible coping strategies has by no means been fully explored. Generally, such strategies may involve either direct action, such as physical avoidance or attack, or intrapsychic processes, such as denial or wish-fulfilling fantasies (Hamburg, 1974; Lazarus, Averill, & Opton, 1974). Factors determining the selection of specific coping strategies will be considered in more detail at a later point.

On the basis of the above discussion, it would appear that a particularly important consideration relevant to these mediating variables concerns the need for flexibility in our consideration of what constitutes resources and deficits. The evidence presented above points to the conclusion that what might be labeled as a deficit for one type of event or at one point in time may be irrelevant or serve as a resource at another time or for another type of event. Other authors have come to the same conclusion (Lieberman, 1975; Lowenthal, 1968; Lowenthal & Chiriboga, 1973; Lowenthal, Thurnher, & Chiriboga, 1975). For example, in his studies on the impact of a change in environment on older adults, Lieberman (1975) reports that the characteristics of the elderly who adapted did not incorporate those elements that would ordinarily be expected to be signs of adjustment or predictors of adequacy in a crisis. Those elderly who were aggressive, irritating, narcissistic, and demanding were the individuals who were most likely to survive the crisis. These findings point to the importance of considering our definition of resources and deficits within a multidimensional context involving event, ontogenetic, and cultural variables.

3. Initial Appraisal of Threat

Once an event occurs, the individual assesses it with respect to the degree of threat posed. The greater the degree of threat posed by the situation, the greater the degree of stress experienced. This phase is similar to what other authors refer to as "appraised significance of the situation," "personal meaning," and "definition of the situation" (Lazarus, 1966; Lazarus, Averill, & Opton, 1974; Lowenthal, Thurnher, & Chiriboga, 1975). This appraisal process is seen as being similar for all individuals, regardless of the type of event or the previous life history of the individual.

The ability of the individual to undertake this process of appraisal depends upon a certain level of adequacy in cognitive functioning. As stated previously, cognitive abilities appear to create a floor effect in this regard (Lieberman, 1975). Cognitive functioning below a certain level would incapacitate the individual's ability to conduct an appraisal of the event sufficient to determine the degree of threat posed. Above this particular level of adequacy, however, increasing cognitive ability would not be correlated with increased ability to carry out the appraisal process.

The degree to which the situation or event is assessed as threatening or stressful depends upon both event and mediating factors. As discussed previously, these will vary depending upon the type of life event, its historical and sociocultural context, the previous life history of the individual, and the point in the individual's life cycle at which the life event occurs. Regardless of these differences, the appraisal process can be considered invariant. This process revolves around the degree of dissonance (Festinger, 1957; Lazarus, 1966) or incongruity (Moss, 1973) experienced by the individual as a result of the occurrence of the life event.

One way of conceptualizing this process is to envision the life event as presenting the individual with certain information or requirements either not previously encountered or which are in conflict with the individual's current information, values, goals, or behavior. It is possible that the information and requirements associated with the life event may be in conflict with some aspects of the individual's functioning and not others. This may indicate the individual is already engaged in some type of internal conflict, for example, between goals and goal-related behavior patterns (Lowenthal, 1971). In this case, the life event would serve to activate this unresolved conflict.

The balance of resources and deficits the individual possesses plays an important role at this point in mediating the degree of threat assessed by the individual. Although the event may be associated with a high degree of dissonance, an individual with a high balance of resources to deficits may see the situation as "challenging."

The outcomes of this initial appraisal of the event range from no threat or stress perceived to intense threat or stress perceived. If no stress is perceived, the individual is essentially unaffected by the life event. If the event is appraised as threatening or stressful, the individual begins to seek some means of resolving the conflict.

4. Resolution Processes

The first phase of the individual's attempts to recreate congruity with the environment involves the selection of coping strategies from among those already in his or her current repertoire. As has already been discussed, previous event sequences and the individual's mastery of these will have resulted in an established repertoire of coping strategies and tendencies. Thus, one can expect interindividual differences in the strategies available and in the selection of strategies.

Selection of coping strategies will also be influenced by the constraints perceived in the immediate context. For example, direct action or manipulation of the environment may be a feasible alternative under some circumstances and not under others. Circumstances under which action tendencies are less likely would be either those in which their expression expose the individual to threat from a different source (Lazarus, 1966) or conditions in which direct action has little or no value (Lazarus, Averill, & Opton, 1974). Conditions which exemplify the latter type of situation are severe injury, terminal illness, and death of a loved one. Here the individual is relatively helpless in the sense that there is little opportunity for direct action on the environment. Although these types of events may occur at any point in the individual's life span, as discussed previously, there is a prevalence of such events later in the life cycle. Older adults also tend to function within a more constricted environmental context in terms of decreased financial resources, decreased status, and decreased options for alternative support networks and employment opportunities (Rosow, 1973). This suggests that the use of intrapsychic coping strategies will tend to increase while the use of direct action coping strategies will tend to decrease over the adult life span.

Another important determinant of strategy selection is the degree of perceived threat. There is some evidence that a high degree of threat leads to a decrease in variability and an increase in stereotyped behavior (Lazarus, 1966). Thus, when the degree of threat is intense, one might expect the selection of defensive maneuvers, including avoidance and denial (Hamburg, Coelho, & Adams, 1974; Lazarus, 1966). Long-term use of such strategies tends to be maladaptive in that the behavioral and psychological flexibility of the individual becomes impaired (Hamburg, Coelho, & Adams, 1974). For example, Lowenthal and Chiriboga (1973) note that among adolescent respondents, the happiest individuals were those with many resources and many deficits. Among young adult respondents, the happiest individuals were those with many resources and few deficits. Among middle-aged respondents, the happiest individuals were those with moderate resources and few deficits. Finally, among older respondents, the happiest individuals were those with few resources and few deficits. It should be pointed out, however, that those individuals with few resources and few deficits also experienced the fewest recent and cumulative stresses. Thus, the pattern may reflect successful avoidance of or insulation from stressful events. Lieberman (1975) reports that those who did not grossly deny the threat and who were able to engage in appraisal and resolution processes consistent with the threat fared better than those who did deny both the affect and acknowledgment of the threat.

Following the initial selection of coping strategies, attempts to cope with the situation using these strategies are undertaken. A variety of outcomes of this process are possible. The individual may find the initial selection of strategies to be adequate to cope with the events. In this case, the current behavior of the individual tends to remain stable. A second possibility is that the individual may find his or her usual strategies of coping inadequate or, at the most, marginally adequate. In this case, a phase of exploration may ensue. This is a time of searching for new solutions, seeking out and evaluating new information, and reappraisal of current assumptions and life goals. A highly unstable period, it is often accompanied by confusion, frustration, disruption of usual behavioral and psychological processes, and a general increase in the susceptibility to pathology (Moss, 1973).

It is important to realize that the resolution process is a continually changing and complex affair. Reappraisal is continually taking place, and a variety of currently available coping strategies may be utilized in the initial stages. Thus, in the process of arriving at new behaviors and reorganization of psychological structures, defensive and avoidance maneuvers may be utilized along the way (Hamburg, Coelho, & Adams, 1974; Lazarus, 1966).

5. Consequences

The outcome of this process depends, to a great extent, on the individual's balance of resources and deficits. With a high ratio of resources to deficits, the individual may be openly responsive to his or her current context and be able to mobilize the energy necessary to undertake learning of new behaviors and reorganization of current psychological structures (Maas & Kuypers, 1974). It is still possible, however, that this outcome will be associated with physical disease, depending upon the genetic and physiological predispositions of the individual (Moss, 1973).

The outcome, however, for the individual who possesses a low ratio of resources to deficits is more likely to be in the direction of physical or psychological dysfunction. This type of individual becomes so preoccupied with defending the self against the perceived threat that he or she is less able to be openly responsive to the environment and, thus, less able to find new solutions. The resulting state of perpetual defensiveness, nonresolution, and instability renders the person particularly susceptible to the development of physical or psychological dysfunction (Hamburg, Coelho, & Adams, 1974; Lazarus, 1966).

It is important to note that what has been offered in this section is a general statement regarding possible outcomes which can be considered applicable to a broad range of life event antecedents. Even in the case where a specific life event antecedent is being examined, one will find that the range of outcomes is extremely broad. The final selection of consequent domains depends upon the nature of the specific life event, the relevant mediators and how they operate to form a balance of resources to deficits, and, finally, the interests of the researcher.

V. Overview

The purpose of this chapter has been to propose a life-span developmental view of life events. It has been argued that examination of life events must consider the basic metamodels within which theory and research related to this issue are articulated. On the one hand, developmental perspectives on life events have typically been rooted in the organismic metamodel. This metamodel stresses the synthesis of organized complexities and the construction of structure–function relationships. On the other hand, nondevelopmental perspectives on life events have typically been rooted in the mechanistic metamodel. This metamodel stresses the analysis of elements and the discovery of antecedent–consequent relations. In this chapter, we have attempted to outline a life-span developmental perspective consistent with this latter approach.

A central feature of this life-span developmental framework is the examination of both individual and cultural event antecedents and their interaction. Within this context, particular attention is drawn to the pattern of life events—their timing, sequencing, duration, and the like. Event antecedents may be concurrent or historical to the present. The impact of life event antecedents is mediated by a variety of biological, psychological, and contextual variables which define a balance of resources and deficits. These antecedents are seen as interacting via a complex adaptation process which involves the appraisal of threat, and potentially, the selection, implementation, modification, and evaluation of coping strategies and changes in psychological and contextual characteristics. This process may result in a variety of consequents including adaptive, homeostatic, and maladaptive outcomes.

References

Adams, J. E., & Lindemann, E. Coping with long-term disability. In G. V. Coelho, D. A. Hamburg, & J. E. Adams (Eds.), *Coping and adaptation*. New York: Basic Books, 1974.

Ahammer, I. M. Social-learning theory as a framework for the study of adult personality development. In P. B. Baltes & K. W. Schaie (Eds.), *Life-span developmental psychology: Personality and socialization*. New York: Academic Press, 1973.

Albrecht, G. L., & Gift, H. C. Adult socialization: Ambiguity and adult life crises. In N. Datan & L. H. Ginsburg (Eds.), *Life-span developmental psychology: Normative life crises*. New York: Academic Press, 1975.

Antonovsky, A. Conceptual and methodological problems in the study of resistance resources and stressful life events. In B. S. Dohrenwend & B. P. Dohrenwend (Eds.), *Stressful life events: Their nature and effects*. New York: Wiley, 1974.

Antonovsky, A., & Kats, R. The life crisis history as a tool in epidemiological research. *Journal of Health and Social Behavior*, 1967, **8**, 15–21.

Baltes, P. B. Prototypical paradigms and questions in life-span research on development and aging. *Gerontologist*, 1973, **13**, 458–467.

Baltes, P. B., Cornelius, S. W., & Nesselroade, J. R. Cohort effects in developmental psychology: Theoretical and methodological perspectives. In W. A. Collins (Ed.), *Minnesota symposia on child psychology* (Vol. 11). Hillsdale, New Jersey: Erlbaum, 1978.

Baltes, P. B., Cornelius, S. W., & Nesselroade, J. R. Cohort effects in developmental psychology. In J. R. Nesselroade & P. B. Baltes (Eds.), *Longitudinal research in the behavioral sciences: Design and analysis*. New York: Academic Press, 1979.

Baltes, P. B., & Schaie, K. W. On life-span developmental research paradigms: Retrospects and prospects. In P. B. Baltes & K. W. Schaie (Eds.), *Life-span developmental psychology: Personality and socialization*. New York: Academic Press, 1973.

Baltes, P. B., & Willis, S. L. Toward psychological theories of aging and development. In J. E. Birren & K. W. Schaie (Eds.), *Handbook of the psychology of aging*. New York: Van Nostrand-Reinhold, 1977.

Bortner, R. W., & Hultsch, D. F. Personal time perspective in adulthood. *Developmental Psychology*, 1972, **7**, 98–103.

Bortner, R. W., & Hultsch, D. F. Patterns of subjective deprivation in adulthood. *Developmental Psychology*, 1974, **10**, 534–545.

Bourque, L. B., & Back, K. W. Life graphs and life events. *Journal of Gerontology*, 1977, **32**, 669–674.

Brown, G. W. Meaning, measurement, and stress of life events. In B. S. Dohrenwend & B. P. Dohrenwend (Eds.), *Stressful life events: Their nature and effects*. New York: Wiley, 1974.

Brown, G. W., & Birley, J. L. T. Crisis and life changes and the onset of schizophrenia. *Journal of Health and Social Behavior*, 1968, **9**, 203–214.

Brown, G. W., Sklair, F., Harris, T. O., & Birley, J. L. T. Life events and psychiatric disorders. Part 1: Some methodological issues. *Psychological Medicine*, 1973, **3**, 74–87.

Bühler, C. Maturation and motivation. *Personality*, 1951, **1**, 184–211.

Bühler, C. The curve of life as studies in biographies. *Journal of Applied Science*, 1953, **19**, 405–409.

Bühler, C. Genetic aspects of the self. *Annals of the New York Academy of Sciences*, 1962, **96**, 730–764.

Cassirer, E. *The philosophy of the enlightenment*. Boston: Beacon, 1951.

Clausen, J. A. The life course of individuals. In M. W. Riley, M. Johnson, & A. Foner (Eds.), *Aging and society: A sociology of age stratification* (Vol. 3). New York: Russell Sage Foundation, 1972.

Cochrane, R., & Robertson, A. The life events inventory: A measure of the relative severity of psycho-social stressors. *Journal of Psychosomatic Research*, 1973, **17**, 135–139.

Coelho, G. V., Hamburg, D. A., & Adams, J. E. (Eds.), *Coping and adaptation*. New York: Basic Books, 1974.

Datan, N., & Ginsberg, L. H. (Eds.), *Life-span developmental psychology: Normative life crises*. New York: Academic Press, 1975.

Dodge, D. L., & Martin, W. T. *Social stress and chronic illness*. South Bend: University of Notre Dame Press, 1970.

Dohrenwend, B. P. The social psychological nature of stress: A framework for causal inquiry. *Journal of Abnormal and Social Psychology*, 1961, **62**, 294–302.

Dohrenwend, B. P. Problems in defining and sampling the relevant population of stressful life events. In B. S. Dohrenwend & B. P. Dohrenwend (Eds.), *Stressful life events: Their nature and effects*. New York: Wiley, 1974.

Dohrenwend, B. P., & Dohrenwend, B. S. The conceptualization and measurement of stressful life events: An overview. In J. S. Strauss, H. M. Babigan, & M. Roff (Eds.), *Proceedings of conference on methods of longitudinal research in psychopathology*. New York: Plenum, 1977.

Dohrenwend, B. S. Social class and stressful events. In E. H. Hare & J. K. Wing (Eds.), *Psychiatric epidemiology: Proceedings of the international symposium held at Aberdeen University 22-25 July 1969*. New York: Oxford University Press, 1970.

Dohrenwend, B. S. Life events as stressors: A methodological inquiry. *Journal of Health and Social Behavior*. 1973, **14**, 167–175. (a)

Dohrenwend, B. S. Social status and stressful life events. *Journal of Personality and Social Psychology*. 1973, **28**, 225–235. (b)

Dohrenwend, B. S. Anticipation and control of stressful life events: An exploratory analysis. In J. S. Strauss, H. M. Babigan, & M. Roff (Eds.), *Proceedings of conference on methods of longitudinal research in psychopathology*. New York: Plenum, 1977.

Dohrenwend, B. S., & Dohrenwend, B. P. Social class and the relation of remote to recent stressors. In M. Roff, L. N. Robins, & M. Pollack (Eds.), *Life history research in psychopathology* (Vol. 2). Minneapolis: University of Minnesota Press, 1972.

Dohrenwend, B. S., & Dohrenwend, B. P. Overview and prospects for research on stressful life events. In B. S. Dohrenwend & B. P. Dohrenwend (Eds.), *Stressful life events: Their nature and effects*. New York: Wiley, 1974. (a)

Dohrenwend, B. S., & Dohrenwend, B. P. (Eds.), *Stressful life events: Their nature and effects*. New York: Wiley, 1974. (b)

Elder, G. H., Jr. On linking social structure and personality. In G. H. Elder, Jr. (Ed.), *Linking social structure and personality*. Beverly Hills: Sage Publications, 1973.

Elder, G. H., Jr. *Children of the Great Depression*. Chicago: University of Chicago Press, 1974.

Elder, G. H., Jr. Age differentiation and the life course. *Annual Review of Sociology* (Vol. 1). Palo Alto: Annual Reviews, 1975.

Elder, G. H., Jr., Family history and the life course. *Journal of Family History*, 1977, **2**, 279–304.

Erikson, E. H. *Childhood and society*. New York: Norton, 1950, 1963.

Festinger, L. A. *A theory of cognitive dissonance*. Stanford: Stanford University Press, 1957.

Fritz, C. E., & Marks, E. S. The NORC studies of human behavior in disaster. *Journal of Social Issues,* 1954, **10,** 26–41.

Grinker, R. R., & Spiegel, J. P. *Men under stress.* New York: McGraw-Hill, 1963.

Gutmann, D. Parenthood: A key to the comparative study of the life cycle. In N. Datan & L. H. Ginsberg (Eds.), *Life-span developmental psychology: Normative life crisis.* New York: Academic Press, 1975.

Hamburg, D. A. Coping behavior in life-threatening circumstances. *Psychotherapy and Psychosomatics,* 1974, **23,** 13–25.

Hamburg, D. A., Coelho, G. V., & Adams, J. E. Coping and adaptation: Steps toward a synthesis of biological and social perspectives. In G. V. Coelho, D. A. Hamburg, & J. E. Adams (Eds.), *Coping and adaptation.* New York: Basic Books, 1974.

Havighurst, R. J. *Developmental tasks and education.* New York: David McKay, 1952, 1972.

Hinkle, L. E., Jr. The effects of exposure to cultural change, social change, and changes in interpersonal relationships on health. In B. S. Dohrenwend & B. P. Dohrenwend (Eds.), *Stressful life events: Their nature and effects.* New York: Wiley, 1974.

Holmes, T. H., & Masuda, M. Life change and illness susceptibility. In B. S. Dohrenwend & B. P. Dohrenwend (Eds.), *Stressful life events: Their nature and effects.* New York: Wiley, 1974.

Holmes, T. H., & Rahe, R. H. The social readjustment rating scale. *Journal of Psychosomatic Research,* 1967, **11,** 213–218.

Hudgens, R. W. Personal catastrophe and depression: A consideration of the subject with respect to medically ill adolescents, and a requiem for retrospective life-event studies. In B. S. Dohrenwend & B. P. Dohrenwend (Eds.), *Stressful life events: Their nature and effects.* New York: Wiley, 1974.

Hudgens, R. W., Morrison, J. R., & Barchha, R. G. Life events and onset of primary affective disorders. *Archives of General Psychiatry,* 1967, **16,** 134–145.

Hultsch, D. F., & Bortner, R. W. Personal time perspective in adulthood: A time-sequential study. *Developmental Psychology,* 1974, **10,** 835–837.

Hultsch, D. F., & Hickey, T. External validity in the study of human development: Methodological and theoretical issues. *Human Development,* 1978, **21,** 76–91.

Janis, I. L. *Psychological stress.* New York: Wiley, 1958.

Jessor, R., & Jessor, S. L. The perceived environment in behavioral science. In G. H. Elder, Jr. (Ed.), *Linking social structure and personality.* Beverly Hills: Sage Publications, 1973.

Kastenbaum, R. Is death a life crisis? On the confrontation with death in theory and practice. In N. Datan & L. H. Ginsberg (Eds.), *Life-span developmental psychology: Normative life crises.* New York: Academic Press, 1975.

Kellam, S. G., Branch, J. D., Agrawal, K. C., & Ensminger, M. E. *Mental health and going to school.* Chicago: University of Chicago Press, 1975.

Kellam, S. G., & Schiff, S. Adaptation and mental illness in the first grade classroom of an urban community. *Psychiatric Research Report,* 1967, **21,** 79–91.

Kohlberg, L. Stage and sequence: The cognitive-development approach to socialization. In D. A. Goslin (Ed.), *Handbook of socialization theory and research.* Chicago: Rand McNally, 1969.

Kuhn, T. S. *The structure of scientific revolutions.* Chicago: University of Chicago Press, 1962.

Lachman, R. The model in theory construction. In M. H. Marx (Ed.), *Theories in contemporary psychology.* New York: Macmillan, 1963.

Lazarus, R. S. *Psychological stress and the coping process.* New York: McGraw-Hill, 1966.

Lazarus, R. S., Averill, J. R., & Opton, E. M., Jr. The psychology of coping: Issues of research and assessment. In G. V. Coelho, D. A. Hamburg, & J. E. Adams (Eds.), *Coping and adaptation.* New York: Basic Books, 1974.

Lerner, R. M., & Ryff, C. D. Implementation of the life-span view of human development: The sample case of attachment. In P. B. Baltes (Ed.), *Life-span development and behavior* (Vol. 1). New York: Academic Press, 1978.

Levine, M. Residential change and school adjustment. *Community Mental Health Journal,* 1966, **2**, 61–69.

Levine, S., & Scotch, N. A. (Eds.), *Social stress.* Chicago: Aldine, 1970.

Levinson, D. J. The mid-life transition: A period in adult psychosocial development. *Psychiatry,* 1977, **40**, 99–112. (a)

Levinson, D. J. Middle adulthood in modern society: A sociopsychological view. In G. DiRenzo (Ed.), *Social character and social change.* Westport, Conn.: Greenwood Press, 1977. (b)

Levinson, D. J., Darrow, C. M., Klein, E. B., Levinson, M. H., & McKee, B. The psychosocial development of men in early adulthood and the mid-life transition. In D. F. Ricks, A. Thomas, & M. Roff (Eds.), *Life history research in psychopathology.* Minneapolis: University of Minnesota Press, 1974.

Levinson, D. J., Darrow, C. M., Klein, E. B., Levinson, M. H., & McKee, B. Periods in the adult development of men: Ages 18 to 45. *The Counseling Psychologist,* 1976, **6**, 21–25.

Lieberman, M. A. Adaptive processes in late life. In N. Datan & L. H. Ginsberg (Eds.), *Life-span developmental psychology: Normative life crises.* New York: Academic Press, 1975.

Lindemann, E., & Ross, N. A follow-up study of a predictive test of social adaptation in pre-school children. In G. Caplan (Ed.), *Emotional problems of early childhood.* New York: Basic Books, 1955.

Loevinger, J. Theories of ego development. In L. Breger (Ed.), *Clinical-cognitive psychology: Models and integrations.* New York: Prentice-Hall, 1969.

Looft, W. R. Socialization and personality throughout the life span: An examination of contemporary psychological approaches. In P. B. Baltes & K. W. Schaie (Eds.), *Life-span developmental psychology: Personality and socialization.* New York: Academic Press, 1973.

Lopata, H. Z. Widowhood: Societal factors in life span disruptions and alternatives. In N. Datan & L. H. Ginsberg (Eds.), *Life-span developmental psychology: Normative life crises.* New York: Academic Press, 1975.

Lowenthal, M. F. The relationship between social factors and mental health in the aged. In A. Simon & L. J. Epstein (Eds.), *Aging in modern society.* Washington, D. C.: American Psychological Association, 1968.

Lowenthal, M. F. Intentionality: Toward a framework for the study of adaptation in adulthood. *Aging and Human Development,* 1971, **2**, 79–95.

Lowenthal, M. F., & Chiriboga, D. Social stress and adaptation: Toward a life-course perspective. In C. Eisdorfer & M. P. Lawton (Eds.), *The psychology of adult development and aging.* Washington, D. C.: American Psychological Association, 1973.

Lowenthal, M. F., Thurnher, M., & Chiriboga, D. *Four stages of life.* San Francisco: Jossey-Bass, 1975.

Maas, H. S., & Kuypers, J. A. *From thirty to seventy.* San Francisco: Jossey-Bass, 1974.

Matson, F. *The broken image.* New York: George Braziller, 1964.

Meyer, A. The life chart and the obligation of specifying positive data in psychopathological diagnosis. In E. E. Winters (Ed.), *The collected papers of Adolf Meyer. Vol. III: Medical Teaching.* Baltimore: Johns Hopkins Press, 1951.

Moss, G. E. *Illness, immunity, and social interaction.* New York: Wiley, 1973.

Myers, J. K., Lindenthal, J. J., & Pepper, M. P. Social class, life events, and psychiatric symptoms: A longitudinal study. In B. S. Dohrenwend & B. P. Dohrenwend (Eds.), *Stressful life events: Their nature and effects.* New York: Wiley, 1974.

Myers, J. L., Lindenthal, J. J., Pepper, M. P., & Ostrander, D. K. Life events and mental status: A longitudinal study. *Journal of Health and Social Behavior,* 1972, **13**, 398–406.

Neugarten, B. L. Continuities and discontinuities of psychological issues into adult life. *Human Development,* 1969, **12**, 121–130.

Neugarten, B. L., & Datan, N. Sociological perspectives on the life cycle. In P. B. Baltes & K. W. Schaie (Eds.), *Life-span developmental psychology: Personality and social processes.* New York: Academic Press, 1973.

Neugarten, B. L., & Hagestad, G. O. Age and the life course. In R. H. Binstock & E. Shanas (Eds.), *Handbook of aging and the social sciences.* New York: Van Nostrand-Reinhold, 1976.

Neugarten, B. L., & Moore, J. W. The changing age-status system. In B. L. Neugarten (Ed.), *Middle age and aging.* Chicago: University of Chicago Press, 1968.

Overton, W. F., & Reese, H. W. Models of development: Methodological implications. In J. R. Nesselroade & H. W. Reese (Eds.), *Life-span developmental psychology: Methodological issues.* New York: Academic Press, 1973.

Pap, A. *Elements of analytic philosophy.* New York: Macmillan, 1949.

Parkes, C. M. Psycho-social transitions: A field for study. *Social Science and Medicine,* 1971, **5**, 101–115.

Pepper, S. C. *World hypotheses.* Berkeley: University of California Press, 1942.

Rahe, R. H., McKean, J. D., & Arthur, R. J. A longitudinal study of life-change and illness patterns. *Journal of Psychosomatic Research,* 1967, **10**, 355–366.

Raush, H. L., Goodrich, W., & Campbell, J. D. Adaptation to the first years of marriage. *Psychiatry,* 1963, **26**, 368–380.

Reese, H. W., & Overton, W. F. Models of development and theories of development. In L. R. Goulet & P. B. Baltes (Eds.), *Life-span developmental psychology: Theory and research.* New York: Academic Press, 1970.

Riegel, K. F. Influence of economic and political ideologies on the development of developmental psychology. *Psychological Bulletin,* 1972, **78**, 129–141.

Riegel, K. F. Adult life crises: A dialectic interpretation of development. In N. Datan & L. H. Ginsberg (Eds.), *Life-span developmental psychology: Normative life crises.* New York: Academic Press, 1975.

Riley, M. W. Age strata in social systems. In R. H. Binstock & E. Shanas (Eds.), *Handbook of aging and the social sciences.* New York: Van Nostrand-Reinhold, 1976.

Rosow, I. The social context of the aging self. *The Gerontologist,* 1973, **13**, 82–87.

Rosow, I. Status and role change through the life span. In R. H. Binstock & E. Shanas (Eds.), *Handbook of aging and the social sciences.* New York: Van Nostrand-Reinhold, 1976.

Ryff, C. D., & Baltes, P. B. Value transition and adult development of women: The instrumentality–terminality sequence hypothesis. *Developmental Psychology,* 1976, **12**, 567–568.

Schon, D. *The displacement of concepts.* London: Tavistock, 1963.

Seeger, R. J. Beyond operationalism. *Scientific Monthly,* 1954, **79**, 226–227.

Selye, H. *The stress of life*. New York: McGraw-Hill, 1956.

Star, S. A. Psychoneurotic symptoms in the army. In S. A. Stouffer, L. Guttman, E. A. Suchman, P. F. Lazarsfeld, S. A. Star, & J. A. Clausen (Eds.), *Studies in social psychology in World War II: Combat and its aftermath*. Princeton, N. J.: Princeton University Press, 1949.

Theorell, T. Life events before and after the onset of a premature myocardial infarction. In B. S. Dohrenwend & B. P. Dohrenwend (Eds.), *Stressful life events: Their nature and effects*. New York: Wiley, 1974.

Thurlow, H. J. Illness in relation to life situation and sick-role tendency. *Journal of Psychosomatic Research*, 1971, **15**, 73–88.

Waring, J. M. Social replenishment and social change: The problem of disordered cohort flow. *American Behavioral Scientist*, 1975, **19**, 237–256.

Problem Solving in Later Adulthood:
Intervention Research[1]

Nancy W. Denney

DEPARTMENT OF PSYCHOLOGY, UNIVERSITY OF KANSAS
LAWRENCE, KANSAS

Abstract

A review of the descriptive studies on problem solving during the adult years indicates that there are age differences in performance, with elderly individuals performing less well than younger adults. The descriptive studies also suggest that these age differences reflect actual age changes as well as cohort differences. However, regardless of the cause of the age differences, it is important to know whether the poorer performance of the elderly can be

[1]This chapter is partially based on a joint paper prepared by Nancy W. Denney and Sherry L. Willis from which each has subsequently developed independent manuscripts. Their joint paper was presented at the Tenth International Congress on Gerontology which was held in Jerusalem, Israel in June 1975.

LIFE-SPAN DEVELOPMENT
AND BEHAVIOR, VOL. 2

changed through intervention programs. A review of the intervention research indicates that most of the intervention techniques aimed at giving individuals direct training on the ability under investigation are effective in increasing performance on that particular ability. However, manipulating peripheral, noncognitive variables, such as motivation, self-confidence, time to develop a strategy, and so forth, has not proved successful.

The fact that the performance of the elderly can be changed with short-term intervention programs suggests that more permanent change could be obtained with more intensive intervention programs. However, it is not yet clear that such changes would be desirable. It has been suggested that elderly individuals may use the problem-solving strategies that are most adaptive given their individual life situations. If this is the case, intervention programs may actually have a detrimental effect. Thus, before intervention programs aimed at producing more long-term change are initiated, both the positive and the negative effects of such change should be clearly established.

I. Introduction

Intervention research is potentially a very useful line of research for furthering knowledge in the area of aging. Not only will intervention studies help to determine the extent to which various abilities are modifiable, which is of theoretical interest, but they will also help to determine the conditions which are conducive to such modification. An understanding of the conditions which lead to modification of various abilities may facilitate a better understanding of the natural developmental antecedents of such abilities as well as facilitate the design of practical intervention programs to ameliorate problems associated with aging if such programs prove to be desirable.

Intervention research in one area of psychological functioning—that of problem solving—will be examined. Both the descriptive research and the interventive research dealing with problem solving during the adult years will be reviewed. The theoretical and practical implications of such research will be discussed and directions for future research will be suggested.

II. Descriptive Research

Although many of the areas in cognitive psychology could be legitimately said to be investigations of problem-solving abilities, only three areas of investigation have been selected for illustrative purposes. The three types of studies selected for review are those involving Piagetian tasks, intelligence tests, and the more traditional problem-solving tasks.

A. PIAGETIAN TASKS

Recent research indicates that elderly adults tend to perform less well on Piagetian tasks, with the possible exception of conservation tasks, than do middle-aged adults. For example, such age differences have been found with classification (Annett, 1959; Denney, 1974a; Denney & Lennon, 1972), multiple classification (Denney & Cornelius, 1975), class inclusion (Denney & Cornelius, 1975), egocentrism (Bielby & Papalia, 1975; Comalli, Wapner, & Werner, 1959; Looft & Charles, 1971; Rubin, 1974; Rubin, Attewell, Tierney, & Tumolo, 1973), animism (Dennis & Malinger, 1949), moral reasoning (Bielby & Papalia, 1975), and various formal operational tasks (Clayton, 1972; Tomlinson-Keasey, 1972). In addition, Storck, Looft, and Hooper (1972) investigated seriation, multiple classification, and egocentrism among individuals 55 years of age and older. Although they reported rather low levels of performance on these tasks, their results are difficult to interpret since they did not obtain a significant relationship between age and performance.

Whereas the results of the preceding studies seem to strongly indicate age differences among adults in performance on Piagetian tasks, with elderly individuals performing at a lower level than middle-aged individuals, the results of studies of conservation are not nearly so consistent. In several cross-sectional studies, elderly individuals were found to conserve less than younger adults. Papalia (1972) found that scores on substance, weight, and volume tests were substantially lower for elderly individuals than for college-aged or middle-aged adults. However, she found no difference between these age groups on a test of conservation of number. Rubin, Attewell, Tierney, and Tumolo (1973) also reported that elderly individuals performed at a significantly lower level than young and middle-aged adults on two-dimensional space, number, substance, weight, and continuous quantity conservation problems. Likewise, Sanders, Laurendeau, and Bergeron (1966) found that elderly individuals conserved less on a conservation of surfaces test than did young or middle-aged adults.

A couple of correlational studies have also been presented as evidence of a decline in performance in old age because of the low conservation performance of the elderly adults tested. Papalia, Salverson, and True (1973) found that the proportions of individuals between 64 and 85 passing substance, weight, and volume conservation tasks were 66.9, 43.7, and 20.9%, respectively. Since the tasks traditionally considered to be more difficult were passed less frequently than the easier tasks, the authors concluded that the elderly participants had lost the ability to conserve on the easier tasks. However, the correlation between age and performance was not significant. Storck, Looft, and Hooper (1972) tested adults ranging in age from 55 to 79 years on weight and volume conservation tasks. All individuals obtained perfect scores on the weight conservation tasks but relatively low scores on the volume conservation task. These authors also concluded that their results provided evidence that elderly individuals exhibit performance decrements on more advanced Piagetian tasks. Again, however, a significant correlation between age and performance on the volume conservation task was not obtained, nor was the correlation between education and performance significant.

Papalia, Salverson, and True (1973) and Storck *et al.* (1972) concluded that the rather low-level conservation performance exhibited by their elderly adults supported the notion that there is a decline in conservation ability in old age. There are at least two problems with such a conclusion. First, it was presumably based on the assumption that younger adults would have performed better on the same conservation tasks. However, since no middle-aged control group was included in either of these studies there is no evidence that middle-aged adults would have performed any better. Second, even if age differences were clearly demonstrated, they might not reflect actual age declines (for a discussion of the problems associated with interpreting such age differences as indicative of age changes, see Baltes, 1968, or Schaie, 1965). Thus, these two studies are inconclusive with respect to both age differences and the hypothesized age declines in conservation among the elderly.

In a third correlational study, Papalia, Kennedy, and Sheehan (1973) found a significant inverse relationship between age and performance on a conservation of surfaces task in adults between 63 and 92. However, a partial correlation between age and performance, with years of education held constant, revealed a nonsignificant correlation. On the other hand, a partial correlation between performance and education with age held constant resulted in a highly significant correlation between the two variables. Thus, the relationship between educational level and performance appeared to be the crucial one rather than the relationship between age and performance.

There is additional evidence that elderly adults and younger adults may not differ in performance on conservation tasks. In addition to studies previously discussed in which elderly individuals attained perfect scores on weight conservation (Storck *et al.*, 1972) and on number conservation (Papalia, 1972), there is also evidence that elderly adults perform as well on continuous and discontinuous quantity conservation tasks as do younger adults. Rubin (1976) reported that 92% of his elderly subjects reached criterion on a test of these two types of conservation. The remaining 8% received scores closely approaching criterion. Furthermore, Rubin emphasized his inability to locate nonconserving individuals even when testing adults of low educational levels, of low socioeconomic class, or living under institutionalized conditions (Rubin, 1975). Likewise, Selzer and Denney (1977) found that elderly adults performed as well on tests of conservation of substance, weight, and volume as middle-aged adults. However, a regression analysis revealed a significant correlation between education and conservation within the elderly group.

While the above studies appear to be conflicting with regard to the effect of age on conservation performance, they do indicate that education may be more closely related to conservation performance than age is. In the Papalia, Salverson, and True (1973), the Papalia, Kennedy, and Sheehan (1973), and the Selzer and Denney (1977) studies, education was found to be significantly related to performance when age alone was not. Only in the Storck, Looft, and Hooper (1972) study was the correlation between education and performance not significant.

Thus, it appears that while definite age differences among adults are obtained on most Piagetian tasks, conservation may be an exception. However, it is important to remember that since all of the studies of Piagetian tasks to date have been cross-sectional, it is not possible to determine whether the age differences that have been found are a result of actual ontogenetic change rather than a result of generational differences.

B.   INTELLIGENCE TESTS

The results of studies of developmental changes in performance on intelligence tests are being included because many of the subtests on intelligence tests tap problem-solving abilities and because a relatively large amount of research has been done in this area. The research suggests that there are different developmental patterns for different abilities. There generally seems to be an increase in verbal abilities throughout most of the life span (e.g., Birren & Morrison, 1961; Horn & Cattell, 1967; Rhudick & Gordon, 1973; Schaie & Strother, 1968; Strother, Schaie, & Horst, 1957), with a possible drop in verbal abilities in the 60s or thereafter (e.g., Birren, 1968; Jarvik & Blum, 1971; Riegel & Riegel, 1972; Schaie & Labouvie-Vief, 1974). With nonverbal abilities (performance, perceptual–motor, etc.), on the other hand, there seems to be a decline that begins in the early adult years and continues throughout the life span (e.g., Birren & Morrison, 1961; Eisdorfer, Busse, & Cohen, 1959; Eisdorfer & Wilkie, 1973; Foulds & Raven, 1948; Horn & Cattell, 1967). Such results have been found with the Wechsler Adult Intelligence Scale which is divided into a verbal portion (includes vocabulary, information, similarities, comprehension, arithmetic and digit span) and a non-verbal portion (includes digit symbol substitution, picture completion, block design, picture arrangement, and object assembly subtests). Such findings were also obtained with the Horn and Cattell (1967; Cattell, 1963) model of fluid and crystallized intelligence. Measures of fluid intelligence are purported to be measures of abilities that are largely determined by the neurophysiological status of the individual (includes such abilities as inductive reasoning, figural relations, and associative memory). Measures of crystallized intelligence are purported to be measures of abilities that are largely determined by learning and acculturation (includes such abilities as verbal comprehension and semantic relations).

Thus, it appears that to the extent that intelligence tests measure problem-solving abilities, and at least some subtests clearly do so, the results of these studies indicate that there are eventual declines in such problem-solving abilities. However, these studies also clearly indicate that the point at which such abilities begin to decline and the rate of decline may vary considerably depending on the type of ability tested. Nonverbal and novel types of problem-solving abilities appear to begin to decline much earlier than more verbal and experience-related types of problem-solving abilities.

Whereas the Piagetian studies reported in the previous section were largely based on cross-sectional designs, much of the research reported in this section was based on longitudinal designs and is therefore much more amenable to conclusions regarding actual age changes (for a discussion of possible biasing effects on such conclusions, see Baltes & Labouvie, 1973).

C. TRADITIONAL PROBLEM-SOLVING TASKS

Some of the more traditional problem-solving tasks have also been administered to middle-aged and elderly adults. Nearly all of these studies have obtained age differences, with the elderly adults exhibiting poorer performances than the middle-aged adults. Such differences have been obtained in cross-sectional studies of performance on traditional concept-learning problems. With these problems the individual is presented with stimuli which vary on a number of dimensions and is told, with each presentation, whether the stimulus is a positive or a negative instance of the concept. The individual's task is, of course, to abstract "the concept." Studies by Arenberg (1968), Brinley, Jovick, and McLaughlin (1974), and Carpenter (1971) have demonstrated that elderly adults perform less well than younger adults on such tasks.

Similar age differences have been found with cross-sectional studies of performance on a variety of "search" tasks in which the individual is supposed to find the "correct" stimulus or stimulus arrangement from a variety of alternatives. In these tasks the subject selects stimulus alternatives and is then told whether the "correct" stimulus or stimulus arrangement is included in the selected sample. The object is to find the correct solution in as few sample selections as possible. Elderly adults have been found to be less efficient on both nonverbal problems in which the subjects select their stimuli with, and received feedback from, a mechanical apparatus (e.g., Arenberg, 1974; Jerome, 1962; Young, 1966, 1971) and verbal problems in which the subjects ask questions and receive verbal feedback from the experimenter (e.g., Denney & Denney, 1973; Rimoldi & Woude, 1971).

Elderly adults also seem to do more poorly than younger adults on tasks which require that they change the concept or strategy that they are using during the experimental session. For example, Heglin (1956) found that elderly adults had more difficulty overcoming set in problems similar to the Luchins' water-jar problems than did younger adults. Likewise, Wetherick (1965) found that elderly adults were less able than younger adults to change an established concept in a typical concept learning session even when they were given feedback which indicated that the concept they were using was no longer correct.

Cross-sectional age differences in verbal reasoning have also been obtained. Bromley (1957) reported that elderly adults performed less well on proverb interpretation tasks than younger adults. Friend and Zubeck (1958) reported similar age differences in "critical thinking"; the test they administered was composed of a number of practical problems. On a test of logical reasoning, Morgan (1956) also obtained age differences, with the elderly adults performing at a lower level than younger adults.

There have been at least two cross-sectional studies of the relationship between problem complexity and age differences. Both Clay (1954) and Kay (1954) found that as the complexity of the problems increase, the difference between the performance of middle-aged and elderly adults also increased.

While the majority of adult developmental studies of performance on traditional problem-solving tasks has yielded age differences, there are a few studies in which such age differences have not been obtained. Since most of the studies in which age differences were not obtained were studies in which the younger and older adults were matched in nonverbal intelligence (e.g., Smith, 1967; Wetherick, 1964), they are difficult to interpret. Since there are age differences in nonverbal intelligence, it is not surprising that when age groups are equated with respect to nonverbal intelligence, age differences on other dimensions are eliminated as well.

Arenberg (1974) conducted a longitudinal study of the more traditional type of problem solving. He tested individuals between the ages of 24 and 87 on logical problem solving and then 6 years later retested the same individuals. His cross-sectional comparisons showed an increase in errors with increasing age; the largest differences occurred between groups under 60 and groups over 60. On the other hand, his longitudinal trends revealed a decline only in individuals over the age of 70.

Generally, studies emanating from different theoretical and historical backgrounds indicate that there are age differences among adults in problem-solving abilities. The cross-sectional studies typically yield larger differences starting at younger ages than the longitudinal studies because age changes are confounded with cohort differences in the cross-sectional studies but not in the longitudinal studies. Thus, it appears that the obtained age differences are a result of both age change (evidenced by the results of longitudinal studies) and cohort effects (evidenced by the fact that age differences are greater in cross-sectional studies than in longitudinal studies).

Kesler, Denney, and Whitely (1976) offered further evidence of the importance of cohort effects in problem-solving ability. They performed regression analyses with performance on problem-solving tasks as criterion variables and age, sex, education, occupation, and nonverbal intelligence as predictor variables. They found that education and nonverbal intelligence were the only significant predictors of problem-solving performance. Nonverbal intelligence could have components of both age-change effects and cohort difference effects and is therefore difficult to interpret. However, since the number of years of education a person has attained is partly a function of his or her cohort and seldom changes as he or she goes from middle to old age, education must be classified as a variable that is indicative of cohort effects rather than of age-change effects. Likewise, Selzer and Denney (1977) included age, education, residence (institution versus community), and sex as predictor variables in a regression analysis with conservation as the criterion variable. They found that among middle-aged and elderly adults education was the only significant predictor. Again, this suggests that there may be cohort effects in performance on Piagetian tasks as well as on some of the more traditional problem-solving tasks.

The issue of whether the obtained age differences are a result of age changes or cohort effects is an important one. However, regardless of whether the obtained age differences are a result of cohort differences or actual age changes, it is important for both theoretical and practical reasons to know whether or not the performance of the elderly can be improved. The purpose of the remainder of this paper is to review research dealing with the issue of whether the problem-solving performance of elderly individuals can be changed, to discuss the theoretical and practical implications of such research, and to suggest directions for future research in this area.

III. Intervention Research

A variety of different intervention approaches has been employed to facilitate problem-solving performance among the elderly. These approaches can be categorized into six basic groups—modeling, direct instruction, feedback, practice, changing response speed, and other indirect noncognitive intervention techniques. Each of these basic approaches and the effectiveness of each approach is reviewed separately.

A. MODELING

One of the types of intervention approaches that has been used with elderly adults is that in which the subject views a model using problem solutions similar to those employed by younger adults. This intervention approach is typically a very effective means of modifying the performance of elderly individuals on a variety of tasks. Denney and Denney (1974) found that modeling improved the question-asking efficiency of elderly adults on a task similar to the 20 Questions game. In this task the subject is presented with a picture of a number of different objects and instructed to identify the object the experimenter is thinking of by asking questions that can be answered with either "yes" or "no." The subject is told to try to find the solution in as few questions as possible. Without training many elderly adults tend to ask questions that eliminate only one item at a time and thus solve the problem more slowly than younger adults whose questions often exclude a whole group of items at a time (Denney and Denney, 1973). However, after simply observing a model ask questions that eliminate more than one item at a time, the elderly begin to ask such questions themselves (Denney and Denney, 1974).

Similar modeling techniques have been used successfully with other types of tasks as well. Denney (1974a) attempted to facilitate classification performance through modeling. She found that after they had observed a model classify the stimuli consistently according to such dimensions as color, shape, or size, the elderly adults were also able to classify consistently according to such dimensions. Meichenbaum (1972) likewise was able to facilitate the performance of elderly adults on concept-learning problems with a modeling procedure. Moreover, Crovitz (1966) found that elderly individuals were better able to learn to sort a deck of cards according to the "relevant" dimension after having observed a model sort the cards three different times according to different dimensions.

In at least two additional studies, modeling approaches have been employed in an attempt to improve performance on inductive reasoning problems. The results of these studies do not provide such clear evidence for the effectiveness of modeling. Labouvie-Vief and Gonda (1976) employed two modeling procedures—one aimed at facilitating cognitive strategies and one aimed at reducing anxiety. They report that both were effective at increasing inductive reasoning but that they were not more effective than a control procedure which consisted of practice with inductive reasoning problems without training. Panicucci (1975) also attempted to increase inductive reasoning by modeling the use of problem-solving strategies. Her modeling procedure was not effective in increasing performance, although performance did improve in her control group which received practice on the problems without any training.

Both the Labouvie-Vief and Gonda and the Panicucci studies illustrate the importance of including practice-only control groups in intervention studies so the effects of practice and training are not confounded. However, since the previously discussed Denney and Meichenbaum studies did include such control groups, the difference between the results of their studies and the results of the Labouvie-Vief and Gonda and the Panicucci studies was not due simply to a difference in the control groups included in the various designs. The differences in the results of the studies are most likely attributable to differences in the effectiveness of the various modeling procedures employed or to differences in the susceptibility of the different abilities studied to training and/or practice effects.

B.   DIRECT INSTRUCTION

A second intervention approach might be called "direct instruction." The studies classified under direct instruction are similar in many ways to the modeling studies. However, rather than being shown how to perform as is done in the modeling studies, the participants in these studies are told how to perform on the relevant task.

Heglin (1956) compared young, middle-aged, and elderly adults on set induction tasks both before and after training. Training consisted of telling the subjects, after they had finished the first series of set induction problems, that their difficulty on some of the latter problems was due to their continued use of a method that they had learned for solving some of the earlier problems although it was no longer efficient or effective on the later problems. The subjects were then told that they would be presented with another series of problems and were warned to try to avoid using just one way of solving the problems. Heglin reported that the middle-aged individuals gained more from the training than did either the younger or older adults; the older adults gained the least. Heglin did not analyze pretraining versus posttraining differences within each age group. However, from the means he presented, it does not appear that his training procedure reduced the elderly adults' susceptibility to set at all. The results of this study demonstrated only that middle-aged adults improved from the first series of set induction problems to the second set of problems. However, since a no-training control group was not included in this study, it is not possible to separate the practice effects from the training effects.

Young (1966) used a direct instruction procedure to facilitate the performance of elderly adults on a nonverbal search task. Her instructions were designed to impose order on the subjects' search strategy and to decrease the demands on short-term memory. Young compared middle-aged and elderly adults. She found that even after rather explicit instructions on how to follow an orderly strategy and how to take notes to lessen the memory load, the elderly subjects still performed at a lower level than did the younger adults. However, since she did not include a control group of individuals who were not given such instructions, it is not possible to determine whether the instructions had a facilitative effect for either age group.

It is difficult to draw conclusions on the basis of the results of the direct instruction studies because of the inadequate research designs and/or inadequate reporting of the statistical analyses and results in the relevant studies. In spite of their problems, these studies do suggest that elderly adults may benefit less from training than younger adults. This is somewhat surprising since elderly adults start out with a lower level of performance and thus should be able to improve more. Whether similar age differences in ability to benefit from training would be obtained with other types of training or with different types of abilities is not clear. Certainly the difficulty of the task under investigation would be a determining factor. The task would have to be difficult enough to preclude the possibility of a "ceiling effect" among the middle-aged group in order to test this hypothesis fairly.

It would be surprising if direct instruction were not effective when modeling appears to be so effective; direct instruction involves just telling the subjects how to perform whereas modeling involves showing the subjects how to perform. However, it is possible that the verbal instructions may be too abstract for the elderly to comprehend as well as they comprehend the more concrete modeling instructions in which they are actually shown how to perform. Since the elderly are apparently functioning at a more concrete level than younger adults (e.g., Arenberg, 1968; Bromley, 1957; Hulicka & Grossman, 1967), such a difference in the concreteness of the intervention approach may actually result in an interaction between age and intervention technique.

C. FEEDBACK

A third intervention approach that has been employed might be called "feedback." The procedures that are included under this heading are really rather diverse, although all of them involve some feedback to the subject regarding the correctness of his or her responses on problem-solving tasks.

Schutz and Hoyer (1976) investigated the effects of feedback on spatial egocentrism in the elderly. The subjects in the training condition were given verbal feedback contingent upon the correctness of their responses. In addition, the experimenter showed the subjects how each pattern appeared from the experimenter's perspective by rotating the matrix 180 degrees. The subjects in the practice condition were given the same number of problems without verbal or perspective-taking feedback. The subjects in the control condition received no problems between the pre-test and the posttest. On the posttest more correct responses were obtained in the feedback condition than in either of the other two conditions.

The Schutz and Hoyer training procedure is difficult to classify. It was classified under feedback techniques because the authors emphasize the feedback component of their training procedure. However, the experimenter's rotation of the matrix is similar to some of the procedures used in the modeling and direct instruction techniques. The experimenter is showing the subject a strategy that he or she can use for solving such problems.

Another training procedure, included under feedback, which also includes direct instruction as well as feedback, is that of Sanders, Sterns, Smith, and Sanders (1975). They assigned the elderly adults in a concept-learning experiment to one of four conditions—reinforced training, training, practice, and control. In the training condition subjects were given verbal feedback after each response to a specific instance and, if necessary, they were also given "strategy hints" and "memory cue cards." In the reinforced training condition they were given tokens for correct responses as well as the verbal feedback, strategy hints, and memory cue cards. In the practice condition if the subject failed a problem, the solution was given before he or she went on to the next problem, but no other feedback was given. In the control condition, the subjects were only given the pretest and the posttest. Both the reinforced training and the training conditions resulted in better performance on the posttest than did either the practice or the control conditions. Thus, as in the Schutz and Hoyer study, practice alone did not facilitate performance. Again, it is apparent that the training procedure involved a great deal more than just feedback. It was very similar to the modeling and direct instruction training procedures in that the subjects were told how to use strategies to solve the problems.

There is at least one study in which only feedback was given without any additional instruction. Hornblum and Overton (1976) attempted to train elderly people to conserve by providing them with feedback contingent upon their responses to conservation problems. The control subjects received the same problems but were not given feedback as to the correctness of their answers. Significantly more conservation responses were obtained on the posttest in the feedback condition than in the control condition.

Since most of the investigations of the effectiveness of feedback have also included procedures similar to those employed in modeling and direct instruction studies, it is difficult to assess the effects of feedback alone. However, since the feedback in the Hornblum and Overton study, which was not confounded with any other procedures, was effective, it suggests that feedback alone may actually have a beneficial effect on problem-solving behavior.

D. PRACTICE ON SIMILAR PROBLEMS

The intervention techniques discussed so far were designed to give the subjects some form of direct training in the problem-solving behavior under investigation. The subjects were either shown how to perform, told how to perform, and/or given feedback regarding their performance. There is another group of intervention techniques which does not involve direct training on the problem-solving behavior in question. Some of these less direct intervention techniques have been used because the investigators have suspected that the elderly have the ability to perform at a higher level on problem-solving tasks than they sometimes exhibit. They suggest that, for some reason, such as lack of practice, lack of motivation, slow response speeds, insufficient consideration of the task demands, or lack of self-confidence, the elderly do not perform as well as they are capable of doing. Thus, these techniques are aimed at trying to change that characteristic which they think is responsible for the less than optimal performance in the first place.

Some researchers have suggested that the elderly may not perform well on problem-solving tasks because they are not frequently required to solve similar problems in their everyday living (e.g., Denney & Denney, 1974; Selzer & Denney, 1977). If this were indeed the case, then practice on similar problems alone might facilitate performance. A number of the previously mentioned studies have included practice-only control groups which are relevant to this issue. In a couple of these studies, practice by itself resulted in improved problem-solving performance (e.g., Labouvie-Vief & Gonda, 1976; Panicucci, 1975). However, there are also studies that show no significant practice effects (e.g., Hoyer, Hoyer, Treat, & Baltes, 1978; Sanders, Sterns, Smith, & Sanders, 1975; Schutz & Hoyer, 1976).

Wetherick (1964) reported an additional study which is relevant to this issue. He presented 20-year-olds, 40-year-olds, and 60-year-olds who were matched on nonverbal intelligence with three problems. The problems involved four switches, each of which could be in any one of three positions. The subject was to find out which position each of the four switches must be in for a light to come on when he pressed a button. In the first problem the subject was told that only one of the switches was "relevant," in the second that two were "relevant," and in the third that either one, two, or three were "relevant." Wetherick concluded that his older subjects did better than either the younger or middle-aged subjects on the third and most difficult problem after having done worse than the other groups on the second problem. Although this study certainly suggests the possibility that elderly individuals gain more from practice than younger individuals, it does not provide very strong evidence for such a hypothesis. Wetherick did not statistically analyze his data and it is therefore difficult to determine whether the age differences he obtained were significant. In addition, since problem difficulty is confounded with order, it would be difficult to determine whether the age effects were a result of differences in the difficulty of the problems or a result of practice effects. Rather than demonstrating the effects of experience or practice, this study must be seen as one that suggests a very promising line of research.

Since the results of the studies that have included practice-only control groups present conflicting results, the effects of practice on cognitive abilities in the elderly are difficult to assess. It may be that practice is more beneficial for some types of tasks than for others, or it may be that the specifics of the practice procedures determine whether the practice is effective.

E.   CHANGING RESPONSE SPEED

Another intervention technique that has been used to change some characteristic of the subject other than problem-solving performance itself is that of changing response speed. Hoyer, Labouvie, and Baltes (1973) hypothesized that the well-established fact that the elderly tend to respond more slowly than younger adults may be a result of experience rather than the result of some biological deficit as is usually assumed. Thus, they attempted to increase the speed of performance of elderly women and then determine whether the resulting improvement in response speed would facilitate performance on intellectual tests that contained a speeded component. Training was conducted with three very simple speed tasks, such as cancelling all of the a's in a series of letters. Three treatment conditions were included. In the reinforced practice condition the subjects were reinforced whenever they completed a trial in less time than they had taken to complete earlier trials. Reinforcement consisted of a light flashing at the end of a trial and subjects were told that they would receive 5 cents for every time the light flashed. In the nonreinforced practice condition the subjects performed all of the tasks but were not given feedback concerning response speed. In the control condition the subjects were not presented with the three training tasks. The results indicated that response speed increased as a function of practice but that the actual reinforcement procedure had little effect. No treatment effects were obtained on the intelligence subtests that were administered after training; thus, neither the training nor the practice had any effect on intellectual performance.

In a similar study, Hoyer, Hoyer, Treat, and Baltes (1978) increased the number of training sessions and changed the reinforcement procedure so that the subjects were given the same number of S & H Green Stamps as the number of items they completed during each 30-sec interval. After the training sessions, the subjects were again given a number of subtests from an intelligence test. No treatment condition effect was found for either response time on the training tasks or performance on the intelligence subtests.

Thus, attempts to increase problem-solving performance indirectly by reinforcing response speed on some unrelated task do not seem to be as effective as some of the more direct methods reported previously.

F. OTHER NONCOGNITIVE INTERVENTION TECHNIQUES

The author conducted a series of studies to determine whether manipulating variables other than problem-solving performance itself might indirectly influence problem-solving performance on the 20 Questions task (Denney, 1977). She hypothesized that the elderly might not perform efficiently on the 20 Questions task because they are not motivated to try to perform well, or because they lack confidence in their ability to perform well, or because they do not take enough time to consider the strategy they are going to use on the task. Thus, she manipulated each of these variables before presenting her elderly subjects with the 20 Questions task in order to see if these manipulations had an effect on performance.

She attempted to increase motivation by setting up a system in which the elderly received more money the fewer questions they used to solve the 20 Questions problems. She found no difference between the performance of the subjects who were reinforced with money for efficient performance and those who were not reinforced. However, money did not appear to be a good reinforcer for the elderly subjects; many of them did not even want to take the money that they earned.

Denney also tried to manipulate self-confidence in the elderly by presenting them with a series of problems, the Raven Progressive Matrices, before the 20 Questions task. The individuals in the experimental condition were told throughout the administration of the Raven Progressive Matrices that they were doing extremely well. The experimenter acted pleasantly surprised at how well they were doing in an attempt to give them the impression that they were doing much better than one might expect. The individuals in the control condition were also given the same problems but they were not given feedback. No difference was obtained between the experimental and control groups in their performance on the 20 Questions task.

Denney also posited that the elderly may not ask constraint-seeking questions on the 20 Questions task because they do not take the time necessary to consider the demands of the task and think of the most appropriate strategy given those demands. She hypothesized that the elderly may require more time than younger adults to decide upon the most appropriate strategy because they have not had as much recent experience with such problem-solving tasks as younger adults. In this study her experimental group was given a forced 3-min delay between the time when the experimenter gave the instructions for the task and the time when they were allowed to begin asking questions. The control group was allowed to begin asking questions as soon as the experimenter finished giving the instructions. Again, no differences between experimental and control groups were obtained on the 20 Questions task.

The results of this series of studies certainly do not prove that manipulation of such variables as motivation, self-confidence, and time to plan a strategy, which are peripheral to problem-solving performance itself, could not be effective. It is possible that better manipulations of these variables might be more effective or that such manipulations might be effective for improving performance on other types of problem-solving tasks. It is also possible that the manipulation of other peripheral variables might be more promising than the manipulation of those studied by

Denney. However, until more research is done in this area, we must conclude that it does not appear that short-term manipulation of such peripheral variables is a very effective means of facilitating problem-solving performance among the elderly.

In summary, the intervention methods that have been used to train individuals, through either modeling, direct instruction, or feedback on the same types of problem-solving tasks that will ultimately be used as the criterion measure, appear to be rather effective. It is, however, difficult to evaluate some of the direct instruction studies because the research designs used do not permit one to draw any clear conclusions regarding the effectiveness of training. The effects of practice on similar or identical problems alone are not clear; in some studies practice seemed to facilitate performance, while in others it did not. Moreover, in all of the other studies in which an attempt was made to manipulate some variable other than problem-solving performance itself, no facilitative effect on problem-solving performance was obtained.

IV. Theoretical Implications

One of the most important findings of these intervention studies is that apparently most, if not all, of the cognitive deficits in problem solving found among the elderly can be at least partially alleviated rather easily with only very brief, short-term intervention techniques. This finding has both theoretical and practical implications. The theoretical implications are discussed first.

A. AGE CHANGE VERSUS COHORT DIFFERENCES

One of the questions that needs to be answered is whether the age differences that have been obtained in problem-solving ability are a result of age changes or cohort differences. As was mentioned earlier, some of the descriptive studies provide evidence relevant to this issue. Both the longitudinal studies of intelligence and Arenberg's longitudinal study of logical problem solving indicate that there are actual intraindividual declines in performance during later adulthood. These studies also indicate that there are cohort differences as well, since the cross-sectional age differences are usually larger than the longitudinal age differences. As was mentioned earlier, the Kesler, Denney, and Whitely (1976) study and the Selzer and Denney (1977) study also provide evidence that there are cohort differences; in both studies, education was a significant predictor of problem-solving performance during the adult years. Number of years of education varies with cohort but not usually with age during the adult years and, consequently, is indicative of cohort effects rather than of age effects.

The intervention studies also have a bearing on the age change versus cohort difference issue. It seems that if the performance of the elderly can be so easily facilitated, their performance deficits may, at least to some degree, be a result of age change. If the deficits were totally a result of cohort differences, it seems that they would be more difficult to alleviate because the elderly individuals would have to learn completely new strategies and, presumably, such learning would involve a more gradual process. Two intervention studies, one with children and one with elderly adults, will help illustrate this point. Both studies were aimed at teaching the subjects to ask constraint-seeking questions on the 20 Questions task. In both studies two different modeling procedures were employed. With one of the procedures the model simply asked constraint-seeking questions (exemplary modeling); with the other, the model both asked constraint-seeking questions and also verbalized the strategy for formulating constraint-seeking questions (strategy modeling). With elderly individuals Denney and Denney (1974) reported that their modeling procedure was highly effective at increasing the use of constraint-seeking questions. They commented that "The ease with which these changes were effected indicates that an intact and efficient questioning strategy lay within the problem-solving repertoires of practically all of the subjects in the study. The modeling procedures apparently served only to elicit this strategy, and this elicitation effect happened very rapidly for most of the subjects" (p. 458). This sudden learning is very different from that observed with children under the same conditions.

Denney and Connors (1974) found that with preschool children the learning process is usually much more gradual and the children seem less able to generalize what they do learn. The percentage of novel, unmodeled constraint-seeking questions that subjects use on the posttest can be used as a measure of the extent to which the subjects are generalizing the strategy modeled by the experimenter. The elderly adults in the Denney and Denney study asked about 27% novel constraint-seeking questions in the exemplary modeling condition and about 40% novel constraint-seeking questions in the strategy-modeling condition. The preschool children in the Denney and Connors study asked about 2% novel constraint-seeking questions in the exemplary modeling condition and about 8% novel constraint-seeking questions in the strategy-modeling condition. So, even though the children in the Denney and Connors study were presented with three times as many training trials as the elderly adults in the Denney and Denney study, they still did not learn to use as generalized a strategy as the adults did. The fact that the elderly adults learn much more quickly and seem to be able to generalize more than the children suggests that they may not be learning a new strategy as the children are but may be just rediscovering a strategy that is already in their repertoire.

In summary, there is evidence that both age changes and cohort differences contribute to the age differences that have been obtained in problem solving among adults. In light of this evidence, the best approach for future research in this area would be to examine the effects of both age changes and cohort differences as well as the interaction between these two factors.

B. ANTECEDENTS OF AGE CHANGES AND COHORT DIFFERENCES

A second theoretical question for which the intervention studies have implications is the question of the antecedents of age differences in problem solving among adults. Until recently most investigators have attributed the deficit in problem solving found among the elderly to declines in neurophysiological functioning that occur in old age (e.g., Dennis & Mallinger, 1949; Hooper, Fitzgerald, & Papalia, 1971; Horn, 1970; Rubin, Attewell, Tierney, & Tumolo, 1973; Young, 1971). More recently, however, investigators have been suggesting that experiential factors may be responsible, at least in part, for some of the obtained age differences. For example, Denney (1974a, 1974b, 1974c) has suggested that some of the cognitive deficits could result from diminished educational and occupational demands encountered by the elderly. Likewise, Looft and Charles (1971) and Rubin, Attewell, Tierney, and Tumolo (1973) have suggested that a decrease in social interaction could contribute to some of the observed deficits.

The results of the intervention studies reported above suggest that many of the problem-solving deficits observed in the elderly are, at least in part, a result of experiential factors. It seems unlikely that deficits caused solely by neurophysiological degeneration could be so easily alleviated by such short-term intervention techniques. If deficits caused by neurophysiological degeneration could be overcome at all, it seems that much more intensive training programs would be required.

Even though the intervention studies indicate that environmental variables may contribute to age differences in problem solving, that does not eliminate the importance of biological factors. It is naive to ask whether age differences are a result of biological factors or of environmental factors; certainly both are important. Rather, it is important to determine under what conditions and how biological factors contribute to age changes and under what conditions and how environmental variables contribute to age changes. It is also important to determine how the less desirable effects of such biologically caused and environmentally caused age changes might be ameliorated.

So far the environmental and biological factors that have been proposed as precursors of age changes have been discussed. Although they have not received nearly as much attention in the literature, the environmental and biological variables that may be responsible for cohort differences need to be considered. The only variable that has received much attention as a possible cause of cohort differences is education. It is clear that the different cohorts of adults living today have received different amounts, and possibly even different types, of education. Since education is one of the most obvious and easily measurable variables that differ across cohorts, it is the most likely candidate for investigation. Education has been examined in a number of studies of different abilities and the results so far have been conflicting. While a number of investigators have reported significant correlations between education and cognitive performance (e.g., Kesler, Denney, & Whitely, 1976; Papalia, Kennedy, & Sheehan, 1973; Papalia, Salverson, & True, 1973; Selzer & Denney, 1977; Young, 1971), some have also reported that education was not significantly related to cognitive performance (e.g., Rubin, 1974; Rubin, Attewell, Tierney, & Tumolo, 1973; Storck, Looft, & Hooper, 1972). Thus, the role of education in effecting performance in later adulthood is not yet clear. However, education is very likely responsible for some of the cohort effects in cognitive abilities. Its role should be investigated in much more depth in future research. In addition, there is a host of other less obvious environmental variables that need to be investigated as potential contributors to cohort effects. For example, time spent in viewing television, in reading books, in traveling, in interacting with other adults, and in leisure time activities over the course of one's life are all factors that vary considerably across cohorts and, thus, may contribute to cohort differences in cognitive performance. The effects of such variables also need to be investigated.

In addition to environmental variables, it is also possible that biological variables may contribute to cohort effects and there is a number of biological variables that seem likely candidates for such a role. For example, cohort differences in nutrition, physical exercise, physical illness, and drug consumption are a few examples of some of the possibilities. These variables, as well as environmental variables, need to be investigated.

C. COMPETENCE VERSUS PERFORMANCE

A third theoretical issue to which the intervention studies are relevant is that of the distinction between competence and performance. Flavell and Wohlwill (1969) originally applied the distinction between competence and performance to the area of cognitive abilities. They defined competence as the "formal, logical representation of the structure of some domain" (p. 71) and performance as that which "represents the psychological processes by which the information embodied in competence actually gets assessed and utilized in real situations" (p. 71). Bearison (1974) has argued that this distinction may facilitate a better understanding of the deficits in cognitive functioning so often found among the elderly. He says that his interpretation of the "disintegration of cognitive functions so common in schizophrenia and apparently in the aged as well is that it represents an increasingly wider gap between competence and performance" (p. 27). Bearison goes on to say, "If certain types of procedures can be shown to reverse or ameliorate a cognitive deficit, then the deficit would seem to be one of performance" (p. 28).

According to Bearison, the results of the intervention studies should be interpreted as indicating that the elderly have a performance deficit but not a competence deficit. However, this formulation seems to be an oversimplification. Whenever someone is able to learn a new skill, does it mean that that person necessarily already had competence in that domain? It seems that a further distinction needs to be made. What Bearison is apparently referring to as competence can be divided into a "having the capacity to learn an ability" component and an "already having the ability" component. The fact that elderly adults can respond in the desired way as a result of some intervention procedure does not indicate that they already have the relevant response in their repertoires; they may have learned a completely new way of responding. If the elderly already have the particular ability in question in their repertoires, then manipulations of variables other than direct training on that particular ability, as well as direct training on that ability, may elicit the relevant performance. However, if the elderly did not have the ability in question in their repertoires, they probably could acquire it only through direct training on that ability. If deficits that result from cohort differences can be overcome, then new learning is most likely involved. If deficits resulting from age changes can be overcome, then either new learning or the elicitation of previously acquired responses may be involved, depending on whether the original ability actually has been lost as a result of increasing age or maintained but not exercised.

The intervention studies presented previously provide conflicting evidence on the issue of whether the intervention techniques are teaching the elderly new abilities or are just eliciting intact abilities. First, a comparison of the effectiveness of the direct and indirect intervention techniques suggests that the elderly are being taught new responses. The investigators who have proposed that the desired responses already exist in the elderly individual's repertoires, and who consequently have tried to enhance performance by manipulating the peripheral noncognitive variables which they think may be responsible for the responses not being exhibited in the first place, have not been very successful in this endeavor. The successful training techniques have been those that entail direct training on the specific ability in question. This suggests that the elderly may not have the abilities in their repertoires; rather, it suggests that they may be learning new responses. However, it is possible that the studies that focused on manipulating peripheral noncognitive variables either did not involve manipulations of the most critical variables or did not involve effective manipulations of the critical variables. Before any conclusions should be drawn the effects of a variety of other potentially important variables should be investigated and some of the previously studied variables should be manipulated in other, possibly more effective, ways.

Second, as was reported previously, the very rapid learning reported in some of the intervention studies (e.g., Denney & Denney, 1974) suggests that new learning is not taking place, but that already present responses are simply being elicited. For example, if the elderly were learning a totally new response when they were taught to use a constraint-seeking strategy on the 20 Questions procedure, their learning might be expected to be more gradual, as is that of young children. It is clear that the young children do not have the ability to use a constraint-seeking strategy in their repertoires; but it is clear that they have the capacity to learn to use a constraint-seeking strategy. On the other hand, even though the elderly may not use a constraint-seeking strategy spontaneously, they appear to already have the ability to use such a strategy because they are able to pick it up so quickly.

Thus, the two preceding lines of research seem to be in conflict with respect to what they suggest regarding whether elderly adults have in their repertoires many of the cognitive abilities that they do not ordinarily exhibit in performance. A great deal more research will be needed before this question can be answered with any degree of confidence. Again, the answer will probably not be a simple one. The elderly may have some abilities that they do not exhibit in performance and they may have lost other abilities that they would still be able to relearn if given training. There may also be some abilities that the elderly are not able to learn but, if so, that limitation is not apparent from the intervention studies reported above. All of the abilities reported were facilitated with at least some of the intervention programs. It is possible that when the elderly are unable to learn a particular ability it is predominantly a result of neurophysiological damage. On the other hand, in the other two cases in which the elderly either retain the capacity to learn the ability or retain the actual ability even though they do not exhibit it in performance, any loss may be predominantly a result of environmental factors. If this were the case, then within any group of elderly individuals some might be unable to learn a particular ability as a result of neurophysiological damage while others might retain the actual ability or, at least, be able to learn the ability. Thus, some elderly individuals may be able to benefit from intervention procedures and others may not. It is not possible to tell from the reports of most of the intervention studies whether there are such individual differences; only group means have typically been presented. It might be interesting to follow up some of the intervention studies to determine which of the subjects were surviving about 5 years after the intervention. If the above hypothesis that individuals who are unable to benefit from intervention are more likely to suffer from neurophysiological damage is correct, it may be that the individuals who gain least from intervention are closer to death than those who show more gain. The phenomenon known as "terminal drop" may occur because neurophysiological deterioration frequently precedes death. When abilities, such as verbal abilities and conservation abilities, that are frequently used by the elderly begin to show a decline, it may be because brain damage has begun to interfere with performance. Other abilities and strategies that are used less frequently by the elderly may simply become less likely to be exhibited through lack of practice. In these cases, however, intervention procedures should be able to elicit or teach such abilities and strategies. However, when the elderly begin to lose abilities that they use frequently in their daily lives, such as verbal abilities and conservation, it seems less likely that intervention procedures would be effective.

V. Practical Implications

The underlying assumption in many of the intervention studies has been that it would be desirable to try to change the problem-solving performance of the elderly if techniques capable of effecting such change are available. Most of the intervention studies to date have been of such a short-term nature, it is unlikely that they would result in permanent change. However, efforts to produce more lasting changes may be undertaken in the future. Such efforts should be undertaken only if it has been demonstrated that the outcome would be beneficial for the elderly individuals involved. Before we can determine whether intervention programs aimed at producing long-term change would be beneficial we need to know a lot more about why the elderly perform as they do. It is possible that the elderly function in the most adaptive way, given their particular circumstances. If that is the case, more harm than good may be done by trying to change their approach to problem solving. At the very least, it might be a waste of time for both the elderly individuals and the investigators.

In fact, the author has previously proposed that the elderly may classify according to criteria that are typically considered less sophisticated because, for them, it is more adaptive. Denney (1974c) concluded that since the elderly can learn so quickly to classify according to more sophisticated criteria than they typically use on their own, they obviously have the ability to classify according to these criteria but they may prefer to use other criteria. The elderly often classify stimuli according to complementary criteria, i.e., they put things together that are different but that share some interrelationship, such as a car and a garage, rather than the more abstract criteria that middle-aged adults tend to use. Denney concluded that both young children and elderly adults may classify according to complementary criteria because complementary criteria are the most natural; objects are grouped according to complementary criteria in the world and therefore in one's natural experience. She also suggested that this natural tendency to group according to complementary criteria may only be overcome when individuals are encouraged to classify in a more abstract way as a result of educational or occupational demands. If this hypothesis is correct, then there would be nothing to be gained by trying to permanently change the way elderly adults classify.

It is also possible that a case can be made that the ways in which the elderly perform on some of the other cognitive tasks also may be more adaptive for them than the ways in which younger adults perform on the same tasks. This possibility needs to be carefully considered. The advantages and disadvantages of intervention programs aimed at effecting long-term change in the elderly need to be carefully assessed before such programs are undertaken.

Another practical question that must be answered if it is determined that it is beneficial to try to change the problem-solving behavior of the elderly is which of the various intervention techniques is the most effective for changing problem-solving performance. However, as was stated earlier, all of the techniques that focus on changing problem-solving performance directly seem to be effective. The more indirect techniques, on the other hand, have not proved to be so effective. Based on the research to date, it is not possible to make relative comparisons of the various direct intervention techniques. Such comparisons will probably not be possible until investigators compare the relative effectiveness of the different techniques directly with a number of different types of problem-solving tasks.

VI. Suggestions for Future Research

The above discussion of the descriptive and intervention studies of problem solving during the adult years points out the importance of a number of methodological considerations for future research in this area. First, there is some suggestion in the literature on intelligence and in the Piagetian literature that problem solving may be composed of more than one factor and that the different factors may follow somewhat different developmental trends. For example, performance on nonverbal measures of intelligence tends to begin to decline at an earlier age than performance on verbal measures of intelligence and performance on most Piagetian tasks apparently tends to begin to decline at an earlier age than performance on conservation tasks. It would be interesting to include a wide variety of problem-solving tasks in the same factor analytic study to see what factors emerge and whether there are different developmental trends for each of the different factors. If different problem-solving factors have different antecedents, lumping the various factors together might just obscure relationships that exist between antecedents and problem-solving behavior. To increase the likelihood of finding such relationships, it is important to first determine whether there are distinct factors and then, if there are, to study them separately.

Once the various factors that make up problem-solving ability have been established, then it will be important to use designs such as those proposed by Schaie (1965) and Baltes (1968) to separate the effects of age changes from the effects of cohort differences. In addition to determining whether the age differences that are obtained are a result of age changes and/or cohort effects, the specific causes of the age changes and/or cohort differences that are obtained need to be investigated. Multiple regression studies in which a variety of potential antecedents (either biological or environmental) is included as predictor variables may be helpful in isolating some of the antecedents.

It would also be useful to compare a variety of intervention techniques and a variety of different types of problem-solving tasks in the same study. Then it could be determined whether some intervention techniques were more effective than others, whether some types of problem solving were more amenable to change than others, or whether there was an interaction between intervention technique and type of problem-solving task. It might also be valuable to compare different types of intervention techniques with different age groups. For example, as was mentioned earlier, modeling may be more effective than direct instruction among elderly adults, but not among middle-aged adults because modeling tends to be a more concrete mode of information transmission.

The remaining suggestions are concerned with the specifics of the design of intervention studies. In future intervention studies both practice-only and no-practice control groups should routinely be included. When just a no-practice control group is included, it is difficult to know whether significant intervention effects are obtained because of the intervention itself or simply because of practice. On the other hand, when just a practice-only control group is included, it is difficult to know what effect the practice has had on performance.

Future intervention studies should include middle-aged individuals as well as elderly individuals. Some of the studies that have not included middle-aged control groups have reported that the performance of the elderly after training was as good as that of middle-aged groups (e.g., Denney & Denney, 1974). This would indicate that the intervention eliminated age differences. However, other investigators who have actually included middle-aged groups have reported that the middle-aged individuals gained more from the intervention than the elderly individuals (e.g., Heglin, 1956; Young, 1966). This finding calls into question the conclusion that the deficit of the elderly is eliminated by the intervention techniques that have raised the elderly's level of performance to that of the untreated middle-aged individuals. Without a middle-aged comparison group, the strongest conclusion that can be drawn is that the elderly improve with training over their initial level of performance.

Although it has seldom been done, intervention studies should routinely include tests of both generalization and durability. In the few studies in which generalization to new tasks was tested, the results have been conflicting; significant transfer effects have been found in some (e.g., Hornblum & Overton, 1976; Labouvie-Vief & Gonda, 1976) and not in others (e.g., Hoyer, Hoyer, Treat, & Baltes, 1978; Schultz & Hoyer, 1976). The results of the studies in which the durability of intervention effects was investigated are more consistent. Typically, the intervention effects are stable over the very short time periods (e.g., 2 weeks) that have been tested (e.g., Labouvie-Vief & Gonda, 1976; Schultz & Hoyer, 1976). It is important to investigate the effects of generalization across tasks and durability across time because of the theoretical and practical importance of the results of such investigations. For example, if it becomes apparent that it would be beneficial to permanently enhance the problem-solving performance of the elderly adults, then we could select to use the intervention technique or techniques that produce the most generalization across tasks and durability across time.

References

Annett, M. The classification of instances of four common class concepts by children and adults. *British Journal of Educational Psychology,* 1959, **29**, 223–236.

Arenberg, D. Concept problem solving in young and old adults, *Journal of Gerontology,* 1968, **23**, 279–282.

Arenberg, D. A longitudinal study of problem solving in adults. *Journal of Gerontology,* 1974, **29**, 650–658.

Baltes, P. B. Longitudinal and cross-sectional sequences in the study of age and generation effects. *Human Development,* 1968, **11**, 145–171.

Baltes, P. B., & Labouvie, G. V. Adult development of intellectual performance: Description, explanation, and modification. In C. Eisdorfer & M. P. Lawton (Eds.), *The psychology of adult development and aging.* Washington, D. C.: American Psychological Association, 1973.

Bearison, D. J. The construct of regression: A Piagetian approach, *Merrill–Palmer Quarterly,* 1974, **20**, 21–30.

Bielby, D. D., & Papalia, D. E. Moral development and egocentrism: Their development and interrelationship across the life-span. *International Journal of Aging and Human Development,* 1975, **6**, 293–308.

Birren, J. E. Increments and decrements in the intellectual status of the aged. *Psychiatric Research Reports,* 1968, **23**, 207–214.

Birren, J. E., & Morrison, D. F. Analysis of the WAIS subtests in relation to age and education. *Journal of Gerontology,* 1961, **16**, 363–369.

Brinley, J. E., Jovick, T. J., & McLaughlin, L. M. Age, reasoning, and memory in adults. *Journal of Gerontology,* 1974, **29**, 182–189.

Bromley, D. B. Some effects of age on the quality of intellectual output. *Journal of Gerontology,* 1957, **12**, 318–323.

Carpenter, W. L. The relationship between age and information processing capacity of adults. *Industrial Gerontology,* 1971, **8**, 55–57.

Cattell, R. B. Theory of fluid and crystallized intelligence: A critical experiment. *Journal of Educational Psychology,* 1963, **54**, 1–22.

Clay, H. M. Changes of performance with age on similar tasks of varying complexity. *British Journal of Psychology,* 1954, **45**, 7–13.

Clayton, V. *The role of formal operational thought in the aging process.* Unpublished manuscript, State University of New York at Buffalo, 1972.

Comalli, P. E., Wapner, S., & Werner, H. Perception of verticality in middle and old age. *Journal of Psychology,* 1959, **47**, 259–266.

Crovitz, E. Reversing a learning deficit in the aged. *Journal of Gerontology,* 1966, **21**, 236–238.

Denney, N. W. Classification abilities in the elderly. *Journal of Gerontology,* 1974, **29**, 309–314. (a)

Denney, N. W. Classification criteria in middle and old age. *Developmental Psychology,* 1974, **10,** 901–906. (b)

Denney, N. W. Evidence for developmental change in categorization criteria for children and adults. *Human Development,* 1974, **17,** 41–53. (c)

Denney, N. W. *The effect of the manipulation of noncognitive variables on problem-solving performance among the elderly.* Unpublished manuscript, University of Kansas, 1977.

Denney, N. W., & Connors, J. C. Altering the questioning strategies of pre-school children. *Child Development,* 1974, **45,** 1108–1112.

Denney, N. W., & Cornelius, S. Class inclusion and multiple classification in middle and old age. *Developmental Psychology,* 1975, **11,** 521–522.

Denney, D. R., & Denney, N. W. The use of classification for problem solving: A comparison of middle and old age. *Developmental Psychology,* 1973, **9,** 275–278.

Denney, N. W., & Denney, D. R. Modeling effects on the questioning strategies of the elderly. *Developmental Psychology,* 1974, **10,** 458.

Denney, N. W., & Lennon, M. L. Classification: A comparison of middle and old age. *Developmental Psychology,* 1972, **7,** 210–213.

Dennis, W., & Mallinger, B. Animism and related tendencies in senescence. *Journal of Gerontology,* 1949, **4,** 218–221.

Eisdorfer, C., Busse, E. W., & Cohen, L. D. The WAIS performance of an aged sample: The relationship between verbal and performance I.Q.'s. *Journal of Gerontology,* 1959. **14,** 197–201.

Eisdorfer, C., & Wilkie, F. Intellectual changes with advancing age. In L. F. Jarvik, C. Eisdorfer, & J. E. Blum (Eds.), *Intellectual functioning in adults.* New York: Springer, 1973.

Flavell, J., & Wohlwill, J. Formal and functional aspects of cognitive development. In D. Elkind & J. Flavell (Eds.), *Studies in cognitive development: Essay in honor of Jean Piaget.* New York: Oxford University Press, 1969.

Foulds, G. A., & Raven, J. C. Neural changes in mental abilities of adults as age advances. *Journal of Mental Science,* 1948, **94,** 133–142.

Friend, C. M., & Zubeck, J. P. The effects of age on critical thinking ability. *Journal of Gerontology,* 1958, **13,** 407–413.

Heglin, H. J. Problem solving set in different age groups. *Journal of Gerontology,* 1956, **11,** 310–317.

Hooper, F., Fitzgerald, J., & Papalia, D. Piagetian theory and the aging process: Extensions and speculations. *Aging and Human Development,* 1971, **2,** 3–20.

Horn, J. L. Organization of data on life-span development of human abilities. In L. R. Goulet & P. B. Baltes (Eds.), *Life-span developmental psychology: Research and theory.* New York: Academic Press, 1970.

Horn, J. L., & Cattell, R. B. Age differences in fluid and crystallized intelligence. *Acta Psychologica,* 1967, **26,** 107–129.

Hornblum, J. N., & Overton, W. F. Area and volume conservation among the elderly: Assessment and training. *Developmental Psychology,* 1976, **12,** 68–74.

Hoyer, F. W., Hoyer, W. J., Treat, N. G., & Baltes, P. B. Training response speed in young and elderly women. *International Journal of Aging and Human Development,* 1978, in press.

Hoyer, F. W., Labouvie, G., & Baltes, P. Modification of response speed and intellectual performance in the elderly. *Human Development,* 1973, **16,** 233–242.

Hulicka, I. M., & Grossman, J. L. Age-group comparisons for the use of mediators in paired-associate learning. *Journal of Gerontology,* 1967, **22,** 46–51.

Jarvik, L. F., & Blum, J. E. Cognitive declines as predictors of mortality in twin pairs: A twenty-year longitudinal study of aging. In E. Palamore & F. Jeffers (Eds.), *Prediction of Lifespan.* Lexington, Mass.: Heath, 1971.

Jerome, E. A. Decay of heuristic processes in the aged. In C. Tibbits & W. Donahue (Eds.), *Social and psychological aspects of aging.* New York: Columbia University Press, 1962.

Kay, H. The effects of position in a display upon problem solving. *Quarterly Journal of Experimental Psychology,* 1954, **6,** 155–169.

Kesler, M. S., Denney, N. W., & Whitely, S. E. Factors influencing problem solving in the middle-aged and elderly. *Human Development,* 1976, **19,** 310–320.

Labouvie-Vief, G., & Gonda, J. N. Cognitive strategy training and intellectual performance in the elderly. *Journal of Gerontology,* 1976, **31,** 327–332.

Looft, W. R., & Charles, D. C. Egocentrism and social interaction in young and old adults. *International Journal of Aging and Human Development,* 1971, **2,** 21–28.

Meichenbaum, D. *Training the aged in verbal control of behavior.* Paper presented at the International Congress on Gerontology, Kiev, Russia, 1972.

Morgan, A. B. Differences in logical reasoning associated with age and higher education. *Psychological Reports,* 1956, **2,** 235–240.

Panicucci, C. L. *The effect of training on inductive reasoning behavior in young and old adults.* Paper presented at the 28th annual meeting of the American Gerontological Society, Louisville, Ky., October 1975.

Papalia, D. E. The status of several conservation abilities across the life-span. *Human Development,* 1972, **15,** 229–243.

Papalia, D., Kennedy, E., & Sheehan, N. Conservation of space in noninstitutionalized old people. *Journal of Psychology,* 1973, **84,** 75–79.

Papalia, D. E., Salverson, S. M., & True, M. An evaluation of quantity conservation performance during old age. *Aging and Human Development,* 1973, **4,** 103–109.

Rhudick, P. J., & Gordon, C. The age center of New England study. In L. F. Jarvik, C. Eisdorfer, & J. E. Blum (Eds.), *Intellectual functioning in adults.* New York: Springer, 1973.

Riegel, K. F., & Riegel, R. M. Development, drop, and death. *Developmental Psychology,* 1972, **6,** 306–319.

Rimoldi, H. G. A., & Woude, K. W. V. Aging and problem solving. *Industrial Gerontology,* 1971, **8,** 68–69.

Rubin, K. The relationship between spatial and communicative egocentrism in children and young and old adults. *Journal of Genetic Psychology,* 1974, **125,** 295–301.

Rubin, K. Personal communication, 1975.

Rubin, K. Extinction of conservation: A life-span investigation. *Developmental Psychology,* 1976, **12,** 51–56.

Rubin, K., Attewell, P., Tierney, M., & Tumolo, P. The development of spatial egocentrism and conservation across the life-span. *Developmental Psychology,* 1973, **9,** 432.

Sanders, J. C., Sterns, H. L., Smith, M., & Sanders, R. E. Modification of concept identification performance in older adults. *Developmental Psychology,* 1975, **11,** 824–829.

Sanders, S., Laurendeau, M., & Bergeron, J. Aging and the concept of space: The conservation of surfaces. *Journal of Gerontology,* 1966, **21,** 281–285.

Schaie, K. W. A general model for the study of developmental problems. *Psychological Bulletin,* 1965, **64,** 92–107.

Schaie, K. W., & Labouvie-Vief, G. Generational versus ontogenetic components of change in adult cognitive behavior: A fourteen-year cross-sequential study. *Developmental Psychology,* 1974, **10,** 305–320.

Schaie, K. W., & Strother, C. R. A cross-sectional study of age changes in cognitive behavior. *Psychological Bulletin,* 1968, **70,** 671–680.

Schutz, N. R., & Hoyer, W. J. Feedback effects on spatial egocentrism in old age. *Journal of Gerontology,* 1976, **31,** 72–75.

Selzer, S. C., & Denney, N. W. *Conservation abilities among middle-aged and elderly adults.* Paper presented at the biennial meeting of the Society for Research in Child Development. March, 1977, New Orleans.

Smith, D. K. The Einstellung effect in relation to the variables of age and training. Doctoral dissertation, Rutgers University, 1966. *Dissertation Abstracts,* 1967, **27B,** 4115.

Storck, P. A., Looft, W. R., & Hooper, F. H. Interrelationships among Piagetian tasks and traditional measures of cognitive abilities in mature and aged adults. *Journal of Gerontology,* 1972, **27,** 461–465.

Strother, C. R., Schaie, K. W., & Horst, P. The relationship between advanced age and mental abilities. *Journal of Abnormal and Social Psychology,* 1957, **55,** 166–170.

Tomlinson-Keasey, C. Formal operations in females from eleven to fifty-six years of age. *Developmental Psychology,* 1972, **6,** 364.

Wetherick, N. E. A comparison of the problem-solving ability of young, middle-aged and old subjects. *Gerontologia,* 1964, **9,** 164–178.

Wetherick, N. E. Changing an established concept: A comparison of the ability of young, middle-aged and old subjects. *Gerontologia,* 1965, **11,** 82–95.

Young, M. L. Problem-solving performance in two age groups. *Journal of Gerontology,* 1966, **21,** 505–509.

Young, M. L. Age and sex differences in problem solving. *Journal of Gerontology,* 1971, **26,** 330–336.

The Primary Mental Abilities in Adulthood: An Exploration in the Development of Psychometric Intelligence

K. Warner Schaie

ANDRUS GERONTOLOGY CENTER
AND DEPARTMENT OF PSYCHOLOGY
UNIVERSITY OF SOUTHERN CALIFORNIA
LOS ANGELES, CALIFORNIA

LIFE-SPAN DEVELOPMENT
AND BEHAVIOR, VOL. 2

Abstract

This chapter recounts the natural history of a longitudinal–sequential study of psychometric intelligence covering the adult life-span from the 20s into the 80s which has now been in progress for 21 years. It presents a summary of findings on age changes and cohort differences, experimental mortality, and differences between results from repeated measurement panels and sequential random samples from the same population frame, for the variables of Verbal Meaning, Space, Reasoning, Number, and Word Fluency, as well as composite indices of intellectual ability and educational aptitude. Implications are discussed for future investigations of psychometric intelligence and for the development of theoretical models of psychometric intelligence in adulthood.

I. Introduction

It is the purpose of this chapter to present the natural history of a program of scientific inquiry which has preoccupied the writer for the past quarter century and to provide a summary of its results and implications. Practically all of the data to be presented here have previously been published, but they are scattered over many journal articles. The historical background important for understanding the material in proper context has been presented only orally, and there is up to now no single convenient account other than a brief discussion suited mostly for an undergraduate audience (Schaie, 1975) to integrate this material.

To introduce the writer's scientific odyssey then, some remarks are in order to signify the original objectives as well as the more programmatic goals that have emerged along the way. These may be conveniently divided into a consideration, first, of the question why one should study the progress of intelligence in adulthood, and second, to give an account of the circumstances which led to the particular research decisions embedded in our studies. As part of this account, moreover, there will be an opportunity to acknowledge the contributions of colleagues and students who have contributed mightily. Much of the credit for that which went well must be ascribed to their contributions, while, of course, the responsibility for what went awry must be mine.[1]

---

[1]The following colleagues and students participated in the various data collections and analyses and/or contributed to the resultant scholarly products: Margret Baltes, Paul

A. WHY STUDY INTELLIGENCE IN ADULTHOOD?

As in many other substantive areas in developmental psychology, early empirical work on intelligence also was directed toward investigating the acquisition of functions and skills in early life. However, early theoretical writers, such as G. Stanley Hall (1922), H. L. Hollingworth (1927), and Sydney Pressey (1939), soon awakened interest in some of the complexities related to attainment of peak performance level, transformations of intellectual structure, and decremental changes occurring in late middle age and the senium. Terman's original standardization on the Binet Intelligence test for American use assumed that intellectual development peaked at age 16 and then remained constant (Terman, 1916). Moreover, Yerkes (1921), in examining World War I soldiers, found that the apparent average level of function for young adults was only 13 years of age. Such assumptions were soon called into question, however, by data from other early empirical studies. Jones and Conrad (1933), on the basis of cross-sectional studies in a New England community, found substantial age differences among adults on some subtests of the Army Alpha intelligence test but little differences on others. Similar findings were obtained in the standardization studies surrounding the development of the Wechsler-Bellevue intelligence test, again emphasizing the fact that growth of intelligence does not seem to end in early adolescence, that peak ages apparently differ for different aspects of intellectual functioning, and that age differences are not uniform across the full spectrum of abilities tapped by most of the major batteries measuring intellectual development (Wechsler, 1939).

Now all these matters might be of purely historical interest if it were not for the fact that omnibus measures of intelligence have generally been found quite useful in predicting a person's competence in dealing with our society's educational system and later on succeeding in vocational pursuits where educationally based knowledge and skills are required. Specific measures of ability, while not terribly successful, have nevertheless had some use in predicting competence in meeting specific situational demands. The analysis of patterns of intellectual performance has also been found helpful by clinicians and in the diagnostic appraisal of psychopathology. When dealing with the elderly, moreover, it is apparent that some determination of intellectual competence may be directly rele-

Baltes, Tom Barrett, Gisela Bertulis, Barbara Buech, Kathy Gribbin, Christopher Hertzog, Pamela Hertzog, Judy Higgins, Eric Labouvie, Gisela Labouvie-Vief, Karen Laughlin, Ann Nardi, John Nesselroade, Iris Parham, Robert Peterson, Alan Posthumer, Margaret Quayhagen, Pat Sand, Coloma Harrison Schaie, Michael Singer, Vicki Stone, Charles Strother, Nathanial Wagner, and Elizabeth Zelinski.

vant to such issues as mandatory retirement, maintenance of individual living arrangements, and the conservation and disposition of property.

For all of these issues it is clearly necessary to know the developmental patterns of different aspects of mental ability and the ages at which developmental peaks occur to be able to differentiate age from cohort differences, to be able to distinguish between obsolescence and decrement, as well as to understand what variables may contribute to the apparent fact that some individuals show intellectual decrement beginning with early adulthood while others maintain and increase their functioning until advanced old age. Our inquiry has tried to address these issues more or less systematically with a purposefully limited and specific set of variables. We will next turn to the natural history of this endeavor.

B. NATURAL HISTORY OF A STUDY

It all began during my junior year at the University of California at Berkeley, where I was much impressed by a well-taught course on psychometric methods with Read Tuddenham. Here I was first introduced to the concept of factor analysis. I inferred that while the work of Wechsler on adult intelligence might be of great importance for clinicians, the Wechsler–Bellevue, because of its factorial complexity, was less than exemplary for the exploration of developmental issues. During my senior year in 1951 I took some directed studies with Tuddenham and proposed to explore what happened to a more clearly defined set of abilities, as defined by the Thurstones' Primary Mental Abilities Test (PMA), into adulthood. Casting about for suitable sources of subjects, I was introduced to gerontology when my family physician (Dr. Robert Perlman) suggested that I consider using his waitng room to test patients in his largely geriatric practice. This I proceeded to do, supplementing my subjects with some recruited through the then pioneer San Francisco Senior Citizen Center directed by Florence Vickery. Lacking much statistical training, I further recruited a classmate (Fred Rosenthal) who had just finished the second statistics course and who joined me in formalizing my first study. This study was designed to test the propositions that there would be differences in age patterns for the five abilities tested by the PMA as well as to test whether such differences would be maintained when the PMA was administered in unspeeded form. My family physician was a member of the Gerontological Society and he encouraged presentation of results at the 2nd International Congress of Gerontology in St. Louis, with eventual publication of findings in the *Journal of Gerontology* (Schaie, Rosenthal, & Perlman, 1953).

During 1951–1952, while I was still at Berkeley, there were some discussions of trying to relate behavioral rigidity to differential patterns of intellectual change with age. This work proceeded at the University of Washington, resulting first in an MA thesis (under the direction of Charles Strother, Paul Horst, and Sidney Bijou) which developed a factored test of behavioral rigidity (Schaie, 1955, 1960; Schaie & Parham, 1975), and then in some pilot work which assessed this relationship in a group of retired college graduates who were also assessed on a variety of other variables with respect to defining limits of optimal functioning (Schaie, Baltes, & Strother, 1964; Schaie & Strother, 1968a, 1968d; Strother, Schaie, & Horst, 1957). More definitive was a doctoral dissertation which tested the relationship between rigidity–flexibility and intelligence but which also served to replicate the earlier work on differential ability patterns across the adult life-span, and which constituted the base for the subsequent longitudinal and sequential studies (Schaie, 1958a, 1958b, 1958c, 1959a, 1959b).

By fortunate coincidence, my mentor, Charles Strother,[2] was president of the board of Group Health Cooperative of Puget Sound, one of the early health maintenance organizations, at the time the dissertation plans matured. A symbiotic arrangement was worked out, which allowed me, with the active cooperation of Group Health management, to recruit volunteer subjects who had been selected by a random draw from the age/sex stratification of the plan membership. My contribution to Group Health was to administer and analyze a membership satisfaction questionnaire at the same time that I obtained psychometric data on the PMA and certain other variables. Results of this study demonstrated a relation of flexibility–rigidity to intelligence at all ages. It did not provide evidence in support of a causal developmental model involving differential patterns for flexible and rigid individuals, but it did provide a sound demonstration of differential patterns for mental abilities across age and provided the basis for the eventual sequential studies.

After an interlude as a postdoctoral fellow at Washington University, St. Louis, I assumed my first academic appointment at the University of Nebraska at Lincoln. While preparing my courses I became aware of the emerging reports from longitudinal studies, such as those by Owens (1953, 1959) and by Bayley and Oden (1955), which suggested maintenance of intellectual function into middle age at least, contrasting with some of the cross-sectional data in the earlier literature and my dissertation data. I soon became convinced that what was needed was the follow-up of a broad cross-sectional sample such as mine by means of short-term longitudinal study. After several years of intermittent discussion, Strother and

[2]The other members of my doctoral committee were Paul Horst, Sidney Bijou, George Horton, Roger Brown Loucks, and Joseph Cohen.

I submitted a grant for such a follow-up study which was funded by the National Institute of Child Health and Human Development (NICHHD) (HD 367-01) in time to collect data in the summer of 1963.

Charles Strother was once again president of the board of Group Health, which by now had grown substantially, and we were able to use their computerized system to retrieve and retest many of the original participants. Heeding Kuhlen's (1940, 1963) admonition, we attended to the question of sociocultural change by drawing a new random sample over the age range covered in the 1956 study plus a new random sample of the age interval now reached by the oldest longitudinal subjects.

Although the 1963 study essentially replicated the earlier cross-sectional findings, the longitudinal comparisons provided substantial surprises. As a consequence, publication of results was delayed while I stewed over possible resolutions. This required some theoretical analyses, leading to the formulations of a general development model (Schaie, 1965, 1967). Findings from both the repeated measurement and comparison of independent samples were eventually reported, to call attention to the matter of cohort differences and to question seriously the universality of intellectual decrement in community-dwelling individuals (Nesselroade, Schaie, & Baltes, 1972; Schaie, 1970; Schaie & Strother, 1968b, 1968c).

Since our longitudinal findings were based on a single 7-year interval (statistically adjusted to 5 years in the reports on the 1963 study), it soon became clear that further replications were in order, not only to buttress the findings on age versus cohort differences but to permit application of all of the new sequential strategies. They were also needed to explore the effect of "experimental mortality," i.e., nonrandom loss of participants in longitudinal studies of cognitive development. Another grant from NICHHD (HD 4476-01), this time to West Virginia University, supported a further follow-up and new data collection during the summer of 1970. Although the 1963 findings were generally replicated (Schaie, Labouvie, & Buech, 1973; Schaie & Labouvie-Vief, 1974; Schaie & Parham, 1977), some interesting discrepancies did occur which have recently fanned a considerable amount of scientific controversy (cf. Baltes & Schaie, 1976; Horn & Donaldson, 1976).

We have been privileged to have had continuing support for this study, located since 1973 at the University of Southern California, from the National Institutes of Health (NIH) (HD 4476-04, AG 480-05), which has permitted full exploration of our data base, as well as relating it to additional information made possible by accessing the health histories of participants and the accumulation of data on environmental complexity and life styles. More important for the purpose of this chapter were studies which examined the aging of the tests we were using, the possibility of shifting from the original sampling without replacement (18,000 member) population frame, to a sampling with replacement (210,000 member) frame, and finally, the fourth 1977 data collection which has just been completed.

None of these studies could have been done without the enthusiastic cooperation of staff and members of the Group Health Cooperative and many interested graduate students and colleagues. In some minor way our study may be a model of how long-range developmental studies can be conducted by meaningful collaboration with organizations which must maintain panel membership for other socially significant reasons. The problems of maintaining continuity in a study which has now been in progress for over 20 years are formidable, but the results of a continuous program have been most rewarding. In the following sections I will attempt to summarize and illustrate by examples some of the findings I find most interesting and significant.

II. The Primary Mental Abilities: Description of the Measurement Variables

Before I proceed with an account of our findings, it will be useful to describe the variables which we have assessed throughout. Although the Wechsler scales have been most widely used with adults for clinical purposes (cf. Matarazzo, 1972; Schaie & Schaie, 1977), they do not have a clear-cut factorial structure. At the initiation of our investigations it seemed therefore more reasonable instead to consider the factored tests provided by the work of the Thurstones (1949), particularly since our initial work (Schaie, Rosenthal, & Perlman, 1953) indicated satisfactory applicability to a group of individuals in the age range from 53 to 78 years, even though the test was originally constructed and normed for adolescents. The Primary Mental Abilities Test (PMA) battery was derived from the factor analysis of about 60 mental tests, resulting in the differentiation of realtively distinct mental abilities (Thurstone & Thurstone, 1941). The form we have used consistently is the 1948 PMA 11-17 version.[3] The PMA test battery consists of five subtests designed to cover the relatively independent factors listed below with descriptions slightly modified from the test manual (Thurstone & Thurstone, 1949).

A. VERBAL MEANING (V)

This is the ability to understand ideas expressed in words. It is used in activities where information is obtained by reading or listening to words.

[3]From *SRA Primary Mental Abilities*, Ages 11–17, Form AM. © 1948, by L. L. Thurstone and Thelma Gwinn Thurstone. Reproduced by permission of the publisher, Science Research Associates, Inc.

The task requires verbal recognition via a multiple-choice format. In the following example the subject must select that alternative which is the best analog of the capitalized stimulus word:

BIG   A. ILL   B. LARGE   C. DOWN   D. SOUR

The test contains 50 items in increasing order of difficulty with a time limit of 4 min.

B.   SPACE (S)

Measured here is the ability to think about objects in two or three dimensions. It may be described as the ability to imagine how an object of figure would look when it is rotated, to visualize objects in two or three dimensions, and to see the relations of an arrangement of objects in space. The more recent technical definition of this ability is *spatial orientation*. Space is measured by 20 test items, with a time limit of 5 min. In the example given below every lettered figure that is the same as the stimulus figure, even though it is rotated, is to be marked. Figures that are mirror images of the first figure are not to be marked.

C.   REASONING (R)

The ability, which in current factor taxonomies is often more specifically identified as *inductive reasoning,* involves the solution of logical problems—to foresee and plan. The Thurstones (1949) propose that persons with good reasoning ability can solve problems, foresee consequences, analyze a situation on the basis of past experience, and make and carry out plans according to recognized facts. Reasoning is measured by such items as the following:

a b x c d x e f x g h x   h i j k x y

The letters in the row form a series based on a rule. The problem is to discover the rule and mark the letter which should come next in the series. In this case the rule is that the normal alphabetic progression is interrupted with an x after every second letter. The solutions therefore would be the letter i. There are 30 test items with a time limit of 6 min.

D. NUMBER (N)

This is the ability to work with figures and to handle simple quantitative problems rapidly and accurately. It is measured by test with items of the following kind:

$$
\begin{array}{r}
17 \\
84 \\
\underline{29} \\
140
\end{array}
\qquad \boxed{R} \quad \boxed{W}
$$

The sum of each column of figures is given. However, some of the solutions given are right and others are wrong. Sixty test items are given, with a time limit of 6 min.

E. WORD FLUENCY (W)

This ability is concerned with verbal recall involved in writing and talking easily. It differs from verbal meaning further in that it concerns the speed and ease with which words are used, rather than the degree of understanding of verbal concepts. The measurement task requires the subject to write as many words as possible beginning with the letter S during a 5-min period.

F. COMPOSITE INDICES

In addition to the factor scores we have consistently reported results on two derived linear composites. These are an index of intellectual ability (or composite IQ) obtained by summing subtest scores weighted approximately inversely to the standard deviation of each test (Thurstone & Thurstone, 1949) according to the formula:

$$\text{Intellectual ability} = V + S + 2R + 2N + W$$

and an index of educational aptitude (EQ) suggested by Thurstone (1958) as a more useful predictor for performance in educational settings with the formula:

$$\text{Educational aptitude } 2V + R$$

Since there were no suitable adult norms available at the initiation of our studies, we generally proceeded to transform all scores to T scores with a mean of 50 and standard deviation of 10, using as the reference group all records at first test available at the time of the particular analysis.

III. Age Differences in Intelligence:
Patterns for Different Abilities

We began our inquiry by addressing the question whether or not factorially defined measures of intellectual functioning would show different
age patterns. This question was first asked in the pilot studies, which also
examined the applicability of the PMA to an older adult population, and
more defintively in our first major cross-sectional study.

A. THE PILOT STUDIES

Sixty-one subjects were tested with the PMA under standard conditions
and for purposes of analysis arbitrarily divided into four groups, aged
53–58, 59–64, 65–70, and 71–80 years, respectively. Since no adult norms
were available, raw scores were converted into percentiles using
Thurstone's conversion table for 17-year-olds. Figure 1 depicts the results
of this study and shows quite dramatically that while our fiftyish group
was slightly above the 50th percentile (suggesting stability of function) for
Number and Verbal Meaning, they performed only at about the 30th
percentile on Word Fluency, and even lower on Space and Reasoning.
This differential pattern obtained for all groups, with apparent further
decrement into the 60s and then maintenance at the lower level into the
70s (Schaie, Rosenthal, & Perlman, 1953).

The first pilot study also gave some support to the construct validity of
the PMA 11-17 when used with older individuals, inasmuch as the inter-

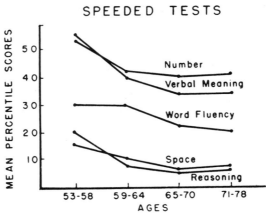

Fig. 1. Performance of older subjects on the primary mental abilities in percentile score
level for a 17-year-old comparison group. (From Schaie, Rosenthal, & Perlman, 1953.
Copyright by the *Journal of Gerontology*. Reproduced by permission.)

correlations remained low and did not differ significantly from those found for adolescents. Split-half reliabilities, moreover, were found to be in the nineties.

A second pilot study occurred in the summer of 1954 as part of a broader investigation of optimal limits of functioning of well-educated community-dwelling older persons (more completely described in Schaie & Strother, 1968b). The sample consisted of 25 male and 25 female college graduates, ranging in age from 70 to 88 with a mean age of 76.5 years, all in fair to superior health with no psychiatric complaints noted by the examining physicians. Again, the differential patterns of abilities was quite clear, with Space and Reasoning well below Verbal Meaning, Number, and Word Fluency. When comparison was made with adolescents, members of this superior adult group in the early 70s were still a standard deviation above the adolescent mean for Number and Verbal Meaning, and even those in their 80s fell at the adolescent mean for several variables (Strother, Schaie, & Horst, 1957). Of course for such a high-ability group the implication is strong that their performance was reduced from their earlier level of functioning. What seemed called for next, therefore, was a parametric study for a representative sample across a broad spectrum of the adult age range.

B. THE FIRST CROSS-SECTIONAL STUDY

As indicated in the section on the natural history of this study, the major base for our sequential studies was laid in 1956 with the assessment of a sample of 500 subjects consisting of 25 males and 25 females in each 5-year age interval from 20 to 70 years. Data based on this carefully stratified and selected sample generally confirm the findings from the pilot study and shed further light particularly on the issue of age of peak functioning. Earlier studies of intellectual development, including those by Wechsler, concluded that peaks occurred in late adolescence or the early 20s (cf. Schaie, 1970). The 1956 study showed an early peak for Reasoning alone. Space did not peak until 26–30, Verbal and Word Fluency until 31–35, and Number reached top performance in the age group 46–50. Figure 2 indicates age differences from peak level in T-score points. Pattern differences were once again confirmed, with Space and Reasoning showing the greatest, and Number and Word Fluency least apparent decrement. In addition, it was noted that until about age 40, the modal pattern was relatively superior performance on Reasoning and Space as compared with Word Fluency and Number, with Verbal Meaning in between. This pattern completely reversed with the 46- to 50-year-old and older groups. Of interest also was the finding that adjusting PMA

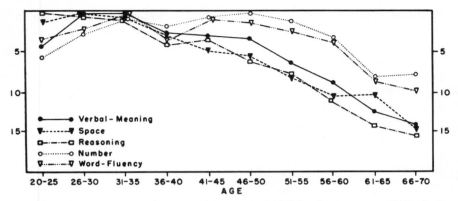

Fig. 2. Mean decrement in the primary mental abilities from mean peak levels in T-score points. (From Schaie, 1958c. Copyright by the American Psychological Association. Reproduced by permission.)

scores for the effect of measures of rigidity and psychomotor speed led to only minor reductions in age differences (Schaie, 1958c), with similar results when covariation was attempted for differences between age groups in income, education, and occupational level (Schaie, 1959a).

IV. Development of Sequential Studies

In the summer of 1963 it was possible to retest successfully 303 (60.6%) of the members of the 1956 panel. A new random sample from the 1956 population stratified by age and sex yielded an additional 995 usable test records. Once the conceptual issues of relating short-term longitudinal to cross-sectional data had been solved (Schaie, 1965, 1967), three distinct issues could be addressed with this data base. The first was concerned with the identification of age changes on the basis of the longitudinal data. The second involved the effects of experimental mortality or dropout from panel studies on the generalizability of longitudinal findings. The third concerned the replication of the age difference findings.

A. THE FIRST LONGITUDINAL FOLLOW-UP

Two substantive findings of considerable significance emerged from analysis of the first follow-up study (Schaie & Strother, 1968b). First, while there was substantial replication of cross-sectional findings, means at comparable ages were systematically higher in 1963 than in 1956 for all variables except for Word Fluency, where the opposite pattern prevailed.

Moreover, when we examined the longitudinal age changes (dotted lines in Fig. 3), it became clear that, again with the exception of Word Fluency, ontogenetic changes are minimal until the 60s. Even then they appear to be largest, in contrast to the cross-sectional findings, for Word Fluency and are quite small for Reasoning, Space, Number, and Verbal Meaning.

It occurred to us next that we could use the cross-sequential method to contrast the effect of age differences between cohorts (cross-sectional differences) with age changes over 7 years (longitudinal change). This analysis led us to conclude that the effect of cohort differences was much more impressive than the effect for aging. Of course, cross-sectional differences confound age and cohort, just as longitudinal changes confound age and time of measurement effects. Our data implied that there might well be age effects within cohorts at both early and late ends of the adult age continuum.

We next concerned ourselves with the problems of constructing appropriate gradients which permitted comparison between cross-sectional and longitudinal findings. We argued that the best comparison would occur by contrasting short-term longitudinal data with cross-sectional data averaged over the time interval bounding the longitudinal segments. For purposes of age-gradient construction we combined data from both sexes and furthermore, to reduce sampling variability, calculated age changes for successive 5-year age intervals averaged over each pair of successive cohorts. Figure 4 provides graphic representations of the estimated average cross-sectional and composite longitudinal gradients. What these graphs compare, in short, are age gradients obtained on the basis of current performance of individuals at different ages who are members of different cohorts with the estimated longitudinal age gradient for a single cohort. Note that if age differences are attributable solely to maturational or otherwise age-related causes, then gradients constructed in either manner ought to coincide. However, if cross-sectional differences include differences in experience or talent between successive cohorts, then the two gradients must diverge. If generational differences go in a positive direction then the cross-sectional between-generation difference gradient must be below the longitudinal within-generation gradient. Conversely, unfavorable change cross generations will yield cross-sectional gradients falling above the longitudinal gradient.

Inspection of Fig. 4, following the above criteria, reveals positive intergenerational differences for Verbal Meaning, Space, and Reasoning, and to a lesser degree for Number. Negative generational differences are clearly shown for Word Fluency, As is generally true for omnibus measures of intellectual ability, ours included, no differences were found between cross-sectional and longitudinal gradients, because the effects of

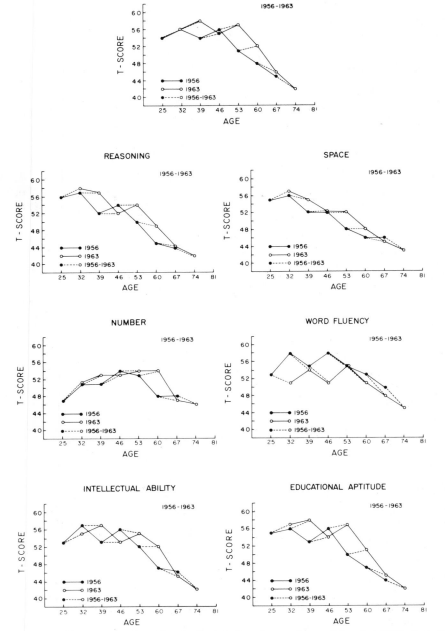

Fig. 3. Cross-sectional and longitudinal findings by age for participants initially tested in 1956 and retested in 1963. (From Schaie & Labouvie-Vief, 1974. Copyright by the American Psychological Association. Reproduced by permission.)

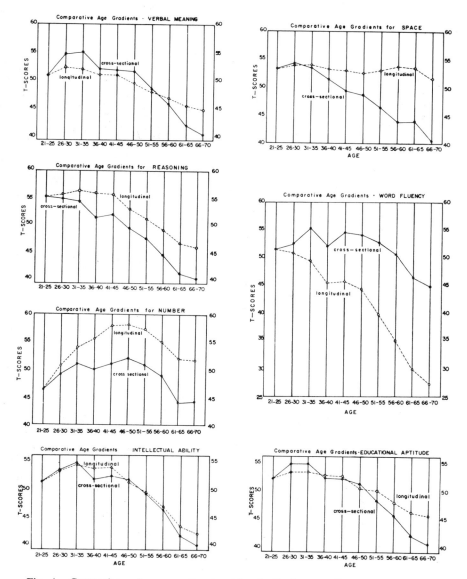

Fig. 4. Comparison of cross-sectional and longitudinal age gradients. (From Schaie & Strother, 1968c. Copyright by *Multivariate Behavioral Research*. Reproduced by permission.)

positive and negative generational differences have been averaged. Of course, the index of educational aptitude showed positive intergenerational differences, being a composite of measures for which similar findings occur.

B. THE FIRST EXPERIMENTAL MORTALITY STUDY

One of the major problems of longitudinal follow-up studies is the concern that nonrandom dropout will tend to impair the validity of one's finding. This issue can, of course, be readily addressed by comparing performance of subjects at entry into a study for those subjects who have been successfully reexamined with the ones who have been lost (Baltes, Schaie, & Nardi, 1971). To provide a more succinct analysis, our entire battery (intelligence and flexibility–rigidity) was factored and second-order factor scores were obtained for all participants at first test ($N=500$). Of interest here is only the first factor, which was interpreted as crystallized intelligence but which I would now rather identify as a second-order general intelligence factor, loading on all our intelligence subtests except Space. The analysis of variance was then applied to a 2 (participation) × 5 (age) × 2 (sex) design, each cell consisting of random draws of either 14 participants or 14 nonparticipants. Differences significant at or beyond the 1% level of confidence were obtained for age and retest survival but not for sex or any of the interaction effects. Factor score means for retest participants at entry into the study were higher for all age decades except for participants in their 20s. We concluded, therefore, that our longitudinal analysis would probably tend to be positively biased with respect to maintenance of functional level, even though slopes of age gradients were not likely to be affected.

C. THE SECOND CROSS-SECTIONAL STUDY

The biasing effects of experimental mortality are but one aspect of the difficulties faced in panel follow-up studies. Another serious limitation is that upon second measurement participants are likely to be much more testwise or, even in the absence of 7-year practice effects, may have different expectational sets. Because of these concerns we decided to provide additional support for our repeated measurement study by collecting data for a new sample randomly drawn from the same population base as the original sample. Although 995 participants were tested (and form the base of our second follow-up study), only the first 25 men and women in each 5-year interval from 21 to 75 years were used in the conjoint independent random samples analysis for comparison with our total 1956 sample.

The report of the analysis of the data comparing the two cross-sectional studies (Schaie & Strother, 1968c), was the first instance in which we tried to apply different sequential models to the same data set. With two time points available it was possible to arrange data in both cross-sequential and time-sequential forms (see Schaie, 1965, 1977). In the first instance we pair for each cohort the measures taken from two samples on the two test occasions. Consequently the sample drawn for each cohort at the second time of measurement will be older by a constant time interval. In this design, if differences between means are due solely to the effect of common environmental change over the intervening period, then only the time main effect would be significant. However, if mean differences are due to generational differences alone, we would expect significant cohort but not time-of-measurement effects. If mean differences were attributable to maturational change alone, then both time and cohort effects would have to be significant, since in this case we would expect both age changes and age differences. This latter situation would, of course, also pertain if there were both cohort and time-of-measurement differences but no maturational effects.

The latter distinction can be made, however, by rearranging data in the time-sequential design. Here we pair the means for participants of the same chronological age but measured on the two test occasions. In this design, if differences in means were attributable to maturational change alone, we would expect a significant age main effect, but no time effect. Now, if there is a reliable time-of-measurement effect it ought to appear in both cross- and time-sequential designs. If mean differences are attributable to generational effects alone, however, we should see both age and time effects in the time-sequential design but only cohort effects in the cross-sequential design. Also, we would expect a relatively lower F ratio for the age than for the cohort effect. The reason for such outcome is that if there are cohort differences but no age changes, then the effect of cohort differences would be spread between the age and time components of variance in the time-sequential designs but concentrated in the cohort component in the cross-sequential design. Finally, the conjoint effects of age and time differences would lead to significant main effects in both designs, but with the age effect greater than the cohort effect and the time effect larger in the cross-sequential than in the time-sequential design. The opposite pattern would, of course, argue for an underlying model involving the joint effect of time and cohort.

Appropriate comparison of cross-sequential and time-sequential data matrices (see Schaie & Strother, 1968c, Tables 1 and 2), given the above considerations, suggests that mean differences between samples for Verbal Meaning, Space, Reasoning, and Number, as well as the composite indices largely represent favorable cohort differences. In contrast, sample differences on Word Fluency appear to be accounted for by the conjoint effects of unfavorable age changes and time-of-measurement differences.

V. Stability of Findings on the Generational versus Ontogenetic Differences Issue

The results of the studies described in the previous section seriously challenged much of the literature on adult intellectual development and consequently it was felt that replications were in order to secure an even stronger empirical foundation for the implicit conclusion that much of the heretofore reported decremental change in adult intellectual function was not attributable to irreversible age changes. Another limitation of a two-point study is further presented by the fact that over a single time period true ontogenetic change could be hidden by unusually favorable compensatory events occuring during such period. Also a two-point study does not permit a direct comparison between age and cohort effects, if both are operating conjointly. That is, to contrast the behavior of two cohorts from one level to another one requires three points in time. Last, but not least, it is the cohort-sequential method which permits the comparison of intraindividual ontogenetic changes with interindividual differences, an interest dear to the heart of developmentalists (cf. Schaie & Baltes, 1975).

During the third data collection wave in the summer of 1970 we were able to reexamine 162 (32.4%) of the members of the 1956 panel, for the third time, and 418 (42.0%) of the members of the 1963 panel for a second time. A third random sample was drawn from the residual membership of the original population frame and 705 participants were initially tested. As in the preceding section we will first consider the longitudinal findings, then turn to the study of experimental mortality in sequential designs, and third consider the replication of cross-sectional age differences over a 14-year period.

A. THE SECOND LONGITUDINAL FOLLOW-UP

Two separate issues could now be addressed on the basis of short-term longitudinal data. Once again we are in a position to describe within-subject age changes for a series of seven successive 7-year cohorts, but now over a 14-year time period, albeit with a further attrited panel (Schaie

& Labouvie-Vief, 1974). Of equal interest, however, is the replication of 7-year changes within subjects for two independent samples carried during two successive time periods. It is this latter comparison which permits application of the cohort-sequential method and thus a direct test of the relative contribution of age and cohort variance (Schaie & Parham, 1977).

1. Changes over 14 years

This aspect of our study can be conceptualized as the simultaneous longitudinal study from 1956 to 1970 of seven cohorts, successively differing by 7 years in average birthdate. Thus, the oldest cohort, with average birth year 1889, is followed from mean age 67 to mean age 81; the youngest cohort, with average birth year 1931, is followed from mean age 25 to mean age 39; and so on. Results of this analysis plotted along a chronological age scale are provided by Fig. 5.

Inspection of Fig. 5 demonstrates clearly the substantial effects of cohort differences. However, it also focuses on the many differences in ontogenetic pattern by type of ability as well as cohort membership. When we consider longitudinal age changes over a 14-year period, reliable decrement ($P > .01$) is observed for Space and Reasoning only for the oldest cohort, from mean age 67 to mean age 81. No reliable 14-year change is found for Number. For Verbal Meaning, however, reliable decrement is observed for both oldest and second-oldest cohort; i.e., as early as from age 60 to 74. Moreover, for Word Fluency decrement is found for all but the two youngest cohorts; that is, beginning from age 39 to 53. Reliable decrement on the composite IQ measure is seen for the three oldest cohorts, from age 53; but for the measure of educational aptitude only for the two oldest cohorts, from age 60. In addition, a reliable 14-year increment from 25 to 39 is found for the youngest cohort for Verbal Meaning and educational aptitude.

2. Replication of 7-Year Changes

The second data set of interest in the 1970 follow-up study comes from those individuals who first entered our study in 1963 and for whom 7-year longitudinal data are available. This data set is an independent replication of the findings reported in Section IV,A of this chapter with one difference. In the first follow-up there were seven cohort groups with initial average age levels from 25 to 67, who at retest were ages 32–74, respectively. Since we also examined one older cohort in 1963 (to be able to do cohort matching with the 1956 sample), we have here an additional cohort group covering the age range of 74 to 81 from initial to follow-up test. In all other respects, Fig. 4 and 6 are directly comparable. Note, however, that every comparable age level in the two studies is of necessity offset by one 7-year cohort; i.e., the 25-year-olds (at first test) in the first follow-up

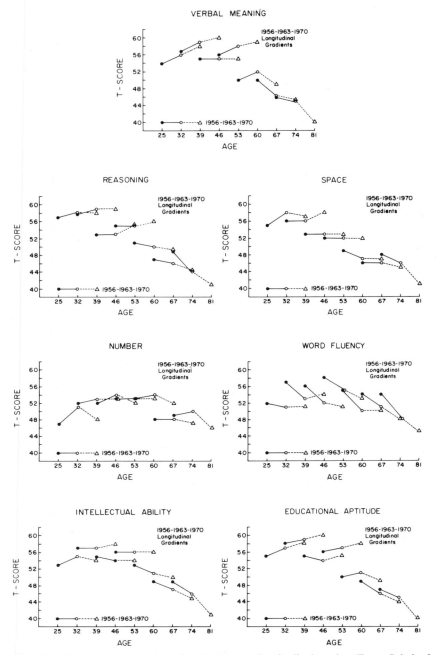

Fig. 5. Mean scores by cohort for the 14-year longitudinal study. (From Schaie & Labouvie-Vief, 1974. Copyright by the American Psychological Association. Reproduced by permission.)

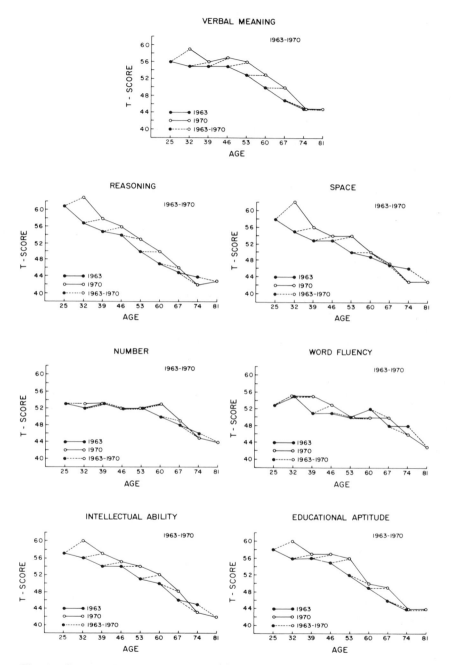

Fig. 6. Cross-sectional and longitudinal findings by age for participants initially tested in 1963 and retested in 1970. (From Schaie & Labouvie-Vief, 1974. Copyright by the American Psychological Association. Reproduced by permission.)

87

study were born in 1931, while those in the second follow-up belonged to the 1938 birth cohort.

Inspection of Fig. 6 shows confirmation of and even clearer patterns for the age/cohort relationship shown in our first study for Verbal Meaning, Space, Reasoning, and the composite indices. For Number there is partial replication; this time without the finding of apparent negative cohort effects for the youngest cohort. However, there is apparent failure to replicate our earlier finding of substantial ontogenetic changes in early middle age. It is apparent then that the longitudinal findings for the first follow-up may have reflected (for the younger cohorts) negative time-of-measurement rather than age decrement effects.

Once again we note cross-sectional gradients which reflect age differences in favor of younger cohorts, but which for the two measurement points are either quite similar or are offset in a favorable direction for the younger cohorts. The stability of the 7-year repeated measurement within cohorts, however, is even more impressive than in the first follow-up. When Duncan's multiple-range test is applied to age changes within cohorts, we do not find a single decrement significant at the 1% level of confidence before age 67. To be specific, no significant 7-year change is found for Reasoning and Verbal Meaning; for the latter there are significant increments from age 25 to 32 and from age 39 to 46. Space shows a significant decrement from age 74 to 81 and a significant increment from 25 to 32; Number a significant decrement from age 67 to 74; and Word Fluency shows significant decrement from age 74 to 81 and increment from 25 to 32. The composite index of intellectual ability increases significantly from 25 to 32 and decreases after age 67. Finally, the index of educational aptitude goes up from 25 to 32 and from 39 to 43, with decrement only from 67 to 74.

These data clearly support our contention of the late onset and relatively limited evidence for ontogenetic decrement in healthy populations. Once again we must stress that the reanalysis of the longitudinal data by Horn and Donaldson (1976) consists of the unsound application of statistical legerdemain and cannot be taken seriously (cf. also Baltes & Schaie, 1976; Schaie & Baltes, 1977). Horn and Donaldson do, however, correctly point to discrepancies in findings between the panel studies and the estimates derived from independent samples. That question is addressed in Section VI of this chapter.

B. THE SECOND EXPERIMENTAL MORTALITY STUDY

Once again, the above findings must be tempered by the effects of selective attrition which impair the degree to which such findings can be generalized widely. The first experimental mortality study was of necessity cross-sectional in nature, since in 1963 we could only examine the 1956 differences between dropouts and retestees. In 1970, on the other hand, it was possible to use the cross-sequential design and contrast base scores for participants and dropouts from the same cohorts who had entered the study in either 1956 or 1963. This design then permits examining both cohort by participation and time-of-measurement by participation interactions for all variables of interest (Schaie, Labouvie, & Barrett, 1973).

Participation effects significant at or beyond the 1% level of confidence were found for all variables. As shown by Fig. 7, participants consistently get higher mean scores, with the exception of the two youngest cohorts on Number, Word Fluency, and the composite intellectual ability measures. The difference between retest participants and dropouts, however, is more pronounced for the older cohorts. In fact, significant age by cohort interactions ($P > .01$) were found for Verbal Meaning, Number, and the composite indices. In addition, there were less pronounced participation by time-of-measurement effects ($P > .05$) for Verbal Meaning and the index of educational aptitude, in the direction of greater differences between retest participants and dropouts in 1963. What is apparent then, is that the discrepancies between members of the longitudinal panel and random samples from the parent population tend to increase over time.

C. THE THIRD CROSS-SECTIONAL STUDY

On the assumption that our three cross-sectional samples represent random draws from the parent population which should differ only with respect to the time when first tested, it would seem appropriate to com-

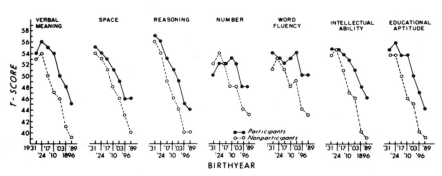

Fig. 7. Cohort differences for retest participants and dropouts. (From Schaie, Labouvie, & Barrett, 1973. Copyright by the Gerontological Society. Reproduced by permission.)

pare cross-sections at equivalent ages. Figure 8 depicts the data for average ages from 25 to 67 for the 1956 sample ($N = 490$), ages 25–74 for the 1963 sample ($N = 960$), and ages 25–81 for the 1970 sample ($N = 701$). Perhaps the most interesting finding here is that at equivalent ages there was a higher level of performance for successive samples for all variables except Word Fluency, where the opposite pattern prevails. It is of some interest to note that what appear to be effects of sociocultural change occurred at a faster rate for the second period, from 1963 to 1970, for the unspeeded tests but slowed for the one highly speeded measure, Word Fluency. Considering the effects of the cohort by time interaction we note particularly large shifts for those individuals in the 40s and 50s during the course of our studies. We might speculate then that these individuals constitute the generation most dramatically effected by rapid educational and technological change (see Schaie, Labouvie, & Buech, 1973, for further details).

The issue of generational changes, as addressed on the basis of replicated cross-sectional studies, can be dramatized further by graphing mean scores by cohort rather than by age. To do so we must compute an estimate of the performance for each cohort at a constant age. This can be done if we assume, for this purpose, that cohort differences account for most of the variance between cross-sectional samples. Even though we have observations for every cohort only at each of three ages, we can estimate the others by obtaining values for the confounded age/time-of-measurement (longitudinal) differences provided by the cross-sequential analysis which can be added as a constant to the observed points. Figure 9 presents projected cohort gradients derived in this manner to show what the expected level of performance was or will be for cohorts with average time of birth from 1889 to 1931, at 53 years of age (chosen because that happens to be the average age of participants in our study). To compute these gradients, we used the means actually observed for each age level as the base level. Age change estimates were then derived from the 1963–1970 interval to predict future missing values and from the 1956–1963 to "postdict" missing values for cohorts who are now beyond the age level of interest. Note that three variables, Verbal Meaning, Space, and Reasoning, showed a constant increment across successive cohorts, but the jump is the steepest between the cohort born in 1910 and that born in 1924, a pattern which also held for the composite indices. Number followed the same trend, but in a far less sharply defined manner, and Word Fluency actually showed a drop from the oldest to the fourth cohort; then there was a rebound similar to the other abilities, but followed by further decrement for the remaining two cohorts.

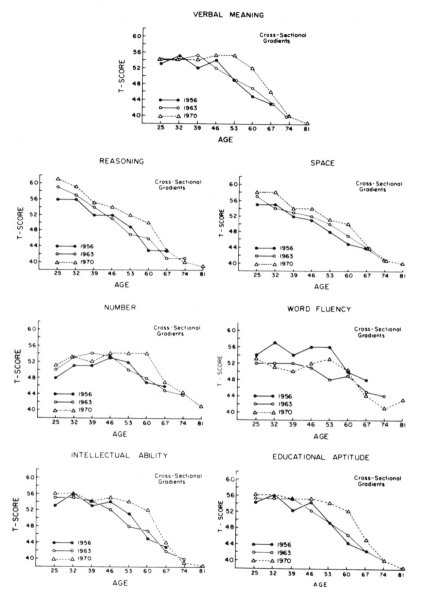

Fig. 8. Mean scores for the independent cross-sectional samples at first test. (From Schaie, Labouvie, & Buech, 1973. Copyright by the American Psychological Association. Reproduced by permission.)

K. *Warner Schaie*

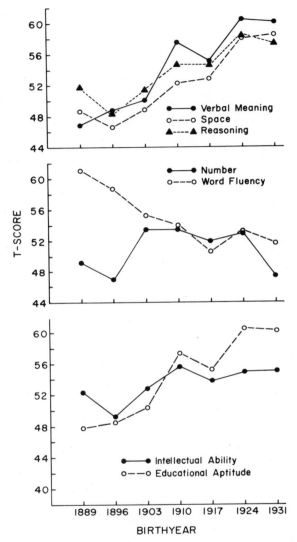

Fig. 9. Cohort gradients for the primary mental abilities. (From Schaie, Labouvie, & Buech, 1973. Copyright by the American Psychological Association. Reproduced by permission.)

VI. The Magnitude of Differences in Adult PMA Performance Across Age and Cohorts

As scientists we frequently get preoccupied with our concern to demonstrate the presence or absence of reliable differences or relationships. We frequently ignore the question of whether or not such differences are substantial enough to warrant advice to those who wish to implement public policy or decide other practical matters on the basis of our findings. In this section we will examine specific estimates of age changes within cohorts over 7-year intervals from 25 to 81 years and similar estimates of cohort differences for cohorts with average birth years from 1889 to 1938 (also see Schaie & Parham, 1977).[4]

For the purpose of these analyses we utilized the cohort-sequential paradigm, which permits segregation of ontogenetic and cohort differences for selected cohorts and ages. Although this design requires the assumption that time-of-measurement effects be trivial, violation of the assumption is not critical in this instance. In the repeated measurement case this design permits a direct contrast between intraindividual age changes and interindividual cohort differences (cf. Schaie & Baltes, 1975). That is, if there is sociocultural change positively affecting our variables of interest, then observed age decrement will be reduced and cohort differences increased; if there is negative sociocultural change, then observed age decrement will be increased and cohort differences will be reduced. However, since these are indeed the practical outcomes of the effects of compensatory or inhibitory environments, the cohort-sequential approach will therefore provide us with the information sought as input to policy decisions (also see Schaie, 1973b).

In addition to dealing with magnitude of change, this section also responds to the criticism that unequal age and cohort ranges used in our earlier analyses favor the reporting of cumulative cohort effects (cf. Botwinick & Arenberg, 1976). Since data were available to conduct such analyses for repeatedly measured as well as for independent samples, we can at the same time address the concern about alternative interpretations provided by projections from attrited panels as opposed to the estimation of age change parameters by comparing relatively random samples of populations at first test across time. Such comparison, of course, directly addresses the recent controversy introduced by the Horn and Donaldson (1976) as well as the Botwinick (1977) reanalyses of our data.

---

[4] A more extensive version of the cohort-sequential analysis, including detailed ANOVA tables and performance indices for all cohorts and ages as a function of the performance of the youngest age and cohort, respectively, may be found in NAPS Document No. 03170.

The design of the data analysis used to estimate age changes and cohort differences involved the set of seven possible comparisons (with both repeated measurement and independent samples) of two cohorts followed over the same age range. In each analysis the older cohort was observed from 1956 to 1963, while the second cohort was followed from 1963 to 1970. From these analyses we concluded that when proportion of variance accounted for (ω^2) is assessed, it is quite clear that cohort effects account for more variance than does aging per se.

Identification of statistically reliable within- or between-group differences, however, does not necessarily imply that such differences have any practical consequence. The latter issue was addressed more directly by summing cumulative age changes as proportions of performance level for the samples tested at age 25. This was done by adding successive within-cohort changes averaged across the two 7-year intervals for which data were available. In the case of the repeated measurement data this would tend to yield rather conservative estimates favoring decrement findings since a panel consisting of favorably selected members will have scores which tend to regress toward the sample mean due to nonrandom attrition (cf. Baltes, Nesselroade, Schaie, & Labouvie 1972).

A convenient and I think quite reasonable approach to appraising the practical significance of cumulative age changes and/or cohort differences is to take recourse to the traditional assumption that one probable error (PE) about the mean defines the middle 50% (average) range of performance on mental abilities, assuming normal distribution within the population (cf. Matarazzo, 1972, pp. 124–126). It follows that cumulative decrement in performance could be judged to be of practical importance in that instance where such cumulative loss reduces the performance of the older sample to a level more than one PE below the mean (i.e., drop to the lower quartile) of the young adult base.

Figure 10 charts performance in 7-year intervals for ages 32 to 81 as a proportion of performance at age 25. The solid bars represent projections from the repeated measurement samples, while dashed bars are estimates from independent samples. Note that in the first study, based on panel members who remain after some of the less favorable endowed individuals have dropped out, within-cohort level of performance was found to be below the midrange of 25-year-olds at 67 for Word Fluency and at 81 for Reasoning and the index of intellectual aptitude, with no drop below this point for the remaining variables. By contrast, when projecting from the independent samples, which are, of course, more representative of the population at large, performance drops below the 25-year average range already at 53 for Reasoning and Word Fluency, at 67 for Space and the

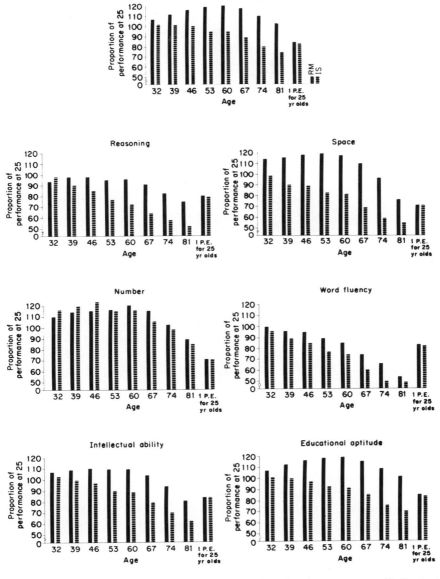

Fig. 10. Performance at various ages as a proportion of performance at age 25. See text for explanation. (From Schaie & Parham, 1977, NAPS Document No. 03170.)

index of intellectual ability, and at 74 for Verbal Meaning and the index of educational aptitude. However, no such drop is shown by Number.

In a manner similar to that for age, we also estimated cumulative cohort differences as a proportion of the performance level of our youngest cohort (that born in 1938) by adding successive cohort differences for each cohort pair averaged over the two points at which each cohort was assessed at the same age. Obsolescence indices were then computed for each cohort from 1889 to 1931 by comparison with the base cohort. Once again we assumed the value of one PE below the mean (the lower quartile) of the youngest cohort as an indicator of obsolescence reaching practical importance.

As would be expected, the effects of cohort obsolescence are more severe in the estimates obtained from independent samples at first test then for the favorably attrited panel study. Judged by our criterion, cohort obsolescence attains practical importance in the random population sample for the cohort born in 1917 for Reasoning, for the 1910 cohort for Space and the composited indices, for the 1903 cohort for Verbal Meaning, and for the 1896 cohort for Number, with no significant finding of obsolescence for Word Fluency. However, even the favorably attrited panel study shows evidence of obsolescence. Here our criterion is reached by the 1924 cohort for Inductive Reasoning, for the 1917 cohort for the composite indices, and for the 1903 cohort for Space. No cohort obsolescence reaching our criterion, however, was found for either Verbal Meaning, Number or Word Fluency. What is surprising from a theoretical view, is the finding that substantial cohort decrement appears to affect most those measures which are likely to be related to the fluid abilities and affect least those which appear to be crystallized.

Before we leave this topic it is interesting to examine what happens when one makes the additional assumption of linear age and cohort decrement and uses the age decrement and obsolescence indices discussed above to fit suitable equations and then estimates rates of annual change. Such rates are presented in Table I, where it is further assumed that the independent samples data would represent lower bound and the panel data upper bound (or perhaps reasonably optimistic) estimates. Such tables may have utility for long-range planning, both in forecasting what the most likely performance level of individuals now under scrutiny will be at any given later age and to predict what the likely difference in performance might be for individuals of a given age in future generations. We could also, of course, attempt to forecast the joint effect of age decrement and cohort obsolescence in predicting the magnitude of age differences to be observed in the future.

TABLE I

Least Square Estimates of the Rate of Annual Age Decrement and
Cohort Obsolescence as Proportions (%) of Performance
at Age 25 and of a Cohort Born in 1938

	Annual age decrement		Annual cohort obsolescence	
	Lower[a] bound	Upper[b] bound	Lower bound	Upper bound
Verbal Meaning	−0.04	−0.53	−0.46	−0.73
Space	−0.64	−0.64	−0.84	−0.89
Reasoning	−0.40	−0.94	−0.80	−1.31
Number	−0.30	−0.60	−0.26	−0.80
Word Fluency	−0.90	−1.04	+0.80	−0.23
Intellectual ability	−0.40	−0.84	−0.16	−0.60
Educational aptitude	−0.13	−0.63	−0.50	−0.91

[a] Estimated age change and cohort differences observed in favorably attrited panel members.
[b] Estimates from age and cohort differences found in the independent random samples.

VII. Adult PMA Performance Related to Health and Environmental Factors

What we have demonstrated so far is that age decrement is not as great or uniform as popular stereotypes would have us believe and that generational (cohort) differences must be taken seriously. What, however, is at the base of these cohort differences? We suspect that one can identify a variety of intrinsic and extrinsic variables on which generations, however defined, do differ. So far we have seriously looked at some gross demographic indicators, have conducted an analysis of cumulative health trauma, and have engaged in the study of interpersonal environments.

A. DEMOGRAPHIC FACTORS

Our concern with these issues began after the initial cross-sectional study when we became sensitized to the fact that there were significant cohort differences on such obvious demographic variables as income, education, and occupational status. We first tried to deal with this issue by applying ANCOVA and by partialling out the effects of these demographic variables on the mental ability scores (Schaie, 1959a). As could be expected, age difference effects were reduced but not eliminated. What we are dealing with, of course, is the fact that the demographic variables are differentially distributed across cohorts; that is, the level of education or income in one cohort does not have the identical meaning to that found in another. While it is clear that considerable variance in mental ability can indeed be explained by gross social status estimators, such estimators are not too helpful in understanding cohort differences directly, because of different ontogenetic patterns in which such status affects change in intellectual ability; but more of that later.

B. HEALTH HISTORY FACTORS

More recently, we have seriously investigated the effect of cumulative health trauma on change in intellectual functions. Since our research participants have all received their health care in a single system we have had access to their complete health histories. However, we soon found that while physicians are very good at recording what they do, little work has been done on retrieving and quantifying such information in ways in which it could be related to behavioral measures. What is needed is a method of characterizing health trauma both in terms of the specific type of illness as well as the likely severity of impact of the disease upon the individual's future life experience (Schaie, 1973a). We addressed this problem by charting each clinic or hospital contact of our participants by the appropriate code from the International Classification of Diseases (ICDA) (United States Public Health Service, 1968). Individual incidents of disease were also linked into episodes referring to the entire set of consecutive visits or contacts for a particular health problem.

Health history records for 150 participants over a 14-year period were charted by incidents and episodes. Although the ICDA contains over 8000 classifications, only about 820 were actually encountered. Collapsing overlapping categories permitted further reduction to 448 classifications, which were then Q-sorted by 12 physicians (six internal medicine and six psychiatry residents) on an 11-point scale ranging from benign to extremely severe, in terms of the impact of each disease entity upon the future health and wellbeing of the patient (Parham, Gribbin, Hertzog, & Schaie, 1975). To our initial surprise, we found only minor relations between cumulative health trauma and mental abilities. These low-level effects occurred for Verbal Meaning and Word Fluency, but only when severity-weighted disease episodes were considered. However, it is of interest to note that at least some variance in verbal behavior decrement can be accounted for on the basis of physical disease.

This line of inquiry was pursued further with respect to individuals with known cardiovascular disease. Several interesting findings occurred as we engaged in the detailed analysis of 155 panel members who had been followed over a 14-year period. At first glance cardiovascular disease results in lowered function on all variables monitored. However, when we control for cohort (age), the effect is no longer significant for either Space or Word Fluency; and when socioeconomic status is taken into consideration, the effect is found only for Number and the composite index of intellectual ability. What we are saying then is that cardiovascular disease is more prevalent in members of older cohorts and those of lower socioeconomic status, who also perform lower on the Primary Mental Abilities Test. We suspect therefore that while cardiovascular disease does indeed contribute to cognitive decline, the variance accounted for is not large, and that there are likely to be rather indirect than specific causal effects. For example, cardiovascular disease may lead to changes in life style which more directly effect cognitive function (cf. Hertzog, Schaie, & Gribbin, 1978). Also, it is conceivable that less healthy life styles shown by individuals of low education and intellectual ability might have modest causal effect upon the development of cardiovascular disease. In addition to these substantive findings, it was also noted that there was a significantly higher incidence of cardiovascular disease among our male dropouts, again emphasizing the importance of collecting data on new random samples when monitoring age changes in panel studies.

C. ENVIRONMENTAL FACTORS

Our next step in trying to understand the effect of environmental factors upon both level of performance and change across age on the mental abilities was an attempt to examine more closely our participants' microenvironment; i.e., a careful selection of those variables present in the day-to-day experience of adults which might be assumed to make a difference in the maintenance of congitive function.

During the spring of 1974, 140 of the participants who had been tested three times were interviewed with a survey instrument which will be referred to as the Life Complexity Inventory (LCI). Initial analysis of the LCI yielded eight item clusters representing: (1) Subjective dissatisfaction with life status; (2) level of social status; (3) a noisy environment; (4) family dissolution; (5) disengagement from interaction with the environment; (6) semi- or passive engagement with the environment; (7) maintenance of acculturation; and (8) female homemaker activities. As expected, there is a significant negative correlation between age and the cluster score for social status and positive correlation between age and disengagement and with family dissolution patterns. On the other hand, neither homemaker status, dissatisfaction with life status, nor maintenance of acculturation is related to age.

We next considered the correlation between LCI cluster scores and the level of intellectual performance at each of our three data points. Systematic positive correlations were observed between all ability variables and the social status cluster, and similar negative correlations occurred with the disengagement cluster. In addition Verbal Meaning, Word Fluency, and educational aptitude related positively to maintenance of acculturation; family dissolution correlated negatively with Reasoning and educational aptitude; female homemaker role correlated negatively with Space; dissatisfaction with life status related negatively to the intellectual ability index and Number; and noisy environment correlated positively with Word Fluency (Gribbin, Schaie, & Parham, 1975). Also considered were the relations between environmental item clusters and change in abilities over a 7-year period. This analysis clearly suggested that an environment characteristic for disengagement and family dissolution seems associated with cognitive decrement, while dissatisfaction with life status appeared to have positive value.

As a final step in this analysis, we examined the distance functions among the profiles of cluster scores for our three-time participants. Our clustering algorithm identified eight clusters of which four had sufficient size to permit interpretation. Type 1 participants were predominantly male, of average social status, with intact families, at an average level of acculturation, and who lived in a relatively noise-free environment, were quite engaged, but voiced relative dissatisfaction with their life status. Type 2 participants have high social status with which they are well satisfied, have intact families, and above average maintenance of acculturation, and live in a noisy and accessible environment. Type 3 participants were almost all women; some were homemakers of average social status, with average life status satisfaction and intact family situations. They were somewhat engaged and low on maintenance of acculturation but lived in accessible and noisy environments and were high on passive engagement items. Type 4 participants were also almost all female. In contrast to Type 3 they were older, had low social status with which they were dissatisfied, and were highest on disengagement items, without even the passive semiengagement pattern. They live in noise-free but also inaccessible environments and are highest on family dissolution.

In terms of environmental complexity it is clear that our typology moves from the high-status–engaged (Type 2), through the average-status–engaged (Type 1), to the semiengaged homemaker (Type 3) and the disengaged homemaker (Type 4). Moreover, when we relate change on the mental abilities to these types, it becomes abundantly clear that there is a substantial relation between life style as inferred from the LCI and maintenance or decrement of cognitive functions. As an example, Table II gives mean change scores for the Primary Mental Abilities Test over a 14-year period for the four types. Clearly Type 1 shows maintenance or increment, while the average pattern for Type 4 represents a similarly clear decrement trajectory, with the other types falling in between between (cf. also Schaie & Gribbin, 1975).

TABLE II

Cumulative Mean Score Change on Cognitive Variables over a
14-Year Period by Subject Type in T-Score Points[a]

	Type 1	Type 2	Type 3	Type 4	All
Verbal Meaning	+3.6	+1.4	−0.2	−4.4	+0.4
Space	+1.0	−1.1	+1.5	−0.1	+0.2
Reasoning	−0.2	+1.1	−1.9	−3.1	−0.7
Number	+1.0	+0.8	−0.9	−1.6	—
Word Fluency	−3.5	−4.2	−6.2	−5.6	−4.8
Intellectual ability	+0.5	−0.2	−1.9	−4.0	−1.1
Educational aptitude	+2.8	+1.3	−0.6	−4.3	+0.1

[a] + denotes incremental change; − denotes decremental change.

VIII. Further Explorations of Adult Development on the Primary Mental Abilities

In the final section of this chapter, I would like to preview briefly what we hope to learn from the new analyses made possible by our most recent (and as yet unanalyzed) data acquisition, since I believe this to be the final stage in the specific program of studies described here. I would then like to go on and suggest where our inquiry should next be directed. In particular, I would like to take this opportunity to show how the initial steps (Schaie, 1977/78; Schaie & Marquette, 1975) I have taken in outlining an approach toward a theory of adult cognitive development relate to the empirical findings described here and provide some guidance for future endeavors.

A. WHAT WE HOPE TO LEARN FROM THE 1977 DATA COLLECTION

1. Substantive Issues

As indicated in the last section, our focus has increasingly been directed toward examining the interaction of two systems of variables (health trauma and microenvironment) which seem to be of particular importance in understanding maintenance or decline of intellectual ability. We will now for the first time have a data system which includes longitudinal–sequential environmental as well as intellectual ability data. We will then be able to apply techniques such as path analysis or Joreskog's (1974) LISREL program to examine causal models specifying alternative hypotheses for the interrelation between environmental impact and cognitive structure.

At a more immediate level, we will be able to test the generalizability of our conclusions on changes over 7- and 14-year time periods, respectively, and have initial estimates of 21-year changes within the survivors of our original panel. Also, of course, within-cohort estimates of age changes can now be extended over a 21-year period. Data such as those provided in Fig. 10 and Table I regarding the level and rate of change across age and cohorts have been replicated on different samples, and the stability of our earlier findings can be tested. We believe these data provide essential information for policy development in such fields as retirement and adult education (cf. Baltes & Willis, 1978; Schaie & Schaie, 1977, 1979; Schaie & Willis, 1978).

With larger samples and data over two 14-year intervals we will also be able to address directly the issue of changes in factor structure across age and cohort. What is at issue here is the possibility of a direct test of the differentiation hypothesis (Reinert, 1970) by means of the new confirmatory factor analysis paradigms (Joreskog & Sorbom, 1976). This is an issue which has considerable implication for the design of measures covering wide portions of the adult life span, as well as implicit theoretical consequences for models of cognitive aging (see Table III summarizing the available data base discussed in this chapter by age, cohort, and time of test).

2. Methodological Issues

The newly acquired data base will permit a number of analyses of methodological interest, paradigms for which have been described previously (cf. Schaie, 1977) but where the needed data are only now available. The most straightforward of these include the application of the cohort-sequential strategy to more than two ages, and the cross-sequential and time-sequential strategies to more than three times of measurement. More complex will be the segregation of practice effects since our data permit analysis of two levels of practice for three times of measurement or three levels of practice for two periods in both cross-sequential and time-

TABLE III

Test Data Available in the Primary Mental Abilities Study
by Age, Cohort, and Time of Measurement[a]

					Years of Birth					
	1886–1892	1893–1899	1900–1906	1907–1913	1914–1920	1921–1927	1928–1934	1935–1941	1942–1948	1949–1955
1956	A1a	A2a	A3a	A4a	A5a	A6a	A7a	—	—	—
	(76)	(72)	(70)	(65)	(71)	(70)	(76)			
Mean age	67	60	53	46	39	32	25			
1963	A1b	A2b	A3b	A4b	A5b	A6b	A7b	—	—	—
	(48)	(40)	(44)	(40)	(47)	(44)	(40)			
	B1a	B2a	B3a	B4a	B5a	B6a	B7a	B8a		
	(77)	(127)	(120)	(143)	(155)	(149)	(123)	(101)		
Mean age	74	67	60	53	46	39	32	25		
1970	A1c	A2c	A3c	A4c	A5c	A6c	A7c	—	—	—
	(11)	(15)	(28)	(32)	(26)	(26)	(21)			
	B1b	B2b	B3b	B4b	B5b	B6b	B7b	B8b	—	—
	(14)	(42)	(39)	(73)	(73)	(77)	(60)	(35)		
	C1a	C2a	C3a	C4a	C5a	C6a	C7a	C8a	C9a	—
	(50)	(88)	(91)	(80)	(89)	(87)	(84)	(65)	(71)	
Mean age	81	74	67	60	53	46	39	32	25	
1977	A1d	A2d	A3d	A4d	A5d	A6d	A7d	—	—	—
	(4)	(10)	(23)	(30)	(23)	(23)	(17)	(17)		
	B1c	B2c	B3c	B4c	B5c	B6c	B7c	B8c	—	—
	(4)	(24)	(24)	(66)	(64)	(66)	(49)	(24)		
	C1b	C2b	C3b	C4b	C5b	C6b	C7b	C8b	C9b	—
	(7)	(30)	(33)	(45)	(53)	(49)	(45)	(32)	(32)	
	D1a	D2a	D3a	D4a	D5a	D6a	D7a	D8a	D9a	D10a
	—	(59)	(69)	(72)	(74)	(76)	(61)	(70)	(61)	(56)
Mean age	88	81	74	67	60	53	46	39	32	25

[a]Notation: Capital letters = samples; i.e., A = sample first tested in 1956 . . . D = sample first tested in 1977. Numbers = cohorts; i.e., 1 = oldest cohort . . . 10 = youngest cohort. Small letters = time of test; i.e., a = first test . . . d = fourth test. Numbers in parentheses indicate cell frequencies.

sequential designs. Similar analyses will be possible with respect to experimental attrition, and for the first time we have data which will allow us to tease apart the effects of prior test exposure and experimental attrition, as well as to apply the cohort-sequential design to the experimental mortality problem. Finally, we have developed scoring procedures which on an expanded data base will provide new insight into such issues as the error structure in psychometric tests over a wide adult age range (cf. Zelinski, Schaie, & Gribbin, 1977).

B. SOME CONCEPTUAL AND THEORETICAL
IMPLICATIONS

I would now like to conclude this account of a systematic exploration of psychometric intelligence in adulthood by examining what I believe has been learned in regard to three issues. The first concerns my current conclusions regarding the empirical facts with respect to the maintenance or decline of intelligence from young adulthood into old age. The second is concerned with the directions in which we must go in the assessment of intellectual competence of individuals both with instruments such as those described here and others which need to be developed (cf. Schaie, 1978). Third, I would like to make some comments as to the status of theoretical models of adult intellectual development in the light of what I think has been learned to date in our explorations.

1. *Does Intelligence Decline?*

When all the evidence presented in this chapter is weighed and due consideration is given to recent reanalyses of some of these data by others (Botwinick, 1977; Horn & Donaldson, 1976), while discounting misquotes and statistical legerdemain (Baltes & Schaie, 1976; Schaie & Baltes, 1977), the reader will, I believe, come to agree with certain conclusions I will now attempt to summarize. First, it is abundantly clear that reliable decrement until very old age (and by that I mean the late 80s) cannot be found for all abilities or for all individuals. Second, it is equally clear that for most individuals there is decrement on those abilities which implicate speed of response, and for those abilities whose measurement is particularly sensitive to relatively modest impairment of the peripheral nervous system. Third, decrement is also likely to be found on most abilities for individuals with severe cardiovascular disease at any age, and for individuals living in relatively undifferentiated or socially deprived environments beginning with the late 50s and early 60s.

Fourth, data from independent random samples (including cross-sectional studies) will tend to overestimate "normal" age decrements for those variables where ontogenetic changes indeed occur, because sampling procedures will tend to include individuals performing at lower levels not because of age, but because of ability-related disease and/or life-style variables. Data from longitudinal and repeated-measurement sequential studies will accurately estimate age changes for individuals living under relatively favorable environmental conditions and in above average health but will overestimate performance maintenance for those living under less favorable conditions and in less than average health. The reason for this statement, of course, is that those who survive to be measured constitute a more favored subset of any population randomly sampled at the origin of a study.

Fifth, I maintain the position that variance for ontogenetic change for most abilities is small relative to that demonstrated for cohort differences. It should be clear, however, that our findings also imply that while cohort differences account for most cross-sectional age difference variance into the mid-60s, we must also be aware of a mix of cohort and age effects, with age effects assuming increasing importance as the 80s are reached.

Finally, I would like to state once again that in healthy well-educated populations ontogenetic change on intellectual ability variables, even where reliably demonstrated, is proportionally small, such that many individuals perform within the middle range of young adults. Generational differences in such samples also are not as pronounced as in the general population, but they do persist. To conclude this section, then, I would note that our exploration suggests once again the tremendous range of individual differences. Some adults show decrement on some abilities quite early in life, but others maintain their function into old age.

2. Implications for the Assessment of Intellectual Competence in Older Adults

There are some eminently practical implications arising out of our studies particularly in view of the recent successful attacks on the concept of mandatory retirement by reason of chronological age. Important here is the recognition that when we assess an older persons' level of function, we must always distinguish whether we wish to know if there has been decrement from previous level of function (i.e., is the person "deteriorating"), or whether we want to know whether the observed functional level is comparable to that expected from a young adult who might be expected to replace the prospective retiree (cf. also Schaie & Schaie, 1977). The first question also requires that we need to know the rate of "aging" on the variables of interest. For what we want to inquire is whether a specific individual is changing faster or slower than expected for a normative group. For example, Table I in this chapter could be used as a primitive aide for such analyses if individuals received annual examinations beyond a critical age in order to provide validation for their continued employment. The second question, of course, requires continued updating of cross-sectional norms, because differences between successive generations are not uniform and generation gradients are not linear or monotonic for all abilities.

I would suggest, then, that assessment of older individuals should include for all variables estimation of both a peer comparison quotient (PCQ) and a base comparison quotient (BCQ). The first, analogous to the well-known Wechsler deviation IQ, would tell us how a given individual would compare to his or her age peers but, in contrast to traditional approaches, would require normative data estimates not just by age, but by age within cohort for those variables where age trends have been found to differ for successive cohorts. This procedure requires that test authors publish estimates of both age and cohort trends (for an example see Schaie & Parham, 1975). Alternatively, of course, they could elect to publish frequent revisions of age norms based on current data, an approach which is probably economically prohibitive. Given such age–cohort means, it is then possible to compute the PCQ by the conventional formula:

$$PCQ = \frac{X - \bar{X}_{ac}}{\sigma_{ac}} \times 15 + 100,$$

where the subscript *ac* refers to cohort specific means and standard deviations for each age of interest.

The second proposed index tells us how an individual compares with norms set by a cohort judged to be at the contemporary culture prime. It is similar to Wechsler's EQ but differs in that the younger reference cohort is not fixed but is determined at the point in time when the comparison is made. Computation of such an index requires knowledge of the means and standard deviations of the age–cohort group to be used as the standard comparison, say age 25, and the standard deviation of the age–cohort to which the assessee belongs. The BCQ can then be estimated in comparable form to the PCQ as follows:

$$BCQ = \frac{X - \bar{X}_{bc}}{\sqrt{\sigma_{ac}\,\sigma_{bc}}} \times 15 + 100$$

where the subscript *ac* again refers to the age–cohort of which the assessee is a member and *bc* refers to the comparison base age–cohort.

A second matter of interest is the possibility that data of the kind provided in our work estimate, for given variables and groups of individuals, the relative proportion of age differences between young and old individuals attributable at any given age to generational difference (or what I have sometimes called cultural obsolescence) and ontogenetic change. I suspect that where the former are predominant educational and other remediable efforts will be most worthwhile.

Not to be glossed over here is the recognition that all measures described in this chapter were constructed for the assessment of adolescents

and young adults. We have noted that those variables where older participants are at greatest disadvantage are also those where abstractness and
novelty are confounded and further, where the technical charactertisics of
the test material (small type size, complexity of answer sheets, poorly
phrased instructions) seem to provide maximal interference, particularly
in group testing situations. In fact, one of the major efforts in my laboratory currently is to design materials which remedy some of these problems so that we can be sure that we are measuring abilities rather than
test-taking skills.

Another major issue not addressed here (cf. Baltes & Willis, 1979;
Schaie, 1978) is the matter of ecological validity. I have here consistently
reported findings on indices entitled "intellectual ability" and "educational aptitude." However, these indices were developed by the
Thurstones for youngsters. We do not know to what extent the primary
abilities sampled in our study are as efficient estimates of the construct of
intelligence in old age as they may be in young adulthood. Only future
comparative factor analyses will tell. Our estimate of intellectual aptitude
may therefore be either inappropriate or at any rate relevant only for a
limited portion of the elderly (say individuals comparable to those in our
repeated measurement panel). We are thus faced with the need for a new
series of investigations which will link both the present and ecologically
more defensible tasks to multiple situational criteria of relevance in the
last third of life (Scheidt & Schaie, 1978).

3. Implications for a Theory of Adult Cognitive Development

Relatively little formal thought can be found in the literature regarding
psychological theories of adult development and aging (for detailed discussion see Baltes & Willis, 1977, 1978), and even less regarding the
development of specific theories of adult cognitive development. It becomes of interest then to speculate whether our experience can be helpful
in moving us towards fruitful theory building. The late Klaus Riegel on
occasion pointed out to the author and his colleagues that we were in a
fashion quite close to taking a limited dialectic position when we were
specifying models which required examining the performance of individuals at given ages within the context of their history and the concurrent
environmental impact (Riegel, 1976, 1977). Indeed, I find myself sympathetic to the dialectic position as long as I may be permitted to make
occasional directional assumptions, if only for the purpose of being able to
test a promising model.

What seems clear to me is that a useful theory of adult cognitive
development must specify a set of latent variables or constructs which
define the domain to be charted. The theory must also specify how the

relationship between observables and the latent constructs may change
over the life course. Moreover, it should speak to the possibility that the
relation among constructs (second-order factors if you prefer) may change
markedly. The theory must further allow for the possibility that there may
be different life courses in intellectual development depending upon the
characteristics of the individuals studied as well as upon the demands of
the environment within which development occurs.

It is not unlikely that such a model will tend to specify discrete appearing stages. Operationally, such stages will likely be detectable whenever a given set of observable measures shows less congruence to a
hypothesized latent construct than does some alternate set. Good theory
building should suggest the form and sequence of efficient studies needed
to detect transformations in cognitive behavior (cf. also Baltes & Schaie,
1973).

Figure 11 reproduces a conceptual scheme which I have found helpful
in organizing my thinking. It derived originally from my reaction to
Flavell's (1970) observation that the Piagetian stages in childhood require
cognitive transformation which occur temporally as a consequence of
changes in the child's morphological structure, whereas in adults there is
little or no isomorphism between physiological structure and cognitive
function. Rather than accepting this to mean that there could be no
further stages, I elected to consider a dialectic position which argued that
changing environmental demands would indeed demand changes in cognitive structure even where there is no physiological instigator.

My scheme (Schaie, 1977/78) would consider much of the traditional

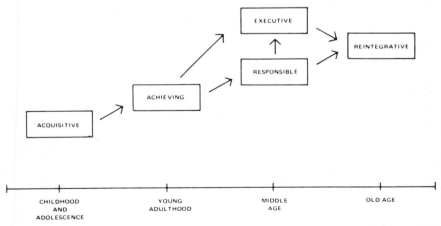

Fig. 11. Schematic for a stage theory of adult cognitive development. (From Schaie,
1977/1978. Copyright by Baywood Publishing Co. Reproduced by permission.)

work on intellectual development, whether utilizing a Piagetian, a Thurstonian, or a Guilfordian framework, as confined to what I have called the period of intellectual skills *acquisition*. What happens next is a life stage during which the individual must now apply intellectual skills to real-life problems. It seems reasonable, then, that during what I called the *achieving stage*, continued growth will occur in achieving individuals on those intellectual skills which are now creatively applied. Note that for our repeated measurement panel, participants showed apparent increments in several abilities, a finding which was not replicated in the independent random samples studies.

Next, I posit a *responsible stage* extending from the 30s to the 60s with the implication that integrative skills are here required to deal with increasingly complex environmental demands. I assume that most modern-day adults have responsibility for extremely complex microsystems both within their home and on the job. It seems not unreasonable that the progressive increment in the complexity of life over historical time should therefore lead to cohort differences in the skills required to deal with such increasing complexity. I also indicate an *executive stage,* which simply implies the application of problem-solving skills to complex systems transcending the nuclear family or self-confined job responsibility. Again, our studies of life complexity as related to maintenance of cognitive function show that individuals of high social status indeed perform at higher levels and show greater tendency to maintain levels of function over time (cf. Table II).

It is at the *reintegrative level,* where I suspect our measures become increasingly inadequate and cease to be adequate estimates of our latent variables, because we must now give serious consideration to the personal meaning of measurement operations as well as to the relevance of the context in which study participants are asked to function. I believe it is at this stage, in the 70s and beyond, where we will find that the same structure of intellect still pertains, but that both the interrelation of the latent constructs (factor structure) and the correlation of specific variables with the latent constructs (factor saturation) are no longer congruent with what we have found at earlier stages.

The principle of parsimony suggests that intellectual structures should become more complex and differentiated as environmental presses do likewise. The extension into old age cannot be dedifferentiation (Reinert, 1970), however; rather it ought to be a selective transformation which can compensate for what otherwise must be progressive information overload, storage, and retrieval problems. That is, the reintegrative stage requires reorganization which permits dealing with significant dimensions of intellect in ways which may superficially seem less efficient but permit

the organism to restrict attention to those aspects of the environment
which continue to be meaningful and adaptive, while ignoring those formal aspects which have lost interest and relevance.

I believe we can deal with some of these issues by applying methods of
longitudinal factor analysis and linear structural analyses to appropriate
sets of person type–cohort–age matrices as described in this chapter. I
think that this is a more promising approach than the attempt to transform
the theory of fluid and crystallized intelligence into a developmental
theory of intelligence. In fact our data base strongly suggests that
crystallized–fluid theory is a strictly cross-sectional model, which does no
more than describe different cohort flows for different abilities. Paradoxi-
cally, our model of cognitive structures changing in response to environmental press would predict that what has been traditionally called fluid
intelligence (Gf) (barring measures which simply reflect fluency of response) should be maintained across the life span, in those instances
where the measurement tasks are meaningful, while so-called crystallized
abilities (Gc) ought to decline where they no longer serve an adaptive
purpose. Examination of our data in this light suggests, indeed, that a
more complex model is needed, for no orderly developmental pattern
which would support the Gf–Gc position can readily be found (also see
Labouvie-Vief, 1977).[5]

One other comment is in order. Much has recently been made of the
need to engage in intervention research in order to examine whether the
test behavior of the old represents disuse or decline and some studies
trying to reverse decrement trends have been reported (e.g., Baltes &
Willis, 1979; Labouvie-Vief & Gonda, 1976; Plemons, Willis, & Baltes,
1978). A concerted program of inquiry along these lines is extremely
important and will contribute to our understanding of the process of
intellectual development in adulthood. However, such efforts make it
even more important to build models which will direct intervention where
intervention can be effective but recognize limitations imposed by
changes in both physiological structures and in environmental support
systems. Again recourse is needed to data bases which permit distinguishing between uncompensated decrement and compensable obsolescence or
lack of prior skill training within the context of the person type–age–
cohort frame of analysis. I hope what has been described in this chapter
can serve both as an initial approximation to such a data base but, even
more importantly, also provide a useful model for the strategies required
to take us to the next level of knowledge and understanding.

[5] A much more powerful and appropriate model for the study of developmental
phenomena was provided earlier by means of Cattell's (1946) covariation chart. The latter
actually provides a possible model for the study of alternate interaction surfaces within a
dialectic framework.

IX. Summary

This chapter has provided an account of the natural history of a longitudinal-sequential study of psychometric intelligence over the age range from the early 20s to the mid-80s. Our account began by discussing the reasons for studying intellectual abilities in adulthood, emphasizing the recently revived interest in the assessment of competence in the elderly due to changes in mandatory retirement practices and the emphasis on maintenance of independent functioning. Variables discussed in this chapter include measures of the primary mental abilities: Verbal Meaning, Space Reasoning, Number, and Word Fluency. Data were presented also for composite indices of intellectual abilities and educational aptitude.

Studies reviewed in this chapter include two pilot studies assessing the applicability of the Primary Mental Abilities Test to older adults, the original cross-sectional study over the age range from 20 to 70 years conducted in 1956, the 1963 7-year follow up and second cross-sectional study, the 1970 14-year follow-up, replicated 7-year follow-up, and third cross-sectional study, as well as the applicable experimental mortality analyses.

Analyses are reported also regarding the magnitude of adult PMA performance across ages and cohorts, as well as the relation between mental abilities and demographic factors, health history factors, and environmental factors. A preview is given of what we hope to learn from our fourth 1977 data collection, as yet unanalyzed. Finally there is a discussion of the conceptual and theoretical implications of this work with respect to the issues of intellectual decline in adulthood, to assessment of competence in older adults, and for psychological theories of adult cognitive development.

References

Baltes, P. B., Nesselroade, J. R., Schaie, K. W., & Labouvie, E. W. On the dilemma of regression effects in examining ability level-related differentials in ontogenetic patterns of adult intelligence. *Developmental Psychology*, 1972, **6**, 79–84.

Baltes, P. B., & Schaie, K. W. On life-span developmental research paradigms: Retrospects and prospects. In P. B. Baltes & K. W. Schaie (Eds.), *Life-span developmental psychology: Personality and socialization*. New York: Academic Press, 1973.

Baltes, P. B., & Schaie, K. W. On the plasticity of intelligence in adulthood and old age: Where Horn and Donaldson fail. *American Psychologist*, 1976, **31**, 720–725.

Baltes, P. B., Schaie, K. W., & Nardi, A. H. Age and experimental mortality in a seven-year longitudinal study of cognitive behavior. *Developmental Psychology*, 1971, **5**, 18–26.

Baltes, P. B., & Willis, S. L. Toward psychological theories of aging and development. In J. E. Birren & K. W. Schaie (Eds.), *Handbook of the psychology of aging*. New York: Van Nostrand Reinhold, 1977.

Baltes, P. B., & Willis, S. L. *Life-span developmental psychology, cognitive functioning and social policy.* Paper presented at the Annual Meeting of the American Association for the Advancement of Science, Washington, 1978.

Baltes, P. B., & Willis, S. L. The critical importance of appropriate methodology in the study of aging. In F. Hoffmeister (Ed.), *The evaluation of old age related changes and disorders.* Heidelberg: Springer, 1979, in press.

Bayley, N., & Oden, M. H. The maintenance of intellectual ability in gifted adults. *Journal of Gerontology,* 1955, **10,** 91–107.

Botwinick, J. Intellectual abilities. In J. E. Birren & K. W. Schaie (Eds.), *Handbook of the psychology of aging.* New York: Van Nostrand Reinhold, 1977.

Botwinick, J., & Arenberg, D. Disparate time spans in sequential studies of aging. *Experimental Aging Research,* 1976, **2,** 55–61.

Cattell, R. B. *The description and measurement of personality.* New York: World Book, 1946.

Flavell, J. H. Cognitive changes in adulthood. In L. R. Goulet & P. B. Baltes (Eds.), *Life-span developmental psychology: Research and theory.* New York: Academic Press, 1970.

Gribbin, K., Schaie, K. W., & Parham, I. A. *Cognitive complexity and maintenance of intellectual abilities.* Paper presented at the 10th International Congress of Gerontology, Jerusalem, Israel, 1975.

Hall, G. S. *Senescence, the last half of life.* New York: Appleton, 1922.

Hertzog, C., Schaie, K. W., & Gribbin, K. Cardiovascular disease and changes in intellectual functioning from middle to old age. *Journal of Gerontology,* 1978, **33,** 872–883.

Hollingworth, H. L. *Mental growth and decline: A survey of developmental psychology.* New York: Appleton, 1927.

Horn, J. L., & Donaldson, G. On the myth of intellectual decline in adulthood. *American Psychologist,* 1976, **31,** 701–719.

Jones, H. E., & Conrad, H. S. The growth and decline of intelligence; A study of a homogenous group between the ages of ten and sixty. *Genetic Psychology Monographs,* 1933, **13,** 223–298.

Joreskog, K. G. Analyzing psychological data by structural analysis of covariance matrices. In R. C. Atkinson, D. H. Krantz, & R. D. Suppes (Eds.), *Contemporary developments in mathematical psychology.* Vol II. San Francisco: Freeman, 1974.

Joreskog, K. G., & Sorbom, D. *User guide to COFAMM: Conformatory factor analysis with model modification.* Chicago: National Education Resources, 1976.

Kuhlen, R. G. Social change: A neglected factor in psychological studies of the life span. *School and Society,* 1940, **52,** 14–16.

Kuhlen, R. G. Age and intelligence: The significance of cultural change in longitudinal vs. cross-sectional findings. *Vita Humana,* 1963, **6,** 113–124.

Labouvie-Vief, G. Adult cognitive development: In search of alternative interpretations. *Merrill–Palmer Quarterly,* 1977, **23,** 227–263.

Labouvie-Vief, G., & Gonda, J. N. Cognitive strategy training and intellectual performance in the elderly. *Journal of Gerontology,* 1976, **31,** 327–332.

Matarazzo, J. D. *Wechsler's measurement and appraisal of adult intelligence.* Baltimore: Williams & Wilkins, 1972.

Nesselroade, J. R., Schaie, K. W., & Baltes, P. B. Ontogenetic and generational components of structural and quantitative change in adult behavior. *Journal of Gerontology,* 1972, **27,** 222–228.

Owens, W. A. Age and mental abilities: A longitudinal study. *Genetic Psychology Monographs,* 1953, **48,** 3–54.

Owens, W. A. Is age kinder to the initially more able? *Journal of Gerontology,* 1959, **14,** 334–337.

Parham, I. A., Gribbin, K., Hertzog, C., & Schaie, K. W. *Health status assessment by age and implications for cognitive change.* Paper presented at the 10th International Congress of Gerontology, Jerusalem, Israel, 1975.

Plemons, T. K., Willis, S. L., & Baltes, P. B. Modifiability of fluid intelligence in aging: A short-term longitudinal training approach. *Journal of Gerontology,* 1978, **33,** 224–231.

Pressey, S. L., Janney, J. E., & Kuhlen, R. G. *Life: A psychological survey.* New York: Hayer, 1939.

Reinert, G. Comparative factor analytic studies of intelligence throughout the human life-span. In L. R. Goulet & P. B. Baltes (Eds.), *Life-span developmental psychology: Research and theory.* New York: Academic Press, 1970.

Riegel, K. F. *The psychology of development and history.* New York: Plenum, 1976.

Riegel, K. F. History of psychological gerontology. In J. E. Birren & K. W. Schaie (Eds.), *Handbook of the psychology of aging.* New York: Van Nostrand Reinhold, 1977.

Schaie, K. W. A test of behavioral rigidity. *Journal of Abnormal and Social Psychology,* 1955, **51,** 604–610.

Schaie, K. W. Differences in some personal characteristics of "rigid" and "flexible" individuals. *Journal of Clinical Psychology,* 1958, **14,** 11–14. (a)

Schaie, K. W. Occupational level and the Primary Mental Abilities. *Journal of Educational Psychology,* 1958, **49,** 299–303. (b)

Schaie, K. W. Rigidity-flexibility and intelligence: A cross-sectional study of the adult life span from 20 to 70. *Psychological Monographs,* 1958, **72,** No. 462 (Whole No. 9). (c)

Schaie, K. W. Cross-sectional methods in the study of psychological aspects of aging. *Journal of Gerontology,* 1959, **14,** 208–215. (a)

Schaie, K. W. The effect of age on a scale of social responsibility. *Journal of Social Psychology,* 1959, **50,** 221–224. (b)

Schaie, K. W. *Manual for the Test of Behavioral Rigidity.* Palo Alto, Ca.: Consulting Psychologists Press, 1960.

Schaie, K. W. A general model for the study of developmental problems. *Psychological Bulletin,* 1965, **64,** 92–107.

Schaie, K. W. Age changes and age differences. *Gerontologist,* 1967, **7,** 128–132.

Schaie, K. W. A reinterpretation of age-related changes in cognitive structure and functioning. In L. R. Goulet & P. B. Baltes (Eds.), *Life-span developmental psychology: Research and theory.* New York: Academic Press, 1970.

Schaie, K. W. *Cumulative health trauma and age changes in adult cognitive behavior.* Paper presented at the annual meeting of the American Psychological Association, Montreal, 1973. (a)

Schaie, K. W. Methodological problems in descriptive developmental research on adulthood and aging. In J. R. Nesselroade & H. W. Reese (eds.), *Life-span developmental psychology: Methodological issues.* New York: Academic Press, 1973. (b)

Schaie, K. W. Age changes in adult intelligence. In D. S. Woodruff & J. E. Birren (Eds.), *Aging: Scientific perspectives and social issues.* New York: Van Nostrand, 1975.

Schaie, K. W. Quasi-experimental designs in the psychology of aging. In J. E. Birren & K. W. Schaie (Eds.), *Handbook of the psychology of aging.* New York: Van Nostrand Reinhold, 1977.

Schaie, K. W. Toward a stage theory of adult cognitive development. *Journal of Aging and Human Development,* 1977/78, **8,** 129–138.

Schaie, K. W. External validity in the assessment of intellectual functioning in adulthood. *Journal of Gerontology,* 1978, **33,** 695–701.

Schaie, K. W., & Baltes, P. B. On sequential strategies in developmental research: Description or explanation? *Human Development,* 1975, **18,** 384–390.

Schaie, K. W., & Baltes, P. B. Some faith helps to see the forrest: A final comment on the Horn and Donaldson myth on the Baltes-Schaie position on adult intelligence. *American Psychologist,* 1977, **32,** 1118–1120.

Schaie, K. W., Baltes, P. B., & Strother, C. R. A study of auditory sensitivity in advanced age. *Journal of Gerontology,* 1964, **19,** 453–457.

Schaie, K. W., & Gribbin, K. The impact of environmental complexity upon adult cognitive development. International Society for the Study of Behavioral Development, Guildford, England, 1975.

Schaie, K. W., & Labouvie-Vief, G. Generational versus ontogenetic components of change in adult cognitive behavior: A fourteen-year cross-sequential study. *Developmental Psychology,* 1974, **10,** 305–320.

Schaie, K. W., Labouvie, G. V., & Barrett, T. J. Selective attrition effects in a fourteen-year study of adult intelligence. *Journal of Gerontology,* 1973, **28,** 328–334.

Schaie, K. W., Labouvie, G. V., & Buech, B. U. Generational and cohort-specific differences in adult cognitive functioning: A fourteen-year study of independent samples. *Developmental Psychology,* 1973, **9,** 151–166.

Schaie, K. W., & Marquette, B. W. *Stages in transition: A biosocial analysis.* Paper presented at the ISSBD Satellite Symposium to the Tenth International Congress of Gerontology, Kiryat Anavim, Israel, 1975.

Schaie, K. W., & Parham, I. A. *Manual for the test of behavioral rigidity.* 2nd ed. Palo Alto, Ca.: Consulting Psychologists Press, 1975.

Schaie, K. W., & Parham, I. A. Cohort-Sequential analyses of adult intellectual development. *Developmental Psychology,* 1977, **13,** 649–653.

Schaie, K. W., Rosenthal, F., & Perlman, R. M. Differential deterioration of factorially "pure" mental abilities. *Journal of Gerontology,* 1953, **8,** 191–196.

Schaie, K. W., & Schaie, J. P. Clinical assessment and aging. In J. E. Birren & K. W. Schaie (Eds.), *Handbook of the psychology of aging.* New York: Van Nostrand Reinhold, 1977.

Schaie, K. W., & Schaie, J. P. Intellectual development. In A. W. Chickering (Ed). *The future American college.* San Francisco: Jossey-Bass, 1979.

Schaie, K. W., & Strother, C. R. Cognitive and personality variables in college graduates of advanced age. In G. A. Talland (Ed.), *Human behavior and aging: Recent advances in research and theory.* New York: Academic Press, 1968. (a)

Schaie, K. W., & Strother, C. R. The cross-sequential study of age changes in cognitive behavior. *Psychological Bulletin,* 1968, **70,** 671–680. (b)

Schaie, K. W., & Strother, C. R. The effects of time and cohort differences on the interpretation of age changes in cognitve behavior. *Multivariate Behavioral Research,* 1968, **3,** 259–293. (c)

Schaie, K. W., & Strother, C. R. Limits of optim functioning in superior old adults. In S. M. Chown & K. F. Riegel (Eds.), *Interdisciplinary topics in gerontology.* Basel: Karger, 1968. (d)

Schaie, K. W., & Willis, S. L. Life-span development: Implications for education. *Review of Research in Education,* 1978, in press.

Scheidt, R. J., & Schaie, K. W. A situational taxonomy for the elderly: Generating situational criteria. *Journal of Gerontology,* 1978, **33,** 848–857.

Strother, C. R., Schaie, K. W., & Horst, P. The relationship between advanced age and mental abilities. *Journal of Abnormal and Social Psychology.* 1957, **55,** 166–170.

Terman, L. M. *The measurement of intelligence.* Boston: Houghton, 1916.

Thurstone, L. L., & Thurstone, T. G. *Factorial studies of intelligence*. Chicago: University of Chicago, Press, 1941.

Thurstone, L. L., & Thurstone, T. G. *Examiner Manual for the SRA Primary Mental Abilities Test*. Chicago: Science Research Associates, 1949.

Thurstone, T. G. *Manual for the SRA Primary Mental Abilities 11–17*. Chicago: Science Research Associates, 1958.

U.S. Public Health Service. *Eighth revision international classification of diseases, adapted for use in the United States*. Washington: Government Printing Office, Public Health Service Publication No. 1693, 1968.

Wechsler, D. *The measurement of adult intelligence*. Baltimore: Williams & Wilkins, 1939.

Yerkes, R. M. Psychological examining in the United States Army. *Memoirs of the National Academy of Sciences*, 1921, **15**, 1–890.

Zelinski, E., Schaie, K. W., & Gribbin, K. *Omission and commission errors: Task-specific adult lifespan differences*. Paper presented at the annual meeting of the American Psychological Association, San Francisco, 1977.

Historical Change in Life Patterns and Personality

Glen H. Elder, Jr.

CENTER FOR THE STUDY OF YOUTH DEVELOPMENT
BOYS TOWN, OMAHA, NEBRASKA

Abstract

A number of developments over the past decade have brought greater sensitivity to issues on the relation between social history and life history, including a sociological perspective on age and the life course. Two approaches to historical change in lives are based on this perspective: the comparative study of successive cohorts and their life patterns, and an assessment of social change in life experience through comparisons of cohort subgroups. The first approach, the study of whole cohorts, tends to limit understanding of historical influence by not attending to explanatory processes and historical variations within cohorts. Cohort subgroups frequently show marked differences in exposure to historical events, as in the Great Depression. Using longitudinal data, this chapter examines and compares the relation of Depression hardship (nondeprived versus deprived) to family patterns, adolescent personality, and adult experience in two well-known cohorts—the Oakland sample (birthdates, 1920–1921) and the Berkeley Guidance sample (birthdates, 1928–1929) at the Institute of Human Development, Berkeley. According to regression and covariance analyses, the differential life stage of these cohorts in the early 1930s made a noteworthy difference in the life consequences of family deprivation, with the most negative effects occurring among the Guidance sample males and especially among those who experienced

LIFE-SPAN DEVELOPMENT
AND BEHAVIOR, VOL. 2

both economic deprivation and parental discord. Yet even in this group the health disadvantage of a deprived background largely vanished over the years to midlife. The results of this study underscore two considerations in the study of historical change in lives; the resources, values, and expectations which people bring to new situations, and their impact on the resulting life course. An understanding of the connection between early historical events in childhood and adult experience requires knowledge of the intervening life course.

I. Introduction

Three developments over the past decade have brought greater sensitivity to questions of historical change in lives: the growth of quantitative studies of families and individuals in social history (Hareven, 1978); the expanding field of life-span developmental psychology, with its identification of cohort variations (Baltes & Schaie, 1973); and the evolution of a sociology of age and the life course (Riley, Johnson, & Foner, 1972; Elder, 1975). Out of this work has come a broad perspective on life-course development in historical context, a view based on the premise that socialization and aging are lifelong phenomena.

Development across the life span is characterized by interacting processes (biological, psychological, social) in the dialectical relation between change in individuals and change in their social–historical world (Riegel, 1976)[1] This chapter examines the psychosocial impact of one major historical event—economic change during the Great Depression—and traces its effect through the adolescent development and adult experience of two longitudinal cohorts (Jones *et al.*, 1971): the Oakland Growth sample with birth dates of 1920–1921 and the Berkeley Guidance sample, birthdates of 1928–1929.

II. Approaches to Historical Change in Lives

Two approaches from the sociology of age bear upon the assessment of historical change in psychosocial patterns: the comparative study of

---

[1]In addressing the debate over two presumed versions of social psychology—as science and as history (Gergen, 1976)—Brewster Smith (1977, p. 723) cogently argues that the dialectic perspective offers a framework for their synthesis. "Through ontogenetic and phylogenetic time, interaction produces human beings and human history, or rather, human beings in interaction and in action in the world produce themselves and history . . . social psychology *must* be developmental *and* historical if it is to be adequately scientific." Programmatic statements of the ecology of human development (Bronfenbrenner, 1977) and of environmental psychology (Proshansky, 1976) also bring these foci together. According to Proshansky, environmental psychology constitutes a "socio-historical behavioral science."

cohorts (e.g., persons born in 1920 and 1930) and of subgroups within a cohort, such as class strata, economic sectors, and geographic location. From a historical standpoint, a cohort approach assumes that rapid change differentiates the options and life patterns of successive cohorts, in part as they experience the same events at different points in the life span and different events at the same point. These life variations constitute a potential set of linkages between historical change and cohort outcomes. Along this line, Leo Srole (1977) has stressed the need for systematic, comparative study of the process by which macrosocial change in life experience is expressed in levels of psychological functioning: "What are the interconnections between trends in macro-social history and temporal trends in the mental health changes within different community populations?" (p. 27).

Periods of drastic change are frequently marked by disparities between the modal dispositions of successive cohorts and options in the social order. Such incongruence may arise from institutional change which provides options that do not mesh with collective mentalities or from change in socialization and personality in an otherwise stable social order (Inkeles & Levinson, 1969). Most cohort studies to date offer little more than speculation concerning the interplay between cohorts and institutions or about historical factors in cohort experience (cf. Davis, 1975; Inglehart, 1977). This deficiency also applies to studies which report cohort variations in developmental trajectories (Nesselroade & Baltes, 1974; Jessor & Jessor, 1977). Typically, cohort-sequential research has focused on the existence of intercohort variation in development, not on historical forces which suggest rationales for expecting such variation (Rosow, 1978). The meaning of "cohort effect" is thereby left ambiguous.

Even with attention to historical circumstances, a cohort approach restricts what we can learn about social change in lives, in large part by obscuring historical variations within successive cohorts. For example, Loewenberg (1972) cites the adverse influence of famine and paternal absence in World War I on the character development of German boys without noting the implications of ecological and social variations in such conditions among the younger population. Consistent with Mannheim's (1952) essay on generation sectors or untis, subgroups in a cohort may differ in exposure to specific historical events, in interpretations of them, and in responses. Subgroup analysis investigates the effects of such intracohort variation by comparing categories that represent contrasts on exposure and impact.

Intracohort variation represents one of the most striking features of life experience in the Great Depression; some children were exposed to severe economic hardship in the family, whereas others managed to avoid misfortune altogether. *Children of the Great Depression* (Elder, 1974) explored some developmental implications of this variation in a longitudinal sample of 167 persons who were born during the early 1920s and grew up in the city of Oakland, California. Using data collected annually during the 1930s and at three points in the adult years, the analysis followed members of relatively nondeprived and deprived families from elementary school through adolescence, young adulthood, and the early years of middle age. Within the middle and working class of 1929, families that lost more than 34% of their 1929 income by 1933 were defined as relatively deprived; all other families were classified as nondeprived. Family adaptations in the Depression, from change toward a more labor-intensive economy to emotional stress, emerged as primary linkages between deprivation and the life experience of the Oakland adolescents. Economic deprivation entailed some disadvantage in career beginnings, but it did not produce noteworthy disabilities in adult accomplishments or health. Instead, the Depression's legacy mainly took the form of values, such as the unusual importance of family among men and women from deprived homes.

There is good reason to expect the Depression experience of the Oakland cohort to differ from that of older and younger cohorts. Members of the Oakland cohort were beyond the critical stage of childhood dependency when the economy hit bottom, and the timing of war mobilization in their lives undoubtedly minimized the handicap of launching adult careers from a background of economic privation. From this vantage point, the Oakland sample clearly occupied a position of relative advantage when compared to the life history of persons who were born during the late 1920s. The latter were subject to extreme family stress in the 1930s as young children and some experienced a long duration of economic hardship up to their departure from the family in the mid-1940s. Both the life stage of this cohort in the Depression and its lengthy exposure to hard times are likely to have enhanced the adverse psychological impact of family deprivation.

A more complete understanding of the Depression experience thus requires a comparative study of economic deprivation in the life course of two or more cohorts. The Berkeley guidance sample (Jones *et al.*, 1971) provides a rare opportunity to employ this analytic design (Fig. 1). With birthdates just prior to the economic collapse (1928–1929), the sample represents a strategic comparison group relative to the older members of the Oakland cohort, and its data archive includes pre-Depression information on family relationships which was not available to the Oakland analysis. The location and management of both studies at the Institute of Human Development also ensures a critical measure of uniformity in data

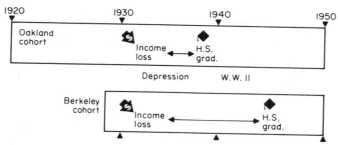

Fig. 1. Interaction of depression hardship and life stage: a comparison of the Berkeley and Oakland cohorts.

collection and measurement, especially on economic deprivation and personality.

III. Objective and Hypotheses

The objective of this chapter is to investigate the effect of Depression hardship (relatively deprived versus nondeprived) on the adolescent development and adult experience of the Oakland and Berkeley cohorts. Using longitudinal data, the analysis centers first on the existence and nature of deprivational effects in the Berkeley cohort and then directly compares the two cohorts on the effects of deprivation in adolescent personality and life patterns to the middle years. Three hypotheses structure the research: (1) *Life stage*—adverse developmental outcomes of economic deprivation in the 1930s will be concentrated in the younger Berkeley cohort; (2) *sex variation*—this differential effect will be most evident in a comparison of males from the two cohorts, owing to the link between economic and paternal deprivation and the primary role of father in the psychosocial development of boys; and (3) the *parental relationship* as a mode of social support—in the Berkeley cohort, the association between family deprivation and developmental impairment will vary according to the emotional strength of the parental relationship before economic loss. The state of this relationship determines the likelihood of erratic, punitive, and divisive parental behavior (see Rutter & Madge, 1976), especially under the pressures of severe economic strain.

Two family outcomes of deprivation in the Oakland study bear directly upon the life-stage hypothesis since they entail greater risk for the well-being of young children who are wholly dependent upon reliable, parental nurturance (Elder, 1974): (1) Change in family relationships—father's loss of income and resulting adaptations in family maintenance increased the relative influence and emotional significance of mother, reduced the level and effectiveness of parental control and supervision in the lives of boys, and diminished the attractiveness of father as a behavior model for sons; and (2) intensified strains—greater social ambiguity, conflict, and emotional stress, resulting from resource exhaustion, disability of the father through depressed feelings and heavy drinking, and inconsistency in the status of the family and its members. While mother assumed a position of strength in deprived families, especially in the lives of the Oakland girls, the problematic behavior of father tends to underscore the developmental vulnerability of boys in this environment who were younger than the Oakland males. The Oakland results and research on father's influence in male development (Lamb, 1976) suggest that the life-stage hypothesis will apply mainly to a comparison of males in the Oakland and Berkeley cohorts.

More than older youth, young girls and especially boys in a disorganized family may learn that they cannot predict how parents will respond to their actions or needs; that emotional expression and autonomy are dangerous and that survival entails withdrawal, passivity, and keeping things to self. The safest course for a young child in a world made unpredictable and hurtful is to avoid initiatives that impinge on arbitrary authority figures. Baumrind (1978, p. 276) observes that "the young child avoids situations which clearly are uncontrollable as though they were aversive, even when the stimuli would otherwise be experienced as positive." Experimental research by Diener and Dweck (1978, p. 460) has documented the self-defeating behavior of helpless children who consistently fail to surmount difficulties. These "children ruminate about the cause of their failure and, given their attributions to uncontrollable factors, spend little time searching for ways to overcome failure. Mastery-oriented children, on the other hand, seem to be directed towards the attainment of a solution."

Though family disorganization is consistently linked to economic stress (Bronfenbrenner, 1974; Wilson & Herbert, 1978), severe income loss during the Depression was least likely to undermine effective family adaptations and recovery when it occurred in a context of marital integration (Elder, 1974, Chapters 1 and 5). Likewise, the emotional support of children in critical life situations, especially by father, is most probable when parents encounter the event with a strong bond of affection and mutual understanding. The weaker the bond, the lower the wife's emotional support of husband and the greater the husband's health risk in stressful situations (Cobb, 1976). Through processes of this sort, a man's inadequacy as spouse and earner tends to generalize to inadequacy as father and conditions that impair male development (Biller, 1971). In

Heath's (1976) longitudinal study, affectionate fathers who devoted time to their offspring were characterized by marital gratification, open communication with spouse, and psychological well-being. If the most negative impact of Depression hardship is found among males in the Berkeley cohort, as the preceding hypotheses suggest, this outcome should be especially pronounced under conditions of marital discord before hard times. Our investigation of the marital context of deprivation is restricted to the Berkeley sample since the Oakland archive does not include pre-Depression data on family patterns.

IV.   The Cohorts: Archival Resources and Measurements

The original Berkeley sample includes two subgroups of equal size: an intensive group, which provided detailed information on family patterns, and a less intensively studied group, which was matched on social and economic characteristics. The basic cohort is comprised of 214 children who participated in the study from 1928 through the 1930s and up to the end of World War II. Most of the children were white and Protestant, and two-thirds came from middle-class families. On each of these characteristics, as well as on native parentage and family stability (both parents present), the Berkeley sample resembles the Oakland cohort. As might be expected from its state university and intellectual tradition, Berkeley represents a different world for young people from that of Oakland, a large center of commerce, industry, and transportation. However, the two cities are part of the same economic region and suffered comparable economic losses in the 1930s. Though most of the work force in Berkeley held jobs outside the city, its middle class does include a larger proportion of professional fathers than the Oakland middle class does, and adjustments will be made for this difference in the analysis.

From the standpoint of comparative study, the two cohorts offer a crucial base of common data sets. Most important, income reports by year were available on the Berkeley families, thereby enabling us to develop an index of economic deprivation that matches the Oakland index. Income change between 1929 and the low year (usually 1933), asset losses, and the decline in cost of living (about 25%) in the Berkeley sample generally confirm the validity of the Oakland definition of economic deprivation (an income loss greater than 34%) and permit us to use the same demarcation between nondeprived and deprived in the Berkeley analysis. This procedure also enabled us to use unemployment and public assistance information to classify some Berkeley families that lacked complete income records. Approximately three-fifths of the working-class families in both cohorts were classified as relatively deprived, compared to about one-third of the middle class. In both cohorts and class strata, economic deprivation refers to decremental change in economic status and thus differs from its usual association with chronic poverty.

The advantage of common data sets also applies to psychological measurements. In both cohorts, an ipsative, Q-sort approach (Block, 1958, 1971) emerged as the best solution to problems of missing information on different individuals and of dissimilar measurements within and across time periods. The 100-item California Q-sort is well suited for longitudinal analysis since clinical judgments take into account the relative salience of each item within a forced normal distribution (nine categories) on each person, a procedure which avoids problems of temporal change in frame of reference. Complications posed by missing data, variant sources of information, and differing times of measurement were minimized by assembling materials for the judging process from multiple sources (parents, child, peers, and staff) in each time period.

Adolescence represents the one early life stage in which archival data and thus Q ratings are available on members of both cohorts. Within this time period, Jack Block (1971) and his research team developed case assemblies for the years of junior and senior high school. Only subjects with satisfactory adolescent and adult data were selected. At least two judges rated each case in each time period, with interrater reliabilities above .65. The senior high assessment includes over 90 of the Oakland subjects and thus provides an adequate base of psychological information on this cohort. However, the number is much smaller in the Berkeley sample, owing partly to the selection criterion on case data. Fewer than 30 boys in the sample have ratings from Block's data set, a subgroup which is too small to permit intracohort analyses. As an alternative, we shall use the judgments of a skilled clinician at the Institute who applied the California Q-sort to case materials on each Berkeley subject. Available evidence indicates that the clinician's ratings describe the subjects in adolescence, even though she had access to information on childhood as well. For cases with ratings by Block's team and by the clinician, measures of the same attributes in this study consistently show an acceptable degree of correspondence. Parallel analyses of the two Q-sorts have also produced comparable outcomes.[2]

[2]Differences in rating procedures between the two studies raise the possibility that cohort and rater patterns are confounded. These differences require a cautionary approach to results from cohort comparisons of deprivational effects in adolescence. However, a large part of the research task involves estimation of deprivational variations in adolescent outcomes within the Berkeley cohort and their explication through family patterns. Moreover, cohort comparisons in the adult years are not handicapped by study differences

Using the Berkeley ratings, we sought to characterize adolescent functioning in terms of at least three prominent elements of a competent self (Smith, 1968; Coan, 1974): (1) goal directedness—concerted and satisfying effort toward the achievement of goals; (2) a sense of personal worth and initiative, including effective coping with life's problems; and (3) social competence—social skills, rewarding associations, consideration of the needs of others. Six item clusters bearing on these dimensions emerged from intercorrelational and factor analyses of ratings on the boys and girls. An index score for each cluster (see below) was obtained by dividing the sum of all item values by the number of component items. With the exception of "open to inner experience," the indexes form an interrelated portrait of adolescent competence; correlations range from .35 to .74.

Goal oriented: "high aspirations," "productive, gets things done," "self-defeating in relation to goals," and "lacks personal meaning." Scores on the latter two items were reflected. Average *r:* boys = .50 and girls, .45. Reliability coefficient (α): boys = .80 and girls, .77.

Self-inadequacy: "satisfied with self" (reflected), "thin-skinned," "feels victimized," "brittle," and "fearful." Average *r:* boys = .42 and girls, .39. Reliability coefficients (α): boys = .77 and girls, .76.

Submissive: "submissive," "withdraws in adversity," "assertive" (reflected), and "reluctant to commit self." Average *r:* boys = .40 and girls, .57. Reliability coefficients (α): boys = .73 and girls, .84.

Social competence: "arouses liking and acceptance," "gregarious," "social poise," "socially perceptive," and "aloof" (reflected). Average *r:* boys = .63 and girls, .58. Reliability coefficients (α): boys = .88 and girls, .87.

Open to inner experience: "insightful," "introspective," and "repressive" (reflected). Average *r:* boys = .46 and girls, .55. Reliability coefficients (α): boys = .72 and girls, .79.

Considerate of others: "giving," "sympathetic," "warm," negativistic" (reflected), and "distrustful" (reflected). Average *r:* boys = .64 and girls, .49. Reliability coefficients (α): boys .90 and girls, .83.

Three of the measures, in particular, represent core aspects of a competent self, "established in benign circles of productive engagement with the environment, and its incompetent counterpart, mired in vicious circles of self-defeat" (Smith, 1968, p. 313): "goal oriented"—the hopefulness of

---

in rating procedure. The analysis of Depression hardship in adult experience employs *Q* judgments which are based on identical rating operations (comparable to those used by Jack Block) in the two cohorts.

high aspirations and personal meaning, coupled with productive efforts in relation to goals; "self-inadequacy"—in internalized devaluation of self which entails vulnerability to others and apprehension; and "submissive"—a passive stance toward life situations, avoidance of hardships, challenges, and commitments involving risk. These clusters and the other three described above were also identified from Q ratings on the Oakland subjects in senior high and formed indexes with properties that are comparable to the Berkeley measurements.[3]

Some individual items offer a more precise test of cohort differences on the effects of economic deprivation than the indexes: for example, the item, "reluctance to commit self to any definite course of action; tends to delay or avoid action." This tendency may be consistent with a young boy's survival interests in the unpredictable environment of a severely deprived family, but we find no evidence of such behavior among older boys in deprived families of the Oakland sample (Elder, 1974). As a group, they were more likely to have paid jobs and an energetic life style than were nondeprived boys; they crystallized their occupational goals at an earlier age and more often embarked on stable lines of work following the completion of education. "Reluctance to commit self" more accurately describes a contrast to this behavior pattern than any other item in the submissive cluster.

Three procedures were employed in assessing the effects of deprivation. First, multiple regression analysis provided estimates of deprivational effects on family relations and personality by subgroups—boys, girls within each cohort, etc.[4] Our emphasis here is not on statistical significance, given the small and variable number of cases, but concerns the overall pattern of differences within and across subgroups on the size and direction of effects. As in *Children of the Great Depression* (Elder, 1974, pp. 6, 329), the strategy differs from the conventional focus on variables which are likely to account for a substantial portion of the

---

[3]Intercorrelation matrices for Q items in the six adolescent measures are available on request for boys and girls in the Berkeley and Oakland cohorts.

[4]Among the Berkeley boys, for example, we regressed each indicator of psychological functioning in adolescence on economic deprivation (1 = deprived, 0 = nondeprived) with class origin (1929) included in the equation. All metric coefficients showing the direct effects of deprivation were compared with their standard errors for evaluative purposes, and coefficients at least equal to twice their standard errors are identified. However, the degree of variation in subgroup size and its relation to the standard error severely limits the usefulness of this test as a criteria for evaluating the results. More informative and helpful are the strength and direction of effects, their correspondence with theory and the research literature. Substantive significance involves considerations of this sort, and in a small sample may bear little relation to statistical significance (see Morrison & Henkel, 1970, pp. 155–198, for an extended discussion of such issues).

variance in a dependent variable. Economic deprivation was selected for study on theoretical and historical grounds, not solely in terms of its potential as a major source of variation in adolescent or adult outcomes.

The process relating deprivation and specific outcomes leads to the family and our second procedure. Wherever appropriate in the Berkeley analysis, selected family correlates of deprivation were added to regression equations as potential linkages which account for the psychological effects of deprivation, e.g., relations with each parent, family disorganization. As the third procedure, covariance analysis was used to test the null hypothesis that linear regressions of personality on economic deprivation do not vary between subgroups. Though probability values are reported for large differences in slopes, they represent only one among other interpretive guides, such as the consistency of outcomes and their relation to the findings of corresponding research. The basic question in this stage of the analysis follows Bronfenbrenner's assumption on the ecological study of human development (1977, p. 518) that *"the principal main effects are likely to be interactions."* Do the psychosocial effects of economic deprivation vary by sex of child, type of parental relationship, and cohort?

V. Depression Hardship in Adolescent Personality: Berkeley Cohort

The first step toward a comparison of Depression hardship in the Oakland and Berkeley cohorts entails analysis of economic loss in the lives of the Berkeley boys and girls, beginning with family relationships and their implications for adolescent development. If developmental change qualifies as one of the most subtle and important consequences of social change, its understanding requires knowledge of the process by which these modes of change are linked, a process that involves family relationships (Greven, 1973). The sex variation hypothesis suggests that economic loss patterned the environment of the Berkeley families in ways that exposed boys to a greater risk of developmental impairment than girls (a pattern marked by an influential mother, weak father, and disorganization) and that deprivation is more predictive of developmental impairment among boys than among girls. We begin with evidence bearing on such outcomes and then investigate whether family relations before and after economic loss account for the observed adolescent effects of Depression hardship. Cohort comparisons in adolescence and the adult years are based upon these results.

A. FAMILY RELATIONS AND ADOLESCENT
PERSONALITY

As represented by the Oakland and Berkeley cohorts, children of differing age experienced similar family conditions in deprived situations, but the same condition did not have similar implications for their developmental course. Deprived families in both cohorts coped with hard times through labor-intensive adaptations, such as the household contributions of children, but only members of the Oakland cohort were old enough at the time to assume major responsibilities. A more important difference is seen in a common family configuration among deprived households; the emotional centrality and power of mother and the more estranged, peripheral status of father. Though observed in both cohorts, this family pattern only made a substantial difference in the family security and development of the young Berkeley children.

From annual interviews with these children in grade school, a staff member judged their warmth toward mother and father (hostile = 1, warm = 5) and their sense of family security on five-point scales. Scores on each rating were averaged across 3 years, ages 8–10 years. With adjustments for class position in 1929, we find that economic deprivation markedly enhanced the affective status of mother relative to that of father among boys and girls.[5] However, boys in deprived families lost more in affection for father and gained less in warmth toward mother when compared to girls. The principal impact of deprivation on parent–child relations thus appears in generational ties among members of the same sex; a weaker tie between father and son, and a much stronger tie between mother and daughter.

Some developmental implications of this difference are indicated by judgments concerning the family security of boys and girls.[6] Boys in deprived homes were rated less secure than the nondeprived, although

[5]The direct effects of economic deprivation are more negative on warmth toward father among boys than among girls ($b = -.32$ versus $-.08$); and more positive on warmth toward mother among girls than among boys ($b = .69$ versus $.33$). Following from these differences, deprivation produced greater closeness to mother relative to father (an index obtained by subtracting the score on father from the score on mother) among girls than among boys ($b = .76$ versus $.57$). Though none of these sex differences is statistically significant, the effects of deprivation on girls' warmth toward mother and relative closeness to mother are reliable outcomes; each coefficient is at least twice its standard error.

[6]The direct effect of economic deprivation on family security is slightly negative among boys ($b = -.12$) and positive among girls ($b = .29$), with social class origin included in each regression equation. Though neither outcome is substantial, the differential effect of deprivation on family security by sex (p of same slope $= .18$) is consistent with the impact of economic loss on boys' and girls' relations with each parent.

this disadvantage is modest when compared to their distant, hostile relation to father. By comparison, a deprived environment offered greater family security for girls than the nondeprived household, a difference which reflects the warmth of mother–daughter relations under conditions of extreme hardship. This female bond stands out as the strongest intergenerational tie among families in the Great Depression (see Elder, 1974, Chapter 4) and represents a more general theme of family and kinship in situations where male support is precarious or absent (Stack, 1974).

From the mid-1930s to the end of the decade, prior analysis suggests that deprived family environments exposed young boys in the Berkeley cohort to the greater developmental risk when compared to girls in the sample (Sacks, 1975). Over this time period, the relation of deprived boys to father was more conflicted than that of the nondeprived in middle- and working-class families (as determined from interviews with mother); and they more often experienced erratic and punitive discipline from father as well. The boys' hostile feelings toward father in childhood reflect such conditions and anticipate their adolescent rejection of father as a behavior model and respected person. Mother generally increased the disadvantage of this life history by her tendency to be less supportive and protective of sons in deprived families, when compared to the nondeprived. Hard times also increased the negative influence of father in the lives of girls, though to a lesser extent. Its impact was countered in large part by the nurturant response of mother and her prominence in household affairs, socialization, and economic support.

These sex differences in family patterns identify two generational cycles relative to Depression hardship: one of comparative advantage through daughters and one of disadvantage through sons (see discussion of generational cycles in Rutter & Madge, 1976). Both of these outcomes emerged among members of our intensive sample from regression analyses of deprivational effects in adolescent personality (Table I—the analysis is restricted to the "intensive" sample which has family information). A background of family deprivation during the 1930s increased the risk of an incompetent self among boys, but not among girls. Apart from the influence of class origin, adolescent boys from deprived families were less likely to be judged ambitious and productive ("goal oriented"), self-confident and resourceful ("self-inadequacy"). Though more responsive than the nondeprived to the needs of others ("considerate"), they were also more vulnerable to the judgments of others and socially inept. Their world view is distinguished by a sense of victimization and meaninglessness. As in Erikson's syndrome of role diffusion, indecision and withdrawal are more characteristic of their responses to life situations

TABLE I

Effect of Family Deprivation on Dimensions of Adolescent Personality among the Berkeley Boys and Girls by Class Origin (1929); Regression Coefficients in Metric (b) and Standard Form (β)

	Effect of family deprivation, in regression coefficients							
	Boys				Girls			
	Total[a] (N = 52)		Middle class[b] (N = 30)		Total[a] (N = 51)		Middle class[b] (N = 32)	
Dimensions of adolescent personality	b	β	b	β	b	β	b	β
Goal orientation	−.54	−.19	−.84	−.29	.35	.12	.48	.17
Self-inadequacy	.66	.24	1.13[c]	.39	−.25	−.09	−.78	−.28
Submissive	.47	.13	1.07	.29	−.59	−.14	−1.48[c]	−.36
Open to inner experience	−.15	−.05	−.43	−.15	.00	.00	.17	.06
Social competence	−.50	−.13	−.76	−.19	.03	.01	.19	.05
Considerate of others	.54	.14	.41	.12	.29	.10	.30	.10

[a] The direct effects of economic deprivation (nondeprived = 0, deprived = 1) on each personality dimension was assessed by multiple regression analysis with class origin (two-factor Hollingshead Index, 1929) included in the equation.

[b] For the middle class, sex differences in the effect of family deprivation are statistically reliable on goal orientation ($F = 3.26$, df = 1,56, $p = .07$), self-inadequacy ($F = 7.09$, df = 1,56, $p = .01$), and submissive ($F = 6.61$, df = 1,56, $p = .01$). Class origin as of 1929 (two-factor Hollingshead index) is controlled in the analysis.

[c] Regression coefficient at least twice its standard error.

("submissive") than of boys who were spared the misfortune of economic hardship and related strain.

The psychological disadvantage of family deprivation in the total sample of boys is modest at best, though it stands out when compared to the adolescent characteristics of girls. Whether due to mother's example or to emotional support, the Berkeley girls fared well in deprived families and appear more goal oriented, self-adequate, and assertive in adolescence than the daughters of nondeprived parents. Not surprisingly, this advantage is most strongly linked to economic deprivation in the middle class, a stratum in which Depression losses were novel and short term. We also find evidence of impairment among deprived boys concentrated in this social class, even though rates of unemployment and public assistance point to greater absolute privation in the working class. This outcome becomes less puzzling when viewed in terms of three considerations.

First, the economic collapse of the 1930s entailed more generalized hardships among working-class families; as a result, differences in well-being between nondeprived and deprived families were less pronounced in this stratum than in the middle class. Second, the past hardship experience of most working-class families meant that adaptations to scarcity were less restricted to the deprived category in this stratum than in the middle class. Third, the contrast between scarcity conditions in the 1930s and wartime prosperity is especially striking among middle-class families that lost heavily in the Depression, owing to the slower recovery of families in the working class.[7]

Three behavioral dimensions in the middle class—goal orientation, self-inadequacy, and submissiveness—represent the major difference between boys and girls on the impact of family deprivation (see note *b* to Table I). Together they link growing up in a deprived family to developmental limitations among boys, on the one hand, and to personal strength, ambition, and initiative among girls, on the other. As we have noted, deprived families generally offered girls an unusual degree of emotional security and support through mother, and both of these factors largely

[7]Unemployment illustrates each of these considerations. Between 1929 and 1936, loss of job is strongly related to degree of economic loss in the middle and working class, as one might expect, but unemployment was more common among blue collar men, even when classified as nondeprived. Second, men from the working class were more likely than those of higher status in 1929 to enter the 1930s with a history of unemployment. Third, the differential recovery pattern has much to do with the concentration of Depression unemployment in the working class. Especially in this stratum, loss of job in the early 1930s forecasts a continuing problem of economic deprivation and worklife instability. Though a good many of the Berkeley unemployed in the working class had reentered the labor force by 1936, they experienced the greatest risk of joblessness during the 1937–1938 depression.

account for their developmental path to resourceful, goal-directed behavior in adolescence. Among middle-class girls, the negative link between deprivation and self-inadequacy virtually disappears ($\beta = -.03$) when we include "warmth to mother" and "security in the family" (ages 8–10) in the regression analysis. These aspects of the family environment also account for a substantial portion of the impact of deprivation on goal orientation and submissiveness, between a third and one-half. Feelings toward father were also consequential in this respect, but they bear little relation to economic misfortune. It is the female lineage and its empathic character that appear most crucial to the developmental assets of girls in deprived families.

These assets may also reflect the behavioral example set by deprived mothers in a period of rapid change in women's options. During the adolescence of the Berkeley girls in World War II, Lawrence Frank (1944, p. 245) noted that in "the confusion and conflict over feminine roles today, the uncertainty about what one does to be a woman . . . [adolescent girls] . . . no longer can find the patterns and the skills they need by following the example of their mothers . . . ." However, the example of a gainfully employed mother was most common among deprived families in the Berkeley cohort and thus established a plausible model for daughters to follow in relation to expanding job opportunities for women. Considering the young age and university setting of the Berkeley mothers, their work and values may have established a broader concept of woman's sphere of activity in the upbringing of daughters, a concept which favors a resourceful, goal-oriented approach to a future with multiple options. This concept applies primarily to the better educated middle class at the time, and it is in this stratum that we find the strongest association between family deprivation and competence among girls.

The family relationships of deprived boys also provide insights concerning their problematic adolescence. Those who felt closer to mother because father counted so little as a recipient of their affection were likely to feel insecure in the family, and both factors illumine the process by which Depression hardship undermined a sense of direction, personal worth, and mastery in the lives of some Berkeley boys. Among middle-class youth, for example, lack of warmth toward father, stronger affection for mother than father, and insecurity in the family (for ages 8–10) account for about two-fifths of the negative effect of family deprivation on "goal orientation"—a pattern of low aspirations and self-defeating behavior (β from $-.29$ to $-.17$). Boys' attitudes toward parents still leave much to be explained in the effect of deprivation, and this is even more true for self-inadequacy and submissiveness. One reason for this limitation may be found in attitude measures which do not capture emotional ambivalence, the presence of both hostility and affection in a son's relation to father and mother. By defining hostility and warmth as opposite ends of the same continuum, the attitude ratings obscure the intensity of each sentiment and its explanatory power.

The return to better times through economic recovery during the late 1930s and war years did not always favor a more involved and effective role among deprived fathers in the lives of their sons. A good many of these men worked overtime in the late 1930s out of fear of job loss and economic need. Moreover, labor shortages during World War II extended this pattern and prompted the labor force participation of mothers. Perhaps even more than the Depression era, civilian mobilization reduced the effective "home" presence of mother and father. One of the Berkeley fathers remarked that there were months at a time in World War II when he "never saw the sun rise or set." In addition to families with a Depression history of economic scarcity, war mobilization served to prolong the "absentee" status of some fathers who were spared economic misfortune in the 1930s, especially within the nondeprived middle class.

Fathers in this sector of the middle class were distinguished by a pattern of overinvolvement in work at the expense of their family contributions and relationships, particularly with spouse and son. From the mid-1930s into the war years, these men tended to work more hours per week than any other subgroup, frequently exceeding their reported work week. Approximately half of the fathers in the nondeprived middle class were minimally involved and effective in family life between 1935 and the 1940s, as defined by evidence on at least one of the following factors: low parental involvement, unusually long hours, and impaired performance of social roles, owing to heavy drinking, illness, etc. The sons of these men ($N = 10$) possessed more attributes of an incompetent self in adolescence than boys with more involved fathers ($N = 9$; no such differences were obtained on girls). The former group ranked higher on self-inadequacy ($p = .19$) and expressed greater dissatisfaction with self ($p = .03$). They also scored lower on social competence and goal orientation. Even though related to hard times, inadequate fathering and its developmental consequences for boys were not restricted to such conditions.

B. THE PRE-DEPRESSION RELATIONSHIP OF PARENTS

The relation between a boy's mother and father may tell us more about his family experience in the Depression than attitudes toward either parent. A boy's attitude toward father is subject to mother's support and approval of father (Lamb, 1976, pp. 30–32), and these conditions were vulnerable to the strain and survival pressures of heavy income losses. Mother's prominence in a young child's world meant that she could shape his understanding of father's behavior through her interpretations, an account which is least likely to be charitable in a divisive marriage. All of these considerations point to the marital context of Depression hardship as a key factor in determining the family environment and psychological effects of economic deprivation among boys.

As a measure of this context, we used a composite index of six interrelated ratings on the marital relationship in 1930–1931 (only available for the intensively studied families); five-point gradient scales on each parent's closeness and friendliness toward spouse, sexual adjustment in the relationship, and the couple's general compatibility. Scores on each rating are based on interviews with husband and wife and represent an average of two judgments, one by the interviewer and the other by a social worker who read the interview transcripts and visited the families. The index, which we shall call "parental integration," precedes in time of data collection the onset of heavy income loss in the Berkeley sample and is unrelated to our measure of economic deprivation. For purposes of analysis, "low parental integration" is indexed by scores below the median; all other families were placed in the high-integration category. Though a middle group would have been desirable, sample size ruled out three categories. Initial analyses with some of the midrange cases removed and included produced comparable results.

The marital context of Depression hardship (whether high or low on parental integration) made a substantial difference in the family and adolescent outcomes of economic deprivation among the Berkeley boys but not among girls. With class origin included in the regression equation, economic loss diminished the family security of boys (ages 8–10) only when parents ranked low on marital integration before hard times ($b = -.43$ versus $.04$ for high integration). By comparison, parental relations were of little consequence for the security advantage of girls in deprived families. If anything, the advantage is slightly more pronounced among girls in less integrated families ($b = .27$ versus $.19$ for high integration), a finding which generally reflects the impact of male inadequacy on mother–daughter relations.

A common observation in the 1930s, that hard times brought some families together and shattered others (see Lynd & Lynd, 1937), finds partial support when we place economic deprivation in the context of marital relations. If parents were relatively close to each other before income loss, economic deprivation enhanced warm feelings toward mother and father among boys and girls (ages 8–10). In a context of marital discord, however, deprivation sharply increased hostility toward father among girls, and particularly boys, while strengthening the relationship between mother and daughter. These differences also appear in the lives of the Berkeley children when they were younger, ages 6 and 7 years. At this time, their attitudes were not influenced by how parents got along before the Depression, but the latter determined how they felt about parents in deprived circumstances (Table II). Instead of producing generational tensions, financial hardship brought the generations together when parents were mutually supportive before hard times. Neither parent stands out as more preferred in these deprived families when compared to the nondeprived. However, mother ranks well above father in deprived families which were characterized by a relatively weak marriage in 1930–1931. This preference mainly indicates estrangement from father among boys and affection for mother in the lives of deprived girls.

As information that leads a child to feel loved and valued (Cobb, 1976), family support amidst economic strain is heavily contingent on the marriage relationship (with its implications for father–son interaction) among boys and on the mother–daughter relationship among girls. Relatively weak marriages before the Depression established a link between drastic income loss and a family environment uniquely conducive to the neglect, abuse, and developmental impairment of young boys in the sample (e.g., Burgess, 1978): greater alienation and hostility between father and son, less warmth toward mother, etc. Broken marriages and father's inadequacy as father and breadwinner (owing to heavy drinking, depressed states, etc.) were concentrated in this group. Girls were more insulated from the psychic costs of this harsh environment by their relationship with mother. By contrast, boys and girls experienced a benevolent side of the Depression when parents faced economic misfortune as one unit, bound together by affection, mutual understanding, and consensus on things that matter. Cohesive families responded to the Depression crisis in ways that favored their survival and a healthful developmental course for offspring, a course in which both mother and father played constructive roles. Goal orientation and aspects of self-competence were most likely to describe the personalities of these youth during their wartime adolescence.

Three measures of adolescent personality (goal orientation, self-inadequacy, and submissive), which showed the strongest effects in Table I, were analyzed by linear regression in relation to economic deprivation among low- and high-integration families, with adjustments for social class in 1929. To appraise the global patterning of behavior by sex, we also included a Q rating on "sex-appropriate behavior" in the analysis. Family deprivation generally enhanced the personal adequacy and social competence of girls, regardless of the pre-Depression quality of their parent's marriage (Table III). Nevertheless, deprivation is slightly more predictive of such attributes when the parental marriage possessed qual-

TABLE II

Attitudes Toward Parents by Family Deprivation, in Categories Defined by Sex and Parental Integration Before the Depression; Regression Coefficients in Metric and Standard Form

	Attitudes toward parents by deprivation, in regression coefficients[b]							
	Boys[c]				Girls[c]			
Attitudes toward parents[a] ages 6–7	Low integration (N = 24)		High integration (N = 22)		Low integration (N = 24)		High integration (N = 25)	
	b	β	b	β	b	β	b	β
Warm toward father	−.76[d]	−.56	.20	.15	−.27	−.17	.45	.25
Warm toward mother	−.08	−.06	.31	.21	.55	.35	.52	.36
Closer to mother than to father	.64	.32	.16	.08	.84[d]	.40	.08	.03

[a] Five-point ratings made by interviewer. Annual scores were averaged to obtain period values. The father and mother ratings are identical—range from "hostile to warm feelings." A relative closeness measure was obtained by subtracting the score on father from the score on mother.

[b] Class origin, measured by the Hollingshead index, is included in each regression analysis.

[c] Covariance analysis was employed to test the probability of similar slopes (deprivational effects) in the two parental groups. A probability of less than .15 was obtained only on the boys' rating, Warm toward father—$F = 3.83$, df $= 1,40$, $p = .05$.

[d] Regression coefficient at least twice its standard error.

136

TABLE III

Adolescent Personality by Family Deprivation among Berkeley Boys and Girls, by Parental Integration Before the Depression; Regression Coefficients in Metric and Standard Form

Dimensions of adolescent personality	Adolescent personality by family deprivation, in regression coefficients[a]							
	Boys[b]				Girls[b]			
	Low integration (N = 24)		High integration (N = 28)		Low integration (N = 28)		High integration (N = 23)	
	b	β	b	β	b	β	b	β
Goal orientation	−.90	−.33	−.31	−.10	.27	.08	.56	.30
Self-inadequacy	1.88[c]	.59	−.26	−.12	−.07	−.02	−.65	−.28
Submissive	1.61	.42	−.34	−.11	−.59	−.13	−.85	−.24
Sex-appropriate behavior	−1.63	−.34	.97	.30	−1.20	−.29	−.10	−.03

[a] Hollingshead's five-level index of class position (1929) is included as a control in each regression analysis.

[b] Covariance analysis was employed to test the probability of similar slopes (deprivational effects) in the two parental groups. Among the boys, a probability of less than .15 was obtained on the following scales: "self-inadequacy," $F = 7.71$, df = 1,46, $p = .01$; "submissive"—$F = 3.29$, df = 1,46, $p = .07$; and "sex-appropriate behavior," $F = 4.68$, df = 1,46, $p = .03$. For the girls, none of the scales produced differences in slopes by parental integration which were other than perhaps a chance outcome.

[c] Regression coefficient at least twice its standard error.

ities of emotional strength and compatibility. Under these conditions, clinical judgments placed girls from deprived families well above the nondeprived on the salience of goal directed and resourceful behavior.

Marital strife enlarged the instrumental scope of mother's behavior in deprived families (i.e., household management, control over children), and we see modest evidence of this managerial stance in the assertive orientation of their daughters. Compared to the nondeprived, these girls were more disadvantaged by lack of affirmative relations with father in which to work out a sense of femininity, and a clinician judged their adolescent behavior as less sex appropriate (effect of deprivation on a nine-point Q rating, $\beta = -.29$). No comparable outcome appears among girls from "integrated" families in which father assumed a more positive, influential role.

Compared to girls, the Berkeley boys show a much greater difference in the effects of deprivation by relations between parents. Under conditions of marital discord, boys from deprived families were less ambitious and productive in goal orientation than were the nondeprived, and they ranked higher on a submissive posture toward life—passivity, reluctance to pursue a line of action, and withdrawal from adversity. This behavior pattern suggests a circle of causation (Smith, 1968, p. 277) in which failure, encountered and imagined, makes one "hesitant to try." By comparison, we see little evidence of this failure syndrome among deprived youth who benefited from the good fortune of a supportive relationship between parents. Self-adequacy and assertiveness stand out as the principal difference (see note *b* to Table III) between these adolescents and the deprived whose problems were compounded by marital discord. In view of such differences, it is not surprising that a clinician described the former as more masculine in behavior than the latter.

Elements of "learned helplessness" (passivity, withdrawal, depressed feelings) distinguish boys who experienced both economic deprivation and marital discord during the early 1930s, and in many ways their family life entailed uncontrollable, aversive outcomes that are known to play a major role in the development of this behavior pattern (Seligman, 1975). Under conditions of low integration, deprivation markedly increased negative parental responses to son, the unpredictability of parental behavior, and the likelihood of father's impairment in family roles. From research in process, we find that mother was most likely to be perceived as dominant by sons in these deprived families, a position typically coupled with less consistency in discipline and affection toward sons. Fathers who suffered heavy income loss and unemployment without the support of close ties with spouse were more hostile or indifferent toward sons than those who could rely upon this support; they were also more likely to be inconsistent in discipline and unable or unwilling to perform family roles effectively. The interaction of deprivation and marital discord heightened the emotional instability of mother and father, as well as a tendency for parents to work at cross purposes. No subgroup ranked higher on ratings of family disorganization than deprived youth in low-integration families. The critical difference between the experience of boys and girls in such families is manifested in the behavior of mother, in her greater affection, protectiveness, and consistency toward daughters.

When viewed as a whole, the family history of boys from deprived and conflicted homes offers many clues to the origin of their developmental limitations in adolescence. Four aspects of family relations and strain during the 1930s provide one account of their self-inadequacy, relative to the nondeprived:

1. Degree of conflict and strain in the father–son relationship—an annual, five-point interviewer rating based on interviews with mother (scores averaged for ages 8–10)
2. Mother's expression of affection toward son—an annual five-point rating based on interviews with mother (scores averaged for ages 8–10);
3. Household disorganization—a five-point rating based on interviews with mother (annual scores averaged for ages 8–10);
4. Evidence of father's impaired functioning in roles from 1932 to 1940—some evidence, coded *1;* no evidence of such impairment, *0.*

With these factors and social class (1929) included in regression equations, the effect of deprivation on goal orientation declines from a β coefficient of $-.33$ to $-.02$; on self-inadequacy, from $.59$ to $-.10$; and on submissive, from $.42$ to $.08$. Parent deprivation in its broadest sense, but with emphasis on father, and the fearful, unpredictable world of a disorganized household chart a plausible course between Depression hardship in the 1930s and the problematic behavior of boys who lacked parental support in a compatible marriage when times became difficult. Many years later painful interactions with father were among their most vivid memories of childhood. As one man recalled, "I don't think he ever really heard me, really understood me . . . usually I related to him as a scared, worried, frightened child."

Summary of Berkeley Analysis. Economic deprivation during the early 1930s is most strongly linked to impaired adolescent development in three subgroups of the Berkeley cohort: boys in contrast to girls, middle-class versus working-class boys, and boys from conflicted versus harmonious families. Economic loss entailed a broad range of parent deprivations among boys, especially in relation to father, but it made little difference in a daughter's relation to father and notably enhanced her tie with mother. These differences are reflected in two versions of the adolescent self: one of incompetence among deprived boys when compared to the nondeprived, and one of resourceful self-confidence among girls with a history of economic deprivation, when compared to those from a more stable family situation. Among the Berkeley boys, family deprivation brought greater disadvantage to youth under two additional conditions: to middle-class offspring, and to the sons of parents who ranked below average on marital compatibility before the onset of hard times. Though sample size precluded simultaneous examination of class and parental compatibility, the latter tells us far more about the family and developmental consequences of Depression hardship in the lives of boys. Parental compatibility before income loss favored closer ties between the generations and developmental assets in the early life course of boys from economically deprived families, whereas initial discord sharply increased their social and psychological disadvantage.

All evidence considered to date, including that reported in *Children of the Great Depression,* supports one version of the *life-stage hypothesis:* that the timing of Depression hardship, relative to developmental age, placed the Berkeley males at greater risk of impaired development and life chances than their older counterparts in the Oakland cohort. This difference is reversed among the girls. Family deprivation appears to be more instrumental in developing the adaptive capacities of girls in the Berkeley than in the Oakland cohort. Each conclusion must be phrased tentatively since they are not based on direct comparisons of the effects of Depression hardship in the two cohorts. Will these conclusions be sustained by this mode of analysis, using common measures of adolescent personality—goal orientation, self-inadequacy, and submissive?

VI. Intercohort (Oakland, Berkeley) Comparisons in Adolescence

Ideally, a direct comparison of the two cohorts would center on critical subgroups defined by the resources parents brought to the Depression (such as marital integration), as well as on the total sample of males and females in each cohort. The Oakland archive is sufficient for cohort comparisons by sex, but it does not include information on family resources before the Depression, except for those implied by class position. Data were not collected on the marriages of the Oakland parents before or after they encountered economic losses. In view of this limitation, we must proceed without attending to the possibility of interaction between economic deprivation and marital relations in both cohorts.

Three measures of adolescent personality (goal orientation, self-inadequacy, and submissive) were selected for the intercohort analysis on the basis of their demonstrated relationship to economic hardship in the Berkeley sample. Each measure is available in identical form in the two archives. However, the Oakland data are restricted to subjects who provided information for Q judgments during adolescence and adulthood. To rule out this cohort difference, we applied the same criterion in selecting Berkeley subjects for the comparison. Cohort variations in family social class (1929) were controlled by adding this variable to both linear regression and covariance analyses.

On the three scales, evidence linking deprivation to aspects of an incompetent self appears only among the Berkeley boys and the Oakland girls (Table IV). Economic hardship made little difference in the adolescent behavior of the Oakland boys, except that members of deprived families scored lower on self-inadequacy, a noteworthy finding when compared to the opposite result in the Berkeley cohort. This is the only adolescent dimension which shows a pronounced cohort difference on the effect of economic deprivation ($p = .12$). In the female comparison, the experience of growing up in a deprived family slightly increased a pattern of self-inadequacy and submissiveness among the Oakland girls, a result which generally corresponds with their domestic obligations and social disadvantage in adolescence. Since neither of these characteristics describes the behavior of deprived girls in the Berkeley sample, they represent a major contrast between the two cohorts on the behavioral impact of economic loss.

Three Q ratings from the scales offer a graphic portrait of helplessness among the Berkeley boys in deprived families: "self-defeating in relation to goals," "feels victimized and cheated by life," and "reluctant to commit self, delays or avoids action." By comparison, deprived boys in the Oakland cohort were characterized more by a sense of hope and buoyant optimism than by the self-pity of a victim of circumstances. Figure 2 shows this cohort difference by presenting the direct effects of deprivation in the two samples. A modest cohort difference appears only on "delays action" (p of same slope = .19), although the pattern of results is compatible with the life-stage hypothesis.

Deprivation is more consistently related to low values on the three ratings among the Berkeley girls than among girls in the Oakland cohort, a difference which is statistically reliable only on "delays action" (p of same slope = .05). Deprived girls in both cohorts were less likely than the nondeprived to be characterized by self-defeating behavior, but deprivation increased feelings of victimization and a reluctance to act in the Oakland sample, while showing the opposite effect among the Berkeley

TABLE IV

Indicators of Adolescent Personality by Family Deprivation among Boys and Girls in Oakland and Berkeley Cohorts; Regression Coefficients in Metric and Standard Form

	Boys						Girls					
	Adolescent personality by family deprivation, in regression coefficients[a]											
Indicators of Adolescent Personality[b]	Oakland (N = 44)		Berkeley (N = 55)		Probability of same slope		Oakland (N = 46)		Berkeley (N = 71)		Probability of same slope	
	b	β	b	β			b	β	b	β		
Goal orientation	−.15	−.05	−.46	−.14	.66		.39	.17	.26	.09	.80	
Self-inadequacy	−.23	−.10	.63	.25	.12		.17	.08	−.55	−.20	.15	
Submissive	.00	.00	.78	.19	.65		.28	.10	−.94[c]	−.24	.07	

[a] Only subjects with adult data (40 years) were selected for this analysis. Class origin (five-point Hollingshead Index, 1929) is included in all regressions.

[b] The item content of these measures for Oakland is identical to that of the Berkeley indicators: Goal orientation—average r for boys and girls = .51 and .37, α reliability = .80 for boys and .68 for girls; self-inadequacy—average r for boys and girls = .50 and .42, α reliability = .83 for boys and .77 for girls; and submissive—average r for boys and girls = .50 and .50, α reliability = .81 for boys and .80 for girls.

[c] Regression coefficient at least twice its standard error.

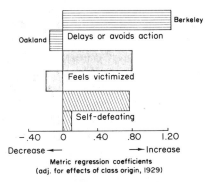

Fig. 2.   Effect of family deprivation on adolescent ratings of personality: Berkeley versus Oakland boys.

girls.[8] In *Children of the Great Depression,* a sense of being victimized or unfairly treated was noted in perceptions of girls from hard-pressed families. On a senior high questionnaire (Elder, 1974, p. 127), they were more likely than the nondeprived to express complaints about classmates who are "snobbish and stuck-up," "won't let others in on the fun," and associate "only with certain pupils." The Oakland girls encountered the social limitations of economic loss during their adolescence in the 1930s, whereas such constraints were largely a matter of history when the Berkeley girls entered adolescence during World War II.

A central theme from this analysis concerns the differential timing of Depression hardship in life experience and its relation to psychosocial development. *The earlier the occurrence of severe economic loss among family units, the greater the psychic costs among boys;* these costs exceed those observed among girls of similar age and among older youth of either sex. As we have seen, family patterns in deprived and conflicted households were more pathogenic for young boys than for young girls in the Berkeley cohort. Studies surveyed by Rutter and Madge (1976, pp. 253–254) also point to this difference on the family support of boys and girls in stressful situations, and to the more severe effects of psychosocial disturbances in the lives of boys.

Cohort variations in sex-typed development provide a global depiction of these age and sex differences. Economic deprivation tended to reverse traditional sex differences in the Berkeley cohort, while reinforcing them

---

[8]Metric regression coefficients for the direct effect of deprivation are as follows, with class origin in 1929 included in the equations: self-defeating, −.32 for Oakland and −.12 for Berkeley; feels victimized, .39 for Oakland and −.41 for Berkeley; and reluctant to commit self, .05 for Oakland and −1.45 for Berkeley.

among the older Oakland youth; the former is expressed in generalized behavior, the latter primarily through social roles and values. When judged by cultural standards, the environment of deprived families minimized observed differences between the Berkeley boys and girls on "sex-appropriate behavior"; boys became more passive and girls less so when compared to their nondeprived counterparts.[9] The Oakland adolescents were influenced less by the misshapen relationships of hard-pressed families than by their roles in the scarcity economy of such households. Boys in deprived families typically held paid jobs and were characterized as more industrious, financially responsible, and adult oriented than the nondeprived. Loss of income enlarged the burden of the Oakland girls, involving them in adultlike responsibilities which assigned priority to a domestic career of marriage and parenthood.

These developmental variations by cohort underscore the risk of generalizing from a single cohort. Similar risks are associated with the cohort comparison. Characteristics of the two samples (e.g., small, nonrepresentative, specific locale) and of longitudinal studies in general (repeated measurements, attrition) obviously discourage generalization to other samples of the birth cohorts represented in the study. Neither sample is remotely typical of the broader membership of their respective cohorts, 1920–1921 and 1928–1929. Data limitations underscore a key premise of secondary analysis—to make the best of available data in research on important questions. From this perspective, the Berkeley sample can be viewed as an unique opportunity to extend the Oakland analysis through a comparative framework. The Berkeley and Oakland samples are not identical on composition, geographic setting, and data, among other factors, but their resemblance is sufficient for an assessment of the effects of economic loss among children of differing age.

Up to this point, the scope of inquiry has not done justice to the full meaning of Depression hardship within the life course. Early experience leaves much to be explained on developmental paths to the middle years (see Clarke & Clarke, 1977); in lives where childhood promise is not matched by accomplishments during the adult years, or where damaged

---

[9]Throughout the analysis we have assumed that economic deprivation produced differences in adolescent personality through related family patterns. This interpretation is based on the premise that such differences were not present before family losses. Though direct empirical support is not available, indirect support is provided by the interaction between economic deprivation and the parental relationship. Our Predepression measure of this relationship is not linked to economic deprivation, but the effects of deprivation on subsequent family patterns and adolescent personality vary by degree of parental harmony or integration before hard times. These outcomes are not readily explained by Predepression variations in child attributes.

life chances are at least partially repaired by growth-producing events later on in life. A poor start in life may anticipate a continuing pattern of disadvantage through cycles of failure, or prompt adaptations that revise the future in more hopeful terms. To provide this broader view of economic deprivation in life-course development, we shall briefly turn to the lives of the Depression children as adults, to their accomplishments, health, and reflections on the past.

VII.   The Depression Children Grown Up

More than 30 years separate a Depression childhood from events at midlife, a time span that ranges from the early events of marriage, parenthood, and full-time employment to a stage marked by rapidly maturing children and aging parents. As we follow members of the Oakland and Berkeley cohorts across these years, the first question that comes to mind involves the developmental and material constraints of Depression hardship on career beginnings. Most important in this regard is educational progress beyond high school, its relation to occupational entry and marital choice. California offered a tuition-free place in higher education for qualified youth during the 1940s, and an unusual number of men and women from the two cohorts took advantage of this opportunity. Over three-fourths of the men and 50% of women entered college, but their chances for completing degree requirements were diminished by a history of family deprivation.

A.   EDUCATION AND LIFE PATTERNS

Family hardship restricted prospects for completion of college among the Oakland boys with origins in the working class, a handicap which also extends to middle-class youth in the Berkeley cohort (Elder & Rockwell, 1978a). Though no less bright on IQ tests than the nondeprived, Berkeley boys from deprived families were more likely to drop out of college in response to financial pressures and personal problems that were manifested during their adolescent years. With few exceptions, only middle-class girls in the two cohorts benefited from the opportunity to enter college, and those with a deprived family history were least likely to follow this course to graduation. Given such limitations one might expect more of the same among children of the Depression in men's worklife and the marital "match" achieved by women.

Young women who did not enter college or complete degree require-

ments presumably had less access to men with a promising future than the
college graduates, but we find no evidence of this disadvantage in the
occupational status of husbands among women from deprived families.
As a group, these women in the two cohorts generally equalled or sur-
passed the marital accomplishments of the nondeprived at the age of 38–40
years. Likewise, Depression hardship did not place men at a disadvantage
on occupational status at midlife. In both cohorts, the sons of deprived
parents frequently rose above the occupational handicap of limited education through a pattern of early career entry, worklife stability, and career
persistence (Elder & Rockwell, 1978a). Whether a member of the Berkeley or the Oakland cohort, these men were more likely than the nondeprived to match or exceed career expectations based on formal education.

Worklife achievement among deprived men is generally consistent
with the inner resources of the Oakland men in adolescence, but it has
little in common with the dispirited self observed among so many deprived boys in the Berkeley cohort. Adolescents engaged in the self-
defeating behavior of indecision and passivity are poor candidates for the
discipline of career progress, and yet a surprising number from the Berkeley sample were successful by any standard of work achievement. Jean
Macfarlane (1963, p. 338), the long-time director of the Berkeley Guidance Study, may have been referring to this group when she observed
that nearly half of the Berkeley men turned out to be "more stable and
effective adults than any of us with our differing theoretical biases had
predicted . . . ." A large percentage of the "most outstandingly mature
adults in our entire group . . . are recruited from those who were confronted with very difficult situations and whose characteristic responses
during childhood and adolescence seemed to us to compound their problems" (1964, p. 121).

In her reassessment, Macfarlane (1963) cites two practices which contributed to the disparity between staff predictions and the adult life
course: (1) failure to recognize the potential maturation value of hardship
experiences—"we have learned that no one becomes mature without
living through the pains and confusions of maturing experiences"; and (2)
insufficient appreciation of such adult experience, including the potential
of late development for altering the trajectory of lives. According to
Macfarlane, a large number of the Berkeley boys and girls did not achieve
a sense of ego identity and strength until adult situations "forced them or
presented an opportunity to them to fulfill a role that gave them a sense of
worth . . . ." Developmental gains were frequently associated with departure from home and community, a large change which provided an
opportunity to "work through early confusions and inhibitions."

Research underway points to five transitions and experiences (Elder &

Rockwell, 1978b) which may have spurred such growth among the Berkeley men who rose above the constraints of a Depression background: entry into college, late marriage and child bearing, military service, a rewarding worklife, and the emotional support of marriage and family life. College entry, delayed family events, and military service are interrelated elements in the ascent of these men, with the latter occupying a key role.

Most of the Berkeley men served in the military at some point between World War II and the end of the Korean Conflict (1953); and among those with deprived origins, the percentage is slightly higher (77 versus 65%, nondeprived). However, the experience of military duty is less important in life-course variation than when it occurred. By the age of 21 (1949–50), fully 60% of all deprived men with a background of military service had joined the Armed Forces, in contrast to only 17% of the nondeprived—a difference that is even greater among men who entered college. Entry into the military typically preceded both marriage and the completion of education in the lives of deprived men, a sequence which accounts for their tendency to marry late and gain access to higher education by means of the G.I. Bill.

Apart from these effects of military service, the essential question is why the event occurred so early in the lives of deprived men. Even though similar to the nondeprived on IQ, these men did encounter more academic problems as adolescents; a life history which may have enhanced the value of military duty over advanced schooling and work, either after high school or in response to a troubled college career (Elder & Rockwell, 1978a). For deprived youth who lacked self-direction and a sense of adequacy, military service offered developmental alternatives to the course charted by their families—separation from maternal control through involvement in a masculine culture, a legitimate "time out" from work and educational pressures in a structured environment, and the opportunity to sort things out in activities that bolstered self-confidence, resolve, and goal setting. Some of these themes appear in the life reviews of veterans from deprived households, especially the "break" from a confused and painful family situation.

One man recalled that he "finally realized what was happening and broke away, entered the Navy." Another described the time he joined the Army at 18 as the end of his mother's domination and the beginning of independence. Several men recalled the novel and rewarding experience of mastery on military tasks, of doing something well and on their own. Across these diverse measures, we see a contrast between descriptions of self before and after time in the military—from the implication of being "such a flop" in adolescence—"I couldn't do anything," to the claim that from "the day I went into the service, I was almost on my own . . .

figured out my own situation and went on from there." Memories of this sort are not restricted to the Berkeley men from deprived families, but they were most in need of such developmental benefits. Their time in the military at least provided a time for growth in adaptive skills that could be employed to advantage in marriage, advanced schooling on the G.I. Bill, and worklife. A substantial number seemed to leave this phase of life with greater harmony between personal resources and the varied demands of adult careers.

Whatever the developmental value of military service, worklife achievement followed hard times in the 1930s primarily among the Berkeley men who managed to enter college, if only for a year or so (66% of the deprived versus 83% of the nondeprived). College entrance established a pathway to career lines with steady advancement possibilities, and college men from deprived families frequently made the best of them even when they failed to complete degree requirements. They were more likely than the nondeprived of college status to fulfill or surpass the promise of their education through occupational attainments by midlife, to enter stable careers at an early age and maintain a commitment to them, to marry relatively late and well in terms of marital gratification (Elder & Rockwell, 1978b). Without at least some college, men with deprived origins experienced more instability of work and marriage than the sons of nondeprived parents.

No group in the two cohorts experienced a more substantial improvement in life situation between adolescence and the middle years than the Berkeley men from deprived middle- and working-class families who were successful in worklife. Moreover, no group over this time span displayed more change in the direction of greater ambition, sense of personal worth, and assertiveness; adolescent Q ratings on these characteristics were not predictive of adult ratings (Elder & Rockwell, 1978a). By the age of 40, these men bore less resemblance to their adolescent personality than to the self-competence of equally successful adults from relatively affluent families.

Direct assessments of adult change were not presented on the Oakland cohort in *Children of the Great Depression,* but the general picture is one of psychological health among the sons and daughters of the deprived middle class. At the age of 38, these adolescents of the Depression ranked well above the nondeprived of similar class origin on clinical ratings that indicated an "ability to surmount difficulties and profit from experience, to postpone immediate gratification for the benefits of long-range accomplishments, and to use talents to their fullest advantage" (Elder, 1974, p. 248). Like deprived men in the Berkeley cohort who did not enter college, Oakland members of the deprived working class ranked lowest on the utilization of skills and resources.

These observations are only suggestive of Depression hardship in the adult health of the two cohorts since they draw upon different sets of materials. To compare the cohorts, we must turn to Q sorts on the Berkeley and Oakland subjects at ages 38–40 and a general index of psychological health constructed from these data in both cohorts.

B. PSYCHOLOGICAL HEALTH AT MIDLIFE

Psychological health at ages 38–40 is measured by the correlation between an individual's Q sort and a criterion composite of the psychologically healthy adult; a composite of Q sorts by clinical psychologists employing the 100-item California Q sort. Livson and Peskin (1967, p. 513) describe the measure as "representing an underlying dimension of psychological health, one which may be regarded as genotypic in its referent, permitting a variety of healthy (and unhealthy) responses." The pool of items that are most and least characteristic of psychological well-being includes a number that are part of the adolescent scales, but it also expands the scope considerably. Among the positive traits are: "seems to be aware of the impression made on others," "genuinely dependable and responsible," "socially perceptive," "behaves in an ethically consistent manner," and "appears straightforward, forthright." The least characteristic traits include "brittle ego-defense system," "feels victimized by life," "gives up and withdraws where possible in face of frustration and adversity," "self-defeating," "negativistic," and "aloof, keeps people at a distance."

By the time the Berkeley and Oakland adults reached middle age, the Depression experience made little difference in their life situation and our global measure of adult health reflects this outcome. Among men and women in the two cohorts with Q ratings in adolescence and adulthood, family misfortune during the 1930s does not tell us much about their adaptive skills and general effectiveness in responding to life's problems at middle age (Table V). The Berkeley men suffered most during adolescence from economic losses in their families and resulting change in relationships and socialization, but this unpromising beginning is not a reliable base from which to predict their well-being in adulthood.[10] They

----

[10]Within the limitations of this analysis, substantial developmental gain among deprived men in the Berkeley cohort seems to have occurred between the ages of 30 and 40, suggesting that the effects of higher education and military experience were expressed through worklife and family. With class origin included in regression analysis, the direct

TABLE V

Adult Psychological Health by Family Deprivation and Class Origin
among Men and Women in the Oakland and Berkeley
Cohorts; Regression Coefficients in
Metric and Standard Form

	Adult Health by family deprivation, in regression coefficients[a]			
	Men		Women	
	Total	Middle class	Total	Middle class
Birth cohort	b β	b β	b β	b β
Oakland cohort	$N = 47$ .10 .12	$N = 28$ .15 .21	$N = 46$ .06 .09	$N = 24$ .11 .17
Berkeley cohort	$N = 55$ $-.08$ $-.12$	$N = 34$ $-.11$ $-.14$	$N = 61$ .02 .02	$N = 41$ .04 .07

[a] The five-point Hollingshead index (1929) is included in all regression analyses for each cohort. Status categories within the middle class (I, II, and III) were added to regression analyses of persons with this background.

are less likely than the nondeprived to rank high on adult psychological health, and in this regard they differ from the health advantage of Oakland men from deprived homes. However, the effect of deprivation in both cohorts is too small to be reliable. Depression hardship shows even less effect in the psychological health of women from the two cohorts. Though membership in a deprived family entailed more beneficial developmental consequences for the Berkeley women during adolescence than for the Oakland women, this contrast does not appear in their health status at midlife. Clarification of this change in deprivational effect awaits more detailed examination of life patterns among women in the two cohorts.

Adults from the deprived middle class were better equipped than working-class offspring (on IQ, grades, parental aspirations) to take ad-

---

effect of family deprivation is more strongly negative in relation to psychological health at age 30 than at age 40 ($b = -.22$ versus $-.08$). The index for age 30 is based on the same measurement procedures as the midlife index. More dramatic evidence of the timing of improved health relative to the deprived origins is shown by comparing the direct effects of deprivation on psychological health in the two periods among men who entered the Depression in conflicted families (above average marital incompatibility in 1930–1931). The negative effect of deprivation is far more pronounced at age 30 than at age 40 ($b = -.40$ versus $-.18$). Among the sons of compatible parents, the direct effect of economic deprivation is small in both time periods and shows very little change (b at age 30 = $-.13$; at age 40, $-.08$). Class position in 1929 is included in each regression equation.

vantage of opportunities which favor well-being, such as higher education and career advancement. While this advantage applies to men and women in both cohorts, it is expressed primarily in the psychological health of the Oakland adults from deprived families. When compared to the nondeprived, these men and women of middle-class origin represent a modest contrast to the health liability of deprived men in the Berkeley cohort.

The notable accomplishments and well-being of most Depression-reared adults may reflect lessons or first-hand experiences of effective coping from the 1930s. A good many of the Oakland men and women from deprived families were called upon to manage adult-life responsibilities, to sacrifice and make do, and to cope with frustrations, family tensions, and disappointments. Some of the men referred to adolescent work experience as a major step toward responsible independence and maturity. Judging from the data at hand, this step did not occur among a large percentage of the deprived Berkeley men until they left home, entered the military, and obtained stable employment. To a considerable extent, they succeeded in putting aside the self-defeating helplessness of their early years, and yet we still find evidence of their dependency experience in families which suffered heavy economic losses during the Depression. More than the nondeprived, these men in high- and low-status occupations were likely to report a loss of energy, heavy drinking, and the use of professional therapy. They also described themselves more frequently as worried and inclined to keep emotions to themselves (Elder, 1977). In view of this pattern of self-containment, it is not surprising that the wives of these men seldom correctly perceived or understood their husbands' inner feelings.

If there is a benevolent legacy of hard times in dealing with problematic situations, it seems likely to appear in two coping mechanisms (Pearlin & Schooler, 1978): the use of *positive comparisons*—adult troubles may fade in significance when compared to the experience of living through the Depression in a severely deprived family; and *selective ignoring*—the process of finding the good even in very difficult times, a noxious event becomes more readily managed by looking for its worthwhile or beneficial aspects. What can we learn about these mechanisms from adult judgments of life periods as good and bad? Are the sons and daughters of deprived families in both cohorts more likely than the nondeprived to regard the adult years as the very best time of life?

C. DEPRESSION HARDSHIP IN LIFE APPRAISALS

Adults from deprived and more fortunate families have much in common, and yet they have different stories to tell concerning the best and worst times of life. Whatever the rewards of adulthood, prior hardship seems likely to have made them more satisfying, better by far than a remembered childhood of privation, fear, and insecurity. Indeed, memories of hard times were associated with objective childhood deprivations among the Oakland adults, and with the "feeling that life had become more rewarding since the Depression" (Elder, 1974, p. 259). The adult years stand out as the very best period of life for those who grew up in hard-pressed families, even when conditions offered minimal grounds for such optimism, such as a dead-end job and a conflicted marriage. Adulthood brought less improvement to the lives of nondeprived adults, and they more often perceived childhood or adolescence as a high point.

The emotional course of life assumes a more varied relationship to Depression hardship among the Berkeley men and women. When asked on a questionnaire (1969–1970) to identify the best and worst periods of life to date, they generally shared the belief that adulthood (especially after age 29) was more rewarding than adolescence or childhood, but this consensus disappears when we take family deprivation into account. Deprived men and women followed divergent life paths to midlife and their representations of the past vary accordingly. Adolescence, in particular, has different meanings and subjective implications in their lives, as our earlier analysis suggests.

Most deprived men in the Berkeley cohort look back on adolescence as the very worst period of life (52 versus 31%, nondeprived), a view which corresponds with their sense of inadequacy and pessimism at this stage. One of the men remembered thinking poor, feeling inferior and rejected by peers, a lack of parental interest, and confusion as to what was expected; "My entire adolescence was a period of painful and frustrating disorientation . . . . I don't know for sure if the depression or the general emotional makeup of my family is responsible, [but] I feel that with loving guidance I might have evolved into a far more useful personality." Though more removed from the economic collapse than childhood, the wartime adolescence of deprived men was shaped developmentally and historically by the intersection of a troubled past and uncertain future. In comparison, adulthood could only fare better as a valued life stage. Indeed, three out of four selected the years after marriage, education, and career establishment—the 30s and 40s—as most satisfying, and they were more likely to do so than the nondeprived even when relatively unsuccessful in work or marriage.

This outlook also describes the life review of nearly two-thirds of the Berkeley women, regardless of their Depression experiences. However, such experience does make a difference in memories of childhood and adolescence. Despite the strains and privations of deprived households, most Berkeley women emerged from such family experience as competent, resourceful adolescents. Consistent with this record, they were less inclined than the nondeprived to look back on the preadult years as the least satisfying period in life (62 versus 79%). With few exceptions, their adolescence did not exceed the satisfactions of adult life, but it provided more positive memories than the troubled adolescence of men who grew up in deprived households. Only a third of the deprived women viewed adolescence as the very worst time of their life.

By moving beyond the dependency years of the Berkeley and Oakland cohorts, we gain a broader context in which to appraise their Depression experience in life outcomes. The scope of analysis obviously precludes a detailed assessment of the adult life course—the timing of early events, such as marriage and parenthood; work and family patterns; civic involvement and value orientations. Nevertheless, it is clear that the initial imprint of Depression hardship, as recorded through adolescence, appears only in very diminished form as we follow lives to the middle years. Even the most severe effect of family deprivation in the 1930s—among the Berkeley males—was frequently countered by growth-promoting events in the adult years. Despite deficient lives, relationships, and options in adolescence, a large proportion of these deprived men were successful in marriage and work. The nature of such turning points deserves priority on the agenda of life-course studies.

VIII. Overview and Conclusions

Two approaches from the sociology of age and the life course have been applied to questions of historical change in psychosocial development: the comparative study of successive cohorts and the investigation of social change in the life experience of individuals within subgroups of one or more cohorts. Both approaches are based on the premise that birth cohorts represent a connection between social change and the life course, between historical time and lifetime; and that the effects of social change vary among persons of differing age or cohort membership. Differing age involves variations in developmental stage and social roles, which imply differences in adaptive potential life outcomes relative to historical events.

Most cohort studies of psychological variables have not specified historical conditions or explored their consequences in life-course development. Moreover, the study of whole cohorts obscures an important feature of social change; that it differentiates life experience within as well as between cohorts. Subgroups in a cohort frequently differ widely in exposure to events of change, in accounts of them, and in responses. Variation of this sort constitutes one of the most striking aspects of life in the Great Depression, the focal event of the present chapter. Though unemployment and economic loss "ravaged numerous homes" (Bernstein, 1970, p. 321), a substantial number of families managed to avoid severe income losses and even benefited from the decline in cost of living.

Children of the Great Depression (Elder, 1974) reports a longitudinal analysis of such variation in life experience of persons who were born in 1920–1921 and grew up in the city of Oakland. Both sons and daughters of relatively nondeprived and deprived families were compared on life patterns and personality from the early years of secondary school to young adulthood and middle age in the 1960s. The Oakland cohort encountered the Depression at a relatively favorable time (e.g., beyond the early dependency years) and the study found no substantial evidence of life disadvantage among the offspring of deprived families. The uniqueness of the Oakland cohort and questions concerning the interaction of life stage and historical change led to the Berkeley Guidance sample (persons born 1928–1929) and the present study: *a comparative analysis of Depression hardship in the adolescent personality and adult life patterns of persons in the Oakland and Berkeley cohorts.* Comparison of the two cohorts is not handicapped by large differences in sample composition and geographic locale, or by the absence of common data sets for key measurements, such as economic deprivation and personality. However, the two samples were not designed originally for purposes of comparison, a limitation which has some consequences that can only be acknowledged, such as differing criteria for member selection (in age, locale) and the role of different staff members of the Institute in the lives of study participants. As such, it is necessary to view the results of this comparative study with appropriate caution.

From a developmental perspective, the Berkeley children were more vulnerable than their Oakland counterparts to family change in the early 1930s and they were exposed to a longer phase of economic deprivation and its persistence up to departure from home. The interaction of this difference in life stage with economic loss is expressed in three hypotheses that structured the study: (1) *Life stage*—the most adverse developmental outcomes of economic deprivation will be concentrated in the Berkeley cohort; (2) *sex variation*—this differential effect will be most pronounced in a comparison of males from the two cohorts, owing to the link between economic and paternal deprivation and its consequences for young boys; and (3) the *relationship between parents* before the Depression—in the Berkeley cohort, marital discord before economic loss will increase the pathogenic effects of family deprivation.

Empirical support for the three hypotheses comes primarily from the Berkeley males. The family relations of deprived households exposed these young boys to greater risk of developmental impairment than girls in the cohort, and deprivation only predicted such outcomes (self-inadequacy, submissiveness, etc., as measured by Q ratings) among the boys. Though stronger in the middle class than in the working class, this effect among the Berkeley boys is primarily restricted to family settings of marital discord before hard times. From direct cohort comparisons, a negative effect of deprivation on boys occurs only in the Berkeley sample, with economic deprivation among girls more strongly linked to self-competence in the Berkeley cohort than in the Oakland sample.

On the basis of this study, the timing of economic deprivation in the course of preadult development has the greatest consequence for the well-being of boys; the earlier the event of economic loss, the more pathogenic its effect on male development. This outcome and the more healthful development of the Berkeley girls in deprived families reflect four types of relationships in hard-pressed families: mother–father, father–son, mother–son, and mother–daughter. Economic loss among the Berkeley families weakened the tie between father and son while increasing the solidarity of mother and daughter. However, both outcomes were contingent on the pre-Depression marital bond. When inadequate as family earner, father's relation to son and daughter was most heavily dependent on the strength of the marital bond and the wife's support. Under conditions of marital harmony, economic loss actually enhanced the relationship of father with son and daughter. In the absence of this precondition, deprived girls acquired closer ties with mother when compared to the nondeprived, whereas deprived boys generally lost emotional support in relation to mother and expecially father.

Adolescence represents the only preadult stage which permits comparisons across the two cohorts, and it provides little more than a snapshot of the Depression experience in lives. In order to view this experience within the life course, we briefly extended the analysis to the adult years, with emphasis on socioeconomic position, psychological health, and life reviews at midlife. Family losses during the 1930s entailed some disadvantage in education and career beginnings, especially among the Berkeley men, but even in this group we find little evidence of a handicap in socioeconomic position at midlife. Men in both cohorts generally managed to overcome the limitations of their deprived background through worklife advancement, while women of similar origins did so through marriage.

The most noteworthy reversal of life prospects appears in the lives of the Berkeley men from deprived families, a change for the better in which military service seems to have played a major role. Psychological health remains a problem in their lives, when compared to the nondeprived, but the effect is small in relation to their disabilities in adolescence. Considering the benefits of adulthood, it is not surprising that the offspring of deprived parents in both cohorts typically view this stage as the best time of life, and, with but one major exception (the Berkeley females), they were more likely than the nondeprived to look back on childhood and adolescence as the worst time of all.

Central themes from this analysis emerge from the interaction of person and situation; of children characterized by a specific life stage, gender, and family environment during the early 1930s, and their developmental course in relation to Depression hardship. The Depression experience was not uniform among members of either cohort, Berkeley or Oakland, or among those who grew up in economically deprived families. The experience differed between males and females, and in different ways between the cohorts as well as between families that met the economic crisis with emotional strength or discord. In short, the impact of historical change in lives varies according to what people bring to the new situation; their resources, interpretations, and relationships pattern modes of adaptation and options.

Conditional outcomes of this sort do not point in the direction of broad generalizations about the developmental consequences of the Great Depression or justify claims of historical particularism. However, they are consistent with principles of a life-course approach to social change and with the empirical results of contemporary research. The psychological impact of stressful events is known to vary by their timing, the social role of the individual, and the availability of social support. We should expect no less from the Depression experience in lives. The need for conditional generalizations about behavioral development may complicate the task of inquiry, but it does not, as Walter Mischel (1977, p. 352) observes, "prevent one from studying human affairs scientifically; it only dictates a respect for the complexity of the enterprise and alerts one to the dangers of oversimplifying the nature and causes of human behavior."

Acknowledgments

This paper is based on a presentation to a thematic session of the Eastern Sociological Association Meetings, Philadelphia, PA, April 2, 1978. Support for the research was provided by the Center for the Study of Youth Development and by Grant MH-25834 from the National Institute of Mental Health to the University of North Carolina at Chapel Hill (Glen H. Elder, Jr., principal investigator). I am indebted to Richard Rockwell, Bert Brim, and Warner Schaie for helpful suggestions.

References

Baltes, P. B., & Schaie, K. W. (Eds.). *Life-span developmental psychology: Personality and socialization.* New York: Academic Press, 1973.

Baumrind, D. Parental disciplinary patterns and social competence in children. *Youth and Society,* 1978, **9,** 239–276.

Bernstein, I. *The lean years: A history of the American worker, 1920–1933.* Boston: Houghton-Mifflin, 1970.

Biller, H. B. *Father, child and sex role.* Lexington, Mass.: Lexington Books, 1971.

Block, J. *The Q sort method in personality assessment and psychiatric research.* Springfield, Ill.: Charles C Thomas, 1958.

Block, J. *Lives through time.* Berkeley: Bancroft, 1971.

Bronfenbrenner, U. *Is early intervention effective?* Washington, D.C.: Office of Child Development, 1974.

Bronfenbrenner, U. Toward an experimental ecology of human development. *American Psychologist,* 1977, **32,** 513–531.

Burgess, R. L. Child abuse: A behavioral analysis. In B. B. Lahey & A. E. Kazdin (Eds.), *Advances in Clinical Child Psychology.* New York: Plenum, 1978.

Clarke, A. M., & Clarke, A. D. (Eds.). *Early experience: Myth and evidence.* New York: Free Press, 1977.

Coan, R. W. *The optimal personality: An empirical and theoretical analysis.* New York: Columbia University Press, 1974.

Cobb, S. Social support as a moderator of life stress. *Psychosomatic Medicine,* 1976, **38,** 300–314.

Davis, J. A. Communism, conformity, cohorts and categories: American tolerance in 1954 and 1972–73. *American Journal of Sociology,* 1975, **81,** 491–513.

Diener, C. I., & Dweck, C. S. An analysis of learned helplessness: Continuous changes in performance, strategy and achievement cognitions following failure. *Journal of Personality and Social Psychology,* 1978, **36,** 451–462.

Elder, G. H., Jr. *Children of the Great Depression.* Chicago: University of Chicago Press, 1974.

Elder, G. H., Jr. Age differentiation and the life course. In A. Inkeles (Ed.), *Annual Review of Sociology,* 1975, **1,** 165–190.

Elder, G. H., Jr. Social structure and personality: A life course perspective. Paper presented at a Conference on Quantitative History and Psychohistory, Mathematics Social Science Board and the National Science Foundation, University of Texas at Dallas, April 24, 1977.

Elder, G. H., Jr., & Rockwell, R. C. Economic depression and postwar opportunity: A study of life patterns and health. In R. A. Simmons (Ed.), *Research in community and mental health.* Greenwich, Conn.: JAI Press, 1978. (a)

Elder, G. H., Jr., & Rockwell, R. C. Historical times in lives. The impact of depression hardship on men's lives and values. In M. Kohli (Ed.), *Soziologie des Lebenslaufs.* Darmstadt: Luchterhand Verlag, 1978. (b)

Frank, L. K. The adolescent and the family. *The Forty-third Yearbook of the National Society for the Study of Education, Part I: Adolescence.* Chicago: University of Chicago Press, 1944.

Gergen, K. Social psychology, science and history. *Personality and Social Psychology Bulletin,* 1976, **2,** 373–383.

Greven, P. J., Jr. Comments for the panel discussion on "change and continuity in family structure." *The Family in Historical Perspective: An International Newsletter,* 1973, **5,** 9–11.

Hareven, T. K. (Ed.). *Transitions: The family and life course in historical perspective.* New York: Academic Press, 1978.

Heath, D. H. Competent fathers: Their personalities and marriages. *Human Development,* 1976, **19,** 26–39.

Inglehart, R. *The silent revolution: Changing values and political styles of western publics.* Princeton, N.J.: Princeton University Press, 1977.

Inkeles, A., & Levinson, D. J. National character: The study of model personality and sociocultural systems. In G. Lindzey & E. Aronson (Eds.), *The Handbook of Social Psychology, Volume 4.* Reading, Mass: Addison Wesley, 1969.

Jessor, R., & Jessor, S. L. *Problem behavior and psychosocial development: A longitudinal study of youth.* New York: Academic Press, 1977.

Jones, M. C., Bayley, N., Macfarlane, J. W., & Honzik, M. P. *The course of human development.* Waltham, Mass.: Xerox, 1971.

Lamb, M. C. (Ed.). *The role of the father in child development.* New York: Wiley, 1976.

Livson, N., & Peskin, H. Prediction of adult psychological health in a longitudinal study. *Journal of Abnormal Psychology,* 1967, **72,** 509–518.

Loewenberg, P. The psychohistorical origins of the Nazi youth cohort. *American Historical Review,* 1972, **76,** 1457–1502.

Lynd, R. S., & Lynd, H. M. *Middletown in transition: A study in cultural conflicts.* New York: Harcourt, Brace and Co., 1937.

Macfarlane, J. W. From infancy to adulthood. *Childhood Education,* 1963, **3,** 336–342.

Macfarlane, J. W. Perspectives on personality consistency and change from the guidance study. *Vita Humana,* 1964, **7,** 115–126.

Mannheim, K. The sociological problem of generations. *Essays on the sociology of knowledge* (P. Kecskemeti, trans.). New York: Oxford University Press, 1952.

Mischel, W. The interaction of person and situation. In D. Magnusson & N. S. Endler (Eds.), *Personality at the crossroads: Current issues in interactional psychology.* Hillsdale, N.J.: Lawrence Erlbaum Assoc., 1977.

Morrison, D. E., & Henkel, R. E. (Eds.), *The significance test controversy.* Chicago: Aldine, 1970.

Nesselroade, J. R., & Baltes, P. B. Adolescent personality development and historical change: 1970–72. *Monographs of Society for Research in Child Development,* 1974, **39** (1, Serial No. 154).

Pearlin, L. I., & Schooler, C. The structure of coping. *Journal of Health and Social Behavior,* 1978, **19,** 2–21.

Proshansky, H. M. Environmental psychology and the real world. *American Psychologist,* 1976, **31,** 303–310.

Riegel, K. From traits and equilibrium toward developmental dialectics. In J. K. Cole & A. J. Arnold (Eds.), *Nebraska Symposium on Motivation, 1975.* Lincoln: University of Nebraska Press, 1976.

Riley, M. W., Johnson, M., & Foner, A. *Aging and society: A sociology of age stratification. Volume 3.* New York: Russell Sage, 1972.

Rosow, I. What is a cohort and why? *Human Development,* 1978, **2,** 65–75.

Rutter, M., & Madge, N. *Cycles of disadvantage: A review of research.* London: Heinemann, 1976.

Sacks, H. L. *Socialization and status change in the development of self.* Unpublished doctoral dissertation, University of North Carolina, 1975.

Seligman, M. E. P. *Helplessness.* San Francisco: Freeman, 1975.

Smith, M. B. Competence and socialization. In J. A. Clausen (Ed.), *Socialization and society.* Boston: Little, Brown, 1968.

Smith, M. B. A dialectical social psychology? Comments on a symposium. *Personality and Social Psychology Bulletin,* 1977, **3,** 719–724.

Srole, L. Long term trends in urban mental health: Old theories and new evidence from the Midtown Manhattan Restudy. Special lecture, American Psychiatric Association, Toronto, Canada, 1977.

Stack, C. B. *All our kin: Strategies for survival in a black community.* New York: Harper & Row, 1974.

Wilson, H., & Herbert, G. W. *Parents and children in the inner city.* London: Routledge & Kegan Paul, 1978.

Family Development Theory and Life-Span Development

Reuben Hill and Paul Mattessich

THE FAMILY STUDY CENTER, UNIVERSITY OF MINNESOTA
MINNEAPOLIS, MINNESOTA

Abstract

This chapter examines the points of convergence among the literatures of family development, individual life-span development, and age stratification/life-course analysis. The history and major concepts of the family development approach to family analysis are

LIFE-SPAN DEVELOPMENT
AND BEHAVIOR, VOL. 2

described. The impacts and deficits of the approach are identified. An explanation of the ways in which a synthesis of the three literatures under consideration might remedy those deficits is presented. Family development is defined in terms of the progressive structural differentiation and the related transformations which the family unit experiences as it moves through its life cycle.

Ten issues which underlie models of psychological development provide a basis for examining the assumptions of the family development model. These issues, along with the appropriate assumptions for the family development model to date, are: locus of the developmental dynamic (internal); qualitative vs. quantitative change (qualitative); openness of the model (semiclosed); continuity of change (discontinuous); structure–function vs. antecedent–consequent (both); nature of family differences (ipsative); chronological age (intrinsic); directionality of development (multidirectional); and universality of development (universal).

Changes in historical context are discussed as they relate to the construction of a nomothetic model of family development. Four dimensions of time are identified: family, individual, chronological, and historical. Implications of the age stratification/life-course literatures lead to conclusions that historical context affects the family developmental dynamic normatively and chronologically, refines and lengthens the family life cycle, and affects the social and physical resources available to families for performing roles at various stages of the life cycle. The age stratification/life-course literatures influence developmental analysis to move toward antecedent–consequent assumptions, to confront the social meaning of chronological age, and to specify precisely the universality of family development.

I. Introduction: Statement of Gains from Interfacing Family Development and Life-Span Development

We are seizing the opportunity in this chapter to open up a dialog between family scholars and life-span developmental psychologists about their common interests in the phenomenon of development. We will want to ascertain in this exchange the extent of isomorphism either between "development" over the life span of humans as biosocial organisms (the focus of life-span psychology) and the "development" of families as they form, as they change in function and structure over their life history (the concern of family development), or between these two phenomena and the "development" in larger aggregations of communities and whole societies over time (about which sociologists, economists, and anthropologists are debating).

Among the half-dozen recognized conceptual frameworks for family study (Hill & Hansen, 1960), the family development perspective is the most appropriate for pursuing this dialogue because it interfaces at many points with life-span psychology without sacrificing its distinctively familial level of analysis and scope. Family development is also the only perspective to have been formulated specifically with the conceptual demands of family research and service in the forefront of concern. Let us illustrate this briefly by referring to the handling of social time. A basic shortcoming of the several frameworks in use prior to the formulation of the family development perspective was their failure to cope systematically with social time. When process concepts dealing with the dynamics of change were utilized by these frameworks they failed to specify time in units appropriate for families and they therefore had limited value in assembling generalizations about family change. This is not surprising since, with the exception of the developmental framework, each of the approaches has originated in domains of social science other than the family: (1) the institutional, the structure–function, and the situational approaches developed out of the effort to understand society and culture; (2) the psychoanalytic, the learning theory, and the psychological habitat framework developed out of the study of personality development; (3) the symbolic–interactional approach similarly was organized to cope with issues of the development of personality and with the phenomenon of socialization—it was only years later that the approach was adopted for the study of the family; finally (4) the household economics approach originated with the analogy of the household as an economic firm and still uses many of the concepts of management and the economics of consumption in its "balance sheet" approach to family living. In sum, no other framework has made a pretense of attending to the issue of *family time,* the orderly changes which occur in most families over the life span.

The scholars who have worked on the family development perspective have unashamedly borrowed and incorporated concepts from a variety of disciplines, paying less attention to issues of theoretical elegance than to substantive relevance, as we shall see in examining the perspective's origins and history. (For a more detailed historical accounting than can be given here, see Hill & Rodgers, 1964, pp. 172–185.)

A. ROOTS OF FAMILY DEVELOPMENT

The genealogy of the family development framework is depicted schematically in Fig. 1 as a type of family tree showing diverse and heterogeneous origins. The ancestors and progenitors from whom concepts and category systems have been borrowed include, on the left-hand side of the tree, economists, demographers, and rural sociologists. They were concerned with the pressure of family needs and demands on a changing but finite set of resources over the life span and they used these elements intuitively to construct categories of the family life cycle. Equally diverse are the developmentally oriented scholars, on the right-hand side of the tree, with their competitive theories of child development

164   *Reuben Hill and Paul Mattessich*

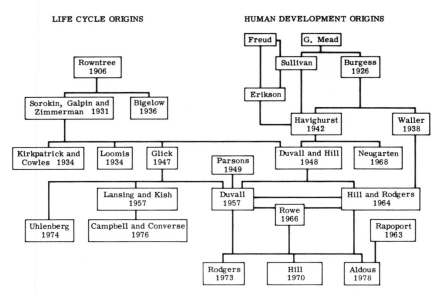

Fig. 1. Genealogy of family development frameworks from human development and family life cycle origins.

and of the impacts of parental child-rearing practices in the formation of personality structures. Almost none of this second set of ancestors gave much attention either to the total life span or to the variability of family organization over its life span.

In their initial conceptualization for the National Conference on Family Life held in the White House in 1948, Duvall and Hill (1948) drew, first, on the symbolic interactionism of George Herbert Mead, E. W. Burgess, and Willard Waller for their view of the family as an arena of interacting personalities and, second, from Robert Havighurst and Erik Erikson for their views on human development as marked by the mastery over the entire life span of progressively more complex developmental tasks. With the two formulations joined, the family of interacting personalities of Burgess and Waller became an organization of growing, changing persons, reciprocally engaged in enabling one another (husband interacting with wife, parents interacting with children, and brothers interacting with sisters) to work through their several developmental tasks as they changed over the life span. This was the original conceptualization of family development, an organization and setting for facilitating growth and development of its members. Left moot was the explanatory question of what types of family organization would best accomplish this matching of members' needs over time.

In its subsequent elaboration in the 1950s, the family development framework continued its imperialistic acquisitions, incorporating the compatible descriptive categories of many other approaches to the study of the family. From the sociology of work and of the professions were borrowed the concepts of career as a series of role sequences and the view of the family as a convergence of intercontingent careers of husband and wife, later of children and parents. From the structure–function approach was borrowed the trio of concepts of position, role, and norm, particularly as these involve age and sex roles and plurality patterns. This approach has also contributed conceptual categories of boundary maintenance and equilibrium seeking of the family as a social system. Joined with these concepts of structure–function are terms from the symbolic interaction framework which modified the concept of role to include role playing, role taking, reciprocity of roles, and role differentiation. These concepts, taken from several disparate approaches, have been assembled in a relatively unified frame of reference that permits the accretion of generalizations about the internal development of families, from their formation in the engagement and wedding to their dissolution in divorce or death.

B. CHIEF CONCEPTUAL ISSUES TREATED BY FAMILY DEVELOPMENT

The most frequently used concepts in the framework, vintage 1970 (Hill, 1971), cluster around four issues of conceptualization:

1. Concepts about the family collectivity as a system in its own right, in which the conceptual categories of its "systemness" are specified; namely, a small group system that is relatively closed, boundary maintaining, equilibrium seeking, purposive, and adaptive, differentiated from other forms of the family rendered residual by the framework, such as the family as a domestic institution, the extended family, the kindred, and the household.

2. Concepts of structure, such as position, role, norm, role cluster, and role complex, which tell us what recurring, repetitive, and reciprocal features may be seen internally when examining the family internally and statically.

3. Concepts of goal orientation and direction, and the corollary concepts of allocation of resources and coordination of activities which illuminate the task performing and functioning features of the family.

4. Concepts dealing with orderly sequences and processes, the sequential regularities observable in the family over its life history, such as role

sequences, careers of family positions, intercontingencies of careers, and stages of development.

In espousing the view of the family as a social system, the developmental approach emphasizes the interrelatedness of parts which exist in the family association. The concept of system carries with it the idea that change in one part of the system brings about changes in other parts. This produces a state of interdependency which in the family involves positions and roles. The units of the system are positions occupied by actors of whom there are a limited number in the family. In family development we concern ourselves primarily with two types of positions: (a) age positions, modified by gender, which in the family may in turn be modified by the norms of ordinal position, and (b) relatedness positions which are interrelated in normatively specified ways as paired positions: husband–wife, brother–sister, father–daughter, father–son, mother–daughter, and mother–son.[1]

Viewing the family as a boundary maintaining system suggests that it is partially closed and semiautonomous and that when coping with internal issues it may exclude the world from its affairs. Nevertheless, the family provides for liaison with other associations, building liaison roles into family positions and rules for transacting business with teachers, employers, and the helping professions. Thus, for example, among the many roles of the wife and mother position is the integrating role of tension management within the family. It follows that the liaison role with the helping professions will be built into the wife–mother position to support the integrative role. The wife–mother position also contains the liaison role with the school, the church, and the retail enterprises of the market place. The breadwinning roles of the husband–father and of the wife–mother link the family to the occupational structure. Thus, both positions have roles linking them to the wider community.

Unique to the family development approach is its capacity to put its concepts to work over the natural history of family formation, expansion,

---

[1]As the family development framework is currently elucidated, interdependence of concepts is evident. The basic structural concept of the position with its associated roles allows one to diagram paired positions of family members both horizontally and hierarchically over the family life cycle. Role relationships depict the internal and external functions of the family, an open system characterized by mutual interactions of members and reorganization of its parts. Processes which relate to the structure of the system emerge as activities undertaken to achieve and/or modify the system's goals. Intrasystem and intersystem interactions and transactions of the invididual, family, and extrafamilial phenomena can be evaluated from the entities conceptualized as individual developmental tasks and family developmental tasks. These tasks are derived from individual and family needs as well as from external cultural demands and societal normative pressures.

contraction, and dissolution. To account for changes in the family system, the developmental approach focuses primarily on the changing role content of positions which occurs chiefly due to changes in age norms for these positions. Since the family is a system, change in the role content of a specific position brings about change in all positions containing roles reciprocal to the changing position.

Human development specialists have extended age role expectations as developmental tasks for every age level, including not only the familiar expectations for infants and children, but also those for young, middle, and late adults. The bridging between position–role theory and developmental task theory was undertaken by Rodgers (1964) in his invoking of the concept of positional developmental tasks. The device of constructing developmental tasks ceases to be individual and becomes positional developmental as the age, sex, ordinal, and relatedness properties of the position in which ego is located are taken into account. Some age and sex compositions of families bring more dovetailing and meshing of developmental tasks of children and parents, and of husband and wife, and of siblings with siblings than others—leading analysts to identify both compatible and incompatible stages over the family's life span. For example, families with children whose births have occurred at regular intervals, within neither an overly narrow nor an overly lengthy time period, will experience a smoother meshing than will families whose new members arrived in distinct "waves," well separated in time. For the latter families, due to their age composition, the performance of stage-specific parental roles will "lapse" during intermediate periods and later recur. For the former type of family, parental role performance will occur as a continuous developmental process with one set of bounding points.

A parallel to the concept of positional developmental tasks is that of family developmental tasks, which bridge the family with the society of which it is a part. Family developmental tasks arise in response to both societal needs and the needs of individual family members. They include, for example, sets of activities associated with reproduction, physical maintenance, socialization, tension management, and conferring of status. The family researcher can specify empirically the stages of the family life cycle during which a particular family developmental family task becomes salient and those during which it recedes from prominence.

The payoff of a dynamic framework is to put it into action, and this can occur at two levels of generality: at the individual family level, as an outline for collecting detailed case histories; and at the modal family level, for research purposes which require the identification of stages of development.

At the level of modalities, it is theorized that all families in a society have enough in common that it is possible to chart their development in stages of the family life span.[2] The family development framework does not cope with short time periods of seconds, or minutes, or days, or months, nor do the categories permit us to be specific in handling brief episodes of interaction, such as the interact (a single unit of interaction) or the interactivity (a sequence of interacts marked by a common focus). We must be content with the uneven time spans covered by the stages of family development. These stages allow the analyst to view the process of development in phases and to concentrate on the role reciprocities and role conflicts in the family at this and that point in its development. In actuality, respondents in retrospective interviews report that the stages often seem to merge into one another so imperceptibly that their impressions of the sequences of development are more of continuity rather than of stages with sharp breaks.

Family development theorists see stages of development changing each time there is a marked break in the complex of positions and in the role content within these positions. New stages of development occur, therefore, with the addition of positions through births or adoptions and the loss of positions through death and through launching of members into jobs and marriage. New stages also occur each time there is a marked change in the age role content of any one of the several positions in the family requiring a rearrangement of role reciprocities. Thus, the family development approach enables one to anticipate stresses which normally accompany "growing up" by families and their members at the beginning of the cycle and "breaking up" toward the end of the life span.

C. IMPACTS AND DEFICITS OF THE PERSPECTIVE

For the record, we might note that the family development perspective has had a distinctive impact on family scholarship, despite a certain number of shortcomings, in the 30 years since its formulation in 1947. The impact of the newly formulated conceptual framework was the greater because Evelyn Duvall kept the framework salient through five successive editions of her widely adopted text, *Family Development* (First Edition, 1957; Fifth Edition, 1977). Two other textbooks have served as markers of trends and changes in the formulations and conceptualizations of family development. Rodgers (1973) pointed to ways of improving the heuristic scope of the perspective by delineating three

---

[2]Problems inherent in the use of the concept of stages with its connotations carried over from embryonic and cognitive development are discussed later in this chapter. At present, the concept is introduced as part of a general orientation to the framework.

facets for expansion: the societal–institutional facet, the group-interactional facet, and the individual psychological facet. Aldous (1978) has introduced new concepts at the individual psychological level from linguistic development (Bernstein, 1971), and cognitive and moral development (Kohlberg, 1969; Piaget, 1948), as well as concepts at the group-interactional level from systems theory (Buckley, 1970), reciprocity theory (Gouldner, 1960), and role-taking theory (Turner, 1970). These may be expected to enrich a revised family development framework if they are shown to vary lawfully over the family's life span. It should also be noted that the framework has been seminal as a stimulator of research. Hundreds of empirical descriptive and a few explanatory studies have used the categories of the perspective.[3]

The framework has also won an accepted place in the competition for attention among family theorists. As early as 1960, Hill and Hansen included family development as one of five distinctive approaches to family study, and Nye and Berardo (1966) devoted an entire chapter to this framework in their book-length treatise. Christensen commissioned Hill and Rodgers to assess the framework's contribution to theory and research in his 1964 landmark *Handbook of Marriage and the Family,* and this has become the definitive position paper establishing the paradigm of family development.

With the exception of the work of Rodgers and Aldous, relatively few additions have been made to the vocabulary of concepts of the framework since 1964 and there has been a benign neglect of the framework's deficits. Relatively little critical examination has been given to the compatibility of the framework's underlying assumptions, despite the open invitation by Hill and Hansen in 1960 to do so (but see Rowe's essay on family development assumptions in Nye & Berardo, 1966). The methodological problems in utilizing the developmental approach in ongoing family research were detailed by Hill (1964), and the steps required to move the framework toward the level of explanatory theory advocated by Zetterberg and Homans were outlined by Rodgers (1964) in his piece "Toward a Theory of Family Development." The unfinished nature of this transformation from descriptive vocabulary to a theory is clearly stated in Rodgers' "The Challenge of an Incomplete Explanation," in his 1973 textbook. The general reaction to the framework by family scholars since its inception, however, has been more favorable than its unfinished nature would justify.

---

[3]The 1969–1976 inventory of family research and theory by Hodgson and Lewis (1979) shows the family development perspective to be "increasingly extending its influence" in the share of studies reported as compared to other frameworks.

In quick summary, although flourishing and cumulative in the research it has stimulated, the family development perspective remains at the descriptive level. Moreover, it appears to have been insensitive to historical contexts and events and to have been exclusively oriented to the developmental cycle of nuclear family units. As yet, no family development theorist has dealt systematically with the pressing theoretical issues that have perplexed life-span development psychologists; namely, issues of reductionism versus emergence, continuity versus discontinuity, idiographic versus nomothetic explanations, and variability versus invariance of stages of development.

We recognize that family development scholarship has been running parallel to three other streams of research and theory: (1) developmental psychology; cognitive development; moral development; linguistic code development; social, emotional, and prosocial development (mostly ending with adolescence); and life-span development with its added accent on career developments of middle adulthood and later maturity; (2) the sociology of age stratification, which includes attention to age roles and social structure, the variable life courses of historical cohorts, and the issues of intergenerational differences, continuity, and social change; and (3) the sociology of participation in, and utilization of, social and kinship networks and voluntary associations. The scholars of the second group (Bengtson & Kuypers, 1971; Brim, 1966; Clausen, 1972; Elder, 1975; Riley, Johnson, & Foner, 1972) have opened up new vistas of personality and social structure through age and generation analyses but have not bridged the family–personality development chasm.[4] The third group of scholars (Bott, 1957; Farber, 1961; Litwak & Szelenyi, 1969; Mitchell, 1969, and others) have linked family and networks provocatively but have not specified the developmental dimension of family transactions. A long-term program in theory reconstruction at Minnesota seeks to integrate the vocabularies, the taxonomies, the propositions, and the theories of these three streams into family development in hopes of achieving a higher informative level (Hill & Mattessich, 1977). In this chapter, we

[4]Orville G. Brim, Jr., past chairman of the Social Science Research Council's Committee on Work and Personality in the Middle Years, indicated in personal correspondence that the sociology of age may be the line of inquiry that will link family development to individual life-span development. He notes that the family represents the strategic point at which to demonstrate how social change alters first the course of family development and, consequently, the course of individual development. Bengtson (1977) has proposed that all social roles have developmental tracks. Positional occupants, since they possess multiple roles, must coordinate these tracks in order to minimize interrole conflict. Gove *et al.* (1972) suggested that the family, with its multiple members, acts as a system of allocation of roles to individuals. They contend that societies may best be conceived as "networks of dynamic family systems."

focus upon the benefits and problems associated with integrating the first two (developmental psychology and age stratification) into family development.

At present, developmental psychology aims to transcend its stalemate between mechanistic and organismic approaches to consider a broader relational model and to consider dyadic and group properties in developmental research. (See Lerner in Burgess & Huston [1978] and Lerner [1978] for a "relational" linkage between individual development and group development.) Thus, it is timely to reduce the distance among the three communities and, in so doing, to increase the sophistication of developmental theory and research. This timeliness is further enhanced by a cross-disciplinary convergence of interests among scholars of both family development and life-span development. Such convergence has emerged as a result of the increasing recognition by social and behavioral scientists that: Socialization occurs as a truly interactional process, not merely as the bestowing of knowledge from an experienced actor to a relatively passive receptor; cognitive behavior is as much "social" as "individual," and it has its roots in the family context[5]; the family constitutes a system which intermingles careers both of children and of adults; and many critical transitions in the life span of the individual occur concomitantly with transitions in the life cycle of the family.[6]

II.   The Nature of Development: Personality, Family, and Society

A.   ASSUMPTIONS CONCERNING HUMAN NATURE AND PERSONALITY DEVELOPMENT

Family development scholars have shared certain basic assumptions about human nature and about personality development, and these have

[5]In fact, Lewis (1977) refers only to "social cognition" and hypothesizes, for future research, the primacy of context over individual capacity as a determinant of linguistic, cognitive, and social knowledge.

[6]The sharing of common methodological problems has also led to this convergence. Meacham's (1977) review of recent books on developmental psychology points to a growing interest in the analysis of the social and historical conditions of individual development. (Issues involved in the separation of ontogenetic universals on the family level from unique contextual effects appear later in this chapter.) Other methodological problems faced by the two groups of scholars include decisions on the advantages and disadvantages of cross-sectional versus longitudinal research and the generalizability of developmental research to populations which include other than white, middle-class individuals.

shaped their preferred models of the way families form, function, and change over the life span.

When Hill and Hansen in 1960 examined the basic assumptions about human nature implicit in family development, they listed five premises which readers will note are quite similar to the basic assumptions of symbolic interaction:

1. The individual in a social relation setting is the basic autonomous unit.

2. The individual is actor as well as reactor.

3. Human conduct cannot be understood apart from human development.

4. Human conduct is best seen as a function of the preceding as well as of the current social milieu and conditions.

5. Individual and group development are best seen as dependent upon stimulation by the social milieu and developed capacities.

These five assumptions have been inferred from the writings of Burgess (1926), Waller (1938), and Duvall & Hill (1948) (see Fig. 1). The perspective they formulated assumed individual autonomy and the utilization of growth experiences of individuals acting as initiators and contributors (in interaction with others) in the creating and shaping of their own social worlds. These views of the primacy of individuals as initiators rather than solely reactors are more compatible with developmental theorists who use the organismic model (Kohlberg, 1969; Langer, 1969; Piaget, 1948) than the social learning theory psychologists who espouse the mechanistic model (Bandura & Walters, 1963; Gewirtz, 1969; Miller & Dollard, 1941). By the same token, the assumptions of family development are incompatible with those of institutionalists or structure–functionalists within sociology, who see individuals basically as reactors and who identify institutions and social systems as the basic autonomous units in social behavior.

The major point of confrontation between conceptualizers of family development and developmental psychology comes from examining the assumptions of different models about the phenomenon of development. We return to the rhetorical question posed as we opened this chapter: Is there any isomorphism either between "development" over the life span of humans as biosocial organisms and the "development" of families as they form and change in function and structure over their life history or between these two phenomena and "development" in larger aggregations of communities and whole societies over time.[7]

---

[7] See Lerner, in Burgess and Huston (1978), for a dialectical model of relationships

B. DEFINITIONS OF DEVELOPMENT

We begin with the degree of correspondence in definitions of "development" among disciplines concerned. Agreement may be small due to the diversity of the phenomena to which the concept "development" refers as well as to the underlying assumptions made concerning the basic nature of developmental processes.

Implied in the most frequently used definitions of development are such terms as "change" and "alteration of structure" (psychological or social). However, the definitions usually go beyond the neutral notion of change to include direction and movement of increasing complexity and growth, changing from simple to complex and from undifferentiated to highly differentiated structures. Nagel (1957, p. 16) exemplifies a minority viewpoint today with his assertion that "changes must be cumulative and irreversible if they are to be labeled development." Actually social scientists vary in the extent to which they incorporate "goals" or "direction" into their definition of development. The closer a discipline's focus lies to the individual as organism, as opposed to communities, polities, economies, societies, or cultures, the more likely are its practitioners to commit themselves to directional, rather than to neutral, concepts of change. For developmental psychologists who subscribe to the organismic model, direction is inferred from the transformation of personality structures accompanying changes in function as the organism achieves maturity (Riegel, 1975a, pp. 6–7).[8]

What is "development" when we turn to the family level of organization? We need a working definition of family development which reflects change in the family as a small group association in its own right as well as the changes within the personalities of individual members. The family is more than an aggregate of residential housemates. We need to incorporate into our definition of family development changes in the family as a social system over its life history. There are implications of unique family level properties in Burgess and Waller's insightful characterization of the family as "a unity of interacting personalities," but there is no implication of orderly change in the Burgess–Waller aphorism. Changes in interpersonal relationships, in dyadic and triadic attachments, in the building and breaking of family bonds, and in family cultural orientations deserve analysis in their own right as families change in form and function over their life span.

---

development which is isomorphic with the model used for explicating individual development.

[8]Lerner points out that there are two types (at least) of the organismic model. The dialectic, "probabilistic epigenetic," model does not carry with it the same views as the older preformed epigenetic organismic version (see Lerner, *Human Development*, 1978).

Two independent concepts are useful for a description of family development: "structural differentiation" and "related transformations." Structural differentiation occurs over time as roles emerge and change to meet the needs of the family at each stage of its development. The family is an entity for which new elements of at least three types appear and disappear during the life cycle: persons, roles, and patterns of roles or other interactive and transactive behavior. The stage notion provides an index for the allocation of roles associated with positions in the family. The changes in this allocation from one stage to the next, which alter the pattern of social relations within the family, manifest the developmental structural differentiation.

The concept of "related transformations" implies that the family moves from one stage to the next, restructuring its pattern of organization, yet with common threads tying all stages together. Each stage influences its successor in two ways. First, each stage contains the embryonic elements which will eventually produce movement into a next stage. Second the decisions made and courses of action pursued by the family at a given stage set limits upon the types of behavior in which it can engage during the next stage.[9]

We propose the following as our working definition of family development:

> Family development refers to the process of progressive structural differentiation and transformation over the family's history, to the active acquisition and selective discarding of roles by incumbents of family positions as they seek to meet the changing functional requisites for survival and as they adapt to recurring life stresses as a family system.[10]

Our readers may well complain that the term "development" in family development has been made to carry, in the above discussion, a host of functional, interactional, and structural changes having in common only that they observe a more or less orderly sequence over the family's

---

[9]The "related transformations" notion parallels the "game tree" model (Magrabi & Marshall, 1965). Such a model could be formalized to include, from aggregate data, probability statements for branches of the tree. One could employ techniques such as cluster analysis to place families onto branches and then, by means of the computed probabilities, construct transition matrices to simulate the flow of family development.

[10]These organizational requisites must be coped with throughout the life span of the family but have a different level of urgency when examined by stages of development in the form of family developmental tasks, such as social control, physical maintenance, morale maintenance, family size control, and socialization.

history. The term "family career" has been coined to encompass the timing and scheduling of these changes. The family career takes on a momentum of its own, but since it is also the convergent product of the intercontingent careers of the incumbents in the family's several positions, these role performances both stimulate and complicate the family's developmental achievements.

The proposed definition of the phenomenon of family development is not constrained by reference to specific, "ideal" activities. It does not propose concrete, arbitrary markers with a value-laden bias, as do some definitions of economic and political development which have provoked endless debate among modernization scholars. Rather, in a straightforward and inherently sociological manner, it focuses attention upon the emergence and alteration over time of norms, roles, and other family group characteristics necessary for the persistence of the family as a social system. It attains its developmental character because the sequence of variations in family organization is a predictable sequence which can be, and has been, identified through family research. Life-cycle categories, such as those of Aldous, Duvall, and Rodgers, represent rough classification schemes for demarcating stages of these sequences, the differentiated phases of the family career.

As yet, the discussion of development has remained abstract. The necessity for developing certain functionally oriented roles has been mentioned but not the activities associated with those roles; the family career has been mentioned, but not the basis for its timing or the ways in which its later stages are in part determined by the events of its earlier stages. The specific activities associated with family roles and the chronology of family change depend, in very large measure, upon social and historical contexts. Families develop over time within such contexts and it is for the implications of contextual effects that we turn later in this chapter to the sociology of age stratification and life-course analysis.

III. The Interface between Life-Span Developmental Psychology and Family Development on Major Issues of Development

We return now to the interface between life-span development and family development. For the benefit of the two sets of scholars who have studied these phenomena independently, this discussion will put into relief the reciprocity of the two types of developmental processes. Life-span development refers primarily to the increasing differentiation of personality structure, including changes in mental abilities, skills, and social competencies. (However, for exceptions to this position, see Lerner & Ryff, 1978.) Such development stimulates changes in family organization but, as well, changes in family organization influence the development of both child and adult personalities.

A. ISSUES OF HIGH SALIENCE ABOUT DEVELOPMENT

Looft (in Baltes & Schaie, 1973) has provided a provocative listing of the basic assumptions about human development on which five of the dominant schools of developmental psychology have taken distinct positions. These assumptions are discussed at length and categorized in a summary table for the five schools (Looft, 1973, Table 1, pp. 48–49).

Looft identifies two dominant paradigms or general models whose basic premises about human nature are at odds on most dimensions: the mechanistic and the organismic. The former assumes humans to be reactive creatures and the latter assumes an active organism. Skinnerian theory and Piagetian theory, respectively, are exemplars. Looft (1973) asserts that, because of the belief that these positions have quite different truth criteria, they are irreconcilable (Overton & Reese, 1973). Looft identifies twelve issues of development on which the two competing models are shown to differ in the positions taken. Lerner (in Burgess & Huston, 1978) modifies this view of unbridgeable, irreconcilable paradigms by suggesting they may constitute a thesis and antithesis awaiting a dialectical synthesis. Such a third model requires conceptual compromises between the organismic orientation and the mechanistic perspective.[11] This third model, which has only recently begun to be elaborated (Lerner, 1976; Looft, 1973; Riegel, 1975b, 1976), is labeled differently by various authors. For example, it is called *relational* by Looft (1973), *transactional* by Sameroff (1975), *dialectical* by Riegel (1975b), and *dynamic interactional* by Lerner (*Human Development, 1978*).

Table I reflects what we have learned from the scholars cited above. We have telescoped four of the five schools listed in Looft's Table I (1973, pp. 48–49) under one or the other of the two opposed paradigms, the

---

[11]Lerner cites contributions in this direction from Heinz Werner's (1957) notion of orthogenesis as developmental change involving both continuous processes (hierarchical integration), on the one hand, and discontinuous processes (differentiation), on the other. T. C. Schneirla's (1957) conceptualization of epigenesis as probabilistic with nature (maturation) in dynamic interaction with nurture (experience) to produce developmental change differently according to the quality and timing of the interactions is clearly a move toward synthesis. The late Klaus Riegel's last papers (1975, 1976) specify a dialectical view which allows development to be either internally or externally derived, either unidirectional or bidirectional, and operating either as an open or a closed system.

mechanistic and the organismic. We have left the fifth, the Chicago Group of Human Development, to appear as a separate model because of its concern for continued development in adulthood and because it did not consistently conform to either of the two dominant models.[12] Table I also adds another model not included by Looft, the emergent dialectical synthesis (referred to above) in which the issue of development is less on personological change than on interactive relations among structures over the life courses.[13] The fifth column registers the deductions we would make for the family as a developing organization from the options shown for personality development on 10 issues incorporated in Table I. Our discussion is confined, however, to the six issues of highest salience for family and life-span development.

To our knowledge, no family scholar has confronted most of these basic issues about the "nature of development" which have been so central to the shaping of models of personality, nor has any considered the implications for changes at the level of family organization. We invite readers to validate or to modify our judgments and will be interested in their assessment of the utility of such a theoretical deduction across the individual–family development chasm.

Before we discuss Table I in any depth, we should add that making the choices on these issues at the family level is a way of opening up, rather than closing, the model of family development. There are, indeed, new areas of uncertainty about family change over time, and choosing one or the other sides of these issues of development, on which psychologists are still in conflict with respect to personality, has the effect primarily of rendering the issues salient and open for discussion among family scholars. This should be perhaps the most productive outcome of the present dialog.

1. External versus Internal Locus of the Development Dynamic

The issue of inner or outer orientation could very well be a fundamental premise with respect to the nature of the family as a closed, relatively closed, or open system. This dimension concerns the question of locus of developmental change. Does it occur because of changes within the organism or because of changes external to it? At the individual level, the

---

[12]Looft (1973) found it difficult to place this group's position on several of the basic issues of development with either the organismic or the mechanistic camp because (a) their guiding theoretical base is still evolving and is not well articulated, (b) the group has tackled more global problems than most researchers operating from other psychological models, and (c) their style of hypothesis formation and data gathering varies from study to study.

[13]We have borrowed generously in making assessments of the stance taken from a major spokesman for the model, Professor Richard Lerner (1978).

TABLE I

A Confrontation of the Psychological Model Assumptions of Four Approaches to the Study of Socialization and Personality Development and the Ways Family Development Resolves These Model Issues at the Family Level of Organization[a]

Model issues	Four selected developmental psychology approaches and family development				
	Organismic model (Kohlberg's developmental approach and Loevinger's ego development approach)	Dialectic model (Riegel's dialectical; Schneirla's probabilistic epigenesis; Lerner's dynamic interactionism)	Mechanistic model (Social-learning theory approach and Cattell's factor trait approach)	Chicago human development approach	Family development approach
A. External vs. internal locus of the developmental dynamic	Internal	Both	External	Internal	Internal, but also responsive to social imperatives
B. Qualitative vs. quantitative change	Qualitative	Both	Quantitative	Qualitative	Qualitative
C. Closed vs. open model	Closed	Semiopen	Open	Closed	Relatively open

D. Continuous vs. discontinuous change	Discontinuous	Both	Continuous	(Continuous?)	Discontinuous between stages but continuous within stages
E. Reductionism vs. emergence	Emergent	Both	Reductionistic	(Emergent?)	Emergent
F. Structure–function vs. antecedent–consequent analysis	Structure–function	Both	Antecedent–consequent	Structure–function but antecedent–consequent in empirical research	Both structure–function and antecedent–consequent
G. Nature of individual or individual–family differences	Classical	(All: classical, differential, ipsative)	(Differential?)	(Differential?)	Ipsative
H. Significance of chronological age (aging)	Intrinsic	Extrinsic	Extrinsic	Intrinsic	Intrinsic
I. Directionality of development	Unidirectional	Multidirectional	Bidirectional	Unidirectional	Multidirectional
J. Universality vs. relativity of development	Universal	Relative	Relative	Universal	(Universal?)

[a] Adapted from Looft, Table 1, 1973 and Lerner, 1978.

179

scholars subscribing to the organismic model view the developmental dynamic as internal to the organism, in contrast with the mechanistically oriented, who assume that the organism changes primarily in response to changes occurring in its environment. The dialectical model sees the two as interactive and interdependent.

In its earliest formulations, the family development perspective posited the family as a closed system and viewed the developmental dynamic as internal to the family. Development occurred in response to changing family members who pressed for a redefinition of their roles in the process of fulfilling their developmental tasks. In subsequent formulations, the family has been seen as selectively open (semiclosed) to societal demands and environmental changes requiring adaptations in family structure (see Hill, 1971; Rodgers, 1973).[14]

The developmental task concept provides a bridging mechanism between the needs of the maturing human organism and societal expectations which dictate that by certain ages, the individual should have mastered certain skills or achieved certain objectives. Networks act as the mediators and enforcers of these expectations: Government enforces regulations on school attendance; grandparents dictate appropriate child-care methods; and so on. Thus, although the family development model considers the stimulus for change as principally internal, some modification of this stance is suggested by the literature on family transactions. External influences comprise a necessary, but not sufficient, cause of family development.

2. Continuous versus Discontinuous Change

Is growth characterized by steady quantitative change, or is it a sequence of spurts of growth suggesting discontinuous change? Choosing the option of discontinuity is associated with the conceptualization of developmental stages. Looft reports that disgruntlement with the stage concept has been increasingly voiced by its users, and Hooper (1973), in a review of the use of stage designations in cognitive developmental psy-

---

[14]Individual task accomplishment and role enactments are unique aspects of the family as an open system. When viewed within the context of an ever-changing, yet persistent, entity the complexity of the family as a composite of role relationships emerges. Change is an ever-present aspect of these relationships. A perception of the family roles gives one clues to the structure or positions in the family, both singular and paired, as well as the functions depicted in roles which family members fill. Descriptive, explanatory and predictive propositions are derived from the explication of the role relationships as they are qualitatively and quantatively documented. Thus, role relationships explicate both the varied structure and the basic functions of the family as a viable, open system.

chology, characterizes this sentiment: ". . . although psychologists are using stages more and more, they appear to be enjoying them less and less."

The mechanistic model assumes continuity of development, and the organismic model assumes discontinuity. The concept of orthogenesis (Werner, 1957) incorporated in the dialectical model sees both continuity and discontinuity occurring in development. Stated as the orthogenetic principle, "Whenever development occurs it proceeds from a state of relative globality and the lack of differentiation to a state of increasing differentiation, articulation and hierarchic integration" (Werner, 1957, p. 126; cited in Lerner, 1976). This issue of continuity versus discontinuity has already been given salience in family development where the family life-cycle stages have been subject to a variety of criticisms (Feldman & Feldman, 1975; Segalen, 1974; among others).

In its earliest formulation, the family development perspective was clearly committed to a discontinuous change precipitated by the transformational sequences of children's behaviors which required major reorganization of the family's role scripts. In later formulations, the conceptualization of "periods of transition" made way for an alternation of periods of continuity and growth, and solidification of attachments within stages as periods of transitions punctuated by discontinuity that marked the beginning of a new stage. Rapoport (1963) has made much of these discontinuities between stages which she called "normal crises" of development. She invoked a crisis theory with its spaces of adaptation to account for the behavior of the family as it moves through these "points of no return" from one stage of development to the next. Klein, Jorgensen, and Miller (1977) have distinguished three models for portraying family developmental time: (1) *discrete stage development,* in which discontinuity is complete and there is no period of transition; (2) *transition period development,* in which discrete stages of development are punctuated by periods of transition and consolidation (Rapoport's formulation); and (3) *dynamic development,* in which the stages seem to merge into one another so imperceptibly that the sequences of development are more continuous than they are stages with sharp breaks. Figure 2 illustrates their formulation for a family life span of four stages.[15]

---

[15]We can see parts of the family cycle where the stage breaks are sharp and discontinuous because of the pileup of changes in plurality patterns, in employment and residential statuses, and in sheer number of role renegotiations required, pointing to Klein's Type 2 model. However, there are just as clearly stage breaks which involve only age changes in children, such as the entrance of the oldest child into adolescence, which suggest Klein's Type 3 model of sequences that are more continuous than discrete.

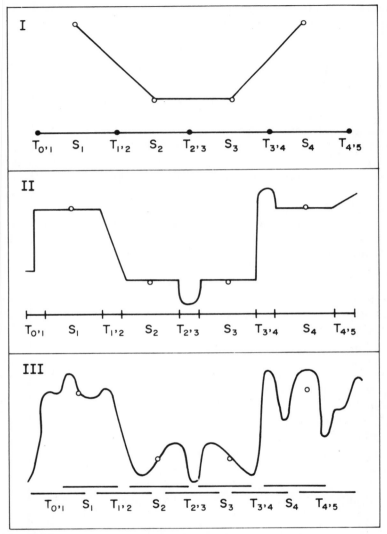

Fig. 2. Three hypothetical models of developmental time. S_i = Stage i; $T_{i,j}$ = transition from Stage i to Stage j. I, Discrete stage development; II, transition period development; III, dynamic development. (Adapted from Klein, Jorgensen, and Miller, 1977.)

3. Reductionism versus Emergence

The mechanistic model assumes reductionism, accounting for phenomena by events at a lower level. It assumes that any behavioral skill or operation can be reduced to simpler, more elementary forms. Emergence is a philosophical alternative to reductionism: Later forms are not reducible to earlier forms. The organismic model takes the emergent position that different levels of complexity of analysis can be defined, and each level has its own set of governing principles that transcend the principles which regulate earlier levels.

Family development to date has tended to skirt the issue of emergence–reductionism but carries over from symbolic interaction a preference for emergence. One consequence of the stage by stage emergence of new regulating principles would be the attenuation of correlations between power and support structures and marital satisfaction and/or parent–child communication, since these might be expected to change by stage of development. The phenomenon of emergence would certainly bear closer examination in evaluating the low incidence of confirmation of hypotheses about marital satisfaction over the family life span (see especially Miller, 1976; Rollins & Cannon, 1974; and Rollins & Feldman, 1970).

4. The Nature of Individual and Family Differences

How do persons in families differ, both between and within themselves? There has been a tendency for developmental analyses to disregard or minimize individual differences. Emmerich (1968) and Van den Daele (1969) are identified by Looft as having developed classification schemes for reflecting the modes of handling individual differences. We are drawing on Emmerich's system here for a classification of developmental theories into three general categories. The classical view assumes an invariant sequence of developmental stages (Freud, Piaget) and generally treats individual differences by their approximations to the age norms of stage or level attainment. Differential approaches are concerned with how persons get sorted into various subgroups, differentiated according to status and behavioral attributes through the course of their development. The third category, the ipsative approach, examines intraindividual consistencies and changes in the organization of attributes over time. Attention is focused on changes within individuals, not between them. An ipsative approach might examine how the interrelationships among attributes change with age, the rate of structural change, or perhaps a change in the number of levels of hierarchical organization.

Family development scholars have been loath to accept the classical view of an invariant sequence of developmental stages, although in their empirical studies they have used a formulation of developmental stages for classificatory purposes that seems to imply such an invariant sequence of stages. Aldous (1975, p. 102), in her caveat about the concept of stage in the family life cycle, departs from the organismic analogy:

> To save ourselves from being misunderstood we should emphasize that our use of the term *stage* does not imply that these stages are invariant, irreversible or always occur in this order, properties that the stage concept has when it is used to refer to the development of organisms. The listed stages are neither prescriptive nor descriptive of all family life cycles. Since there is not rigid chronological sequence of events, multiple variations of stages are possible within the general overall sequence.

When the research method is one of taking individual family histories, however, the ipsative approach is utilized which permits overlapping of stages, opens the way for multiple developmental tracks, and allows for a wide variety of time intervals from one stage to another.[16] Magrabi and Marshall (1965) have proposed a "game tree" model with crucial turning or decision points as a corrective of the imagery of the invariant stages in the life cycle for families. The Magrabi–Marshall model offers an excellent way to deal with the emergence of individual family differences in development that are masked under the present family life-stage classificatory system.

5. The Significance of Chronological Age

Critics say that use of age grades as a cataloguing system to impose order on the diversity of people has produced an age psychology, not a true developmental psychology. Baer (1970, p. 239) puts the case colorfully:

> The age psychologist studies children only because they represent a condition of the organism in which a great deal of the behavior does in fact vary in an orderly way. Typically, as age increases beyond childhood, behavior changes become less thoroughly ordered by it, and the interest of the age psychologists wanes correspondingly. Late in life, age change may again take on a powerful function in correlating behavior change; thus a developmental psychology, concerning this time of senescence, again is possible.

Many mechanistic scholars are relatively unconcerned about age, for age can be reduced to time, and time itself causes nothing. From their standpoint, the same general processes or mechanisms underlie behavioral changes at all ages, and therefore age itself, as a focus of attention, is relegated to minor status. There is really no need to explain age

---

[16]In constructing stages for one-child families the impression is one of homogeneity not achieved in families with several children of different ages and needs.

differences at all; the task at hand is to account for behavioral change in terms of the determining mechanisms.

In contrast, preformed organismic theories which posit stages of development are characterized by their chronological age boundaries. Age is intrinsic to a sequence of stages and the many attempts to modify or replicate age-normed cognitive development functions attest to the salience of chronological age in the organismic model. Birren (1964) notes that the term *aging* is closely tied to chronological age change but is not identical to it. In gerontological research, aging has been used both as an explanation for behavioral change and as something to be explained.

Psychological models can be viewed as treating age as intrinsic or extrinsic to development. The intrinsic category would include those approaches that assume age is correlated with invariant, sequential changes; these approaches are likely to hold implicit or explicit assumptions about the importance of maturation underlying the changed sequence. The extrinsic category, in contrast, would include those approaches which relegate age consideration to very minor status and which do not take the age norm seriously since age is not inherent to the behaviors observed.

Transposing age from the personological level to the family organizational level anticipates a confrontation with the age stratification and life-course analysis set of scholars to be discussed later in this chapter. The time marker for a family's history is marital duration but this is so closely related to calendar time, as such, that it has relatively little heuristic or classificatory value. Family structure changes in its age composition from the childless period in family formation through the addition of children and their aging over the child-rearing period. In the launching of leave taking, the age composition changes once again and, as far as the nuclear household is concerned, the family becomes a group of age similars until the end of the family cycle. Virtually all of the stages of the family life-cycle systems which serve as markers of "family time" currently use age of oldest, or age of youngest, child and age at retirement as ways of identifying changes in the family's role complex for purposes of stage differentiation. The challenge to scholars in family development would be to identify markers of behavior change processes over a family's history that are not age determined yet are sequentially normative regularities, such as:

1. Changes in residential status: lodger, renter, homeowner, resident in nursing home
2. Status changes: marriage, parenthood, grandparenthood, widowhood

3. Job changes: student, apprentice, employee, supervisor, manager, employer, retired

4. Of a different order, historical events which would identify event cohorts: World War I, the Great Depression, World War II, Korean Conflict, War on Poverty, urban riots, anti-Vietnam protests, Watergate, recession–inflation–energy crisis of the 1970s, and so on

As things stand, family theorists would probably see age and other time markers as intrinsic to family development, as have the organismic and age stratification scholars, because of the central use of age norms and age compositions in formulating stages of development.

6. *Universality versus Relativity of Development*

Is the course of developmental change common to all human beings, or does each person traverse a unique developmental pathway? This sounds like a rehash of Issue G in Table I on individual differences in development, but this time the issue of cultural and subcultural differences appears salient. All people are alike in some respects due to the existence of certain biologically endowed personality determinants that are universal to the species; some people are like some other people because of their membership in certain statuses (culture, ethnicity, gender, vocation); and in some ways, each person is unique because of his or her unique genetic composition and unique experiential encounters (Kluckhohn & Murray, 1949). Lerner (1978) asserts that the dialectic model is compatible with all three of these views of humankind; biologically universal, culturally variant, and genetically–experientially unique.

Taking a less eclectic stance, the active-man organismic model essentially posits developmental universals: Each individual evolves through an invariant sequence of developmental stages that are common to all biologically intact human beings. Empirical research, to a limited extent, supports these claims of universality.[17]

Proponents of the reactive model of humans, on the other hand, would be likely to assume that development proceeds uniquely for each human being. A person reacts to and is shaped by the forces of stimuli existent in his or her surroundings. Since each person experiences a unique surrounding for a multitude of reasons (gender, birth, culture, parental char-

---

[17]Cross-cultural and cross-sectional strata studies have shown that sensory–motor, preoperational, and concrete operational forms of thought are apparently displayed by children everywhere (Goodnow, 1969; Levine, 1970). Formal operational thought, however, seems to be more relative and dependent upon certain forms of educational and social experiences (Rohwer, 1971). Kohlberg and others have marshalled evidence that progression through well-articulated stages of moral development (Kohlberg & Kramer, 1969) is also apparently universal.

acteristics, etc.), he or she displays a set of behaviors that are in many ways unlike those of anyone else.

Hill and Rodgers (1964) faced the issue of cultural relativity in acknowledging that the family development framework may have reflected its origins and may have been culture bound to the United States, possibly to urban middle-class American families, since it had not yet been empirically tested for variations outside the United States or among subcultures within the United States. Subsequently, evidence in support of the universality of family developmental processes as stages of increasing and decreasing complexity comes from the work of anthropologists (Goody, 1962) and from sociologists in India (Desai, 1964) and Japan (Koyama, 1961; Morioka, 1957; Suzuki, 1942). The much criticized family life-cycle categories have seen widespread use as proxies for family development in the reconstruction of family developmental histories for 18th Century Europe and colonial America by family historians (Berkner, 1972; Hareven, 1974) and by a number of Asian and European scholars whose work was reported in the Thirteenth International Family Research Seminar in Paris in 1973 (Cuisenier, 1978).

Family scholars seeking to establish whether or not family development is universal or culturally relative face first of all the question of the universality of the nuclear family as a small group association (see Reiss, 1965, for a thoughtful assessment). Personality psychologists do not face as great a problem in establishing the universality of the human species or the phenomenon of personhood. A second and somewhat more troublesome problem is whether or not the phenomenon of family development is invariant cross-culturally. The present authors would be inclined to see high cross-cultural variability in the phenomenon of family development in the timing and duration of developmental processes, as well as in the age composition of family membership, but would hypothesize that the ordering and sequence and general shape of family development do approximate universality across cultures.

B.   WHAT WE HAVE LEARNED FROM THE EXAMINATION OF DEVELOPMENTAL PSYCHOLOGY CONCERNING THE ISSUES OF DEVELOPMENT

From the transpositions we have made for the family development perspective in confronting the basic issues about "development" by four sets of life-span scholars, a profile has been deduced. We should, however, express some caveats about the profile which is to be found in the fifth column of Table I. We found the accumulated wisdom about family development quite inadequate to guide us in our choices on most of the basic issues. In contrast with the well-articulated theories of the mechanistic and organismic scholars, whose positions on the nature of development on all 10 issues were theoretically predetermined by the logically interdependent premises they make about the nature of man, the family development perspective brings to bear few principles of family organizational change which respond to the issues confronted here. We opted again and again (as do the dialectical model scholars) for more pluralistic and less constrained solutions than those offered by either the mechanistic or the organismic theorists. That is, we opted for multiple but orderly paths of development, for variable growth patterns, for reversible processes over nonrecursive processes, and we drew on empirical descriptions to guide us when our theory came up empty handed.

Is it possible that there is more multidimensionality of "development" in families than in personalities? Family change over time involves simultaneously changing numbers of participants, changing needs to be met, and changing competencies of participants. Orchestrated somehow are changing role scripts and family structures, mediated by developmental processes so complex that pluralism of theories and of strategies of research for describing family development phenomena is surely required!

What does the profile reveal about the nature of family development? Although recognizing the importance of exogenous factors contextually, the dynamic determinant of life-span development of families is seen as internal, arising from the responsiveness of the family to the changing needs of its growing members. Family functions are disproportionately performed for members and secondarily as a service to society. Almost as a corollary, family development weds structure to function. Thus, structure–function characterizes the family developmental stance with respect to Issue F in Table I. The family actively manipulates its environment rather than being primarily acted upon by its environment. Even in transaction with its support networks, over time, the family operates more from internal than from external cues.

To the extent that family development can be charted in distinct stages (much debated among users of the framework) it is qualitative and discontinuous. Current observations recommend, however, that we take a middle position of qualitative change in confronting major life event stresses producing discontinuity of structural forms which punctuates quantitative changes and continuity of adaptive changes in the transitions between stages (see Fig. 2).

Family development as a perspective conceptualizes the family as a semiclosed system varying over its life span in the permeability of its boundaries and in the degree of its linkages with external associations and networks. Utilizing Emmerich's categories for characterizing the handling of individual differences among families in their developmental achievements, the preferred strategy of family development theoretically is an ipsative one which emphasizes intrafamily consistencies while permitting large interfamily variability in the direction and paths of development—thus joining ipsative patterning (Issue G) with miltidirectionality (Issue I).

While recognizing both that age may be flawed as a "cause" of development at the personality level and that its equivalent for the family, "number of wedding anniversaries" (marital duration), may be even more subject to criticism as an explanation for family development, we are not ready to write off either of these "time markers" as cues for developmental sequences. Age norms are found in all societies and are used to schedule rites of passages for families and for their members. We therefore see age as intrinsic to family development. Moreover, we draw on the universality of age differentiated stages of family development to hypothesize that many of the generalizations about family development will eventually be shown to be universal rather than culture bound.

IV. Implications of the Age Stratification and Life-Course Literatures for Family Development

The preceding discussion has highlighted the interrelationship between processes of individual life-span development and of family development. An implicit, long-range goal provided by the discussion to this point would be the building of an integrated model of family development and individual development wherein the complementary processes of each type of development would be clearly explicated. Invariances in developmental sequences, discovered empirically, could bolster our confidence in such an integrated model.

If societal norms and expectations were "frozen," so to speak, the task of building such a model would be straightforward. We could observe the movement of individuals and families from one rung to the next along each of several ladders of development. In reality, however, such movement along easily identifiable ladders does not occur for two reasons. First, society changes the "rules" of development by altering the sets of expectations and roles assigned to individuals of certain ages. Second, historical events occur; so that even if the rules remain constant, different cohorts have dissimilar opportunities for attaining goals. Since social and historical contexts do influence individual and family developmental sequences, and since no two cohorts of individuals or families ever pass through exactly the same series of contexts, much of what we would like to call a universal pattern of development may, in fact, be situationally determined. This presents a problem which scholars of both family development and life-span development have recognized (see Elder, 1975; Glick, 1947; Riley *et al.*, 1972). Elder (1978) posited the necessity of a synthesis of family development and life-course analysis if we hope to understand the movement through time of individual family members and the family organization itself.[18]

A. LEVELS OF ANALYSIS AND DIMENSIONS OF TIME

Family development, as a process, begins and ends at two distinct points in historical time for each nuclear family. If the developmental perspective is to have utility, then whatever intervenes between these two time points should in some way be similar for all families. Although the historical period through which the developmental cycle runs will influence many aspects of family behavior, do life-cycle regularities exist regardless of historical context? The central challenge is to sift invariances on the individual and family developmental levels from the pecularities and uniqueness of cohorts on the historical level.

Figure 3 contains a diagram which might be used to sort out visually changes which occur on the individual, family, and societal levels. Lines marked A represent individual developmental processes; those marked B represent development of an interpersonal attachment over time; those marked C represent the development of an entire family. The effect of context is represented by starting each "family" life cycle at a different point in time (i.e., at t_1 and t_2). The diagram renders visual at least four dimensions of time: family time, individual life time, chronological time, and historical time.

Family time is represented by stages (1), (2), and (3), which demarcate significant disjunctures in the processes of family change. Each stage constitutes a different organization of the family's role cluster.

Individual life time (or the life course) is the sequence of stages through which the role sets of individuals move. It includes role transitions, such as those from infant to toddler, from young person to adult, from childless to parent, from breadwinner to retiree, and so on. In the exhibit, its stages are not differentiated from those of family development, and at times significant transitions for both the individual and the family group will

---

[18]Strictly speaking, the age stratification and life-course perspectives grew up separately in different disciplines, at times borrowing concepts from one another. For our present purposes, however, we will treat them together because they share an emphasis upon the contextual component of individual and family development.

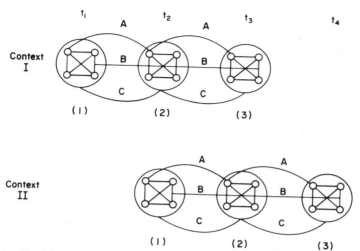

Fig. 3. Graphic representation of individual time, family time, and historical time. A→, individual development; B→, dyadic attachment development; C→, family development.

occur simultaneously. However, this does not imply that individual life stages and family life stages are necessarily or even frequently congruent. (There is more congruence for only and eldest children than for younger siblings or for the adult family heads.)

Chronological time is the number of years which happen to correspond to the length of life-cycle stages. It is represented in the exhibit by $t_1, \ldots, t_4$. (The years between the chronological markers are not intended to be equal.) Chronological time derives its meaning from historical contexts. Such meaning thus changes, dependent upon the progression of historical time.

Historical time refers to the sets of social, political, scientific, and all other events which constitute the contexts within which individuals are born, develop, and die. These sets of events, when they can be qualitatively distinguished one from the other along a civilization's chronological time line, are popularly termed ages, epochs, eras, periods, and so on.

B. COHORT DIFFERENCES IDENTIFIED BY THE AGE STRATIFICATION AND LIFE-COURSE LITERATURES

As a strategy for distinguishing between variance in family organization over time which is developmental in nature and that which is contextual, we can discuss a number of issues pointed up by the confrontation of family development with the age stratification and life-course literatures. Discussion will occur in terms of cohorts of families, that is, aggregates of

families which come into being during some time interval (e.g., within a
1-year or 5-year interval). All families within a cohort experience roughly
the same historical events. Therefore, intercohort differences in the typical developmental cycles of families are manifestations of the effects of
historical time or of context.

1. Sources of Family Change

Although family development occurs primarily in response to internal
pressures (e.g., changing plurality patterns, changing age composition),
historical time affects the developmental dynamic in at least two ways.
First, it affects the developmental dynamic chronologically by defining
appropriate role transitions at certain chronological ages for members of
the family. These individual role transitions (e.g., entrance into school,
achievement of adulthood) provide the impetus for reorganization of the
family's role complex and, thus, its transition into a new stage of development. Second, historical time affects the developmental dynamic
normatively by establishing prescriptions for family behavior appropriate
to particular stages of its development.

2. Refinements and Elongation of the Family Life Cycle

Childhood, adolescence, and the teenage years have appeared as stages
of individual development only during the past few centuries, concomitant with rapid development on the societal level (see Aries, 1962; Demos
& Demos, 1969). The new family role complexes necessary to cope with
the developmental needs of family members in these individual life-cycle
stages have emerged as refinements of the developmental cycle of the
family group.

Elongation of the sequence of family developmental stages has occurred due to the increased life expectancies of spouses (see Glick, 1977).
The lengthened period of time which spouses spend together after the
launching of children introduces new developmental tasks for them, some
of which, remarkably, may resemble the couple tasks of the early childless companionate stage.

The effects of historical time offer some of the best evidence for the
openness of the family development model, as discussed earlier. Historical time impinges directly upon family time through the introduction of
new family time units. Its effects, therefore, are not limited merely to
changes in the specific behavioral phenomena which are the manifest
expressions of underlying family role complexes.

3. Historical Impacts upon Interstage Discontinuities

Interstage differences between sets of roles for positional occupants or
between sets of norms for roles which remain constant take form from

prevailing prescriptions within a historical context. Cohorts will differ with respect to behavior appropriate for families in certain stages, for example, with respect to child-rearing standards. However, the fact that the specific type of qualitative changes may differ among cohorts does not imply that the sequence of changes differs among cohorts. So, for example, families of any cohort will likely evince the same type of roles when the transition to parenthood occurs, although the specific behaviors associated with those roles and the assignment of the roles to positional occupants will vary contextually.

Historical contexts also affect the chronology of developmental sequences. Certain occurrences (e.g., unique historical events, demographic trends) speed up or slow down the process of status transition and they smooth out or increase interstage discontinuities. Glick (1977) has suggested that the effects of 20th Century demographic trends include: a lengthening of the family career; shorter child-bearing periods; larger periods, both early and late in the family career, during which spouses live without children present; small families, with consequent greater opportunity for parent–child interaction; and a postponement to later ages, especially among women, of marital and parental roles.

The implications of chronological timing of family events have not received detailed treatment by family development scholars, although the long-term effects of age at marriage upon such family characteristics as stability, size, ability for physical maintenance, and spouse's labor force participation have been revealed (e.g., Bumpass & Sweet, 1972; Elder & Rockwell, 1976; Freedman & Coombs, 1966). On the aggregate level, changes in the chronology of status transitions are reflected not only by changes in average or modal behavior (which indicate at least indirectly changes in age norms) but also by changes in variances of distributions around means or modes (which indicate the strength of age norms and/or the opportunities present to fulfill such norms). Normative constraints limit the types of family structures considered acceptable within a society and thereby affect their frequency. Other components of context (e.g., sex ratios, mortality rates) also affect the frequency of appearance of family structures which depart from "typicality" in their development. (See Uhlenberg's [1974] description of such changes over time for United States women, and Modell, Furstenberg & Hesberg [1976] for evidence of less dispersion around markers of transition to adulthood for men in 1970 than in 1880.)

Integration of aggregate level demographic data with research on internal family processes might reveal the microlevel effects of shifts in age norms which influence movement into marriage, the labor force, parenthood, and so on. For example, large variance around a typical age for status transition might imply that families can accommodate the timing of events to their own particular resources and contingencies. On the other hand, it might also cue us to search for large numbers of families whose members suffer from indeterminacy in planning or from frustration at lacking the resources or opportunities to achieve those things which most families achieved at an earlier age.

4. Age Stratification, Life-Course Analysis, and Development of Models

In the extreme, life-course analysis would push the developmental framework into an antecedent–consequent model. The situational or historical determinism implied by an extremely conservative life-course perspective admits only idiographic sequences of changes rather than nomothetic processes of development.[19] Homogeneity within cohorts and heterogeneity among cohorts occur because the cohorts experience the same events but at different ages of life or at different stages of the family life cycle.

The age stratification literature similarly has only an antecedent–consequence flavor: Age norms and age grading shape individual behavior. The literature attends to systemic processes on a macrolevel where, in societies with fluid strata, systems of age norms and age grading may change over time. (In such societies, the young individual cannot accurately predict the future expectations to be confronted as an adult.) Age stratification writing leaves residual, however, the dynamics of smaller social organizations, such as families.

5. Social Meaning of Chronological Age

The status of chronological age has proved problematic in developmental psychology, as our earlier discussion indicated. Is age simply a marker, or is it something more important? From the diagram (Fig. 3), chronology appears irrelevant to a definition of development since the same developments occur over differing periods of time (e.g., the lengths of childless and child-bearing stages for families). Marital duration, the chronological age, so to speak, of the family organization, does not determine family role complexes.

Age stratification scholars (Riley *et al.*, 1972) have noted, however, the social meaning of chronological age which arises in the form of age expectations. Indeed, its only importance to social scientists may derive from its social meaning. Historical context imparts to chronological age its social dimension. So, predominant norms may prescribe that marital

---

[19]In fact, Elder (1978) has noted that life-course analysis follows in the tradition of W. I. Thomas' situational approach.

unions occur with a limited age span and, after some appropriate length of time, produce children. The individual confronts society's expectations upon reaching certain ages. Thus, chronological age is somewhat important for determining the temporal rate of a developmental sequence, but such a rate is contextually variant. Social expectations (sometimes formalized as laws) regulate status transitions of children and of adults. Such expectations change over the course of historical time, even to the extent of creating new life-cycle periods, such as "childhood" or the "teenage years." Biological changes in the population, another component of historical time, affect mortality rates, with consequent elongation of role sequences, positional careers, and family careers.

6. Universality versus Relativity of Development

This dimension approaches the heart of the interface between the age stratification–life-course literatures and family development. Its centrality is, in some respects, surprising, since no processes seem so universal across the ages as birth, mating, and death. Yet the life-course analyst will rightly suggest, first, that no two cohorts of families ever experience exactly the same events at exactly the same points in their life cycles. Phenomena, such as wars, depressions, prosperity, influence the life outlooks of family members, their goals, planning strategies, and decision-making processes. These phenomena are idiosyncratic; they cannot be incorporated into an overall model of development. Second, predominant social expectations within a historical context dictate the appropriate chronology of family life-cycle events. Thus, cohorts will differ in timing and spacing of significant family events. Third, as we noted earlier, the units of family time differ for different cohorts, with refinements and elongation of the life cycle occurring most clearly during the last few centuries.

Do any of these issues which the life-course analyst might raise suggest the necessity for major renovation of the family development model? For the first, we might reiterate an earlier comment that families are, in some ways, like all other families, like some other families, and like no other families. Certainly, unpredictable, idiosyncratic events will occur and they will partly shape family behavior. The effect of such events (in which a cohort of families is like no other cohort) cannot be incorporated into a general model, although case materials on families within one historical context can handle them. However, the significance of cohort membership in the explanation of variance in family behavior depends upon the dependent family phenomenon in question. Regardless of historical context, families will need to develop patterns of interaction suitable to meet the developmental needs of their members. The general shape of family development will thus likely attain uniformity across historical contexts. Clausen (1972, p. 483) similarly concluded:

> The usefulness of the concept of the family cycle and the data generated by its application in research derive from the expectations and requirements that are imposed upon husband and wife as their children appear and progress along their own life courses. Families may be broken at any stage of the cycle, of course, but the constraints upon parents posed by the ages of their children continue to operate. The stages of different occupational careers are so diverse as to defy systematic analysis except within narrowly defined occupations; age predicts increased stability, seniority, and satisfaction and, to a degree, increased responsibility but not much more. The stages of the family life cycle, on the other hand, permit us to say a good deal about pervasively important developments in the lives of most individuals. [From "The Life Course of Individuals," by John A. Clausen, in *Aging and Society,* vol. 3 (M. W. Riley, M. Johnson, and A. Foner, eds.) © 1972 by Russell Sage Foundation, New York]

The second issue, that of timing, depends upon the importance of chronological age in the developmental model. As mentioned previously, the chronology of development can be substantially altered without a major modification of the developmental process itself.

The refinements in family time which have occurred concomitant with general societal development represent the strongest impingement of historical context upon family development. Clearly, universality, in a narrow sense of the term, diminishes if families of all historical periods do not proceed through the same series of stages (e.g., when families of one period launch their children to marriage or to the productive sector at puberty, while those of another period retain them through the teenage years). Yet, in another sense, the families of different periods are simply creating the structures necessary to satisfy the developmental needs of their members. Such needs will change, depending upon historical context, and the openness which is characteristic of the family developmental model permits the refinements in the developmental process consequent to these changes.

C. CONCLUDING COMMENTS ON AGE STRATIFICATION, LIFE-COURSE ANALYSIS, AND FAMILY DEVELOPMENT

The foregoing discussion did not do justice to the many contributions of age stratification and life-course scholars in their analyses of social change. As of this preliminary confrontation, however, the age stratification and life-course materials seem more valuable for description than for explanation and theory building. Scholars in these areas have established well the fact that cohorts of families pass through different sets of historical events at different points in their life cycles. Families have different opportunities, suffer from different social problems, espouse different predominant values, and so on. Each cohort over time is unique because even when two cohorts share a common historical experience, they do so at different points in their life cycles.

Yet despite all the dissimilarities among cohorts there are undeniably rhythms to family life which all cohorts have shared since the earliest days of the human species. In fact, perhaps no other rhythmic social processes possess the universality of those which are associated with family formation, growth, and dissolution. Interviews with the oldest great-greatgrandmothers and the youngest mothers of the present day would probably reveal that roles involving nurturance, social control, physical maintenance, and other aspects of family functioning, while phenomenally different in content, have remained conceptually quite similar over the years. Progress in research and theory which would sift developmental invariances from family behaviors contingent upon historical events remains as yet unachieved. Such progress, the most crucial outcome of an amalgamation of family development, age stratification theory, and life-course analysis, will reveal the existence of nomothetic, developmental processes, if indeed they do exist. It will result in the specification of types of family behavior which are epiphenomenal to historical context and those for which context (except insofar as it offers the cultural tools for social interaction) has little relevance.

V.   New Dimensions Requiring Attention for the Improvement of the Family Development Perspective in Order to Describe and Explain Family Phenomena

There have been fruits in this chapter's strategy which juxtaposed with family development two major intellectual enterprises: (1) life-span developmental theory; and (2) age stratification and life-course analysis. The payoff has come principally from closer attention to new dimensions for careful description of the phenomena of life-span family development in historical context, but as we shall see, there have also been implications for issues of explanation.

An examination of 10 basic assumptions about the nature of personality development, held by four sets of theorists of life-span development, pointed up several theoretical issues which family developmentalists have largely skirted in their descriptions of development at the level of family organization. With some trepidation, the authors of this paper have asserted a position about the nature of family development: on the locus of its dynamic (internal); about the degree to which family changes over the life span are qualitative (yes), discontinuous (yes), unidirectional (no), and universal (yes); about the closedness of the family as a system (semiclosed); and about the extent to which development is regulated by similar or different principles as the family is transformed over the several stages of its life cycle (both).

The perspectives examined—developmental psychology and the sociology of age stratification—triangulated clearly enough on these several issues of development to make us cautious about wedding family development to either of these perspectives. On several issues, they offered support for a pluralistic stance both in description and explanation.

The tasks of description of the phenomenon of family development have been incremented by this discussion:

1. What are the basic elements of family composition which enter into the changing shape and direction of family development over the life span?

2. How does interaction between parents and children, and among siblings, change as the mix of competencies (cognitive, perspective taking, moral reasoning, and linguistic abilities) changes over the family's life span?

3. What are the modal profiles of family development over the life span?
   a. Continuous, cumulative, and steady growth, irreversible and progressive?
   b. Spiral-like, moving forward only to backtrack and start again, reversible and discontinuous?
   c. Curvilinear, moving from simple to complex and then returning to simple again, with discrete "gappiness" between stages?

4. Do life-cycle invariances in family behavior persist regardless of historical context?

5. Are family developmental processes conceptually, if not phenomenally, equivalent across historical and cultural contexts?

6. How can the concepts of timing and scheduling of status changes be incorporated into the family development perspective? (The perspective is currently indifferent to the variability of such scheduling for different generations and cohorts, yet intercohort variability is great in the timing of marriage, parenthood, home ownership, and other status transitions in our own society; see Hill, 1970).

The confrontations in which we have been engaged lead us also to delve further into the explanations of family development. To take one of these issues, continuity versus discontinuity, as an example: Is it continuity or discontinuity of development which requires explanation?

Lerner and Ryff (1978, p. 12) state that explanation of continuity refers to invariant causes operating across age levels (translate: at the family level, across family stages of development), whereas explanation of discontinuity offers reasons for behavior which differs by age levels (by stages of development).

Beyond the issue of continuity versus discontinuity there are implications for explanation in many other issues highlighted in this chapter. Moreover, the literature domains reviewed appear to offer hints of explanation congruent with their peculiar perspectives.

We offer three intriguing developmental phenomena which are pressing for explanation:

1. What accounts for the point of inflection in families' microsocial organization which moves during the life span from simple to increasingly complex forms and then scales down in complexity in the later years?
   a. Are the precipitators of changes in direction internal or exogeneous to the family?
2. Are different regulating principles and theories of explanation required to account for family behavioral changes within each of the stages of development?
3. Noting the wide range of family behaviors and achievements over the life span which are curvilinear in shape (marital happiness, crisis vulnerability, power and task allocations, family economic well-being, and social participation), what explanations may be offered?
   a. What of the structural constraints of changing numbers of members who press on resources of space, time, energy, and goods (the life-cycle squeeze)?
   b. What of the counterpart of numbers in interactional complexity— numbers of interpersonal relations to be sustained with their own rise and fall in complexity?
   c. Do the "livability" properties of growing children mitigate or exacerbate the family's vulnerability to crisis—decreasingly egocentric and burdensome and increasingly competent, resourceful, and responsible? (Actually, the net impact of children appears paradoxical: They are most lovable when they are most egocentric and most disruptive and threatening to family morale in adolescence when they have become most competent and prosocial).
   d. Do we have a variety of general variables, including changes in interactional complexity, autonomy striving of maturing children, breakdown of consensus about rules and roles, and pressures on margins of available time, energy, and revenue resources, which interact to produce the life-cycle patterns which we observe?

Explanations of life-span family development will likely never receive as neat a packaging as laboratory designed experimental models. Our targets for explanation are moving targets rather than "stages" or "products": multidirectional paths of development which depart from the usual unidirectional linear models; and reversible, recursive relations among the indicators of family development. Explanations themselves will need to be arrayed by their properties as distal versus proximal, direct versus indirect, and endogenous versus exogenous versus contextual. At this writing, we are in a better position to prescribe what needs to be done than to describe the means to achieve defensible explanatory models.

We conclude this chapter by reminding our readers that the ultimate goal of this enterprise is the generation of two types of substantive theory: (1) theories of the phenomenon of family development and (2) an improved family development theory of the economic and social achievement of families. The first makes variety in life-span family development the consequent or dependent variable to be explained. The second makes "family development" the antecedent or determinant variable in a cause–effect sequence model. Both are important, the latter to family-oriented economists, demographers, and political scientists and the former to family developmentalists for whom the phenomenon of life-span ups and downs of family organizational change is the puzzle to be explained. We invite help in working toward this largely unfinished goal of reworking and reformulating family development theories.

References

Aldous, J. *The developmental approach to family analysis.* Athens, Georgia: University of Georgia, Department of Child Development, 1975. Mimeo.

Aldous, J. *Family careers: Developmental change in families.* New York: Wiley, 1978.

Aries, P. *Centuries of childhood.* New York: Random House, 1962.

Baer, D. M. An age-irrevelant concept of development. *Merrill Palmer Quarterly,* 1970, **16**, 230–245.

Baltes, P. B., & Schaie, K. W. (Eds.), *Life span developmental psychology: Personality and socialization.* New York: Academic Press, 1973.

Bandura, A., & Walters, R. H. *Social learning and personality development.* New York: Holt, 1963.

Bengtson, V. L. *Reconstruction of family development theory: An exercise in the study of micro-social organization through time.* Discussion paper of Hill & Mattessich for the Theory and Methodology Workshop, National Council on Family Relations, San Diego, 1977.

Bengtson, V. L., & Kuypers, J. A. Generational differences and developmental stake. *Aging and Human Development,* 1971, **2**, 249–259.

Berkner, L. K. The stem family and the developmental cycle of the peasant's household: An 18th century Austrian example. *American Historical Review.* 1972, **77**, 398–418.

Bernstein, B. *Class, codes and control.* (Vol. 1). London: Kegan Paul, 1971.

Bigelow, H. F. *Family finance.* Philadelphia: Lippincott, 1936.

Birren, J. E. *The psychology of aging.* New York: Prentice-Hall, 1964.

Bott, E. *Family and social network.* London: Tavistock, 1957.

Brim, O. G., Jr. Socialization through the life cycle. In O. G. Brim & S. Wheeler (Eds.), *Socialization after childhood: Two essays.* New York: Wiley, 1966.

Buckley, W. *Sociology and modern systems theory.* New York: Prentice-Hall, 1970.

Bumpass, L. L., & Sweet, J. A. Differentials in marital instability: 1970. *American Sociological Review,* 1972, **37,** 754–766.

Burgess, E. W. The family as a unity of interacting personalities. *The Family,* 1926, **7,** 3–9.

Burgess, R. L., & Huston, T. L. (Eds.), *Social exchange in developing relationships.* New York: Academic Press, 1978.

Campbell, A., Converse, P. E., & Rodgers, W. L. *The quality of American life.* New York: Russell Sage Foundation, 1976.

Christensen, H. (Ed.) *Handbook of marriage and the family.* Chicago: Rand McNally, 1964.

Clausen, J. A. The life course of individuals. In M. W. Riley, M. E. Johnson, & A. Foner (Eds.), *Aging and society. Vol. 3: A sociology of age stratification.* New York: Russell Sage Foundation, 1972.

Cuisenier, J. (Ed.) *Le cycle de la vie familiale dans les sociétés européenes.* Paris: Mouton, 1978.

Demos, J., & Demos, V. Adolescence in historical perspective. *Journal of Marriage and the Family,* 1969, **31,** 632–638.

Desai, I. P. *Some aspects of the family in Mahuva.* Baroda, India: Sadhana Press, 1964.

Duvall, E. M. *Family development.* Philadelphia: Lippincott, 1957.

Duvall, E. M. *Marriage and family development.* (5th ed.) Philadelphia: Lippincott, 1977.

Duvall, E. M., & Hill, R. L. *Report of the Committee on the Dynamics of Family Interaction.* Washington, D.C.: National Conference on Family Life, 1948.

Elder, G. H., Jr. Age differentiation and the life course. In A. Inkeles, J. Coleman, & N. Smelser (Eds.), *Annual review of sociology* (Vol. 1). Palo Alto: Annual Reviews, 1975.

Elder, G. H., Jr. Approaches to social change and the family. *American Journal of Sociology, Supplement,* 1978, **84,** S1–S38.

Elder, G. H., Jr., & Rockwell, R. C. Marital timing in women's life patterns. *Journal of Family History,* 1976, **1,** 34–53.

Emmerich, W. Personality development and concepts of structure. *Child Development,* 1968, **39,** 671–690.

Farber, B. The family as a set of mutually contingent careers. In N. Foote (Ed.) *Household decision making.* New York: N.Y. University Press, 1961.

Feldman, H., & Feldman, M. The family life cycle: Some suggestions for recycling. *Journal of Marriage and the Family,* 1975, **37,** 277–284.

Freedman, R., & Coombs, L. Childspacing and family economic position. *American Journal of Sociology,* 1966, **31,** 631–648.

Gewirtz, J. L. Mechanisms of social learning: Some roles of stimulation and behavior in early human development. In D. A. Goslin (Ed.), *Handbook of socialization theory and research.* Chicago: Rand McNally, 1969.

Glick, P. C. The family cycle. *American Sociological Review,* 1947, **14,** 164–174.

Glick, P. C. Updating the life cycle of the family. *Journal of Marriage and the Family,* 1977, **39,** 5–13.

Goodnow, J. J. Problems in research on culture and thought. In D. Elkind & J. H. Flavell (Eds.), *Studies in cognitive development: Essays in honor of Jean Piaget.* New York: Oxford University Press, 1969.

Goody, J. (Ed.) *Developmental cycle in domestic groups*. Cambridge, England: Cambridge University Press, 1962.

Gouldner, A. The norm of reciprocity. *American Sociological Review*, 1960, **25**, 161–179.

Gove, W. R., Grimm, J. W., Motz, S. C., & Thompson, J. D. The family life cycle: Internal dynamics and social consequences. *Sociology and Social Research*, 1972, **57**, 182–195.

Hareven, T. K. The family as process, the historical study of the family cycle. *Journal of Social History*, 1974, **7**, 322–329.

Havighurst, R. J., Prescott, D. A., & Redl, F. Scientific study of developing boys and girls as set up guideposts. In B. L. Johnson (Ed.), *General education in the American high school*. Chicago: Scott Foresman, 1942.

Hill, R. Methodological problems with the developmental approach to family study. *Family Process*, 1964, **31**, 186–206.

Hill, R. *Family development in three generations*. Cambridge, Mass.: Schenkman, 1970.

Hill, R. Modern systems theory in the family: A confrontation. *Social Science Information*, 1971, October, 7–26.

Hill, R., & Hansen, D. A. The identification of coneptual frameworks utilized in family study. *Marriage and Family Living*, 1960, **22**, 299–311.

Hill, R., & Mattessich, P. W. *Reconstruction of family development theories: A progress report*. Paper prepared for the Theory Development and Methodology Workshop, National Council on Family Relations, San Diego, 1977.

Hill, R., & Rodgers, R. The developmental approach. In H. Christensen (Ed.), *Handbook of marriage and the family*. Chicago: Rand McNally, 1964.

Hodgson, J., & Lewis, R. Pilgrim's progress III: A trend analysis of theory and methodology. *Family Process*, 1979.

Hooper, F. H. Cognitive assessment across the life span: Methodological implications of the organismic approach. In J. R. Nesselroade & H. W. Reese (Eds.), *Life span developmental psychology: Methodological issues*. New York: Academic Press, 1973.

Kirkpatrick, E. L., Cowles, M., & Rough, R. *The life cycle of the farm family*. Madison: University of Wisconsin, Agricultural Experiment Station, Research Bulletin #121, 1934.

Klein, D. M., Jorgensen, S. R., & Miller, B. C. *Methodological issues and strategies for assessing the influence of children on marital quality and family interaction over the life span*. Unpublished manuscript presented at Pennsylvania State University Conference on Human and Family Development: Contributions of the child to marital quality and family interaction across the life span, State College, Pa, April 21–23, 1977.

Kluckhohn, C., & Murray, H. A. *Personality in nature, society and culture*. New York: Knopf, 1949.

Kohlberg, L. Stage and sequence: The cognitive developmental approach to socialization. In D. A. Goslin (Ed.), *Handbook of socialization theory and research*. Chicago: Rand McNally, 1969.

Kohlberg, L., & Kramer, R. Continuities and discontinuities in childhood and adult moral development. *Human Development*, 1969, **12**, 93–120.

Koyama, T. *The changing social position of women in Japan*. Paris: UNESCO Press, 1961.

Langer, J. *Theories of development*. New York: Holt, Rinehart & Winston, 1969.

Lansing, J. B., & Kish, L. Family life cycle as an independent variable. *American Sociological Review*, 1957, **22**, 512–519.

Lerner, R. M. *Concepts and theories of human development*. Reading, Mass.: Addison-Wesley, 1976.

Lerner, R. M. Nature, nurture and dynamic interactionism. *Human Development*, 1978, **21**, 1–20.

Lerner, R. M. A dialectical concept of individual and social relationship development. In R. L. Burgess & T. L. Huston (Eds.), *Social exchange in developing relationships.* New York: Academic Press, 1978.

Lerner, R. M., & Ryff, C. D. Implementation of the life span view of human development: The sample case of attachment. In P. B. Baltes (Ed.), *Life span development and behavior* (Vol. 1). New York: Academic Press, 1978,

Levine, R. A. Cross-cultural study and child psychology. In P. H. Mussen (Ed.), *Carmichael's manual of child psychology.* Vol. 2. New York: Wiley, 1970.

Lewis, M. Early socioemotional development and its relevance for curriculum. *Merrill-Palmer Quarterly,* 1977, **23,** 279–286.

Litwak, E. and Szelenyi, I. Primary group structures and their functions: Kin, neighbors, friends. *American Sociological Review,* 1969, **34,** 465–481.

Looft, W. Socialization and personality throughout the life span: An examination of contemporary psychological approaches. In P. Baltes & K. W. Schaie (Eds.), *Life span developmental psychology: Personality and socialization.* New York: Academic Press, 1973.

Loomis, C. P. *The growth of the farm family in relation to its activities.* Raleigh: North Carolina State College, Agricultural Experiment Station, 1934.

Magrabi, F. M., & Marshall, W. H. Family developmental tasks: A research model. *Journal of Marriage and the Family,* 1965, **27,** 454–461.

Meacham, J. A. The decentration of developmental psychology: A review of recent books. *Merrill-Palmer Quarterly,* 1977, **23,** 287–295.

Mitchell, J. C. *Social networks in urban situations.* Manchester: Manchester University Press, 1969.

Miller, B. C. A multivariate developmental model of marital satisfaction. *Journal of Marriage and the Family,* 1976, **38,** 643–657.

Miller, N. E., & Dollard, J. *Social learning and imitation.* New Haven: Yale University Press, 1941.

Modell, J., Furstenberg, F., & Hesberg, T. Social change and transitions to adulthood in historical perspective. *Journal of Family History,* 1976, **1,** 7–34.

Morioka, K. Life cycle patterns in Japan, China and the United States. *Journal of Marriage and the Family,* 1957, **29,** 595–606.

Nagel, E. Determinism and development. In D. B. Harris (Ed.), *The concept of development.* Minneapolis: University of Minnesota Press, 1957.

Neugarten, B. L. (Ed.) *Middle and aging: A reader in social psychology.* Chicago: University of Chicago Press, 1968.

Nye, F. I., & Berardo, F. (Eds.) *Emerging conceptual frameworks in family analysis.* New York: Macmillan, 1966.

Overton, W. F., & Reese, H. W. Models of development: Methodological implications. In J. R. Nesselroade & H. W. Reese (Eds.), *Life span developmental psychology: Methodological issues.* New York: Academic Press, 1973.

Parsons, T. *Essays in sociological theory: Pure and applied.* Glencoe, Ill.: Free Press, 1949.

Piaget, J. *The moral judgment of the child.* Glencoe, Ill.: Free Press, 1948.

Rapoport, R. Normal crises, family structure, and mental health. *Family Process,* 1963, **2,** 68–80.

Reiss, I. L. The universality of the family: A conceptual analysis. *Journal of Marriage and the Family,* 1965, **27,** 443–453.

Riegel, K. F. Structure and transformation in modern intellectual history. In K. F. Riegel & G. Rosenwald (Eds.), *Structure and transformation: Developmental historical aspects.* New York: Wiley, 1975. (a)

Riegel, K. F. Toward a dialectical theory of development. *Human Development,* 1975, **18,** 50–64. (b)

Riegel, K. F. From traits and equilibrium toward developmental dialectics. In W. Arnold (Ed.), *Nebraska Symposium on Motivation.* Lincoln: University of Nebraska Press, 1976.

Riley, M. W., Johnson, M. E., & Foner, A. (Eds.) *Aging and society: A sociology of age stratification.* Vol. 3. New York: Russell Sage Foundation, 1972.

Rodgers, R. H. Toward a theory of family development. *Journal of Marriage and the Family,* 1964, **26,** 262–270.

Rodgers, R. H. *Family interaction and transaction: The developmental approach.* New York: Prentice Hall, 1973.

Rohwer, W. D. Prime time for education: Early childhood or adolescence? *Harvard Educational Review,* 1971, **41,** 316–341.

Rollins, B. C., & Cannon, K. L. Marital satisfaction over the family life cycle: A reevaluation. *Journal of Marriage and the Family,* 1974, **36,** 271–282.

Rollins, B. C., & Feldman, H. Marital satisfaction over the family life cycle. *Journal of Marriage and the Family,* 1970, **32,** 20–27.

Rowe, G. P. The developmental conceptual framework to the study of the family. In I. Nye & F. Berardo (Eds.), *Emerging conceptual frameworks in family analysis.* New York: Macmillan, 1966.

Rowntree, B. S. *Poverty: A study of town life.* London: Macmillan, 1906.

Sameroff, A. Transactional models in early social relations. *Human Development,* 1975, **18,** 65–79.

Schneirla, T. C. The concept of development in comparative psychology. In D. B. Harris (Ed.), *The concept of development.* Minneapolis: University of Minnesota Press, 1957.

Segalen, M. Research and discussion around the family life cycle. *Journal of Marriage and the Family,* 1974, **36,** 814–819.

Sorokin, P. A., Zimmerman, C. C., & Galpin, C. J. *A systematic sourcebook in rural sociology.* Vol. 2. Minneapolis: University of Minnesota Press, 1931.

Suzuki, E. On cyclical regularity in generational development of the Japanese family. In T. Toda & E. Suzuki (Eds.), *Family and rural village.* Tokyo: Nikko-shoin, 1942.

Turner, R. *Family interaction.* New York: Wiley, 1970.

Uhlenberg, P. Cohort variations in family life experiences of U. S. females. *Journal of Marriage and the Family,* 1974, **36,** 284–289.

Van den Daele, L. D. Qualitative models in development analysis. *Developmental Psychology,* 1969, **1,** 303–310.

Waller, W. *The family: A dynamic interpretation.* New York: Dryden, 1938.

Werner, H. The concept of development from a comparative and organismic point of view. In D. B. Harris (Ed.), *The concept of development.* Minneapolis: University of Minnesota Press, 1957.

Prolegomena to a History of Life-Span Developmental Psychology

Guenther Reinert

DEPARTMENT OF PSYCHOLOGY
UNIVERSITY OF TRIER
TRIER, WEST GERMANY

Abstract

The history of human developmental psychology, defined as the science dealing with changes in human behavior within the time continuum of the life span, is outlined. Four historical periods are distinguished: The preliminary period, from the beginning of European intellectual history to the end of the eighteenth century; the formative period, from the end of the eighteenth century to the end of the nineteenth century; the period of foundation and specialization, from the end of the nineteenth century to the beginning of World War II; and the period of differentiation and integration, from the beginning of World War II to the present time. The first three periods are described in a relatively detailed fashion, but the fourth period is only briefly discussed. The organizational status of psychology as a scientific discipline is adopted tentatively to identify and delineate the division of these four historical periods.

I. Objective and Background

This chapter examines the history of human developmental psychology as a specific developmental psychology dealing with changes in human behavior within the time continuum of the life span (conception to death). In other words, the historical development of the science of the ontogeny of human behavior in the sense of Thomae (1959) and Baltes and Goulet (1970) is the topic discussed here.

All of the desirable methodological approaches to a historical under-standing of developmental psychology cannot be discussed. Unfortu-

LIFE-SPAN DEVELOPMENT
AND BEHAVIOR. VOL. 2

nately, biographical, regionally specific, and the so-called historical problem debates cannot be traced individually. However, they will be considered, when important, within the chronological perspective chosen for its apparent necessity. The accepted organization of psychology as a science is adopted tentatively as a model for the always problematic division of the historical process, which is connected in numerous ways. Four historical periods (i.e., the preliminary, formative, foundation and specialization, and differentiation and integration periods) are distinguished in the current perspective as sufficient for describing relatively important divisions in the development up to the present time. From this framework (i.e., historical development until about the end of the 1930s), our portrayal will only briefly touch upon the fourth period.

Concerning the present state of the historiography of developmental psychology, it is tempting to say, generalizing a hope expressed by Debesse (1970) regarding child psychology, that developmental psychology is still waiting for its historian. Although this expectation probably ought to be expressed again at each point in history, progress in the historiography of developmental psychology cannot be overlooked. Until now most treatments have dealt only with specific segments of the whole span of human development. On the one hand, the early authors (e.g., Fritzsch, 1910; Götz, 1918; Schumann, 1921) attended exclusively to the history of child psychology. C. Bühler and Hetzer (1929) and Dennis (1949) also have focused on the history of child psychology, but the former two authors offer a brief view of adolescent psychology and in neither work is the span of adulthood completely excluded. Höhn (1959), who discusses the history of child and adolescent psychology, speaks only briefly about the entire life span. Debesse (1970) does this also, though less explicitly, in his attempt to contribute to the understanding of childhood from the perspective of the history of psychology. This attempt, however, turned out to be more like a history of child and adolescent psychology. On the other hand, authors who were interested in the history of psychological gerontology (Birren, 1961; Munnichs, 1966; Riegel, 1973) could not restrict themselves only to the period of old age. More recently a few developmental psychologists interested in historical aspects have finally worked out the beginnings of a history of developmental psychology as a discipline encompassing the life span (Charles, 1970; Groffmann, 1970; Havighurst, 1973). They have followed a trend that was already discernable in more recent comprehensive portrayals of the history of psychology (e.g., Hehlmann, 1963). Comprehensive portrayals of the history of psychology are in other respects quite pertinent for not allowing us to forget that the history of developmental psychology is embedded in the developmental context of the history of psychology—a history which is in danger of being lost in scarce individual (historical) portraits (Wohlwill, 1973).

II. The Preliminary Period: Up to the Late Eighteenth Century

It may seem improper to summarize more than 2000 years of European intellectual history in a single historical period. Although such a summary would not be justified from the perspective of a historian of philosophy, the historiographer of psychology need not have any particular reservations about this. Although psychology was known by name since Philipp Melanchthon (1497–1560) and by subject matter much earlier, it did not take an organized form during this long period of time. There were neither institutions for teaching and research nor journals and societies for interaction.

One can debate whether the statements of the thinkers of antiquity, the middle ages, and segments of the modern period belong in the same class as the one to which later psychological statements are assigned. It is, however, indisputable that throughout these centuries human behavior and behavioral development were observed and reflected upon, even if behavior was not systematically and empirically researched. In this respect, this historical period is very often called the prescientific period of developmental psychology. It seems more appropriate to call it an introductory or preliminary period.

Groffmann (1970) justifiably remarks that birth, death, "growth and decline" are so clearly recognizable and important in the social organization of a society that they could not have been overlooked in any culture. To state all the evidence available to support this assertion is beyond the limits of this chapter. However, several interesting and, perhaps, even important ones ought to be mentioned.

The pre-Socratic philosopher Democritus (460 B.C.–370 B.C.) compared the advantages of youth and old age and distinguished between natural disposition and education as requirements for development. Plato (427 B.C.–327 B.C.) and Aristotle (384 B.C.–322 B.C.) dealt more extensively with characteristics of different ages. The ideas of both men (Plato in his *Politeia* and in *Nomoi* and Aristotle in his *Politics*) are confined to the topics of growth and development but remain for the most part relatively restricted to pedagogical issues. Aristotle, in his *Rhetoric*, made a comparison between youth, adulthood, and old age. Likewise, the eclectic Cicero (106 B.C.–43 B.C.) compared childhood, youth, the adult years, and old age in his *Cato maior de senectute* but to some extent arrived at very different evaluations than Aristotle's.

Although other divisions of the life span than those mentioned here have been proposed in developmental psychology, the historical continuity of developmental thought is apparent. The Czech pedagog J. A. Comenius (1592–1670) in his *Didactica magna* (1638) divided the first 24 years of the life span "as does nature itself" into four levels, each of which encompasses 6 years: childhood, boyhood, adolescence, and incipient manhood. A less valid but apparently more popular conception was the old division of the periods of life according to the number seven. This division was praised by Solon (640–560); repudiated by Aristotle (*Politics,* seventh book); perpetuated by Philo Judaeus (25 B.C.–50 A.D.), according to Hofstätter (1957), by the scholastics of the middle ages, and by the baroque preacher Abraham a Santa Clara (1644–1709); and represented probably in its most extreme form by the physiologist K. F. Burdach (1828).

Finally, there are a number of autobiographies scattered throughout the preliminary period. Beginning with the *Confessions* of the 43-year-old Augustine (354–430) through *De vita propria* by the physician of the Italian renaissance Cardanus (1501–1576) up to the autobiography of Jung-Stilling (1740–1817), autobiographies have illuminated their authors' capacity to observe, reflect upon, and describe their own development. Literary descriptions of the course of development as the precursors of the *Entwicklungsromane* have appeared—such as *Parzival* by Wolfram von Eschenbach (1170–1220) and *Der abentheuerliche Simplicissimus teutsch* as well as its feminine counterpart *Lebensbeschreibung der Landstörtzerin Courage* by Hans Jacob Christoffel von Grimmelshausen (1620–1676). These fictional portrayals of development appear to be less useful for developmental psychology than are autobiographical accounts.

At first glance it is surprising that over many centuries only minor progress was achieved in actual knowledge about human ontogenesis, despite the significant interest in and the long tradition of thinking and writing about human development. This is especially striking because the most important philosophers of the classical philosophy of antiquity, Plato and Aristotle, and patristic philosophy, Augustine, were also developmental philosophers in the ontogenetic sense. However, these philosophers were first and foremost ethicists and metaphysicists. Because of their decisive prominence in ethics and metaphysics, succeeding generations were sufficiently occupied not only with disseminating but especially with integrating these ethical and metaphysical concepts into the theologically oriented world view of scholasticism.

Empirical experience, which could have improved knowledge about human ontogenesis, was hardly considered in this task. Albertus Magnus (1200–1280) argued that affairs of nature could be not only derived from theology but also researched empirically. However, from Augustine almost 1500 years elapsed before the insights of Albertus Magnus were realized in activity relevant to developmental psychology. Empirical developmental research was preceded by various postulates. The "Renaissance psychologists," particularly the Spaniard Juan Luis Vives (1492–1540) and the Italian Bernardinus Telesius (1508–1588), argued that contemplation about man ought to be freed from metaphysical speculation and that provisions ought to be made instead for experience. Francis Bacon (1561–1626), the great reformer of science who lived at the threshold of the modern period, sought to place science at the service of the world, base scientific understanding on empirical experience, and begin with observation and experimentation. Finally, there were the empirical requirements of the English experiental philosophers from John Locke (1632–1704) to David Hume (1711–1776) that were so important for the development of the sciences. If all of these men had not made their important demands, the history of psychology and the history of developmental psychology would probably have developed along a different path. Acknowledging this, one can note without worry that Hume considered "observing a child totally worthless for science" (C. Bühler & Hetzer, 1929, p. 211) and suggested that "the way in which . . . a man of the stature of a Locke speaks about the development of the child [is] like a reflective private tutor obliging us with his wisdom" (C. Bühler & Hetzer, 1929, p. 206).

Calls for psychological observation and experimentation were issued in German-speaking regions even before English empiricism reached its zenith with David Hume, or at the very latest by the time the rationalist Christian Wolff (1679–1754) distinguished *psychologia rationalis* and *psychologia empirica* in the early 1730s. Georg Bernard Bilfinger (1693–1750), a follower of Wolff, had already clearly made this request (Bilfinger, 1725). A quarter of a century later the physician Johann Gottlieb Krüger (1715–1759), who was also influenced by Wolff, demanded an "experimental psychology" (Krüger, 1756). For the development of developmental psychology, demands of this type introduced the first period of intensive activity in human ontogenesis. The methodological foundation of this activity, however, was still not established. There continued to be reports of hard-to-control observations, regrets about not having observed adequately, unspecific reference to experience, and new demands for qualified empirical experience.

Friedrich Engel, a private tutor for a count, was a minor precursor of Rousseau and the man to whom Götz (1918) attributed the beginnings of child psychology. Engel (1753) wanted to judge men by children according to the "great law of the sages: follow nature." He described characteristics of children's behavior and attempted to explain them but only began to deal with developmental changes. It is different with Jean-Jacques Rousseau (1712–1778). His *Émile* (Rousseau, 1762), explicitly an educational anthropology, is implicitly a partial developmental psychology. Rousseau portrayed his fictitious Émile in five stages of development— from infancy through puberty to the age of a young adult. Even if these stages are not clearly defined or in particular very profitable for psychology, and although earlier Rousseau interpretations (Bourjarde, 1937; Claparède, 1932) and more recent ones (e.g., Debesse, 1970) are dubious of Rousseau's stages because they are too exclusive, Rousseau nonetheless deserves credit for bringing ontogenetic thinking "with pulse and breath" (C. Bühler & Hetzer, 1929) to the consciousness of his contemporaries.

Rousseau's ideas were adopted most directly by pedagogical authors interested in childhood. His influence was especially pronounced on the philanthropists to whom Fritzsch (1910) attributes the beginnings of child psychology. This group adopted the ideas of the pedagog Johann Bernhard Basedow (1723–1790) the founder of a pedagogical institute in Dessau in 1774. The institute published its ideas since 1777 through *Pädagogische Unterhandlungen* wherein the observation of and experimentation with children as well as the writing of "educational histories" were continually encouraged. The first published educational history was a translation from Danish (Sneedorf, 1778). The first rules for the observation and preparation of educational histories with respect to age, among other characteristics, were outlined by the philanthropists Wezel (1778) and Trapp (1780).

Aside from and even before the philanthropic movement, similar trends may be discerned at the same time. Among others, the writings of pastor David Nikolaus Schönfeldt (1764) in Norway should be noted. He proposed that "capable minds," especially educators, should be encouraged by means of established rewards to improve knowledge about the psyche, especially of children. Shortly afterwards the wish for "having a continued history of everything that happens in the psyche of a child . . . from the first movement of its life up to the first use of its reason" was expressed in a translation of a work by an anonymous English author ("Wichtigkeit der Untersuchung," 1767, p. 595). An essay by Garve (1769) submitted to the Berlin academy for a writing contest can also be mentioned. The work offers examples that distinguish themselves by "the genetic observation dealing extensively with childhood" (Dessoir, 1902, p. 264). Finally, Desmonceaux's work (1775) on the life of newborns, which has since been lost, can also be noted (see Debesse, 1970).

We can deal only briefly with the "still unwritten history of the child prodigies,'' which Schumann (1921, p. 209) cites as the beginnings of child psychology. Schumann mentions Christian Heinrich Heinecken, a child from Lübeck who died at the age of four (''Merkwürdiges Ehrengedächtnis,'' 1726), and Johann Philipp Baratier from Schwabach, who died at age 19 (Formey, 1742). Certainly one must agree with Schumann that the extraordinary frequently captured the attention and was described first. However, the spectacular early biographies of child prodigies, as interesting and instructive as they might be, are separate from the historical path of psychology. The same is true for the numerous reports from those times about children who supposedly grew up in the wilderness and were classified by the Swedish taxonomist Carl Linnaeus (1707–1778) as *homo sapiens ferus.* Hecquet's story of a young girl (1761) is an example of such a report. Finally, the sketches of the childhood of the later king Louis XIII (1601–1643) by his physician Héroard, which have become widely known through Crump (1929) and Ariès (1960) and were published by Soulié and Barthélémy (1868) more than 200 years after the observations, also lie apart from the history of developmental psychology.

Particularly important for the history of psychology and developmental psychology is an author with whom we shall complete this sketch of the preliminary period: Johann Nikolas Tetens (1736–1807). Tetens was a professor of philosophy in Kiel, a theoretician of ''natural science,'' and an experimenter in psychology. Tetens' contributions to the development of psychology have been fittingly praised by Dessoir (1902), Hehlmann (1963), and Pongratz (1967). Until now his importance for the history of developmental psychology, although previously recognized by Groffmann (1970), has not been described with sufficient clarity. His two-volume main work (Tetens, 1777) deals with ''the perfectibility and development of man'' in which the author says he has expressed the actual goal of his thought. In the last chapter of this work, Tetens shows himself to be a true giant among the precursors of developmental psychology. Neither before nor since Tetens (1777) has the true program of human developmental psychology been so impressively formulated: ''The question 'What can man become, and what and how should one make him?' can be answered thoroughly and definitively only when the theoretical question 'What is man? What does he become and how does he become it under the circumstances and under the influence of the moral and physical causes to which he is subject in the world?' has been answered definitively and clearly beforehand'' (Vol. 2, p. 377).

Tetens' comprehensive perspective, including the development of both the individual and mankind, is important for the development of developmental psychology in at least three ways. First, by emphasizing the search for general developmental laws, Tetens severed developmental thought from its connection to direct practical application in education—a connection that had been paramount until that time. In opposition to the preformist C. Bonnet and the epigeneticist C. F. Wolff, he formulated "epigenesis through evolution" as a fundamental hypothesis about the "development of the psyche." Second, by leaving no doubt that one could proceed only by the method of "natural philosophy," i.e., natural science, he solidified the methodological approach to the investigation of development. Based on John Locke and "experiential psychology," he emphasized that the method of psychological analysis should be observation. Tetens said that the strength of this method was dependent upon how well the generalizations of the experiential principles obtained from individual cases would succeed. Such generalizations would be derived on the basis of hypotheses and arguments by analogy, especially between physical and psychical development. Moreover, this would indicate how well the coordination of "raisonnement" and observation, hypotheses and experiential principles, and certainty and probability could be accomplished. Third, by directing his attention less to specific, concrete periods of life and more to the courses of development and their conditions, he changed the viewpoint of developmental psychology and focused on the whole span of human development from conception to death. The term "developmental courses" means interindividual, differentially accelerated processes. Such processes consist of increase, reaching a high point and temporary stability, as well as the ensuing decrease (no return to a previous condition) of "mental powers" or "mental capabilities" (e.g., intellectual achievement, the power to reason, memory, self-determination). Besides interindividual differences in abilities, Tetens saw differentially effective environmental influences (e.g. cultural, status-related, educational, experience-related influences, the effect of other individuals as models) as the most important conditions for development. Certainly Tetens only hinted at many things and was unable to fulfill his program. However, he did introduce it in an impressive manner and thereby directed the path for his successors.

III. The Formative Period: Up to the Late Nineteenth Century

In the latter part of the European Enlightenment, the preliminary period approached its end and psychology entered a new period. It withdrew from the greater union with experiential philosophy, in which it was included until then, and achieved self-consciousness as an individual science. The first psychological journals, in which the new science of psychology was given a type of initial organizational form, are external indicants of the development of this consciousness. The earliest journal was a periodical founded by Carl Philipp Moritz, *Gnoti Sauton oder Magazin zur Erfahrungsseelenkunde,* published from 1783 to 1793 and followed by the *Allgemeines Repertorium für Empirische Psychologie und Verwandte Wissenschaften* of I. D. Mauchart starting in 1792 and by the *Psychologisches Magazin* of C. C. E. Schmid starting in 1796. The contents of these journals has basically remained unchanged for psychology, and the fundamental methodological approach—empirical experience—has also remained. The formative or initial period spans from 1783 (Moritz), mentioned above, to the next important date generally recognized in psychology, 1879 (Wundt). For developmental psychology, this period is distinguished because it contains the first important empirical initiatives in addition to other essential theoretical ideas.

Many things of secondary importance to the history of psychology are scattered throughout the formative period, such as autobiographies or *Entwicklungstromane,* such as Carl Philipp Moritz's *Anton Reiser* (1785–1790); reports about child prodigies, such as the one by Kästner and Kirsten (1796); and reports about children who grew up in the "wilderness," such as that of Itard (1798). If one disregards such things and focuses instead on things more relevant to the history of psychology, three events or chains of events in the formative period are important for the history of developmental psychology. Events associated with physical development in childhood are linked to Dietrich Tiedemann, professor of philosophy and Greek at Marburg. Events associated with the entire span of human development are connected with the names of Friedrich August Carus, professor of philosophy at Leipzig, and Adolphe Quetelet, a Belgian astronomer and mathematician.

The systematic, longitudinal investigation of the behavioral development of young children, based on the technique of observation, began with Tiedemann (1748–1803). In any case, his book *Observations on the Development of Mental Capabilities in Children* (Tiedemann, 1787) was based on observations conducted between 1781 and 1784 during the first $2\frac{1}{2}$ years of the life of his son Friedrich. This work represents the first known psychological diary of the development of a young child. Of course, early in 1774—and thus before Tiedemann—Heinrich Pestalozzi (1746–1827) kept a diary on his then 4-year-old son Jacqueli, as reported by Niederer (1828) after Pestalozzi's death. However, Pestalozzi's data are of a pedagogical rather than developmental nature. On the other hand, Tiedemann, as the "first psychologist . . . who . . . also took an interest in child psychology" (C. Bühler & Hetzer, 1929, p. 209), interpreted his data in a manner befitting developmental psychology. His data are furnished with denotations of time and consist of a broad spectrum of behaviors (e.g., motor skills, mental achievement, emotional and social behavior, speech and thought).

It is possible that Tiedemann was encouraged to publish his diary by the pedagog Joachim Heinrich Campe (1746–1818). Fritzsch (1910) accepts the idea, a bit euphorically, as "almost certain." In 1785 in the second volume of the 12-volume *General Revision of the Entire School and Educational System* (1785–1793) which he edited, Campe established a prize of 69 ducats for the best "journal by a father about his child from the hour of his birth on, including" among other things the portrayal of the "progress of bodily and intellectual development." Two of the submitted diaries were published. The first ("Tagebuch eines Vaters," 1789/1790) dealt mainly with physical development; the second (Dillenius, 1789/1790) focused more on psychic development. Neither study, however, approached the sophistication of Tiedemann's.

The influence of Tiedemann's work from 1787 on developmental psychology during his time and the subsequent period has been judged relatively pessimistically until today. Debesse (1970) suggests that his work had very little direct influence and was then forgotten for almost a century. C. Bühler and Hetzer (1929) even believe that "around 1800 . . . his influence and child psychology for the moment" (p. 209) were over. These assessments do not appear to be completely justified. As we know mainly from Dessoir (1902) and Schumann (1921), Posewitz (1799), a physician from Giessen, made a portion of Tiedemann's observations available again to the scientific community in synoptic form. After Tiedemann's death, the editor of his *Handbook of Psychology* (see Tiedemann, 1804) referred to his observational study once again, as did Schwarz (1804, 1829) in both printings of his pedagogics and Perty (1865) several decades later in a comparison of the psychic development of animals and children. Following Tiedemann's model, Schwarz also gathered several observational data on the development of a boy in his first year of life and included as well quite a broad portrayal of physical and intellectual development in childhood and adolescence. Following the translation of Tiedemann's work into French (Michelant, 1863), Pérez (1881) again dealt with Tiedemann extensively. Mandelli (1889) offered a critique shortly afterwards, and then Ufer (1897a) finally published a new edition.

Diaries about children, which were produced between 1800 and 1850 but were published only later, indicate that there was no cessation of work in developmental psychology after Tiedemann in the first half of the nineteenth century, as C. Bühler and Hetzer (1929) suggest for the period of childhood. Jean Paul made diary sketches of his three children for the preparation of *Levana* (1807) at the beginning of the nineteenth century (see, e.g., Miller, 1963). Likewise, Bronson Alcott kept a diary on his daughter who was born in 1831 (see Talbot, 1882), as did Charles Darwin in 1840 on his son Francis (Darwin, 1877), and Ludwig Adolf von Strümpell in 1846 and 1847 on his daughter (von Strümpell, 1880). The only observational study of the early development of a child, which has been discovered so far, was prepared as well as published at that time by an American named Willard (1835). It is also the first such study in English. There is a number of other studies which verify the interest in child development in the first half of the nineteenth century. Several of the studies are discussed in subsequent sections. Here we shall cite the following: the sketch of a general and specialized age-oriented science of youth by Weiller (1799); the *Psychology of the Childhood Years* by Grohmann (1812) and his *Ideas on a History of the Development of the Childhood Years* (Grohmann, 1824), which clearly express the idea of phylogenetic–ontogenetic parallelism; the description of the main periods of intellectual development in childhood and adolescence by the pedagog Denzel (1817); the works of the physiologist Rudolphi (1823) about the sensory–perceptual development of young children; the work of the physician Feldmann (1833) on the beginning of running and speaking; and, finally, the sketches by Miss Peabody (Alcott & Peabody, 1835, 1836/37) about conversations of adults with children—sketches which are informative for the understanding of childrens' thinking and, according to Charles (1970), reminiscent of Piaget's style of questioning.

With this in mind, one can hardly agree with the appraisal of C. Bühler and Hetzer (1929) that at the beginning of the first half of the nineteenth century there was a "reaction against this first movement in psychology which centered around Tiedemann" (p. 210) and not until the middle of the century did a sudden reversal occur leading to modern child psychology. C. Bühler and Hetzer suggest this reaction occurred mainly with the rise of idealistic philosophy. They argue that a division between child psychology and pedagogy and a significant reduction in interest in biological and psychological data and thereby research in child psychology resulted from: (a) Kant's objections to a scientific psychology and his pedagogics (resulting from the categorical imperative which was oriented toward maxims and which "appeal only to the intellectual life of man"); (b) the intensification of these tendencies by Hegel (1770–1831) and Fichte (1762–1814); and, (c) the intellectualism and mathematicism of Herbart (1776–1841), which had the most disastrous effect. Both authors attribute the sudden reversal at the middle of the nineteenth century secondarily to a few attempts to establish a therapeutic pedagogy. However, the primary causes are attributed to two trends leading to the biological–genetic movement in which modern child psychology toward the end of the nineteenth century had its roots. One of these trends was from natural science and medicine, and the other was from ethnology and linguistics. C. Bühler and Hetzer say that the confluence of these two trends was expressed symbolically when Hippolyte Taine, who dealt with the development of his child from the perspective of linguistics (Taine, 1876), encouraged the naturalist Charles Darwin to publish his Francis diary (Darwin, 1877).

The interesting "reaction and sudden reversal" hypothesis of C. Bühler and Hetzer (1929) in its essence seems to be formulated too simplistically to do justice to the historical process to which developmental psychology, like every other scientific discipline, is subject. First, there was probably no distinct movement in child psychology connected with Tiedemann. Based on the diary he published, Tiedemann was a prominent and influential psychologist during his time; his work was obviously widely read and quoted for a long time. However, he had no direct successors in the writing of diaries. In view of Tiedemann's model diary, which was quite sophisticated for its time, it would be surprising if there had been many successors right away. The insights into the difficulty of both empirical observation in a longitudinal study continuing over a few years and subsequent developmental-psychological interpretations of the results probably frightened off many potential successors. Following Tiedemann's work of 1787, the aforementioned Campe prize winners (Dillenius, 1789/1790; "Tagebuch eines Vaters," 1789/1790), Schwarz (1804, 1829), and Willard (1835), there were no pure diaries on children published again until the middle of the 1870s (Darwin, 1877; Ferri, 1879; Semming, 1879; Taine, 1876). This was at a time when, according to the interpretation of C. Bühler and Hetzer, the aforementioned symbolic confluence had already occurred. Proceeding from Tiedemann, if only the pure diary publications are considered, one can conclude that Taine, perhaps influenced by Michelant's (1863) translation of Tiedemann, again stimulated interest in writing and publishing diaries on children. From this consideration one would not conclude that research in child psychology experienced a setback between 1800 and 1850 from which it did not recover until the middle of the century. Certainly child and developmental psychology were not enhanced by Kant and idealistic philosophy, but neither were they severely hindered in their further development. The fact that Tiedemann was an anti-Kantian was probably unimportant in this process. However, Herbart played a more ambiguous role. As a pedagog he recognized connections between the education and development of children. As a psychologist he emphasized psychology as an independent experiential science more than any other person of his time. Certainly his agenetic psvchological system did not exactly promote thinking in developmental psychology, but it did not block it either, as can be seen from the work of several of his pupils—above all von Strümpell, and Lazarus and Steinthal. Characteristically physiology, the foundation for the physiological psychology in the second half of the nineteenth century, reached its first high point at this time (Bell, 1811; Fourens, 1824; J. Müller, 1826; Weber, 1834). Moreover, even idealistic philosophy itself had in the multifacted Hegel an authoritative developmental thinker.

The biological–genetic movement appeared for the first time not toward the end of the nineteenth century but about a century earlier. Dessoir (1902), a specialist in the history of psychology of that period, wrote: "In almost every textbook in psychology which appeared after 1775 there are studies on epigenesis and evolution, on the origin of language and the history of civilization, and on natural development" (p. 161). Ideas on the origin of language are rooted particularly in the second half of the eighteenth century. Since Süssmilch's attempt in 1756 to prove to the Berlin Academy that the origin of language could be explained only by divine revelation, and Herder's subsequent rejection of this explanation in his *Treatise on the Origin of Language* (1772), this ethnological–linguistic "branch" was an indigenous part of psychology. The results of this movement for developmental psychology can be found in Moritz's *Gnoti Sauton* (1783–1793) and Pockels (1784), among others. Obviously it continued to grow relatively consistently throughout the nineteenth century, carrying with it concepts from genetics, ethnopsychology, and comparative psychology (Bastian, 1968; Lazarus & Steinthal, 1859; von Humboldt, 1836). At the beginning of the twentieth century, it brought into the Wundtian "ethnological developmental psychology" a large part of the energy it had carried with it. Its impact on the developmental psychology of ontogeny is found in the second half of the nineteenth century, for example, in the biographies of children by the Frenchmen Taine (1876) and Egger (1879) and by the Englishman Pollock (1878).

The branch of natural science and medicine followed two separate lines. First, there was the further development of the science of evolution in the 18th Century. It is well known that these theories experienced a decided growth (with important modifications) in the 19th Century, especially by the French natural scientist Jean-Baptiste de Lamarck (1744–1828), the British thinker and systematist Herbert Spencer (1820–1903), and the Briton Charles Darwin (1802–1882). Conceptions of development propagated by these researchers do not appear to have found their way into developmental psychology to any great extent until the end of the 19th Century. However, this fact and Darwin's direct contributions to developmental psychology (Darwin, 1872, 1877) should not lead to the conclusion that Darwin had a decided impact on the origin or progress of developmental psychology (see e.g., Heckhausen, 1974; Höhn, 1959; among many others).

Second, as C. Bühler and Hetzer (1929) properly note, medicine in the nineteenth century made an important contribution to developmental psychology, especially through physiologists, or more precisely, physiologists interested in the embryo and the newborn. Rudolphi (1823), who was the teacher of Johannes Müller, has already been mentioned. After Rudolphi in the second half of the nineteenth century, a large number of physiologists presented additional observational and experimental studies of the mental development of newborns. In the formative period the studies of Kussmaul (1859) and Genzmer (1873) have become the most well known. Löbisch (1851), a doctor, provided the first more general description of development in the first years of life. The beginning of therapeutic pedagogy mentioned by C. Bühler and Hetzer (1929) also made a contribution during this period. Löbisch belonged to a group of doctors and educators from Vienna who founded a therapeutic pedagogical institute in Liesing in 1856. They named it "Levana Institute" in honor of Jean Paul. Similar but more general observations of development in early childhood, based partially on the authors' own diary sketches, were published by Sigismund (1856), Heyfelder (1857), Altmüller (1867/1913), and Pérez (1878). The work of Pérez (1878) deserves to be emphasized as especially valuable for developmental psychology. More specialized works dealing with the developmental psychology of the childhood years which appeared during the formative period cannot be elaborated on. Only a few themes will be mentioned: fairy tales and fantasy, play, the scope of imagination, and abnormalities, such as mental retardation and speech anomalies.

Friedrich August Carus (1770–1808) was a developmental psychologist of a completely different type than Tiedemann. This scholar, a relative of the well-known romanticist Carl Gustav Carus, died at a young age and has been quite unjustly neglected in the historiography of psychology until now. Ament (1899) deserves the credit for discovering F. A. Carus' role in history of developmental psychology. Works by Friedrich August Carus published posthumously include a two-volume *Psychology* (F. A. Carus, 1808a) and a *History of Psychology* (F. A. Carus, 1808b). His statements on developmental psychology are found in *Specialized Psychology*, the title of the second part of the former work. F. A Carus distinguishes there the "characteristics of the psychic-types" from the "science of the conditions of the psyche." Under the first topic, F. A. Carus discussed differences between the sexes, and among various age levels, temperaments, and nationalities. Under the latter topic, he referred to the "characteristics of the psychic-type of age" (F. A. Carus, 1808a, pp. 27–91). According to the almost 50-year-old judgment of C. Bühler and Hetzer (1929), F. A. Carus employed a "type of questioning which appears extraordinarily modern" (p. 209). Indeed, F. A. Carus' position is not only "modern" for 1929 but for contemporary times as well.

F. A. Carus (1808a) was not the first to try to describe the characteristics of different ages. In the discussion of the preliminary period, very early examples have already been mentioned. In addition, several years before F. A. Carus, Pockels (1801) had sketched a "character portrait of age." What is fascinating about F. A. Carus—likewise with Tetens—is the breadth of his conception. In contrast to Tetens, however, F. A. Carus achieved a concretization that was astonishing for his time and presumably would have succeeded even more impressively if the fragmentary character of his posthumous psychological writings could have been eliminated.

The foundation of F. A. Carus' (1808a) developmental concept involves the interplay of forces in psychophysical parallelism and in the parallelism "between nature and freedom." In relation to the latter parallelism he asked two questions. First, "What does nature do for man in each period?" whereby nature he meant man's "total environment," i.e., "everything that is not his ego." Second, "What does man do in regard to this continuing influence?" by which he meant what are the possibilities of action in man's conflict with nature, possibilities that are given to the individual in various periods of the life span.

Building on this foundation, F. A. Carus (1808a) strove to develop a "general age-oriented science," i.e., an ideal description of human ontogenetic development from conception to death. He distinguished a general age-oriented science from a "specialized age-oriented science" in which modifications of development that occur through special conditions are included—foremost among these conditions is living in a particular historical period. Here he discussed not only the former "natural individual" and the present "bourgeois individual" but also the conditions of future historical periods. For F. A. Carus, the goal of a general age-oriented science was a nomothetic, general "psychology as a history of the inner life . . . as if fitting a normal biography for all people."

F. A. Carus (1808a) divided the life span into two main periods: the first encompassed "childhood and youth" and the second "manhood and old age." He understood that "in and of itself chronological age" . . . was not a "psychological determinant." Hence, "the freedom of human development" should not be bound to years. Instead of speaking of age, he preferred to speak "more psychologically" of "periods of life," or chronological stages that are not clearly separable. Such periods, therefore, are more aptly described as "inwardly psychological," stages that all individuals must "go through or at least run through." He demanded fundamentally that such periods or stages should be applicable "to the continual development in man," and specifically to "all classes of individuals" and "to all the capabilities of the individual." In his conceptualization, each stage was a preparation for the next, and stages were not sharply divided but rather flowed gradually into one another. He also was sensitive to the danger of enumerating only specific characteristics of each stage rather than "portraying the gradual gradations of the individual in view of his various sides." F. A. Carus also provided a psychological description of four periods (childhood, youth, adulthood, and old age). His description focused on developmental aspects and, therefore, also included interindividual variations despite the claim of being "general."

One cannot expect the developmental psychology of 1808 to yield individual facts corresponding to our present state of knowledge. Much of what is known today is lacking in F. A. Carus (1808a), and much of his work would have to be expressed differently today. This is unimportant here. Likewise, it is even less important that F. A. Carus obviously conducted no systematic studies or experiments. In many psychological matters, especially regarding adolescence and old age, he proved himself to be an extremely sensitive and astute observer who could distinguish what is essential, but this did not bring him any lasting fame. However, his anticipation of the principle of scientifically observing human development as a series of stages is of greater importance. In addition, his early avoidance of the naive mistakes or carelessness of so many subsequent theoreticians in developmental psychology concerning stages or periods is of utmost importance. Friedrich August Carus occupies a position in the history of developmental psychology because he was the first person to offer a psychologically based description of human development over the entire life span. His description really does justice to the term "human developmental psychology." The significance of his achievement can be noted from the fact that after F. A. Carus about 130 years elapsed before anyone made another attempt of this kind (Pressey, Janney, & Kuhlen, 1939). The extent to which F. A. Carus was ahead of his time is also evidenced by the fact that, as far as the author has discovered, the next fundamental discussion of the status and role of the chronological age variable for observation in developmental psychology did not occur until about 160 years after him (Wohlwill, 1970).

In comparison to Friedrich August Carus, the developmental psychology of Carl Gustav Carus (1789–1869) appears to be in various respects poorly conceived. This may have resulted because the psychological, philosophical, and poetic became united in an often inseparable trinity in

C. G. Carus' writing. Therefore, he was led less by direct observation of human behavior than by confidence in the power of the "inner sense." C. G. Carus' statements on developmental psychology are found most easily and in the most concrete form in *Lectures on Psychology* (1831/ 1931), in a more condensed form in *Psyche* (1846/1964), and in a very specialized form in *Symbolism of the Human Gestalt* (1853/1962). The *Lectures,* which the exuberant Lorenz Oken mistakenly called the book with which "the embryo of psychology came into the world" (Bernoulli, 1925, p. 2), expressed his desire most clearly. He wanted "to apply to psychology the theory of developmental history, which has given such important information in the natural sciences" (C. G. Carus, 1831/1931, p. *xli*) He believed that only the "genetic method" was appropriate for achieving this goal. For C. G. Carus, the genetic method meant pondering the course of development by means of the "inner sense" with the cooperation of the external senses.

Using this method C. G. Carus devised a three-stage model of development that he called a "pattern of a history of the psyche." He classified the psyche of plants and lower animals in the first "stage of unconsciousness" the psyche of higher animals was part of the second "stage of world-consciousness" and, the third "stage of self-consciousness" consisted of the psyche of man. C. G. Carus (1831/1931) then assumed "that the [normal] person acts as a restatement of the world, to the extent that every individual relives a kind of pattern of world history in his development" (p. 447). According to him, the developing individual is at the stage of unconsciousness before birth; at birth the individual enters into the stages of world-consciousness; and, self-consciousness gradually develops in the child by means of the intellectual influence of people in his environment. C. G. Carus suggested that there were two additional lines of development related partially to the development of mankind and partially to adult individuals of different nations. He thought that unconsciousness prevailed among peoples living "in an uncivilized condition," and that in the "population of Europe and its colonies" a world-consciousness prevailed. However, a representation of self-consciousness would apply not to an entire nation but only to an individual person. Finally, he tried to conceptualize mental illness as a developmental phenomenon. Sickness was defined as "disharmony in several or all functions within the context of a developmental process which is foreign to the whole" (C. G. Carus, 1831/1931, p. 211–212). He viewed the mental health of youth differently than that of adulthood and old age. These three periods of life are more characteristically labeled by C. G. Carus as "period of adolescent immaturity," "period of maturity," and "the psyche in the latter years." An abnormal mental condition occurs when a condition which is healthy in one period of life appears in another period. Furthermore, mental illness can be conceived of as a repetition of an earlier stage.

Because C. G. Carus' (1831/1931) descriptions of three periods of life do not appreciably extend our knowledge about human ontogenesis, one might be tempted in an outline of developmental psychology to mention him only briefly. Indeed, he is not discussed in detail here. In many ways these descriptions even represent a regression from F. A. Carus' *Psychology* (1808a), which C. G. Carus was familiar with, because C. G. Carus built his three chronological periods on Burdach's (1828) ludicrous 7-year reckoning, which C. G. Carus accepted as being scientifically based. However, C. G. Carus did set a precedent in developmental psychology. His idea of recapitulation, which followed the spirit of the times (see Grohmann, 1824), foreshadowed in principle the "basic law of psychogenetics" (i.e., stages of human evolution are repeated in individual development; ontogeny recapitulates phylogeny) that was discussed extensively several decades later in developmental psychology. However, C. G. Carus very early viewed as "comical extravagence" (C. G. Carus, 1831/1931) the idea of strict parallelism between human embryonic and racial development. This idea of parallelism was widely discussed by biologists in the first half of the 19th Century and was propagated further in 1868 by the zoologist Ernest Haeckel as a "basic law of biogenetics" which served as the model for the "basic law of psychogenetics." Heinz Werner (1926), long after C. G. Carus' death, called his concept of illness and recapitulation a "careless identification."

Arthur Schopenhauer (1788–1860) was a famous thinker and contemporary of C. G. Carus. He is occasionally referred to in the context of developmental psychology and deserves brief mention because he, like both Caruses, dealt with life-span psychic development in his observation "on the distinctions of the periods of life" (Schopenhauer, 1851). For example, his remarks on the subjective experience of time in different life periods are rather interesting. Schopenhauer's (1851) essay also delves into obscure ptolemaic connections between the periods of life and planets or planetoids. Overall, the essay is more of a philosophical "feuilleton" than a contribution to developmental psychology: "The psychologist is not concerned with the spirit without the individual" (F. A. Carus, 1808a, Vol. 2, p. 35).

Adolphe Quetelet's (1796–1874) approach to knowledge about human ontogenesis was unlike that of F. A. Carus and substantially different from the approaches of C. G. Carus and Schopenhauer. Similar to the

Caruses and Schopenhauer, Quetelet (1835) was interested in individual development across the life span. Like several other men before him, he also strove to discover developmental laws. To this extent, his work was not new as he was aware. What was new in Quetelet's approch was his methodology. He counted observable changes in the course of human development by measurement and estimation and related these data to the statistically average individual *(l'homme moyen)*. In other words, Quetelet conducted cross-sectional research.

Acknowledging all the human characteristics for which statistics were at his disposal and often covering age spans from birth to old age, he investigated physical development (size, weight, strength, heartbeat, and breath rate, among others), the development of "moral characteristics" (suicide and criminal acts, among others), and mental illness. In this way he described courses of development and developmental curves that showed maximal magnitude at a given point in the life span and minimal magnitudes toward the beginning and end of life. Quetelet's efforts to assess the development of intellectual abilities are especially interesting for psychology. He viewed intellectual development as a large field of research and made the first attempts at investigation. He thought about memory tests among other things, but above all he recognized the possibility of relating concrete actions to intellectual capabilities and their development. He examined paradigmatically works of the dramatic theater, related the time of their origin to the period of the dramatists' lives, weighed each work according to its relative value, and thereby devised a developmental curve of dramatic talent.

Hofstätter (1938; see also Baltes, this volume) had paid extensive tribute to Quetelet's achievements in developmental psychology. Hofstätter (1938) argued that it was an "act of historical justice . . . to give the deserving Belgian researcher his proper place" (p. 327). It appeared to Hofstätter (1938) that Miles' (1933) well-known review, which appeared 100 years after Quetelet's work, contained "almost nothing.that had not already been called for in Quetelet's program, and almost nothing about which the Belgian astronomer had not already carried out the first investigations" (pp. 273–274). Hofstätter (1938) also commended Quetelet for "a simply ingenious perspective in methodological significance" (p. 275) because Quetelet had already articulated the need to reduce multidimensional quantities to single-dimensional quantities—the basic concern of factor analysis. As an additional sign of Quetelet's methodological foresight one can mention, as Groffmann (1970) has, that Quetelet (1835) had already recognized the advantages of the longitudinal over the cross-sectional method which he used. However, one must see this insight relatively and note that the idea of statistical average had been anticipated previously by Tetens (1777, Vol. 2, p. 608). In any case, Quetelet can be seen in a certain sense as the empirical executor of Tetens' thought.

In recognizing Quetelet's achievements it should also be acknowledged that F. A. Carus saw the important role of the chronological age variable for the methods of developmental psychology much more clearly than Quetelet. Although Quetelet attributed the observed variance not only to chronological age but also to other "sampling-characteristics" (see Groffmann, 1970), he at least implied that this chronological reference quantity was to be ascribed to a direct influence.

Quetelet (1869) pondered the relation between the development of the individual and the development of mankind. Although he assumed that there was generally only a weak connection between the two developmental processes, he still tended to use the same developmental laws for intellectual development in the individual, on the one hand, and in the history of the sciences as represented in the works of great men, on the other hand. In relation to the statistically average individual he believed that over the course of centuries his developmental laws had almost remained the same. He suggested that only the magnitude of the respective developmental maxima increased depending on historical progress over the centuries in scientific development.

For a long time in continental European psychology, apparently little attention was paid to Quetelet's work of 1835, even though a German translation published in 1838 and an inexpensive pirated edition published in French (see Quetelet, 1869) were circulated widely. There are presumably many reasons for this (see Hofstätter, 1938). One reason is that Quetelet (1869) changed the superscriptions and captions in the second edition of his book and emphasized the perspective of "social physics" rather than the developmental aspect.

In England, however, where a translation of Quetelet's work (Quetelet, 1835) was published in 1842, Quetelet's ideas influenced Sir Francis Galton (1822–1911). Later Quetelet further developed his ideas, particularly in his anthropometric works (Quetelet, 1871). Two other sources which nourished Galton's thought were the works of Charles Darwin, his relative, and Herbert Spencer. It is difficult to characterize simply Galton's specific influence on developmental psychology. According to Flugel (1933), he was "a wanderer in the realm of science who scattered riches on the streets as he went" (p. 110). Generally, Galton's importance for developmental psychology probably has resulted from his propagation of evolutionary theory, emphasis on interindividual differences, and methodological ideas (e.g., the technique of using questionnaires). Most notably in *Hereditary Genius* (Galton, 1869) and in his study of twins (Galton, 1876), Galton emphasized the nature–nurture problem, which is important for developmental psychology. His book *Inquiries into Human Faculty and Its Development* (Galton, 1883) combines in a revised and condensed form a number of his previously published essays that were difficult to acquire. This book (Galton, 1883) provides the best picture of Galton's multifaceted ideas relevant to developmental psychology.

IV. The Period of Foundation and Specialization

It has become customary to recognize the year 1879, when Wilhelm Wundt established the first psychological laboratory at the University of Leipzig, as an especially important historical date in psychology. Even though the exact date of this event is unimportant (see the historical work by Boring, 1965), it indicates that psychology reached a new level of organization at that time. Wundt's establishment of a laboratory, though, is only one of many indicators. At approximately the same time as Wundt, William James set up rooms for psychological experimentation at Harvard University. In 1883 G. Stanley Hall founded a psychological laboratory at Johns Hopkins University. A little later, in 1889, the first French institute for psychology was established at the Sorbonne in Paris with the cooperation of Alfred Binet. Shortly after these early institutes were established, the first important periodicals encompassing the total scope of psychology began to appear. These periodicals were of supraregional importance and still exist today (e.g., the *American Journal of Psychology* beginning in 1887/1888, the *Zeitschrift für Psychologie* beginning in 1890, and *L'Année Psychologique* beginning in 1894). In 1889 the first international congress of psychology met in Paris. In the following decades, the institutionalization of psychology, which commenced in 1879, accelerated at different rates in different countries—undoubtedly the fastest in the United States. Relatively steady progress was made, and psychology was not dramatically affected by World War I. Then in the 1930s an abrupt and worldwide disruption occurred when national socialist rule was established in Germany and Austria.

During this period, psychology as a total (fictitious) discipline became rooted in the field of scientific disciplines. Developmental psychology became rooted as a subdivision of psychology and, in union with it, a part of the sciences. The metaphor should be taken literally. One cannot discern a single, individual root, but several more or less interwoven cords of roots can be disentangled from the entire network. One can tease apart one root representing the developmental psychology of childhood, another the developmental psychology of adolescence, and yet another the developmental psychology of adulthood and aging. Thus, there are two aspects to the development of developmental psychology during this period. On the one hand, it became linked to scientific psychology in the sense of an institutional connection, and on the other hand, subareas of concentration within developmental psychology developed. Hence, this third phase of developmental psychology is aptly characterized as the period of foundation and specialization. Acknowledging the aspect of specialization, progress in developmental psychology during this period is discussed separately according to the three aforementioned segments of life.

Both the scope and intensity of research in the developmental psychology of childhood are much more prominent than in the formative period. The initiatives of the previous period were developed further. Besides numerous specialized studies encompassing a wide variety of topics that cannot be considered here, monobiographical portraits in the tradition of Tiedemann's diary as well as more general comparative portrayals of psychic development in childhood appeared in rapid succession. Among the diaries the following deserve special mention: in German-speaking regions, von Strümpell (1880), Preyer (1882), Dix (1911, 1912, 1914), and Scupin and Scupin (1907, 1910, 1931); in French, Espinas (1883), Cramaussel (1909), and St. Ybars (1909/1910); and in English, Shinn (1893, 1900, 1907), Moore (1896), and Major (1906). From the group of general portrayals the following can be noted here: from France, Pérez (1878, 1886, 1888), Compayré (1893), and Claparède (1905); from England, Sully (1895); and from North America, Tracy (1893), Baldwin (1895), and King (1903).

Among these authors the physiologist Wilhelm Preyer (1841–1897), who was active in Jena and later in Berlin, must be singled out. He has been called the "first classicist of child psychology" (Debesse, 1970). Preyer's book *The Psyche of the Child* (Preyer, 1882) was based primarily on observations and small experiments with his son Axel. This work has been evaluated as the "basic text of contemporary child psychology" (K. Bühler, 1918), the "first work of modern child psychology" (W. Stern, 1914), and a "monument of German assiduousness" (Compayré, 1893). However, Preyer was certainly "no pioneer" (Debesse, 1970), and his book was more like a developmental psychophysiology than a developmental psychology. It was, in any case, "a noteworthy book full of interesting and conscientious observations and—deficient in ideas" (K. Bühler, 1918, p. 49). Perhaps this was the reason that Preyer rather than the more imaginative Pérez (1878) achieved fame. In addition, Preyer's success may have occurred because the spirit of the times was favorable to psychophysiology—Wundt's *Outline of Physiological Psychology* appeared in 1873. As Ament (1899) has argued, it is perhaps especially important that Preyer's precise and clearly recognizable method inspired others to conduct observational studies of child development. The good model provided by Preyer stimulated research: Shortly after the publication of Preyer's book, an extraordinary enthusiasm for research with children spread throughout the whole Western world.

The child study movement reached its high point around the turn of the century. At that point, the Swedish writer Ellen Key (1900), a woman thoroughly imbued with developmental thinking and inspired by child psychology, proclaimed "the century of the child." In a similar burst of enthusiasm, G. Stanley Hall (1900) eloquently characterized child psychology as "part of a large cultural movement." Hall acted as the main proponent of this movement. Compayré (1893) proposed the word "Paidoskopie" to identify a general science of the child, and Chrisman (1896), a student of Hall, proposed the term "Paidologie." In 1893 Hall founded the National Association for the Study of Children in the United States, and several similar societies were established in many European countries in the following years. A number of journals began publication. For instance, in 1891 Hall began the *Pedagogical Seminary,* which was later retitled the *Journal of Genetic Psychology* and continues to be published today under the latter title.

The excessively high aspirations which many people, especially numerous pedagogs, held for the child study movement were unfulfilled. The movement was "overdrawn," too ideological, and consequently potentially dangerous for scientific developmental psychology. Several psychologists quickly recognized this problem. In America, Hugo Münsterberg (1898) emphasized the differences between the approches of scientific psychologists and practical pedagogs. William James (1899), Münsterberg's colleague at Harvard, warned pedagogs not to expect too much from child psychology. In Germany, Wilhelm Ament (1899), a student of Külpe, committed "pure scientific research in child psychology to the psychologists, and their results to the pedagogs" (p. 26). This counterargument was justified in view of the earlier proposal of Heydner (1894) to grant the right to execute research in child psychology only to school teachers. Occasionally it was asserted (e.g., Ufer, 1897b) that Wilhelm Wundt also warned of the danger of a "nursery psychology" (Kinderstubenpsychologie). As Ament (1899) discovered, the term "nursery psychology" came from the Englishman Max Müller (1887). He had argued that psychologists should not mistakenly assume that insight into the earliest developmental processes of the human intellect could be gained through the observation of children. However, judging from its meaning, this warning really could have emanated from Wundt. Wundt

(1900, 1912) was interested in the psychological developmental history of mankind (i.e., historical development of psychological processes). For him, the psychology of nations (i.e., cross-cultural psychology) was "in the eminent sense of the word, developmental psychology" (Wundt, 1912, p. 4). Therefore, he believed it would be "wrong if one should think that child psychology could solve the last problems of psychogenesis" (Wundt, 1912, p. 4).

Psychologists interested in human development did not subscribe to Wundt's view. Rather, the majority focused on the period of childhood where they expected to find the solution to the "last problems of psychogenesis." Karl Bühler (1921) expressed this idea as follows: "The great evolutionary steps of mental development are focused in the first years of life" (p. 59). On the other hand, during the period of foundation child developmental psychologists did not neglect the similarities between child development and the development of mankind (i.e., evolutionary or historical human development). Hardly anyone among the successors of Grohmann (1824), C. G. Carus (1831), and Taine (1876) ignored this issue. Some authors (e.g., Ament, 1899; Hall 1894, 1897, 1904; W. Stern, 1906) discussed it excessively, some (e.g., K. Bühler, 1918; Claparède, 1905; W. Stern, 1914) moderately, others (e.g., Baldwin, 1895; Koffka, 1921) in a critical or reflective manner, and still others (e.g., Groos, 1911) with disapproval. At the same time, some of these psychologists also tried to prevent child psychology from becoming connected to everyday pedagogical practice. They thought such a connection would have endangered the progress of child psychology. Rather, they tried to incorporate child psychology "in the broad context of general psychological questions" (C. Bühler & Hetzer, 1929, p. 221) by building on the foundation of natural science established by Wundt.

In order to consider the contributions of all specialists in psychology to research in the psychology of childhood during the period of foundation, a considerable number of scientifically active psychologists during this period would have to be mentioned. This necessity may be indicative of the close connections between the various interests in the entire field of psychology of this period. The following portrayal is limited to a few persons and some research that was especially important for progress in developmental psychology. The countries or language groups where the most important contributions occurred are identified.

The character of child psychology in the United States was molded extensively by G. Stanley Hall. Psychology owes much to his dynamic personality, diversity of ideas, and ability to organize. However, the developmental psychology of childhood was not advanced significantly by either Hall's excessive questionnaires or his all too fanciful ideas of recapitulation. More important stimulation for developmental psychology was initiated by other researchers. First, the contributions of the Princeton psychologist James M. Baldwin should be noted. If his book *Mental Development in the Child and the Race* (Baldwin, 1895) had not been misunderstood by his contemporaries (e.g., Ament, 1899; Claparède 1909) and was not misunderstood today as well (see Anandalakshmy & Grinder, 1970), it could have produced a change from a general child research to developmental psychological research guided by theory. Inspired by the developmental theoreticians Herbert Spencer and George J. Romanes, Baldwin pursued the developmental processes of intellectual activity in childhood without falling prey to superficial ontogenetic–phylogenetic parallelism. He presented the advantages gained by observation and experimentation with children compared with the study of animal behavior and pathological phenomena. He emphasized the problems of a strict classification of children's behavior on the basis of their initial occurrence and position in the chronological course of life. He argued that child psychologists must be knowledgeable of general psychology. Finally, Baldwin achieved extraordinarily different insights into the beginning processes of cognitive development. The importance which Baldwin attached to children's imitative actions for their mental development and his "circular reaction" explanation of imitative action was acknowledged and accepted (e.g., Groos, W. Stern, Koffka). The true brilliance of Baldwin's theory of psychological development as an interplay of the processes of assimilation and accommodation was first recognized by Piaget. Piaget's theory of early cognitive development is a broad application and magnificient execution of Baldwin's basic concept.

Besides Baldwin, the most important American developmental psychologists were John B. Watson and Arnold Gesell. Watson and Gesell espoused opposite positions in the controversial discussion of the relative importance of heredity and environment (maturation–learning, nativism–empiricism) in individual development. Obviously, the staunch and vigorous standpoints of these two researchers produced a stimulating effect on the debate. J. B. Watson was the most important spokesman for behaviorism (Watson, 1914, 1919) and, according to Hehlmann (1963), the *enfant terrible* of psychology at that time. Based on his observations of children, Watson devalued the importance of aptitude and emphasized the great importance of environmental influences through his impressive conditioning experiments with children (see above all Watson & Rayner, 1920). Watson's exaggerated enthusiasm for the environmental modifiability of developmental processes is evidenced foremost in his informative work on educational psychology (Watson, 1928); this book was dedicated characteristically to "the mother, who above all others raises a happy

child.'' On the other side, Arnold Gesell conducted extensive and very
meticulous observational studies of children at the Yale Clinic of Child
Development (Gesell, 1925, 1928; Gesell & Thompson, 1934; Gesell,
Thompson, & Amatruda, 1938). He concluded that maturation is the most
important determinant of early child development. He thought that maturation, which manifests itself in traits of anatomy, physiology, and behavior of children, would guarantee a development characterized by an
ordered sequence. Gesell (1925) argued that because behavioral traits are
especially suited for assessing the level of maturity, the young child is as
old as his behavior. Therefore, Gesell linked the child's forms of behavior
to the degree of maturity in his developmental diagnosis (see Reinert,
1964).

American psychologists have made an especially characteristic contribution to developmental psychology through their extensive longitudinal studies. Following Tiedemann's example, the early child biographies
generally pursued the development of a single child over a few years. In
contrast, the extensive longitudinal studies were begun with more or less
comprehensive random samples of children born during the same year,
and then these samples were observed several times in subsequent years
and decades at certain time intervals. Moreover, besides data on physical
development, direct observational data were collected. Interviews, questionnaires, and standardized testing procedures were also established for
assessing developmental changes. The average values obtained in this
manner for physical growth and behavioral variables furnished developmental psychology with important factual information. It is equally important that these studies have provided insight into the methodological
complications of a basic research technique in developmental psychology.
Terman's study of gifted children, begun in 1920, was the first and best
known longitudinal investigation. Several other longitudinal studies also
were begun with normal children—the *Berkeley Growth Study* by Nancy
Bayley, the *Guidance Study* by Jean M. Macfarlane, and the *Fels-Study
of Human Development* by Lester W. Sontag, among others. Kagan
(1964) provides a valuable overview of these and other longitudinal
studies.

At the beginning of the period of foundation, Alfred Binet was the
director of the psychological laboratory at the Sorbonne and an extraordinarily broad and productive researcher. By the end of the 1880s, Binet
already began to study problems of child and developmental pscyhology
related to perception. Because of Binet's method of experimentation and
questioning children in his perception research (Binet, 1890a, 1890b, 1895;
Binet & Henri, 1894), Pollack (1971) identified him as a methodological
precursor of Piaget. Shortly after the turn of the century, Binet led the

child study movement in France. In 1920 he assumed the presidency and scientific leadership of the recently founded Société Libre pour l'Étude Psychologique de l'Enfant—an organization analogous to Hall's Association. Binet's most significant contribution to developmental psychology clearly was the development of the "échelle métrique de l'intelligence" in collaboration with Simon (Binet, 1911; Binet & Simon, 1905a, 1905b, 1905c, 1908). This was the first developmental test of intelligence. In the first decades of this century, no other testing instrument attracted as much attention among developmental psychologists throughout the world as this procedure (see Groffmann, 1964).

   The most important advocate of the child study movement in French-speaking Switzerland was Edouard Claparède, a professor at the University of Geneva. One of his contributions to developmental psychology was a stage theory of the development of interests in childhood and adolescence (Claparède, 1909). From a historical perspective, much importance is attributed to Claparède's organizational work. In 1912 Claparède and Pierre Bovet founded a pedagogical–psychological facility for the scientific study of children in Geneva—the Institut Jean-Jacques Rousseau. In 1921 Claparède attracted the then 25-year-old Jean Piaget as a co-worker for the institute. Piaget had previously worked in the Binet laboratory at the Sorbonne but not during the lifetime of Binet, who died in 1911. Piaget's great importance in developmental psychology is so well known today that a detailed exposition of his work and that of his collaborators can be dispensed with here. Rather, only the "leitmotifs" of Piaget's developmental psychology are noted to the extent that they belong to the period of foundation (see Petter, 1960). They are "the hypotheses of egocentrism and realism in children" (Piaget, 1923, 1924, 1926, 1927, 1932) and "adaptation as a balance between assimilation and accommodation" (Piaget, 1936, 1937). For a co-worker of the pedagogically oriented Claparède, it is surprising that from the commencement of his career to the present Piaget has pursued almost exclusively interests in developmental psychology and by necessity also in epistemology. Obviously, the "egocentric" attitude toward this single area of interest, which has lasted for decades, has made Piaget the important developmental psychologist that he is.

   In contrast to research in English and French, general portrayals of child development in German appeared at a later time in the period of foundation. Ament (1899) restricted his work to the development of speaking and thinking. Likewise, Groos (1911) did not portray the total development of the child but approached child psychology with general psychological problems. The turning point came with Wilhelm Stern's (1914) *Psychology of Early Childhood*. This book provides a comprehensive portrayal of child development. Höhn (1959) described it as a "milestone in the history of developmental psychology" (p. 24). Before publication of this book, William Stern, a professor of psychology first in Breslau and then in Hamburg after 1916, had already achieved widespread recognition as an experimental perceptual psychologist (e.g., W. Stern, 1894), the founder of differential psychology (W. Stern, 1900, 1911), and author of numerous works on child and developmental psychology (e.g., W. Stern, 1903, 1904, 1908, 1909; C. Stern & W. Stern, 1907, 1909). W. Stern's research in child developmental psychology was conducted with an intentional ontogenetic focus. Unlike any other psychologist of his time, W. Stern was in a position to introduce appropriate viewpoints of general psychology into child developmental psychology. As a representative of "personalism" he was also able to view individual psychic functions within the context of the total person. As a differential psychologist, W. Stern was capable of drawing attention earlier than others could to developmental variations associated with environmental influences (e.g., the influence of differential social class membership). The clarity and coherence of W. Stern's thought is embodied most clearly in his "convergence theory" (W. Stern, 1914; see also W. Stern, 1908). In this context one should recall the heredity–environment controversy, which was mentioned in the discussion of the contributions of Watson and Gesell. According to W. Stern's "convergence theory," the question of whether a psychic characteristic comes from without or within is improperly stated from the very beginning. Rather, the question should be what comes from without (learning) and within (maturation), because psychic development is always "the result of a convergence of internal elements with external developmental conditions" (W. Stern, 1914). An examination of the successive revisions that W. Stern's developmental psychology underwent in the course of its various editions is enlightening for the history of developmental psychology. These revisions (the Sixth and since then unchanged edition was published in 1930) resulted from the confrontation of his personalism with the psychology of thought, perception, Gestalt psychology, psychoanalysis, and individual psychology.

One year after the appearance of W. Stern's (1914) book on child development, Felix Krueger outlined the approach of a general developmental psychology in his programmatic work *On Developmental Psychology* (1915). Krueger was Wundt's last assistant at Leipzig and held a position as professor of psychology at the University of Halle when this book was published. Krueger strove for a comparative psychology that would encompass all forms of early development (children, animals, primitive races, psychopathological phenomena). He thought that a comparative psychology was the "most urgent task of psychology" and would truly fulfill what Wundt meant by developmental psychology. Through this work Krueger wanted to stimulate progress in developmental theory and discover the form and coherency of "psychic structures." Krueger's idea basically was not a new one (e.g., recall C. G. Carus; G. S. Hall, 1899, may also be mentioned here). However, Krueger's (1915) book did become a kind of "guideline" for the so-called "Leipzig School" also identified as "genetic holistic psychology" (Sander, 1933; Wellek, 1954). "General developmental psychology" reached its height in the work of Heinz Werner (1926). Numerous monographs, which in part have been profitable for developmental psychology, were published in the "Arbeiten zur Entwicklungspsychologie," edited by Krueger between 1914 and 1941. The articles on "experimental child psychology" and "the image-forming child" published by Felix Krueger and Hans Volkelt in the *Neue Psychologische Studien,* beginning in 1931 and 1933, respectively, are also important for developmental psychology. After Wolfgang Köhler published his famous *Intelligence Experiments with Anthropoids* (Köhler, 1917, 1921), the Gestalt psychology of the "Berlin School" paid special attention to comparisons between the achievements of children and animals in child and developmental psychology. This type of comparison occupied a dominant role in the developmental psychology of Kurt Koffka (1921) as well as in Kurt Gottschaldt's (1933) analysis of child behavior. Koffka, by the way, intentionally did not treat the child "as an object of its own worth," as the child study movement had done, but "as the carrier of development" (Koffka, 1921, p. *iii*).

In addition to interests in language theory, thought, perception, and Gestalt psychology, interests in comparative psychology directed one of the most theoretically gifted German-speaking psychologists: Karl Bühler. He was already receptive to questions of developmental psychology before World War I (K. Bühler, 1913). During the last years of the war, K. Bühler was working at the University of Munich as the interim successor of his deceased mentor Oswald Külpe and published one of the most stimulating books on "the mental development of the child" (K. Bühler, 1918). In the following years he added an "outline" on the same topic (K. Bühler, 1919). Karl Bühler's developmental psychology was biologically oriented and emphasized the aspect of systematic maturation that manifests itself in ontogenetic–phylogenetic parallels. Furthermore, the methodology and substantive focus was psychologically oriented. The multidimensional approach was prominent in his methodology; all relevant sources of data, from anatomical to experimental, were considered. Substantively, he dealt mostly with the development of perception, language, imagination, thinking, and the ability to draw, while incorporating relevant knowledge from the general psychology of his day. Finally, Karl

Bühler's developmental psychology was substantially theoretical (especially beginning with the second edition of *Die geistige Entwicklung des Kindes* in 1921). Mental development was conceived of as a process of stages where each stage was defined by a characteristic field of action and a specific motivation for action ("Lebenskraft"). The stage of instinct is defined by acts of enjoyment and the desire for satisfaction ("Befriedigungslust"); the stage of training by playing and the desire for activity ("Funktionslust"); and, the stage of the intellect by creative acts and the desire to create ("Schöpferlust"). Unfortunately, Karl Bühler did not complete the intended elaboration of this nascent theory by incorporating life values.

In his book on developmental psychology, Karl Bühler referred to a psychological analysis of children's fairy tales prepared with his encouragement by his wife Charlotte. This analysis (C. Bühler, 1918), which appeared several months after Karl Bühler's book, was Charlotte Bühler's first pertinent publication in developmental psychology. It marked the beginning of a lengthy series of further achievements in developmental psychology by this self-confident researcher. Her achievements in their totality were extraordinarily influential. After accepting a faculty appointment at the University of Vienna, Karl Bühler moved from Dresden in 1922. Shortly afterwards Charlotte followed him to Vienna and established a scientific center for developmental psychology through a lively intellectual exchange with her husband (see Reinert, 1974) and with vigorous support from her colleague Hildegard Hetzer. In its dynamics, the center was probably superior to all other research facilities in developmental psychology at that time. The outcomes of these research projects for child developmental psychology may be found foremost in the books *Childhood and Youth* (C. Bühler, 1928) and *Tests for Small Children* (C. Bühler & Hetzer, 1932). A developmental model characterized as a "sequence of stages of closed structural systems" (C. Bühler, 1928, p. *vii*) was adopted in the book *Childhood and Youth*. The stage model of ontogenetic development (see Bergius, 1959) was employed more extensively by Charlotte Bühler than it had been until that time. Of course, it had been cultivated in its prescientific form since antiquity, critically and scientifically examined by F. A. Carus, and later favored by many developmental psychologists (e.g., Sigismund, 1856, already had used it for the graphic description of the behavioral progress of infants). C. Bühler's theory of stages reappeared in another form in *Tests for Small Children* (C. Bühler & Hetzer, 1932). The form of the stages was analogous to Binet's "échelle," but the content encompassed a much broader spectrum of behavior including not only intelligence. Like the somewhat different method of Gesell, the tests provided an objective means for assessing the developmental level of children (see Reinert, 1964).

The developmental psychology of adolescence was not invented in the period of foundation any more than the developmental psychology of childhood was. For instance, the description given by Rousseau in *Émile* (1762) and by F. A. Carus in *Psychology* (1808a) appeared earlier—in the preliminary and formative periods, respectively. As far as the author can detect, the first independent description of puberty appeared in France at the end of the formative period (Bacqué, 1876). More intensive and widespread efforts to understand the developmental psychology of adolescence did begin in the period of foundation. The establishment of child developmental psychology that began earlier appears to have been both detrimental and beneficial to this process. The handicap involves the special fascination many psychologists had for developmental processes only in childhood. Childhood was seen as the real period of development. For example, Compayré's (1893) interest in ontogenetic development dwindled at that point in childhood when the child "learns to read and write, when the child becomes a pupil" (p. 18). For some authors of child biographies, there was obviously a spontaneous need to continue their observations into the next period of childhood. An early example is Egger (1879) who, following Compayré (1893), extended his observations at least until the 10th year. Scupin and Scupin (1907, 1910, 1931) can be noted as a later example. The vigorous interest in solving educational problems shared by pedagogs involved in the child study movement and their psychological colleagues obviously benefited a developmental psychology of adolescence. Concurrently, one must also recognize that several psychologists identified early the favorable opportunities provided by schools for psychological research.

Hall (1882), borrowing from the example of Bartholomäi (1870), was one of the first psychologists to concentrate on school-aged children. He (1894) also provided his first tentative descriptions of adolescence in relation to educational problems. For Hall the question of what one should do with adolescents in this difficult period of life could be clearly answered: First, one should study them. Hall (1894) also pointed out that the study of adolescence had already begun. He was probably referring to work by Burnham (1891) that had appeared in his *Pedagogical Seminary*. Debesse (1938, 1970), who was especially interested in the history of adolescent psychology, thought that his work could be regarded perhaps as the manifesto for research in adolescent psychology. Debesse (1970) identified an article by Lancaster (1897) appearing several years later in the *Pedagogical Seminary* as the first short general review of adolescence. Eventually Hall (1904) published a two-volume comprehensive overview entitled *Adolescence*. The subtitle gives an impression of the breadth of Hall's attempt: "Its Psychology and Its Relation to Physiology, Anthropology, Sociology, Sex, Crime, Religion, and Education." Hall viewed "adolescence" as a special period of life distinct from childhood and as a "new birth" rather suddenly initiated by physical maturation. He applied his theory of recapitulation to this period of life as well. Hall's views were spread very rapidly first in the United States and soon after in France by Compayré (1906) and in England by Slaughter (1911). A negative reaction to Hall followed shortly thereafter primarily in the United States. Criticisms were directed to Hall's technique of interrogation, statements on recapitulation, and especially his idea of adolescence as a period of abrupt behavioral changes. A few decades later, Debesse (1970) commented that Hall was seen in the United States only as a "venerable pioneer" of adolescent psychology. For example, Arlitt's (1937) book on adolescence does not even mention Hall in the text but only in the bibliography.

Hall's proponents were not the only researchers who dealt with adolescence before the turn of the century. In France Biérent (1896) and in Italy Marro (1897) also wrote about adolescence. After the turn of the century there was a sudden increase in Europe in the number of publications on adolescence. Most of the publications were related to fringe areas of psychology, such as medical and pedagogical problems, as well as general and specific problems in the "knowledge of adolescence." Prior to World War I, several publications oriented toward adolescent psychology in a narrower sense deserve mention: from France, Mendousse (1909); from Switzerland, Lemaître (1910) and Evard (1911); and, from Germany, Bauer (1911) and Groos (1912). After World War I progress in research in adolescent psychology was somewhat retarded in most European countries. However, several important works appeared: in England, Burt (1925); in Belgium, Vermeylen (1926); and, in France, Mendousse (1928). At this time, the locus of European research in adolescent psychology, especially during the 1920s, was in German-speaking regions. Obviously, this change of interest among German psychologists was advanced rather significantly by extensive discussions—both inside and outside the field of science—of the youth movement that had begun to spread in Germany since the turn of the century.

Since adolescence was a relatively unfamiliar area of investigation, German researchers in adolescent psychology were preoccupied with developing new methodological approaches at that time. The most extensively used method was the psychological analysis of diaries, which had not been used before in developmental psychology. Fritz Giese (1914) made the first comprehensive attempts to psychologically analyze literary productions of children and adolescents. Several years later a suprisingly interesting *Diary of a Teenage Girl* was published by a psychoanalyst (Hug-Hellmuth, 1919). Sigmund Freud, in the foreword of the book, called it a "jewel." Soon, however, it was shown to be a hoax (Burt, 1921; Krug, 1926). At first only three and then shortly later 14 diaries by adolescents provided the foundation for Charlotte Bühler's (1922a, 1923; also see C. Bühler, 1922b, 1925, 1927) attempt to analyze "the inner life of the adolescent." Although C. Bühler, in reviewing the relatively imprecise method of diary analysis, later wrote of the "completely illegitimate origin . . . with which adolescent psychology began" (C. Bühler & Hetzer, 1929, p. 223), one must recognize that she achieved the most psychologically satisfactory description of the period of adolescence (prepuberty, puberty, adolescence) of that time. William Stern, whose interests in developmental psychology began to shift from child to adolescent psychology (Stern, 1922, 1923, 1924, among others) at the time of World War I (see above all W. Stern, 1916), considered adolescents' diaries important documents for psychology. Stern (1925) analyzed a diary psychologically, but he also noted that sketches in a diary could be properly used in psychology only in conjunction with other data. Besides data from diaries, Busemann (1926) and others demonstrated to German-speaking adolescent developmental psychologists of that time that systematically conducted self-evaluations of adolescents were profitable sources of data. In contrast, eidetic ability as a source of data for adolescent psychology did not fulfill the hopes that E. R. Jaensch and others had placed in it (e.g., Jaensch & Jaensch, 1921; Kroh, 1922).

During this time, the pedagog Eduard Spranger also searched for a new approach to adolescent developmental psychology. His *Psychology of Adolescence* (Spranger, 1924) dealt mainly with the educated young man's entrance into the culturally specified value system of adults or, as Spranger described it, the "objective and normative spirit" of the times. The tenor of Spranger's book was not independent of this focus but at the same time was more important than the theme itself. Spranger wanted to refute a large part of adolescent psychology that had been conducted up until then. Polemicizing against Theodor Ziehen's (1922) *The Inner Life of the Adolescent,* Spranger thought that it was necessary to completely deny the importance of anatomical and physiological maturation—in particular the maturation of the sex glands—for the psychological understanding of puberty. Spranger essentially adopted the ideas of Wilhelm Dilthey (1894, 1910) but presented as his own the idea of an "understanding psychology of adolescence," i.e., a humanistic psychology that would seek to derive the adolescent's psychic structure from knowledge of the "superindividual structure" of the "objective spirit" (cf. the "inner sense" of C. G. Carus). Karl Bühler (1927) sharply criticized Spranger's position on developmental psychology. However, K. Bühler's critique hardly reached any of Spranger's readers outside the field of psychology. Judging from the number of editions, Spranger's book was quite successful. Except for Oswald Kroh's (1928) *Developmental Psychology of the Elementary School Child,* which was very popular with educators, probably no other developmental psychology book outsold Spranger's in German-speaking regions until the end of World War II.

As far as the author can detect, the developmental psychology of adulthood and old age was established relatively late in the linguistic region from which Quetelet came (e.g., Courbon, 1927; Ehinger, 1927, 1931). In French-speaking regions, Claparède's (1909, p. 141, p. 204) views on adulthood ("crystallization," "petrifaction") and old age ("the period of need," "un pis-aller") possibly had a lasting influence. Earlier beginnings and more numerous and important contributions on adulthood and old age originated in German-speaking areas and the United States.

The psychology of aging began in the United States (see Riegel, 1973) in the last decade of the nineteenth century (Richardson, 1891; Scott, 1896), whereas the earliest contributions to the psychology of adult development began during the first decade of the twentieth century (e.g., Dorland, 1908; Sanford, 1902). More intensive interest and research in the psychology of adult development and aging began in the United States only after World War I. The increase in research was partly a function of the success American psychologists experienced with intelligence tests, especially the group intelligence tests (i.e., Army Tests) used extensively by the United States Army beginning in 1917 (see Yerkes, 1921). The majority of this research from the 1920s and 1930s investigated the development of cognitive functions (e.g., intelligence, reaction time, motor and verbal abilities). Miles (1933), Hofstätter (1938), and Riegel (1958, 1959) give the best overviews of this research. American works from that period that deserve special recognition dealt with the developmental psychology of learning (Ruch, 1933; Snoddy, 1926; Sorenson, 1930; Thorndike *et al.*, 1928), the development of interests (e.g., Gray & Munroe, 1929; Strong, 1931; Thorndike, 1935), and the development of scientific and literary productivity (e.g., Lehmann, 1936).

Again, G. Stanley Hall ought to be singled out. At the age of 76, just 2 years before his death, he published a two-volume book *Senescence, the Last Half of Life* (Hall, 1922). Like *Adolescence* (Hall, 1904), this book also covers a broad scope of topics: Data from history, philosophy, and physiology were presented. The more precise psychological statements are based on interrogations and introspection. From a historical perspective, the importance of this work does not result from its content, but from the fact that Hall presented "senescence" as a distinct period of life and recommended a special psychological treatment of it. It is interesting that Hall's psychological gerontology included not only the last years of life but also the greater part of adulthood. Because he viewed "senescence" as beginning already in the fourth decade of life, Munnichs (1966) proposed that a more appropriate subtitle would have been "the second half of life."

In German-speaking areas the first separate approach to understanding the second half of the life span is found foremost in criminological and medical studies (e.g., Bresler, 1907; Hübner, 1910; Mendel, 1910). It was not until the middle of the 1920s that professional psychologists began to become interested in this segment of the life span. First, there were psychotechnicians who dealt especially with the relation between age and achievement (e.g., Berliner, 1924; Moede, 1926; Schorn, 1930; Skutch, 1925; Weiss, 1927). A little later "experiential forms of age" (Giese, 1928) were studied. Afterwards several more general works in gerontological psychology were produced (e.g., Gruhle, 1938; E. Stern, 1931; von Bracken, 1939).

Independent of the aforementioned works, the most important contributions to research in developmental psychology in the German-speaking psychology of the prewar period were made by Charlotte Bühler's Viennese group. C. Bühler (1932, 1933) considered "the course of human life" to be "a psychological problem." The ideas of finding a kind of psychological analog to biological life curves (growth in childhood and youth, relative stability in adulthood, and regression in old age) is evident in C. Bühler's analysis of the diaries of adolescents and the experimental and theoretical studies conducted for her book *Childhood and Youth* (C. Bühler, 1928). It became clear to C. Bühler that one could not do justice to the dynamics of human development if individual spans of life were considered separately. Therefore, she and her colleagues collected a large amount of data on the course of life (reminiscences, biographies, documents, statistics). Based on her analysis of these data, she described five periods in the human life span: (a) childhood and youth as the "entrance into life"; (b) the period of the expansion of life and provisional self-determination; (c) the middle of life as the time of modifications of needs and tasks; (d) the period in which the person retreats behind his achievement; and, (e) the period of intensified occupation with one's own past and future.

In C. Bühler's conception of a developmental psychology covering the entire life span, she "rediscovered" in principle the comprehensive human developmental psychology that F. A. Carus had outlined more than a century before. Even before she emigrated from Europe, C.

Bühler's "new" idea of developmental psychology had already become known in the United States (C. Bühler, 1935a, 1935b; Frenkel, 1936). One year before C. Bühler immigrated to the United States, Pressey, Janney, and Kuhlen (1939) published the first textbook of life-span developmental psychology entitled *Life: A Psychological Survey.* After World War II the integrated concept of developmental psychology encompassing the whole life span was adopted in a number of textbooks (Anderson, 1949; Hurlock, 1968; Pressey & Kuhlen, 1957; Zubeck & Solberg, 1954) and was pursued both theoretically and methodologically in symposiums (Baltes & Schaie, 1973; Goulet & Baltes, 1970; Nesselroade & Reese, 1973).[1]

Because individual research in developmental psychology has been conducted in an extraordinarily differentiated fashion after World War II, the kind of integrative effort represented by life-span developmental psychology appears to be urgently needed. In many ways the process of differentiation and integration which has been recognizable for a time in human developmental psychology appears to coincide with corresponding processes in the organization of the total field of scientific psychology. However, a detailed illustration of this is not part of the contents of this outline of the history of developmental psychology.

V. Summary

Most of the previous historigraphical treatments of developmental psychology have dealt only with specific segments of the whole span of human life, such as child psychology, adolescent psychology, or psychological gerontology. More recently, a few developmental psychologists have begun to delineate the history of developmental psychology as a discipline encompassing the whole life span. In this chapter an attempt has been made to further understanding of the history of developmental psychology from this latter perspective.

The methodology of presentation is primarily chronological; biographical, geographically specific, or topic-specific aspects assume only secondary importance in the organization of the material. The history of developmental psychology is described as a transition through four periods—the preliminary period, the formative period, the period of foundation and specialization, and the period of differentiation and integration.

---

[1]Baltes (this volume) identifies another early life-span work by Hollingworth (1927) entitled "Mental Growth and Decline: A Survey of Developmental Psychology." It is surprising that this text has been neglected in historical considerations as it antedates both Charlotte Bühler and Pressey, Janney, and Kuhlen.

The organizational status of psychology as a scientific discipline is adopted tentatively as a criterion to identify and delineate these four historical periods.

The approximately 2000 years of European intellectual history, extending from the writings of Democritus to the end of the eighteenth century, are designated as the preliminary period. Psychology as a science had no organizational structure during this long period of time. There was no institutional framework for scientific activity; there were no journals or societies for scientific interaction.

Human development was the object not of empirical research but of philosophical reflection and description. Evidence of such endeavors is found primarily in summaries of the characteristics of persons of different ages (e.g., Democritus, Plato, Aristotle, Cicero, Comenius) and in autobiographies (e.g., Augustine, Cardanus, Jung-Stilling). The importance of empirical observation is recognized in this period in the writings of Albertus Magnus, whose attitudes were primarily amplified in the postulates of "Renaissance psychologists" (e.g., Vives, Telesius) and the English empirical philosophers (e.g., Locke, Hume). Beginning in the middle of the eighteenth century, demands for empirical observation led to a period of intensive activity in human ontogenesis. Of particular importance during this time are J.-J. Rousseau's *Emile*, which may be implicitly understood as a partial developmental psychology, and the "educational histories" encouraged by the philanthropists. This work culminated in J. N. Tetens' *Perfectibility and Development of Man*.

The years between the end of the eighteenth century and the end of the nineteenth century are designated the formative period. It was during this time that developmental psychology withdrew from the greater union with experiential philosophy and acquired a sense of self-consciousness as an individual discipline. The publication of the first psychological periodicals (the first journal, *Gnoti Sauton*, edited by C. P. Moritz, appeared in 1783) may be considered an indication of this new self-consciousness.

Three events are of particular importance for the history of developmental psychology in the formative period. The first of these is D. Tiedemann's diary of the development of a young child, which may be considered the first known longitudinal study. It served as a prototype for a large number of similar diaries by other authors. The second was F. A. Carus' outline of a "general age-oriented science"—the first psychologically based description of human development over the entire life span. The third important event was A. Quetelet's attempt to trace the course of human development with the help of empirical curves based on varying types of cross-sectional data.

The third phase in the history of developmental psychology, beginning at the end of the nineteenth century and continuing to the start of World War II, is designated the period of foundation and specialization. The new level of organization reached at the beginning of this period is reflected in the establishment of the first university laboratories for psychology, the first psychological periodicals of supraregional importance, and the first international congresses of psychology.

During this period, developmental psychology achieved the status of a well-founded, empirically oriented subdivision of psychology. Since the investigation of human development was separately oriented toward the development of children, adolescents, adults, and the aged, this period may be justifiably designated as that of specialization. Among these areas of specialization, child development was pursued most intensively—perhaps as a result of the effects of the child study movement, which enjoyed worldwide interest at that time. Several noteworthy scientists in this era were Wilhelm Preyer, William Stern, Felix Krueger, and Karl and Charlotte Bühler in the German-speaking countries, Alfred Binet, Edouard Claparède, and Jean Piaget in the French-speaking countries, and G. Stanley Hall, James M. Baldwin, John B. Watson, and Arnold Gesell in the United States. In the area of adolescent development, which reached it peak in the 1920s, G. Stanley Hall in the United States, Charlotte Bühler in Austria, and Eduard Spranger in Germany made the most significant contributions. The intensive investigation of adulthood and old age first began after World War I. Among the scientists active in the United States, G. Stanley Hall was the most prominent; in Europe, Charlotte Bühler was outstanding. Her conception of a developmental psychology covering the whole life span is, in principle, a rediscovering of the comprehensive approach outlined by F. A. Carus one century earlier.

The last period in the history of developmental psychology, which may be interpreted as one of differentiation and integration, began at the end of World War II. This period is characterized not only by increased differentiation, but also by more consistent integrative efforts in developmental psychology, as well as in psychology as a whole. K. Warner Schaie, L. R. Goulet, and Paul B. Baltes, in their West Virginia Symposia on Life-Span Developmental Psychology, are considered to have given a truly integrated psychology of human development its most important impetus.

Acknowledgments

The author would like to acknowledge the important contributions of Christian W. Hallstein and Steven W. Cornelius in the preparation and editorial revision of this contribution for publication in this series.

A similar version of this paper is published in German as "Grundzüge einer Geschichte der Human-Entwicklungspsychologie," in H. Balmer (Ed.), *Die europäische Tradition. Tendenzen, Schulen, Entwicklungslinien*, Vol. 1 of *Die Psychologie des 20. Jahrhunderts.* Zürich: Kindler, 1976, pp. 862–896.

References

Alcott, B., & Peabody, E. P. *Record of a school*. Boston: Munroe, 1835.

Alcott, B., & Peabody, E. P. *Conversations with children on the Gospels*. Boston: Munroe, 1836/1837.

Altmüller, F. *Über die Entwicklung der Seele des Kindes: Blüten aus dem Garten der Kindheit*. Langensalza: Beyer, 1913. (Originally published, 1867.)

Ament, W. *Die Entwicklung von Sprechen und Denken beim Kinde*. Leipzig: Wunderlich, 1899.

Anandalakshmy, S., & Grinder, R. Conceptual emphasis in the history of developmental psychology: Evolutionary theory, teleology, and the nature–nurture issue. *Child Development*, 1970, **41**, 1113–1123.

Anderson, J. E. *Psychology of development and personal adjustment*. New York: Holt, Rinehart & Winston, 1949.

Ariès, P. *L'enfant et la vie familiale sous l'ancien regime*. Paris: Plon, 1960.

Arlitt, A. H. *Adolescent psychology*. New York: Cincinnati American Book, 1937.

Bacqué, S. *Considerations médico-physiologiques sur la puberté (Thèse)*. Argenteuil/Paris: 1876.

Baldwin, J. M. *Mental development in the child and the race: Methods and processes*. New York: Macmillan, 1895.

Baltes, P. B., & Goulet, L. R. Status and issues of a life-span developmental psychology. In L. R. Goulet & P. B. Baltes (Eds.), *Life-span developmental psychology: Research and theory*. New York: Academic Press, 1970.

Baltes, P. B., & Schaie, K. W. (Eds.). *Life–span developmental psychology: Personality and socialization*. New York: Academic Press, 1973.

Bartholomäi, F. Der Vorstellungskreis der Berliner Kinder beim Eintritt in die Schule. *Berliner Städtisches Jahrbuch*, 1870, **4**.

Bastian, A. *Beiträge zur vergleichenden Psychologie: Die Seele und ihre Erscheinungsweisen in der Ethnographie*. Berlin: Dümmler, 1868.

Bauer, H. *Psychologie des Jugendlichen*. Berlin: Ostdeutscher Jünglingsbund, 1911.

Bell, C. *Ideas of a new anatomy of the brain*. London: Strahan & Preston, 1811.

Bergius, R. Entwicklung als Stufenfolge. In H. Thomae (Ed.), *Entwicklungspsychologie*. Göttingen: Hogrefe, 1959.

Berliner, A. Einfluß des Alters auf die Geschwindigkeit bei leichter Arbeit. *Zeitschrift für Angewandte Psychologie*, 1924, **23**, 196–204.

Bernoulii, C. *Die Psychologie Carl Gustav Carus und deren geistesgeschichtliche Bedeutung*. Jena: Diederichs, 1925.

Biérent, L. H. *Étude sur la puberté chez l'homme et chez la femme*. Paris: Société d'Éditions Scientifiques, 1896.

Bilfinger, G. B. *Dilucidationes philosophicae de deo, anima humana, mundo et generalibus rerum affectionibus*. Tübingen: Cottae, 1725.

Binet, A. La perception des longueurs et des nombres chez quelques petits enfants. *Revue Philosophique*, 1890, **30**, 68–81. (a)

Binet, A. Perceptions d'enfants. *Revue Philosophique,* 1890, **30,** 582–611. (b)

Binet, A. La mesure des illusions visuelles chez les enfants. *Revue Philosophique,* 1895, **40,** 11–25.

Binet, A. Nouvelles recherches sur la mesure du niveau intellectuel chez les enfants d'école. *Année Psychologique,* 1911, **17,** 145–201.

Binet, A., & Henri, V. Recherches sur le développement de la mémoire visuelle des enfants. *Revue Philosophique,* 1894, **37,** 348–350.

Binet, A., & Simon, T. Sur la nécessité d'établir un diagnostic scientifique des états inférieurs de l'intelligence. *Année Psychologique,* 1905, **11,** 163–190. (a)

Binet, A., & Simon, T. Méthodes nouvelles pour le diagnostic du niveau intellectuel des anormaux. *Année Psychologique,* 1905, **11,** 191–244. (b)

Binet, A., & Simon, T. Application des méthodes nouvelles au diagnostic du niveau intellectuel chez les enfants normaux et anormaux d'hospice et d'école primaire. *Année Psychologique,* 1905, **11,** 245–336. (c)

Binet, A., & Simon, H. Le développement de l'intelligence chez les enfants. *Année Psychologique,* 1908, **14,** 1–94.

Birren, J. E. A brief history of the psychology of aging. *Gerontologist,* 1961, **1,** 69–77, 127–134.

Boring, E. G. On the subjectivity of important historical dates: Leipzig 1897. *Journal of the History of the Behavioral Sciences,* 1965, **1,** 5–9.

Bourjarde, J. *L'intelligence et la pensée de l'enfant.* Paris: Alcan, 1937.

Bresler, J. *Greisenalter und Criminalitaet.* Halle: Marhold, 1907.

Bühler, C. Das Märchen und die Phantasie des Kindes. *Zeitschrift für Angewandte Psychologie,* 1918, Beiheft 17.

Bühler, C. *Das Seelenleben des Jugendlichen: Versuch einer Analyse und Theorie der psychischen Pubertät.* Jena: Fischer, 1922. (a)

Bühler, C. *Tagebuch eines jungen Mädchens.* Jena: Fischer, 1922. (b)

Bühler, C. *Das Seelenleben des Jugendlichen: Versuch einer Analyse und Theorie der psychischen Pubertät* (2nd ed.). Jena: Fischer, 1923.

Bühler, C. *Zwei Knabentagebücher: Mit einer Einleitung über die Bedeutung des Tagebuches für die Jugendpsychologie.* Jena: Fischer, 1925.

Bühler, C. *Zwei Mädchentagebücher.* Jena: Fischer, 1927.

Bühler, C. *Kindheit und Jugend: Genese des Bewußtseins.* Leipzig: Hirzel, 1928.

Bühler, C. Der menschliche Lebenslauf als psychologisches Problem. In G. Kafka (Ed.), *Bericht über den 12. Kongreß der Deutschen Gesellschaft für Psychologie in Hamburg 1931.* Jena: Fischer, 1932.

Bühler, C. *Der menschliche Lebenslauf als psychologisches Problem.* Leipzig: Hirzel, 1933.

Bühler, C. *From birth to maturity.* London: Kegan Paul, 1935. (a)

Bühler, C. The curve of life as studied in biographies. *Journal of Applied Psychology,* 1935, **19,** 405–409. (b)

Bühler, C., & Hetzer, H. Zur Geschichte der Kinderpsychologie. In E. Brunswik, C. Bühler, H. Hetzer, L. Kardos, E. Köhler, J. Krug, & A. Willwoll (Eds.), *Beiträge zur Problemgeschichte der Psychologie: Festschrift zu Karl Bühlers 50. Geburtstag.* Jena: Fischer, 1929.

Bühler, C., & Hetzer, H. *Kleinkindertests: Entwicklungstests vom 1. bis 6. Lebensjahr.* Leipzig: Barth, 1932.

Bühler, K. Kinderpsychologie. In K. Bühler, H. Klose, A. Vogt, & W. Weygandt (Eds.), *Geschichte der Erforschung und Fürsorge des jugendlichen Schwachsinns.* Jena: Fischer, 1911.

Bühler, K. Die Entwicklung der Abstraktionsfähigkeit bei Schulkindern. In F. Schumann

(Ed.), *Bericht über den 5. Kongreβ für Experimentelle Psychologie in Berlin 1912.* Leipzig: Barth, 1913.

Bühler, K. *Die geistige Entwicklung des Kindes.* Jena: Fischer, 1918.

Bühler, K. *Abriss der geistigen Entwicklung des Kindes.* Leipzig: Quelle & Meyer, 1919.

Bühler, K. *Die geistige Entwicklung des Kindes* (2nd ed.). Jena: Fischer, 1921.

Bühler, K. *Die Krise der Psychologie.* Jena: Fischer, 1927.

Burdach, K. F. *Über die Zeitrechnung des menschlichen Lebens.* Leipzig: Voss, 1828.

Burnham, W. H. The study of adolescence. *Pedagogical Seminary,* 1891, **1**, 174–195.

Burt, C. A young girl's diary (Review). *British Journal of Psychology,* 1921, **1**, 353–357.

Burt, C. *The young delinquent.* London: University of London Press, 1925.

Busemann, A. *Die Jugend im eigenen Urteil.* Langensalza: Beyer, 1926.

Carus, C. G. *Vorlesungen über Psychologie, gehalten im Winter 1829/30 zu Dresden.* Zürich: Rotapfel, 1931. (Originally published, 1831.)

Carus, C. G. *Psyche: Zur Entwicklungsgeschichte der Seele.* Darmstadt: Wissenschaftliche Buchgesellschaft, 1964. (Originally published, 1846.)

Carus, C. G. *Symbolik der menschlichen Gestalt: Ein Handbuch zur Menschenkenntnis.* Darmstadt: Wissenschaftliche Buchgesellschaft, 1962. (Originally published, 1853.)

Carus, F. A. *Psychologie: Zweiter Theil: Specialpsychologie.* (Nachgelassene Werke, Zweiter Theil: Der Psychologie zweiter Band). Leipzig: Barth & Kummer, 1808. (a)

Carus, F. A. *Geschichte der Psychologie* (Nachgelassene Werke, Dritter Theil). Leipzig: Barth & Kummer, 1808. (b)

Charles, D. C. Historical antecedents of life-span developmental psychology. In L. R. Goulet & P. B. Baltes (Eds.), *Life-span developmental psychology: Research and theory.* New York: Academic Press, 1970.

Chrisman, O. *Paidologie: Entwurf zu einer Wissenschaft des Kindes* (Dissertation). Jena: Universität, 1896.

Claparède, E. *Psychologie de l'enfant et de pédagogie expérimentale.* Geneva: Kündig, 1905.

Claparède, E. *Psychologie de l'enfant et de pédagogie expérimentale* (2nd ed.). Geneva: Kündig, 1909.

Claparède, E. *Psychologie de l'enfant et de pédagogie expérimentale* (4th ed.). Geneva: Kündig, 1911.

Claparède, E. *J.-J. Rousseau et l'éducation nouvelle.* (In L'éducation fonctionelle). Neuchâtel: Delachaux & Niestlé, 1932.

Comenius, J. A. Didactica magna. (1638). Deutsche Bearbeitung: H. Ahrbeck: Jan Amos Comenius. *Große Didaktik.* Berlin: Volk und Wissen, 1961.

Compayré, G. *L'évolution intellectuelle et morale de l'enfant.* Paris: Hachette, 1893.

Compayré, G. *L'adolescence. Études de psychologie et de pédagogie.* Paris: Alcan, 1906.

Courbon, P. Sur la psychologie de la vieillesse. *Journal de Psychologie,* 1927, **24**, 455–463.

Cramaussel, F. *Le premier éveil intellectuel de l'enfant.* Paris: Alcan, 1909.

Crump, L. *Nursery life 300 years ago.* London: Routledge, 1929.

Darwin, C. *The expression of the emotions in man and animals.* New York: Appleton, 1872.

Darwin, C. A biological sketch of an infant. *Mind,* 1877, **2**, 285–294.

Debesse, M. Les grands courants de la psychologie de l'adolescent. *L'Information Pédagogique,* Octobre 1938.

Debesse, M. L'enfance dans l'histoire de la psychologie. In H. Gratiot-Alphandéry & R. Zazzo (Eds.), *Traité de psychologie de l'enfant. Vol. 1: Historie et généralités.* Paris: Presses Universitaires de France, 1970.

Dennis, W. Historical beginnings of child psychology. *Psychological Bulletin,* 1949, **46**, 224–235.

Denzel, B. G. *Einleitung in die Erziehungs- und Unterrichtslehre*. Stuttgart: Metzler, 1817.

Desmonceaux. *Lettres et observations sur la vie des enfants naissants*. 1775. (Cited in M. Debesse, L'enfance dans l'histoire de la psychologie. In H. Gratiot-Alphandéry & R. Zazzo (Eds.), *Traité de psychologie de l'enfant. Vol. 1: Histoire et généralités*. Paris: Presses Universitaires de France, 1970.)

Dessoir, M. *Geschichte der neueren deutschen Psychologie* (2nd ed.). Berlin: Duncker, 1902.

Dillenius, F. W. J. Fragmente eines Tagebuches über die Entwicklung der körperlichen und geistigen Fähigkeiten und Anglagen eines Kindes. *Braunschweigisches Journal Philosophischen, Philologischen und Pädagogischen Inhalts*, 1789, **3**, 320–342; 1790, **4**, 279–298.

Dilthey, W. Ideen über eine beschreibende und zergliedernde Psychologie. *Sitzungsberichte der Königlich-Preussischen Akademie der Wissenschaften*, 1894, pp. 1309–1407.

Dilthey, W. *Der Aufbau der geschichtlichen Welt in den Geisteswissenschaften*. Berlin: Verlag der Königlichen Akademie der Wissenschaften-Reimer, 1910.

Dix, K. W. *Körperliche und geistige Entwicklung eines Kindes. 1. Heft: Die Instinktbewegungen der ersten Kindheit*. Leipzig: Wunderlich, 1911.

Dix, K. W. *Körperliche und geistige Entwicklung eines Kindes. 2. Heft: Die Sinne*. Leipzig: Wunderlich, 1912.

Dix, K. W. *Körperliche und geistige Entwicklung eines Kindes. 3. Heft: Vorstellen und Handeln*. Leipzig: Wunderlich, 1914.

Dorland, W. A. M. *The age of mental virility*. New York: Century, 1908.

Egger, M. E. *Observations et reflexions sur le développement de l'intelligence et du langage chez les enfants*. Paris: Picard, 1879.

Ehinger, G. Age et déclin des aptitudes. *Archives de Psychologie*, 1927, **20**, 318–323.

Ehinger, G. Déclin des aptitudes avec l'age. *Archives de Psychologie*, 1931, **23**, 67–73.

Engel, F. *Versuch einer Theorie von dem Menschen und dessen Erziehung*. Berlin: Lange, 1753.

Espinas. *Observations sur un nouveau-né*. Bourdeaux: Annales de la Faculté des Lettres, 1883.

Evard, M. *L'adolescence*. Neuchâtel: Delachaux & Niestlé, 1911.

Feldmann, H. *De statu normali functionum corpis humani animadversiones quandam*. Bonn: Georgie, 1833.

Ferri, L. Note su una bambina. In *Filosofia delle Scuole Italiane*, Roman, 1879. (Cited in M. Debesse, L'enfance dans l'histoire de la psychologie. In H. Gratiot-Alphandéry & R. Zazzo (Eds.), *Traité de psychologie de l'enfant. Vol. 1: Histoire et généralités*. Paris: Presses Universitaires de France, 1970.)

Flourens, M. J. P. *Recherches expérimentales sur les propriétés et les fonctions du système nerveux dans les animaux vertébrés*. Paris: Crevot, 1824.

Flugel, J. C. *A hundred years of psychology, 1833–1933*. London: Duckworth, 1933.

Formey, J. H. S. *La vie de Mr. Jean Philippe Baratier, Maître des Arts et Membre de la Société Royal des Sciences de Berlin*. Utrecht: 1742. (Cited in P. Schumann, Aus den Anfängen der Kinderpsychologie. *Zeitschrift für Pädogogische Psychologie*, 1921, **22**, 209–218.)

Frenkel, E. Studies in biographical psychology. *Character & Personality*, 1936, **5**, 1–34.

Fritzsch, T. Die Anfänge der Kinderpsychologie und die Vorläufer des Versuchs in der Pädagogik. *Zeitschrift für Pädagogische Psychologie*, 1910, **11**, 149–160.

Galton, F. *Hereditary genius: An inquiry into its laws and consequents*. London: Macmillan, 1869.

Galton, F. Twins, as a criterion of the relative power of nature and nurture. *Journal of the Royal Anthropological Institute*, 1876, **5**, 391–406.

Galton, F. *Inquiries into human faculty and its development*. London: Macmillan, 1883.

Garve, C. *Ob man die natürlichen Neigungen vernichten oder welche erwecken könne, die die Natur nicht erzeugt hat*. Berlin: Königliche Akademie der Wissenschaft, 1769.

Genzmer, A. *Untersuchungen über die Sinneswahrnehmungen des neugeborenen Menschen* (Dissertation). Halle: Niemeyer, 1873.

Gesell, A. *The mental growth of the pre-school child: A psychological outline of normal development from birth to sixth year, including a system of developmental diagnosis*. New York: Macmillan, 1925.

Gesell, A. *Infancy and human growth*. New York: Macmillan, 1928.

Gesell, A., & Thompson, H. *Infant behavior, its genesis and growth*. New York: McGraw-Hill, 1934.

Gesell, A., Thompson, H., & Amatruda, C. S. *The psychology of early growth, including norms of infant behavior and a method of genetic analysis*. New York: Macmillan, 1938.

Giese, F. Das freie literarische Schaffen bei Kindern und Jugendlichen. *Zeitschrift für Angewandte Psychologie*, 1914, Beiheft **7**.

Giese, F. *Erlebnisformen des Alters*. Halle: Niemeyer, 1928.

Götz, H. Zur Geschichte der Kinderpsychologie und der experimentellen Pädagogik. *Zeitschrift für Pädagogische Psychologie*, 1918, **19**, 257–268.

Gottschaldt, K. Der Aufbau des kindlichen Handelns: Vergleichende Untersuchungen an gesunden und psychisch abnormen Kindern. In *Schriftenreihe zur Entwicklungspsychologie* (Band 1). Leipzig: Barth, 1933.

Goulet, L. R., & Baltes, P. B. (Eds.). *Life-span developmental psychology: Research and theory*. New York: Academic Press, 1970.

Gray, W. S., & Munroe, R. *The reading interests and habits of adults*. New York: Macmillan, 1929.

Groffmann, K. J. Die Entwicklung der Intelligenzmessung. In R. Heiss (Ed.), *Psychologische Diagnostik*. Göttingen: Hogrefe, 1964.

Groffmann, K. J. Life-span developmental psychology in Europe: Past and present. In L. R. Goulet & P. B. Baltes (Eds.), *Life-span developmental psychology: Research and theory*. New York: Academic Press, 1970.

Grohmann, J. C. A. *Die Psychologie des kindlichen Alters: An Eltern und Erzieher in Briefen*. Hamburg: Campe, 1812.

Grohmann, J. C. A. *Ideen zur einer Geschichte der Entwicklung des kindlichen Alters: Psychologische Untersuchungen*. Hamburg: 1824.

Groos, K. *Das Seelenleben des Kindes: Ausgewählte Vorlesungen*. Berlin: Reuther & Reichard, 1911.

Groos, K. Zur Psychologie der Reifezeit. *Internationale Monatsschrift für Wissenschaft, Kunst und Technik*, 1912, **6**, 1331–1351.

Gruhle, H. W. Das seelische Altern. *Zeitschrift für Alternsforschung*, 1938, **1**, 89–95.

Hall, G. S. The contents of children's minds on entering school. *Princeton Review*, 1882, **11**, 249–272.

Hall, G. S. Child study, the basis of exact education. *Forum*, December 1893.

Hall, G. S. The new psychology as a basis of education. *Forum*, August 1894.

Hall, G. S. A study of fears. *American Journal of Psychology*, 1897, **8**, 147–249.

Hall, G. S. *Decennial celebration of the Clark University*. Worcester, Mass.: Clark University, 1899.

Hall, G. S. Child-study and its relation to education. *Forum,* August 1900.
Hall, G. S. *Ausgewählte Beiträge aus Kinderpsychologie und Pädagogik.* Altenburg: Bonde, 1902.
Hall, G. S. *Adolescence: Its psychology and its relation to physiology, anthropology, sociology, sex, crime, religion, and education.* New York: Appleton, 1904.
Hall, G. S. *Senescence: The last half of life.* New York: Appleton, 1922.
Havighurst, R. J. History of developmental psychology: Socialization and personality development through the life span. In P. B. Baltes & K. W. Schaie (Eds.), *Life-span developmental psychology: Personality and socialization.* New York: Academic Press, 1973.
Heckhausen, H. Entwicklung, psychologisch betrachtet. In F. E. Weinert, C. F. Graumann, H. Heckhausen, & M. Hofer (Eds.), *Funk–Kolleg Pädagogische Psychologie* (Band 1). Frankfurt/M: Fischer, 1974.
Hecquet. *L'histoire d'une jeune fille sauvage trouvée dans les bois à l'age de dix ans.* 1761. (Cited in M. Debesse, L'enfance dans l'histoire de la psychologie. In H. Gratiot–Alphandéry & R. Zazzo (Eds.), *Traité de psychologie de l'enfant. Vol. 1: Histoire et généralités.* Paris: Presses Universitaires de France, 1970.)
Hehlmann, W. *Geschichte der Psychologie* (Kröners Taschenausgabe, Band 200). Stuttgart: Kröner, 1963.
Herder, J. G. *Abhandlung über den Ursprung der Sprache.* Berlin: 1772.
Heydner, G. *Beitrag zur Kenntnis des kindlichen Seelenlebens.* Leipzig: Richter, 1894.
Heyfelder, O. *Die Kindheit des Menschen: Ein Beitrag zur Anthropologie und Psychologie.* Erlangen: Enke, 1857.
Höhn, E. Geschichte der Entwicklungspsychologie und ihrer wesentlichsten Ansätze. In H. Thomae (Ed.), *Entwicklungspsychologie.* Göttingen: Hogrefe, 1959.
Hofstätter, P. R. Tatsachen und Probleme einer Psychologie des Lebenslaufs. *Zeitschrift für Angewandte Psychologie,* 1938, **53,** 273–333.
Hofstätter, P. R. *Psychologie* (Fischer-Lexikon 6). Frankfurt/M.: Fischer, 1957.
Hübner, A. *Zur Psychologie und Psychopathologie des Greisenalters.* Medizinische Klinik, 1910.
Hug–Hellmuth, H. *Tagebuch eines halbwüchsigen Mädchens.* Leipzig: Internationaler Psychoanalytischer Verlag, 1919.
Hurlock, E. B. *Developmental Psychology.* New York: McGraw-Hill, 1968.
Itard, J. M. G. *Mémoire sur le sauvage de l'Aveyron.* Paris: Alcan, 1798.
Jaensch, E. R., & Jaensch, W. Über die Verbreitung der eidetischen Anlage im Jugendalter. *Zeitschrift für Psychologie,* 1921, **87,** 91–96.
James, W. *Talks to teachers on psychology and to students on some life's ideals.* New York: Holt, 1899.
Kästner, A. G., & Kirsten, A. F. *Der Erinnerung eines Kindes und seiner Mutter gewidmet.* Göttingen: Scheider, 1796.
Kagan, J. American longitudinal research on psychological development. *Child Development,* 1964, **35,** 1–32.
Key, E. *Barnels århundrade.* Stockholm: Bronnier, 1900.
King, I. *The psychology of child development.* Chicago: University of Chicago Press, 1903.
Koffka, K. *Die Grundlagen der psychischen Entwicklung: Eine Einführung in die Kinderpsychologie.* Osterwieck: Zickfeldt, 1921.
Köhler, W. *Intelligenzprüfungen an Anthropoiden I: Abhandlungen der Preussischen Akademie der Wissenschaften, Physikalisch-Mathematische Klasse Nr. 1.* Berlin: Reimer, 1917.
Köhler, W. *Intelligenzprüfungen an Menschenaffen: Abhandlungen der Berliner Akademie*

der Wissenschaften, Physikalisch-Mathematische Klasse Nr. 1 (2nd ed.). Berlin: Reimer, 1921.

Kroh, O. *Subjektive Anschauungsbilder bei Jugendlichen.* Göttingen: Vandenhoek & Ruprecht, 1922.

Kroh, O. *Entwicklungspsychologie des Grundschulkindes.* Langensalza: Beyer, 1928.

Krueger, F. *Über Entwicklungspsychologie: Ihre sachliche und geschichtliche Notwendigkeit.* Leipzig: Engelmann, 1915.

Krüger, J. G. *Versuch einer Experimental–Seelenlehre.* Halle: Hemmerde, 1756.

Krug, J. Kritische Bemerkungen zu dem Tagebuch eines halbwüchsigen Mädchens. *Zeitschrift für Angewandte Psychologie,* 1926, **27**, 370–381.

Kussmaul, A. *Untersuchungen über das Seelenleben des neugeborenen Menschen.* Heidelberg: Winter, 1859.

Lancaster, E. G. Psychology and pedagogy of adolescence. *Pedagogical Seminary,* 1897, **7**, 61–128.

Lazarus, M., & Steinthal, H. (Eds.). *Zeitschrift für Völkerpsychologie und Sprachwissenschaft,* 1859, **1** ff.

Lehman, H. C. The creative years in science and literature. *Scientific Monthly,* 1936, **43**, 151–162.

Lemaître, A. *L'adolescent: La vie mentale de l'adolescent et ses anomalies.* St. Blaise: Foyer, 1910.

Löbisch, J. E. *Entwicklungsgeschichte der Seele des Kindes.* Wien: Haas, 1851.

Major, D. R. *First steps in mental growth.* New York: Macmillan, 1906.

Mandelli, B. *Perez e la psicologia dell' infanzia.* Milano: 1889. (Cited in P. Schumann, Aus den Anfängen der Kinderpsychologie. *Zeitschrift für Pädagogische Psychologie,* 1921, **22**, 209–218.)

Marro, A. *La pubertà studiata nell'uomo e nella donna.* Turin: 1897.

Mendel, K. Die Wechseljahre des Mannes. *Neurologisches Zentralblatt,* 1910, **29**.

Mendousse, P. *L'âme de l'adolescent.* Paris: Alcan, 1909.

Mendousse, P. *L'âme de l'adolescent.* Paris: Alcan, 1928.

Merkwürdiges Ehrengedächtnis des weyland klugen und gelehrten Lübeckischen Kindes Christian Henrich Heiniken. Hamburg: 1726.

Michelant, H. Observations sur le développement des facultés de l'âme chez les enfants. *Journal Général de l'Instruction Publique,* 1863, 251–291, 309–319.

Miles, W. R. Age and human ability. *Psychological Review,* 1933, **40**, 99–123.

Miller, N. Anmerkungen zu Levana oder Erziehungslehre. In Jean Paul, *Werke* (Fünfter Band). Darmstadt: Wissenschaftliche Buchgesellschaft, 1963.

Moede, W. Kraftfahrereignungsprüfungen beim deutschen Heer 1915–1918. *Industrielle Psychotechnik,* 1926, **3**, 23–28.

Moore, K. C. The mental development of a child. *Psychological Review,* 1896, **1**(3).

Moritz, K. P. *Anton Reiser.* Darmstadt: Wissenschaftliche Buchgesellschaft, 1960. (Originally published in Berlin, 1785–1790.)

Müller, J. *Zur vergleichenden Physiologie des Gesichtssinnes der Menschen und Thiere nebst einem Versuch über die Bewegungen der Augen und über den menschlichen Blick.* Leipzig: Gnoblock, 1826.

Müller, M. *The science of thought.* 1887.

Münsterberg, H. Psychology and education. *Educational Review,* 1898, **16**, 105–132.

Munnichs, J. M. A. A short history of psychogerontology. *Human Development,* 1966, **9**, 230–245.

Nesselroade, J. R., & Reese, H. W. (Eds.). *Life-span developmental psychology: Methodological issues.* New York: Academic Press, 1973.

Niederer, J. *Notes on Pestalozzi.* Aix-la-Chapelle: 1828. (Cited in W. Dennis, Historical beginnings of child psychology. *Psychological Bulletin,* 1949, **46,** 224–235.)

Pérez, B. *La psychologie de l'enfant: Les trois premières années de l'enfant.* Paris: Baillière, 1878.

Pérez, B. *Thierri Tiedemann et la science de l'enfant.* Paris: Baillière, 1881.

Pérez, B. *La psychologie de l'enfant: L'enfant de trois à sept ans.* Paris: Alcan, 1886.

Pérez, B. *La psychologie de l'enfant: L'art et la poésie chez l'enfant.* Paris: Alcan, 1888.

Perty, M. *Über das Seelenleben der Thiere: Thatsachen und Betrachtungen.* Leipzig: Winter'sche Verlagshandlung, 1865.

Petter, G. *Lo sviluppo mentale nelle ricerche die Jean Piaget.* Florence: Editrice Universitaria, 1960.

Piaget, J. *Le language et la pensée chez l'enfant.* Neuchâtel: Delachaux & Niestlé, 1923.

Piaget, J. *Le judgment et le raissonnement chez l'enfant.* Neuchâtel: Delachaux & Niestlé, 1924.

Piaget, J. *La représentation du monde chez l'enfant.* Paris: Alcan, 1926.

Piaget, J. *La causalité physique chez l'enfant.* Paris: Alcan, 1927.

Piaget, J. *Le jugement moral chez l'enfant.* Paris: Alcan, 1932.

Piaget, J. *La naissance de l'intelligence chez l'enfant.* Neuchâtel: Delachaux & Niestlé, 1936.

Piaget, J. *La construction du réel chez l'enfant.* Neuchâtel: Delachaux & Niestlé, 1937.

Pockels, K. F. Ursprung der Wortsprache. *Gnoti Sauton,* 1784, **II**(3), 93 ff.

Pockels, K. F. *Versuch einer Charakteristik des weiblichen Geschlechtes: Ein Sittengemälde des Menschen, des Zeitalters und des geselligen Lebens.* Hannover: Ritscher, 1801.

Pollack, R. H. Binet on perceptual-cognitive development or Piaget-come-lately. *Journal of the History of the Behavioral Sciences,* 1971, **7,** 370–374.

Pollock, F. An infant's progress in language. *Mind,* 1878, **3,** 392–401.

Pongratz, L. J. *Problemgeschichte der Psychologie.* Bern: Francke, 1967.

Posewitz, J. F. S. Ätiologische Entwicklung der Äußerungen des Sensoriums beim Foetus und beim jungen Kinde sogleich nach seiner Geburt bis zum 247. Tage. *Journal für Medizin, Chirurgie und Geburtshülfe vorzüglich mit Rücksicht auf Ätiologie und Semiotik,* 1799, Heft 1.

Pressey, S. L., & Kuhlen, R. G. *Psychological development through the life span.* New York: Harper & Row, 1957.

Pressey, S. L., Janney, J. E., & Kuhlen, R. G. *Life: A psychological survey.* New York: Harper, 1939.

Preyer, W. *Die Seele des Kindes: Beobachtungen über die geistige Entwicklung des Menschen in den ersten Lebensjahren.* Leipzig: Grieben, 1882.

Quetelet, A. *Sur l'homme et le développement de ses facultés, ou essai de physique sociale.* Paris: Bachelier, 1835.

Quetelet, A. *Über den Menschen und die Entwicklung seiner Fähigkeiten.* Stuttgart: Schweizerbart's Verlagshandlung, 1838.

Quetelet, A. *Physique sociale ou essai sur l'homme et le développement de ses facultés.* Paris: Bachelier, 1869.

Quetelet, A. *Anthropométrie ou mesure des différentes facultés de l'homme.* Brussels: Muquart, 1871.

Reinert, G. Entwicklungstests. In R. Heiss (Ed.), *Psychologische Diagnostik.* Göttingen: Hogrefe, 1964.

Reinert, G. The giant and the first lady: Karl and Charlotte Bühler, and their contribution to developmental psychology. *Trierer Psychologische Berichte,* 1974, **1**(4).

Richardson, B. W. Memory as a test of age. *Aselepiad*, 1891, **8**, 230–232.

Riegel, K. F. Ergebnisse und Probleme der psychologischen Alternsforschung. *Vita Humana*, 1958, **1**, 52–64, 111–127, 204–243; 1959, **2**, 213–237.

Riegel, K. F. On the history of psychological gerontology. In C. Eisdorfer & M. P. Lawton (Eds.), *The psychology of adult development and aging*. Washington, D.C.: American Psychological Association, 1973.

Rousseau, J.–J. *Émile ou de l'éducation*. Amsterdam: Néaulme, 1762.

Ruch, F. L. Adult learning. *Psychological Bulletin*, 1933, **30**, 387–414.

Rudolphi, C. A. *Grundriss der Physiologie*. Berlin: Dümmler, 1823.

Sander, F. Kindes- und Jugendpsychologie als genetische Ganzheitspsychologie. *Vierteljahresschrift für Jugendkunde*, 1933, **3**, 1–14.

Sanford, E. C. Mental growth and decay. *American Journal of Psychology*, 1902, **13**, 426–456.

Schönfeldt, D. N. *Anweisung zur Erkenntnis seiner selbst nach der natürlichen Beschaffenheit seiner Seele*. Bützow: Bödner, 1764.

Schopenhauer, A. Aphorismen zur Lebensweisheit. In A. Schopenhauer, *Parerga und Paralipomena* (Vol. 1: Parerga). Berlin: Hayn, 1851.

Schorn, M. Lebensalter und Leistung. *Archiv für die Gesamte Psychologie*, 1930, **75**, 168–184.

Schumann, P. Aus den Anfängen der Kinderpsychologie. *Zeitschrift für Pädagogische Psychologie*, 1921, **22**, 209–218.

Schwarz, F. H. C. *Erziehungslehre* (Vol. 2). Leipzig: Göschen, 1804.

Schwarz, F. H. C. *Erziehungslehre* (2nd ed.). Leipzig: Göschen, 1829.

Scott, C. A. Old age and death. *American Journal of Psychology*, 1896, **8**, 67–122.

Scupin, E., & Scupin, G. *Bubis erste Kindheit: Ein Tagebuch über die geistige Entwicklung eines Knaben in den ersten drei Lebensjahren*. Leipzig: Grieben, 1907.

Scupin, E., & Scupin, G. *Bubi im vierten bis sechsten Jahr: Ein Tagebuch über die geistige Entwicklung eines Knaben während der ersten sechs Lebensjahre. Zweiter Teil: das vierte bis sechste Lebensjahr umfassend*. Leipzig: Grieben, 1910.

Scupin, E., & Scupin, G. *Lebensbild eines deutschen Schuljungen*. Leipzig: Grieben, 1931.

Semming, H. *Das Kind: Tagebuch eines Vaters*. Leipzig: Hartung, 1879.

Shinn, M. W. *Notes on the development of a child*. Berkeley: University of California, 1893.

Shinn, M. W. *The biography of a baby*. Boston: Houghton Mifflin, 1900.

Shinn, M. W. *Notes on the development of a child. II. The development of the senses in the first three years of childhood*. Berkeley: University of California, 1907.

Sigismund, B. *Kind und Welt: Vatern, Müttern und Kinderfreunden gewidmet*. Braunschweig: Vieweg, 1856.

Skutsch, R. Lebensalter, Berufsleistung und Eignungsprüfung. *Industrielle Psychotechnik*, 1925, **2**, 90–91.

Slaughter, W. J. *The adolescent*. London: 1911.

Sneedorf. Die Geschichte eines Kindes von 2 Jahren und 5 Monaten. *Pädagogische Unterhandlungen*, 1778, **2**, 758–765.

Snoddy, G. S. Learning and stability. *Journal of Applied Psychology*, 1926, **10**, 1–36.

Sorenson, H. Adult ages as a factor in learning. *Journal of Educational Psychology*, 1930, **21**, 451–457.

Soulié, E., & Barthélémy, E., de (Eds.) *Héroard, Jean: Journal, 1601–1628*. 1868, (Cited in W. Dennis, Historical beginnings of child psychology. *Psychological Bulletin*, 1949, **46**, 224–235.)

Spranger, E. *Psychologie des Jugendalters*. Leipzig: Quelle & Meyer, 1924.

Stern, E. *Anfänge des Alterns*. Leipzig: Thieme, 1931.

Stern, W. Die Wahrnehmung von Bewegungen vermittelst des Auges. *Zeitschrift für Psychologie,* 1894, **7,** 321–386.

Stern, W. *Über Psychologie der individuellen Differenzen.* Leipzig: Barth, 1900.

Stern, W. Die Kindespsychologie als angewandte Wissenschaft. *Zeitschrift für Pädagogische Psychologie,* 1903, **5,** 394.

Stern, W. Die Sprachentwicklung eines Kindes, insbesondere in grammatischer und logischer Hinsicht. In F. Schumann (Ed.), *Bericht über den 1. Kongress für experimentelle Psychologie in Giessen 1904.* Leipzig: Barth, 1904.

Stern, W. *Person und Sache: System der philosophischen Weltanschauung. I: Ableitung und Grundlehre.* Leipzig: Barth, 1906.

Stern, W. Tatsachen und Ursachen der seelischen Entwicklung. *Zeitschrift für Angewandte Psychologie,* 1908, **1,** 1–43.

Stern, W. Die Entwicklung der Raumwahrnehmung in der ersten Kindheit. *Zeitschrift für Angewandte Psychologie,* 1909, **2,** 412–423.

Stern, W. *Die differentielle Psychologie in ihren methodischen Grundlagen.* Leipzig: Barth, 1911.

Stern, W. *Psychologie der frühen Kindheit bis zum sechsten Lebensjahr.* Leipzig: Quelle & Meyer, 1914.

Stern, W. *Die Jugendkunde als Kulturforderung: Mit besonderer Berücksichtigung des Begabungsproblems.* Leipzig: Quelle & Meyer, 1916.

Stern, W. Vom Ichbewusstsein des Jugendlichen. *Zeitschrift für Pädagogische Psychologie,* 1922, **23,** 8–16.

Stern, W. Über die Entwicklung der Idealbildung in der reifenden Jugend. *Zeitschrift für Pädagogische Psychologie,* 1923, **24,** 34–45.

Stern, W. Das "Ernstpiel" der Jugendzeit. *Zeitschrift für Pädagogische Psychologie,* 1924, **25,** 241–252.

Stern, W. *Anfänge der Reifezeit: Ein Knabentagebuch in psychologischer Bearbeitung.* Leipzig: Quelle & Meyer, 1925.

Stern, W. *Psychologie der frühen Kindheit bis zum sechsten Lebensjahr* (6th ed.). Leipzig: Quelle & Meyer, 1930.

Stern, C., & Stern, W. *Die Kindersprache: Eine psychologische und sprachtheoretische Untersuchung.* Leipzig: Barth, 1907.

Stern, C., & Stern, W. *Erinnerung, Aussage und Lüge in der ersten Kindheit.* Leipzig: Barth, 1909.

Strong, E. K. *Change of interests with age.* Stanford, Calif.: Stanford University Press, 1931.

St. Ybar, I. *De un jour à dix ans: Notes d'une mère.* 1909–1910. (Cited in E. Claparède, *Psychologie de l'enfant et de pédagogie expérimentale* (4th ed.). Geneva: Kündig, 1911.)

Sully, J. *Studies in childhood.* London: Longmans, 1895.

Tagebuch eines Vaters über sein neugeborenes Kind. *Braunschweigisches Journal Philosophischen, Philologischen und Pädagogischen Inhalts,* 1789/1790, **2,** 404–441.

Taine, H. Note sur l'acquisition du langage chez les enfants et dans l'espèce humaine. *Revue Philosophique,* 1876, **1,** 3–23.

Talbot, E. *Papers on infant development.* American Sociological Science Association, 1882.

Tetens, J. N. *Philosophische Versuche über die menschliche Natur und ihre Entwicklung.* Leipzig: Weidmanns Erben und Reich, 1777.

Thomae, H. Entwicklungsbegriff und Entwicklungstheorie. In H. Thomae (Ed.), *Entwicklungspsychologie.* Göttingen: Hogrefe, 1959.

Thorndike, E. L. *Adult interests.* New York: Macmillan, 1935.

Thorndike, E. L., Bregman, E. O., Tilton, J. W., & Woodyard, E. *Adult learning.* New York: Macmillan, 1928.

Tiedemann, D. Beobachtungen über die Entwickelung der Seelenfähigkeiten bei Kindern. *Hessische Beiträge zur Gelehrsamkeit und Kunst,* 1787, **2**(2–3; whole No 6–7).

Tiedemann, D. *Handbuch der Psychologie, zum Gebrauch bei Vorlesungen und zur Selbstbelehrung.* Leipzig: Barth, 1804.

Tracy, F. *The psychology of childhood.* Boston: 1893.

Trapp, E. C. *Versuch einer Pädagogik.* Berlin: Nicolai, 1780.

Ufer, C. (Ed.), *Dietrich Tiedemanns Beobachtungen über die Entwickelung der Seelenfähigkeiten bei Kindern.* Altenburg: Bonde, 1897. (a)

Ufer, C. Kinderpsychologie. In W. Rein (Ed.), *Encyklopädisches Handbuch der Pädagogik* (Vol. 4). Langensalza: Beyer, 1897. (b)

Vermeylen, G. *Psychologie de l'enfant et de l'adolescent.* Brussels: Lamertin, 1926.

von Bracken. H. Die Altersveränderungen der geistigen Leistungsfähigkeit und der seelischen Innenwelt.. Übersichtsreferat. *Zeitschrift für Alternsforschung,* 1939, **1**, 256–266.

von Humboldt, W. *Uber die Verschiedenheit des menschlichen Sprachbaues und ihren Einfluss auf die geistige Entwicklung des Menschengeschlechts.* Berlin: Dümmler, 1836.

von Stümpell, L. A. Notizen über die geistige Entwicklung eines weiblichen Kindes während der ersten zwei Lebensjahre. In L. A. von Strümpell, *Psychologische Pädagogik.* Leipzig: Böhme, 1880.

Watson, J. B. *Behavior: An introduction to comparative psychology.* New York: Holt, 1914.

Watson, J. B. *Psychology from the standpoint of a behaviorist.* Philadelphia: Lippincott, 1919.

Watson, J. B. *Psychological care of infant and child.* New York: Norton, 1928.

Watson, J. B., & Rayner, R. Conditioned emotional reactions. *Journal of Experimental Psychology,* 1920, **3**, 1–14.

Weber, F. H. *De pulsu, resorptione, audita et tactu: Annotationes anatomicae et physiologicae.* Leipzig: Köhler, 1834.

Weiller, K. *Über die gegenwärtige und zukünftige Menschheit: Eine Skizze zur Berichtigung unserer Urteile über die Gegenwart und unsere Hoffnung für die Zukunft.* München: Lindauer, 1799.

Wellek, A. Die genetische Ganzheitspsychologie der Leipziger Schule und ihre Verzweigungen. *Neue Psychologische Studien,* 1954, **15**(3).

Weiss, E. Leistung und Lebensalter. *Industrielle Psychotechnik,* 1927, **4**, 227–245.

Werner, H. *Einführung in die Entwicklungspsychologie.* Leipzig: Barth, 1926.

Wezel, J. K. Über die Erziehungsgeschichten. *Pädagogische Unterhandlungen,* 1778, **2**, 21–43.

Wichtigkeit der Untersuchung des menschlichen Verstandes. *Berlinisches Magazin oder Gesammelte Schriften und Nachrichten für die Liebhaber der Arzneywissenschaft, Naturgeschichte und der Angenehmen Wissenschaften überhaupt,* 1767, **3**, 595 ff.

Willard, E. Observations upon an infant during its first year by a mother. In Necker de Saussure (Ed.), *Progressive education.* Boston: Ticknor, 1835.

Wohlwill, J. F. The age variable in psychological research. *Psychological Review,* 1970, **77**, 49–64.

Wohlwill, J. F. *The study of behavioral development.* New York: Academic Press, 1973.

Wundt, W. *Grundzüge der physiologischen Psychologie* (3 vols.). 1873.

Wundt, W. *Völkerpsychologie: Eine Untersuchung der Entwicklungsgesetze von Sprache, Mythos und Sitte* (Erster Band: Die Sprache). Leipzig: Engelmann, 1900.

Wundt, W. *Elemente der Völkerpsychologie: Grundlinien einer psychologischen Entwicklungsgeschichte der Menschheit.* Leipzig: Kröner, 1912.

Yerkes, R. M. (Ed.). *Psychological examining in the United States Army.* Washington, D.C.: Memoirs of the National Academy of Sciences, 1921 (No. 15).

Ziehen, T. *Das Seelenleben des Jugendlichen.* Langensalza: Beyer, 1922.

Zubeck, J. P., & Solberg, P. A. *Human development.* New York: McGraw-Hill, 1954.

Life-Span Developmental Psychology: Some Converging Observations on History and Theory

Paul B. Baltes

COLLEGE OF HUMAN DEVELOPMENT, THE PENNSYLVANIA
STATE UNIVERSITY
UNIVERSITY PARK, PENNSYLVANIA

Abstract

Observations are offered on the confluence of history, theory, and method of life-span developmental psychology. Contrary to most current beliefs, it is shown that throughout the history of developmental psychology, beginning in the late eighteenth century, a life-span approach to the study of behavioral development has been espoused repeatedly though in an insular fashion. Life-span developmental psychology stretches the boundaries of any developmental orientation because of its primary concern with long-term processes. Therefore, a life-span approach is apt to accentuate, amplify, and articulate important theoretical and methodological issues and principles beyond the level of clarity suggested in age-specific developmental specialties, such as child development or gerontology. Examples are used to illustrate the enduring significance of several theoretical and methodological themes. These themes include (a) the reformulation of the concept of development to encompass models other than only biological growth models, (b) the expansion of the substantive scope of developmental constructs, (c) the linkage of ontogenetic and biocultural change in an interactive and contextual framework, and (d) the formulation of appropriate development-specific methodologies. It is argued that life-span researchers should continue to focus on explicating the methodological and theoretical uniqueness and challenge of the developmen-

LIFE-SPAN DEVELOPMENT
AND BEHAVIOR, VOL. 2

tal orientation expressed in these themes. Continual awareness of and concern for these themes will not only increase the general impact of a life-span orientation but also promote more significant research endeavors.

I. Introduction

It is often observed that the field of life-span developmental psychology has emerged during the 1960s and 1970s. There is a tremendous outpouring of life-span work both in psychology and in neighboring disciplines, such as sociology (e.g., Brim & Wheeler, 1966; Clausen, 1972; Elder, 1975; Hill & Mattessich, this volume; Hill & Rodgers, 1964; Riley, 1976, 1978; Riley, Johnson, & Foner, 1972; Rosenmayr, 1978; Van Dusen & Sheldon, 1976). However, this recent growth of life-span research has been preceded by a lengthy historical gestation of life-span developmental ideas. The field of adult development and aging has played a pivotal role in this development, most likely because aging is easily conceptualized as an outcome of life history. Eminent psychological gerontologists, such as Pressey, Kuhlen, Havighurst, Shock, Birren, Neugarten, Riegel, and Schaie, all, at one point or another, have argued for and contributed to the advancement of life-span developmental conceptions.

The explosion of life-span work in psychology is evident in numerous types of publications. Following earlier contributions by Bayley (1963), Birren (1964), Bühler and Massarik (1968), Erikson (1959), Havighurst (1948), and Neugarten (1969), the volumes resulting from the West Virginia Conferences (e.g., Baltes & Schaie, 1973a; Datan & Ginsberg, 1975; Datan & Reese, 1977; Goulet & Baltes, 1970; Nesselroade & Reese, 1973) are illustrative and notable examples of life-span work during the last decade. There are also several handbooks on human development and aging that exhibit a life-span framework. The first was a German handbook of developmental psychology edited in 1959 by Thomae; the second was a handbook on socialization edited in 1969 by Goslin. Moreover, life-span perspectives are evident in the recently published handbooks on aging (Binstock & Shanas, 1976; Birren & Schaie, 1977) in which close to 10 chapters pay explicit tribute to a life-span conception of sociological and psychological aging. Furthermore, there are at least a dozen textbooks or readers on developmental psychology and human development claiming a life-span orientation, conception, and coverage (e.g., Baltes, Reese, & Nesselroade, 1977; Charles & Looft, 1973; Craig, 1976; CRM, 1971; Goldberg & Deutsch, 1977; Hurlock, 1959; Kaluger & Kaluger, 1974; Kuhlen & Thompson, 1963; Lugo & Hershey, 1974; Newman & Newman, 1975; Oerter, 1978; Pikunas, 1976; Pressey &

Kuhlen, 1957; Rebelsky, 1975). Finally, results from long-term longitudinal investigations covering extended periods of the life span are appearing. Research by Block (1971), Elder (1974, and this volume), the Sears' (Sears, 1977; Sears & Barbee, in press), and Schaie (this volume) are good examples of the increasing nourishment of life-span developmental psychology by solid empirical work.

A number of neglected questions need to be addressed, however. For example, is this explosion in the quantity of life-span work paralleled by an increasing insight into its historical, theoretical, and methodological foundations? To what degree is this surge of life-span thinking reflected in a change in actual empirical developmental work, data interpretation, and theoretical conception? Moreover, are there any reasons to believe that this recent outpouring is more than a short-lived fad and that we are not dealing with mere rhetoric rather than with a cogent theoretical argument and framework?

One option for addressing these questions is to present a conceptual framework for life-span developmental psychology. This would be repetitious since a number of recently published and unpublished papers aimed at this goal are available (Baltes & Schaie, 1973b; Huston-Stein & Baltes, 1976; Lerner & Ryff, 1978; Riley, 1978). However, comment on the meaning of life-span developmental psychology is relevant here for clarification: The term "life span" is not intended to imply that chronological age is the primary organizing variable for life-span developmental work. Rather, the primary focus is on developmental processes that attain their salience in a life-span or life-course context. It is important not to commit the fallacy of equating life-span developmental work with age-developmental work because this would result in an extremely limited model of life-span development. Indeed, recent discussions of life-span developmental models (e.g., Baltes & Willis, 1977, 1978; Hultsch & Plemons, this volume; Lerner & Ryff, 1978) have emphasized that a life-span orientation suggests conceptions of development which, especially in the latter part of life, go beyond the use of chronological age as an important theoretical variable. Thus, the term "life span" is not intended at all to communicate a sole concern with age change. Rather, developmental processes occurring through life are of major concern. Age changes and age-related explanations represent only one class of ontogenetic change sequences.

The primary goal of this chapter is to place the recent surgence of a life-span orientation into a historical perspective by specifying some of its theoretical and methodological underpinnings and by articulating some recurrent themes that may serve as guides in the current period of quantitative explosion in life-span work. A life-span orientation is surprisingly old in the history of developmental psychology. In fact, it will be argued that there are a number of theoretical and methodological themes which have been identified repeatedly throughout the history of life-span work. These themes may help to explicate and amplify the special role of a developmental approach to the study of behavior and to place in perspective current endeavors in life-span work.

II. Notes on the History of Life-Span Developmental Psychology

A. EARLY PRECURSORS: TETENS, CARUS, QUETELET

A number of reviews on historical facets of developmental psychology (Birren, 1961a, 1961b; Charles, 1970; Groffmann, 1970; Hofstätter, 1938; Munnichs, 1966a; Reinert, 1976; Riegel, 1977) are available. Together, they provide much insight into the origins of life-span developmental psychology. Let me, however, begin my notes on the history of life-span developmental psychology by quoting from the Preface to a textbook of developmental psychology:

> The author . . . has for many successive years conducted a course in developmental psychology. . . . With the remarkable progress in psychology during those years, two things have happened. The older volumes on genetic psychology have become inadequate. . . . The more recent volumes have been devoted to rather narrow sections of human growth, such as "preschool age," "adolescence," and "senescence." (p. *vi*)

The author continues:

> But the general student is interested in the whole career of human life, not merely in its infancy and school days. (p. *vii*)

These statements reflect the search for life-span coverage and are very representative of what many authors of current developmental psychology textbooks maintain. The fact is, however, that these quotations are 50 years old! They are found in the Preface to a forgotten, but excellent textbook by H. L. Hollingworth (1927) titled *Mental Growth and Decline: A Survey of Developmental Psychology.*

The quotations from Hollingworth (1927) illustrate an important though often overlooked historical fact. The emergence of life-span developmental psychology is seen as a recent event; this is not true. On the contrary, a life-span view of behavioral development has origins that antedate the emergence of any age-specific developmental speciality, such as child psychology. A strong life-span emphasis in the formative stages of developmental psychology is due largely to a group of European scholars.

Review articles by Hofstätter (1938), Groffmann (1970), and particularly a recent *tour de force* historical review by Reinert (1976, and this volume) have provided massive evidence. These authors have identified at least three major developmental-psychological works of the eighteenth and nineteenth centuries advocating an explicit life-span orientation toward the study of human development. These are publications by Tetens in 1777, F. A. Carus in 1808, and Quetelet in 1835 (1838 in German; 1842 in English). Indeed, a careful examination of these heralds of developmental psychology is most educational and humbling. Their works exemplify both depth and scope in theory and methodology rarely witnessed in the early stages of a field. It is unfortunate that they did not have much impact on subsequent developments.

As already suggested in 1938 by Hofstätter, Quetelet's (1842) volume, *A Treatise on Man and the Development of his Faculties,* merits particular attention because of its comprehensiveness and methodological quality. Quetelet's book is full of empirical data covering the entire life course and considering a host of demographic (birth, fecundity, mortality), physical growth (stature, weight, height, strength, swiftness, respiration), and psychological variables (crime, morality, intellectual qualities). Quetelet's theoretical conceptions are equally impressive for his joint concern for general developmental laws and the import of sociohistorical change. Last, but not least, Quetelet's nascent insights into methodological issues in the study of development are most astonishing. For example, close to 150 years ago, Quetelet, when evaluating his empirical findings, carefully enumerated a large number of problems in research design. Thus, he (Quetelet, 1842) identified the notion of critical periods (pp. 31, 57) in the life span, elaborated the effects of period-specific historical events on age functions (see also Süssmilch, 1741), suggested the need for multiple-period (rather than time-specific) data in the study of age changes (pp. 33, 97–100), touched on salient issues in measurement validity and equivalence (pp. 72–74), and drew attention to selective survival effects (pp. 62–63). In many respects, Quetelet presented not only the first comprehensive account of life-span developmental findings but also the first glimpse of many issues in developmental research methodology. Unfortunately, his contributions to developmental psychology lay dormant for more than 100 years.

B. TWENTIETH CENTURY PRECURSORS

It is beyond the scope of this manuscript (see, however, Reinert, 1976 and this volume) to elucidate why the late nineteenth century and early twentieth century did not see a continuation of this early ascendance of a life-span conception of developmental psychology developed in the works of Tetens, F. A. Carus, and Quetelet. Except for rare exceptions, the dominant focus in the study of behavioral development, both in Europe and the United States, became clearly that of child development and child psychology.

In the first decades of the twentieth century occasional contributions to an understanding of all stages of the human life-span appeared, including the establishment of the field of gerontology (Hall, 1922; see Birren, 1961a, 1961b; Riegel, 1977, for reviews of the history of gerontology). Gerontology is particularly prone to suggest a life-span conception because of its concern with life processes which lead to aging. However, with one notable exception (Sanford, 1902), it was not until the late 1920s and 1930s that a concerted effort to develop an integrative view of life-span development was again attempted. The exception is a largely unknown review article by Edmund Clark Sanford published in 1902 in the *American Journal of Psychology* with the title "Mental Growth and Decline." In this article, Sanford treats development as a continuous process from birth to death, applying this view of development to "the course of mental development from the first beginnings of mind . . . at birth . . . to old age" (p. 426).[1]

In the third and fourth decades of the 20th Century, there are three books which mark the reappearance of a life-span conception: Hollingworth (1927), Charlotte Bühler (1933), and the coauthored volume by Pressey, Janney, and Kuhlen in 1939. The 1927 text by Hollingworth, although the earliest of the three, is perhaps the least known.[2] Each of these books is inherently life-span developmental in that the authors do not simply present an accumulation of age-specific information (infancy, childhood, adolescence, etc.) but attempt to articulate life-span developmental processes. It is interesting that, although these three books were published within a dozen years of each other, they exhibit more or less complete independence in citation and practically no reference to their 19th Century precursors (Charlotte Bühler makes a reference to F. A.

[1]A quote from Browning is often used in gerontological writings to communicate an optimistic view of behavior change in aging and the need for a life-span conception of aging: Browning makes Rabbi Ben Ezra say: "Grow old along with me! The best is yet to be, The last of life, for which the first was made." Sanford (1902, p. 448) appears to be the first to have used Browning's quote.

[2]There is one additional monograph published in 1928 by E. L. Thorndike and his colleagues, on *Adult Learning* (Thorndike, Bregman, Tilton, & Woodyard, 1928), which has distinct life-span features. This monograph, however, is less developmental than general–experimental in that it focuses on ontogenetic differences in learning rather than on the description and explanation of development via learning or learning histories.

Carus in a footnote). This is particularly surprising in the case of the Pressey *et al.* book which did not acknowledge the 1927 American text by Hollingworth while acknowledging Charlotte Bühler's 1933 German work.

In any case, each of these books is unique and quite remarkable in conception and in-depth treatment of life-span developmental events and processes. Similar to Quetelet's early 1835 work, the Hollingworth (1927) and Pressey, Janney, and Kuhlen (1939) books especially present a basic conception of human development that is empirical, process oriented, multidimensional, multidirectional, contextual, and clearly cognizant of the impact of social change and ecological contingencies. For example, Hollingworth (1927, p. 326) presents a chart that summarizes the complexity of life-span development in a format which is standing the test of modern times. Furthermore, Pressey's and his co-workers' rich exposition of the macro- and microlevel "conditions and circumstances of life," embeddedness of human development in a changing culture, and conern with the real-life behaviors represent a powerful forerunner of what is now termed an ecological (Bronfenbrenner, 1977), dialectical (Riegel, 1976a, 1976b), and external-validity (Hultsch & Hickey, 1977) orientation. Pressey and his co-workers' empirical data may lack precision. However, their basic theoretical orientation is amazingly similar to what the current trends in developmental psychology appear to be: a movement toward models of development which are nonpersonological, contextualistic, and multilinear.

The fact that practically all the historical marker publications dealing with a life-span orientation (Hollingworth, Pressey *et al.*, Quetelet) present a very explicit concern with what are now seen as contemporary trends (e.g., contextualism, social-evolutionary change, and development-specific methodology) is a noteworthy situation in my view. This is especially remarkable because the cross-references in these works are so few. It indicates that the involvement of current life-span researchers in such themes as cohort effects, social change, and other macro-level features might be intrinsic to a life-span orientation rather than a reflection of the personal interest of the individual researchers. In fact, it is this hitherto unrecognized historical continuity in ideas and issues which is the focus of the remainder of this chapter.

III. Recurrent Themes in Life-Span Developmental Theory

What are some of the current themes in life-span developmental theory and research that exhibit historical continuity? Moreover, what are some of the reasons why I judge the recurrence of these themes to be significant for an evaluation of their theoretical power? Four themes are discussed as illustrative examples.

It will become evident that each of the themes covered has achieved a high degree of articulation and resolution primarily because studying human development from a life-span perspective stretches the conceptual boundaries of the developmental approach (Baltes & Schaie, 1973b; Huston-Stein & Baltes, 1976). Life-span processes extend over long time periods, involve explanatory mechanisms requiring an explicit concern for distal and cumulative causation (historical paradigms), and accentuate the continuity–discontinuity dimension for both the description and explanation of behavior. These extreme conditions of life-span research are apt to exemplify and magnify the basic rationale and foundation of developmental psychology.

A. REFORMULATING THE CONCEPT OF DEVELOPMENT

Most of the publications aimed at identifying the key features of life-span developmental research (e.g., Baltes & Schaie, 1973b; Bayley, 1963; Brim & Wheeler, 1966; Elder, 1975; Huston-Stein & Baltes, 1976; Labouvie-Vief & Chandler, 1978; Lerner & Ryff, 1978; Neugarten, 1969; Schaie & Willis, 1978, in press; Thomae, this volume) emphasize that the traditional concept of development needs expansion or modification when applied to life-span change. Typically, it is argued that the developmental "growth" concept borrowed from biology, while useful for some purposes, has some features that are inappropriate or too restrictive for the study of ontogenetic change in a life-span framework. Most historical forerunners, with the exception of Charlotte Bühler, rejected implicitly the application of simple biological growth models as good representations of life-span change. This is particularly true for Quetelet (1835), Hollingworth (1927), and Pressey *et al.* (1939).

1. Definition of Development

Let me illustrate this argument in greater detail. Traditionally, conceptions of developmental change (e.g., Harris, 1957; Lerner, 1976; Wohlwill, 1973) have focused on a definition of development as behavioral change manifesting characteristics of: (a) sequentiality, (b) unidirectionality, (c) an end state, (d) irreversibility, (e) qualitative–structural transformation, and (f) universality. This definitional position has much conceptual strength and good support from biological approaches to child development, especially maturational–personological ones.[3] Research on life-span development in a variety of areas, most notably cognitive and social development, however, has resulted in the conclusion that such a conception of development is unduly restrictive (Baltes & Willis, 1977, 1978).

During the recent decades in the United States, dissatisfaction with the aforementioned definition of development was probably first expressed in Havighurst's (1948) concept of developmental tasks and the contention of several gerontologists (see also Benedict, 1938; Birren, 1964; Neugarten, 1969) that there is much discontinuity between child development and the remainder of the life span. Similarly, in the extensive German literature on life-span development after World War II (for reviews, see Löwe, 1977; Thomae, 1959, and this volume), it has been consistently argued that "one-factor" (biological) and unidimensional (growth–decline) conceptions of life-span development are inappropriate. On the contrary, German writers have espoused a position that includes multidimensionality, multidirectionality, and discontinuity as key features of any theory of human development through the life span.

Figures 1A and B are taken from Baltes and Willis, 1978. They illustrate such a view of development that is more complex than those represented in simple cumulative and unidirectional conceptions. Figure 1A (upper part) depicts the notion that interindividual variability in behavior increases as life-span change evolves.[4] Furthermore, the lower part of Figure 1A suggests that life-span changes can be rather diverse in nature: Multidimensionality and multidirectionality of behavior-change processes are frequent outcomes.

Figure 1B further portrays the complexity of life-span development. Besides the notions of large interindividual differences, multidimensional-

---

[3]Child development as a field represents a rather diversified set of approaches, some of which (e.g., social learning) do not follow the biological growth-oriented perspective to the degree described in this section. Therefore, it needs to be recognized that the present discussion, for heuristic purposes, is an oversimplification. The implication is that the requirements outlined for appropriate life-span models of development are similar more to some than to other models of child development. For instance, a cognitive structural model of development (Piaget, etc.) represents an extreme point of contrast. A similar note of caution applies to the discussion of biological growth models. The intent here is not to summarily classify all developmental biologists as advocates of a simple maturational–personological growth model. This would be inappropriate (Lerner, 1976). However, it is maintained that this conception historically has been extremely influential.

[4]Although the evidence is less clear, it may be possible to argue that an age-correlated increase in interindividual differences is paralled by an age-correlated decrease in intraindividual variability (plasticity). The author intends to examine this proposition in future writings.

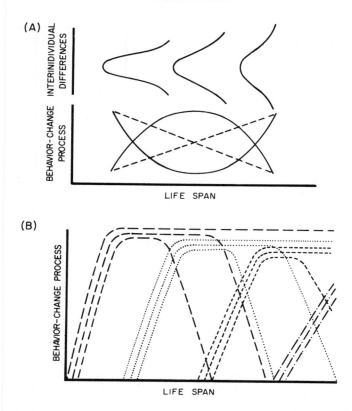

Fig. 1. Selective examples of life-span developmental processes: Figure 1A illustrates multidimensionality, multidirectionality, and age-correlated increases in interindividual variability. Figure 1B summarizes notions of life-course grading and discontinuity. Developmental functions (behavior-change processes) differ in terms of onset, duration, and termination when charted in the framework of the life course; moreover, they involve both quantitative and qualitative aspects of change (see also Baltes, Cornelius, & Nesselroade, 1979, in press). (From Baltes & Willis, 1978).

ity, and multidirectionality (Figure 1A), possible discontinuity due to life-course grading (Neugarten, 1969) is graphically shown in Figure 1B. Behavior-change processes in life-span development do not always extend across the entire life span nor are they always outcomes of continuous influences and processes. Thus, behavior-change processes can differ in terms of onset, duration, and termination when charted in the framework of the life course. Moreover, as illustrated in Havighurst's (1948) formulation of developmental tasks, novel behavior-change processes can emerge at many points in the life span, including old age.

Among current research, the area of intellectual functioning is perhaps the best example to support the views on development expressed in Figure 1. Here, a number of researchers (e.g., Baltes & Schaie, 1976; Baltes & Willis, 1978; Labouvie-Vief & Chandler, 1978; Riegel, 1973b) have argued that life-span intellectual development is less a unidirectional continuation of childhood intelligence with universal sequences, than that it evidences features of multilinearity, multidimensionality, large interindividual differences, and much contextual plasticity. Evidence on cohort effects, differential change functions for distinct dimensions of intelligence, and sensitivity to intervention programs in the elderly support, in concert, such a conclusion.

As researchers consider development after childhood, then, there is a need for a conception of development which includes the traditional growth-oriented views of development as one important but special class of developmental phenomena. A more comprehensive taxonomy of developmental-change models is needed to permit us to go beyond the restrictive constraints specified by our early colleagues in biology and so eagerly embraced by many child developmentalists. For the most part, we do not yet have a good grasp of what the salient behavior dimensions for life-span developmental models are. However, it appears that restricting developmental events to those which have the features of a biological growth concept of development is more of a hindrance than a help.

2. Explanation of Development

This expansion or modification of a monolithic concept of development is important not only in answering the descriptive question: What does development look like? It also applies to its explanatory counterpart: Where does development come from? Again, Quetelet, already in 1835, and surely Pressey *et al.* in 1939, adopted a multicausal position and enumerated a large list of potential determinants of life-span change. Only some of the determinants, moreover, are usefully related to simple cumulative age-associated factors and mechanisms. Similarly, they espoused interactive–contextual rather than personological modes of explanation.

In the current scene, similar expansive views in regard to developmental explanations can be noted. For example, Hultsch and Plemons (this volume) have reviewed the concept of "significant life events" as an organizing explanatory principle for adult-developmental change; Bengtson and Black (1973) and Riley (1976) have used structural features of intergenerational and age–cohort relations as explanatory principles for ontogenetic change; and Reese (1976) and Kohlberg (1973) have argued that in the areas of memory and moral judgment, respectively, explanatory discontinuity is predominant. Different modes of developmental explanation (e.g., mechanistic versus organismic and maturational versus environmental) become attractive to account for developmental changes at different segments of the life span. As a final example, Labouvie-Vief's (1977) review of cognitive development through the life span emphasized the need for alternative conceptions of intelligence that would include multilinear and contextual explanatory features rather than only the traditional models that have emphasized simple cumulative explanations based on invariant mechanisms.

Figure 2, modified from Baltes, Cornelius, and Nesselroade (1979, in press; see also Baltes & Willis, 1978), summarizes a multicausal view that appears to be necessary to account for the complexity of life-span development. The scheme outlined in Fig. 2 postulates three major sets of antecedent factors influencing individual development: normative age-graded, normative history-graded, and non-normative life events. The three sets of influences interact in the production of developmental change processes. The scheme outlined does not represent a theory of development. It is a heuristic device aimed at generating a new set of coordinated questions about the causes of life-span development.

Normative age-graded influences refer to biological and environmental determinants exhibiting a high correlation with chronological age. They are the ones usually considered in traditional developmental psychology. Examples of such age-graded influences include biological maturation and socialization when it is viewed as consisting of the acquisition of a series of normative age-correlated roles or competencies.

Normative history-graded influences consist of fairly general events or event patterns experienced by a given cultural unit in connection with

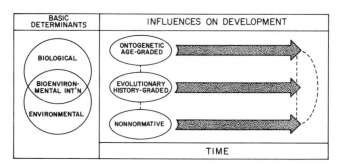

Fig. 2. Three systems of influences regulate the nature of life-span development: ontogenetic (age-graded), evolutionary (history-graded), and non-normative. Further explanation of the figure is contained in Baltes, Cornelius, and Nesselroade (1979, in press) and Baltes and Willis (1978). (Modified from Baltes *et al.*, 1979, in press.)

biosocial change, for example, as evidenced by cohort effects (Baltes, Cornelius, & Nesselroade, 1978). As was true for normative age-graded influences, history-graded influences can involve both environmental and biological characteristics. Such biosocial change effects vary with historical time and can produce unique cohort-related constellations of influences (Elder, this volume; Riley, 1976).

Nonnormative influences on life-span development, finally, refer to environmental and biological determinants which, while significant in their effect on individual life histories, are not general. They do not occur for everyone or necessarily in easily discernible and invariant sequences or patterns. Events and event patterns related to occupational careers (unemployment), family life (divorce, death of a significant other), or health (serious sickness) are examples.

Figure 2 suggests that these three sets of influences interact with each other. The arrows to the right also indicate that they accumulate in their effects and may change over time. It is also important to recognize that there is a convergence between the complexity of life-span development depicted in Fig. 1 and the multicausal system of influences postulated in Fig. 2. This results because diversity and discontinuity in influences (in terms of content, sequencing, duration, patterning, etc.) are prerequisites for diversity in developmental outcomes.

Furthermore, it might be useful to speculate about the relative significance of age-graded, history-graded, and nonnormative influences on development at varying points in the life span or on a given behavior-change process. For instance, one could hypothesize that age-graded influences are primarily important in child development and perhaps in advanced aging, whereas history-graded and nonnormative influences become the dominant influence systems in early and middle adulthood. Such a *differential life profile* of the relative magnitude of the influence systems would explain why much work in child development has been focused on age-graded influences, whereas the reverse has been true for recent work in adult development (see also Hultsch & Plemons, this volume).

In short, a biological growth concept of development, predominant in the early stages of the field, is being recognized increasingly as a special case, or subclass of a larger class of developmental phenomena. Moreover, in accord with the basic position espoused by historical proponents of a life-span approach, simple personological and cumulative forms of description and explanation are judged to be of restricted value. While the trend toward complex, multilinear, and multivariate models of development is likely to be useful, it is necessary to be aware, however, of potential dangers that may result from overgeneralizing this trend. For example, it would be unwise to let this expansion of the concept of development evolve into a total lack of specificity, i.e., of equating any behavioral change with developmental change. Indeed, it will be important to specify some minimum definitional criteria or boundaries so that the uniqueness of a developmental orientation is not lost in toto.

B. EXPANDING THE SCOPE OF DEVELOPMENTAL CONSTRUCTS

The expansion of the concept of development is paralleled by an expansion in substantive developmental constructs. A life-span approach is apt to draw attention to new classes of developmental behavior. Again, historical forerunners, such as Quetelet (1835) and Pressey *et al.* (1939), had already proposed a much larger array of substantive areas to be the province of developmental psychology than is evidenced in the territory claimed by contemporary standard textbooks. In Pressey's and his co-workers' 1939 text, for example, such areas as work, occupation, leisure, and family life were given much more prominent consideration than a topical review of developmental psychology (especially of the child developmental ilk) of recent decades would indicate.

The expansion of classes of developmental behavior suggested by life-span research follows in principle two directions. One is to expand a specific construct to include life-span perspectives; the other is to delineate classes of behavior that workers in age-specific fields, such as child development, would easily overlook.

Let me use attachment as an example of the first strategy, where the expansion in scope of a construct is likely to occur when conceptualized in a life-span framework. As discussed recently by Lerner and Ryff (1978; see also Hartup & Lempers, 1973), attachment behaviors do not occur only in early life in the context of parent–child relations, but attachments may be developed at many occasions in the life span, such as in the formation and transformation of adolescent and adult friendships; occupational settings; family systems such as marriage, divorce, or remarriage; and the death of spouses and friends. As soon as the life-span nature of attachments is recognized, it becomes apparent that the methodology and theory of attachment needs expansion in descriptive and explanatory scope. Moreover, a life-span perspective of attachment makes it apparent that studying the acquisition of attachments is only one significant feature. Attachment behaviors are likely to undergo many subsequent transformations involving not only acquisition but aspects of maintenance, dissolution, and transfer. Similar expansive perspectives may be applied to other constructs such as achievement motivation, love, self-concept, or the development of life ideologies. In the case of achievement motivation, for example, it has been suggested that the traditional focus on childhood acquisition needs to be supplemented by midlife behavior-change studies aimed at clarifying the maintenance (or extinction) of achievement motivation and its transformation into alternative behavior constructs required for successful life adjustment during adulthood.

The second strategy of identifying novel developmental classes of behavior suggested by a life-span perspective is most easily evident in classical research on the nature of life biographies or life histories (Bühler, 1933; Dollard, 1949), but also in examples from research in adult development and aging. In life-history research, Elder (1977, and this volume) has provided recently a comprehensive and insightful review of the need for temporal constructs aimed at delineating the social course of lives. This strategy of identifying novel classes of behavior is also illustrated by some research in adult development and aging. Work by Clayton (1975) on wisdom; Munnichs (1966b) and Marshall (1975) on finitude; Bortner and Hultsch (1974) on time perspective; Brim (1975) on the sense of personal control over one's life; Neugarten, Havighurst, Fiske, and Chiriboga on life styles (Neugarten, 1964; Lowenthal *et al.* 1975); or Bengtson and Black (1973) on generational relations are all examples where somewhat new classes of developmental behavior have been identified. In a simple age-specific approach, particularly when oriented toward childhood, one would easily overlook such constructs. These constructs acquire immediate saliency, however, when a life-span perspective is adopted as a guiding principle.

C. LINKING ONTOGENETIC AND BIOCULTURAL CHANGE

Another theme emerging both from a historical review and the current scene is that individuals change in a changing biocultural context. Research on cohort effects and intergenerational relations are examples. This theme implies that the study of development must deal with at least two streams of interactive changing systens: the individual and society broadly defined, or ontogeny and biocultural evolution (e.g., Baltes, 1968; Baltes, Cornelius, & Nesselroade, 1978; Elder, 1975; Neugarten & Datan, 1973; Riegel, 1976a, 1976b; Riley, 1976; Schaie, 1965, this volume; Van Dusen & Sheldon, 1976). The focus on age-graded and history-graded influences in Fig. 2 already has indicated a concern with linking individual and biosocial change. Again, it is the extreme conditions of a life-span developmental perspective that accentuate this theme. When long-term processes are the focal concern, the assumption of an invariant biocultural or ecological context is not generally a fruitful one.

The role of historical change in the study of individual development can take several forms and may vary according to conceptual beliefs in a given research area. Baltes, Cornelius, and Nesselroade (1978), for example, suggest four distinct conceptual treatments of cohort effects on behavioral development. They argue that the cohort variable or cohort variance can be seen as (a) error, (b) momentary disturbance, (c) a dimension of quantitative generalization, or (d) a theoretical process variable similar to a process view of chronological age. None of these strategies is true or false. A life-span approach, however, because of its extension in both individual and historical time (Neugarten & Datan, 1973), makes it less likely that a history-irrelevant or error-type approach would be a viable option (see also Elder, this volume).

It is again impressive to see how our historical forerunners have forcefully tackled this issue. Quetelet in 1835, for example, discussed extensively the roles of evolutionary change and historical periods as modifiers of specific age-developmental functions. Similarly, he provided a lengthy discussion of conditions under which it would be possible to discern in a changing world what he called "general developmental laws." General developmental laws, as defined by Quetelet (1835), transcend the perturbations created by period-specific effects. Quetelet's view on general developmental laws, incidentally, is similar to Wohlwill's (1973) conceptualization of developmental functions.

The same is true for Quetelet's successors in the history of life-span developmental psychology. Thus, Hollingworth (1927, p. 34) is apparently the first American to have examined intensively the relative advantages of cross-sectional and longitudinal methods. Moreover, he does this in the context of two types of change: individual and societal–institutional. Furthermore, the issue of historical–cultural change is paramount in the 1939 textbook of Pressey, Janney, and Kuhlen. They devote considerable attention to an elaboration of the effects of the changing conditions of a molar cultural context on the nature of human development through the life span. Thus, it is not surprising that R. B. Kuhlen (1940, 1963) wrote in 1940 the perhaps classical historical paper on cohort effects and, thereby, antedated in principle the work of many present investigators.

In short, there is an impressive continuity evident in life-span writings on the relationship between individual and biocultural change. An understanding of current discussions about the meaning and import of cohort effects is greatly aided by a historical perspective. For example, it helps to separate important arguments regarding developmental theory from relatively trivial questions concerning the empirical magnitude of cohort effects (Horn & Donaldson, 1976). Paraphrasing Anastasi's (1958) classical paper on the nature–nurture issue, the central question is not "How much cohort variance?'' but rather "*How* do historical and ontogenetic factors interact in codetermining individual development?''

D. ADVANCING DEVELOPMENT-ADEQUATE METHODOLOGY

The fourth theme in the history as well as the current scenario of life-span developmental psychology deals with the need for methodologies that are specifically designed for the analysis of ontogenetic change.

As an illustration, Hayne Reese, John Nesselroade, and the author (Baltes, Reese, & Nesselroade, 1977) recently have attempted to summarize development-specific research methods. The general conclusion (see also Nesselroade & Baltes, 1979; Petermann, 1978; Rudinger, 1978) was that many of the methods produced by general psychology in its methodological arsenal are ill suited to the study of developmental change. In fact, existing methods often result in a situation where the phenomenon of development is either ruled out on an a priori methodological basis or only captured in an inadequate manner due to a lack of development-sensitive methodology. This situation has resulted because the traditional focus in psychological research methodology has been oriented toward such features as optimal prediction (rather than representation of change), stability (rather than change), and interindividual differences (rather than patterns of intraindividual change).

Again, because of the radicalism in the developmental formulation of a life-span approach, this perspective highlights the inappropriateness of existing methodologies. For example, if one acknowledges that change is pervasive, that individuals live in a changing biocultural context, that the explanation of long-term processes is apt to involve complex historical paradigms, and that long-term processes are likely candidates for explanatory discontinuity rather than simple cumulative causal explanations, then the search for new methodologies becomes a critical task. The need for new development-specific methodologies is amplified to such a degree by life-span thinking that it cannot be avoided.

In our historical review an immediate concern for development-specific methodologies was expressed by practically all our precursors. From Quetelet in 1835, to Hollingworth in 1927, to Pressey, Janney, and Kuhlen in 1939, there have been repeated efforts to discuss methodological issues in the study of development and to formulate appropriate methodologies. Quetelet's (1842) concerns, noted earlier, with critical periods in the life span (pp. 31, 57), selective survival (pp. 62–63), measurement equivalence (pp. 72–74), and the impact of social change and specific historical moments on age functions (pp. 33, 97–100) exemplify this immediate interest in development-specific methodologies. Likewise, as alluded to earlier, Hollingworth, Pressey, and Kuhlen, all devoted considerable attention to development-specific methodology, as did Charlotte Bühler (1933), who proposed the use of life biographies as a major tool of developmental analysis.

Thus, it is not surprising that the search for development-appropriate methodology continues among current researchers with life-span interests. For instance, in addition to methodological discussions on cohort-sequential methodology, there are efforts by life-span oriented researchers to advance models aimed at assessing developmental changes in measurement validity (Schaie, 1978), consider external validity as a research dimension not only as equal in significance to internal validity but also as a contextual component intrinsic to any developmental explanation (Hultsch & Hickey, 1978), and to advance the use of structural equation models in identifying long-term causal chains (Kohn & Schooler, 1977; Labouvie, 1974; Rogosa, 1979). In my judgment, there is a logic to life-span thinking in each of these cases which pushes the formulation of development-specific methodology beyond a level of articulation that is likely to be accomplished by any age-specific developmental specialty, such as child development or gerontology. In other words, the fact that many life-span researchers are interested in theoretical and methodological issues is not accidental. Rather, it reflects the stimulation resulting from the conceptual extremities inherent in life-span conceptions. Moreover, the conceptual extremity required by life-span questions requires the formulation of new methodologies that will likely advance the state of developmental design generally.

IV.   Conclusions

All these examples from the history and current state of life-span developmental psychology illustrate two features. First, a life-span approach is attracting an increasingly large audience and, therefore, is in a critical stage of testing its limits and honest potential. Second, my suggestion is that the strong continuity of historical themes expressed in life-span work will be helpful for guiding future research. Thus, these themes may help us to see the forest for the trees as Schaie and Baltes (1977), for example, have argued in the area of intellectual development. This emphasis will also increase the likelihood that life-span researchers will be able to offer something unique to colleagues in the behavioral and social sciences. Moreover, the conceptual challenges provided by the historical themes identified in life-span work emphasize and highlight what classical developmental psychology is all about. That is, the foundation, basic paradigms, and potential weaknesses of a developmental approach only become easier to grasp when placed in the amplifying context of a life-span framework.

At the same time, the history of life-span thinking has emphasized the need for close interaction between theory and methodology as reflected in the importance of ideas, such as the ones presented here, that have survived the test of history. Twentieth Century developmental psychology in the United States has been in danger of forgetting its conceptual uniqueness or "challenges," as McCall (1977) so aptly expressed it in a recent issue of *Child Development*. In the often expedient experimental study of individual age differences rather than individual change and developmental processes, much of the unique and historical foundation of developmental research is easily neglected. Therefore, what is impressive in this historical excursion is the clear recognition that not much is gained by taking shortcuts when attempting to describe and explain behavioral development. Insufficient data bases, expediently collected with little use of developmental methodology and little concern for salience in a life-span framework, can quickly lead to an explosion of data. At the same time, however, such research fades away quickly with little lasting impact.

The basic ideas about what it means to study development and how a particular developmental event is embedded in a larger context of life-span development have a long tradition. These ideas have survived more or less unperturbed and still await the true developmental scholars who mean what they say. In this sense, if we trust my collection of historical observations, a life-span approach, because of its apparent concern with the extreme boundaries of a developmental approach, helps to keep us honest as developmental psychologists and, thereby, functions as a conceptual guide for the importance of ideas. Studying development from a life-span perspective makes it difficult to forget the paradigmatic basics and larger context of developmental psychology and to succumb to the selection of an expedient course of action rather than what is "right" or potentially useful in the long run.

Let me conclude these observations on the history and theory of life-span developmental psychology by citing a passage from the Preface to Solzhenitsyn's (1973) *Gulag Archipelago*. Solzhenitsyn quotes a Russian proverb that nicely illustrates the dilemma and danger developmentalists face when choosing between the "right" but tedious developmental–historical approach and the expedient, nondevelopmental shortcut. He says: "Dwell on the past and you will lose one eye. . . . Forget the past and you'll lose both eyes'' (Solzhenitsyn, 1973, p. *x*). Such appears our future in the study of development and aging. On the one hand, if we commit ourselves to a life-span orientation, it will promote the application of proper developmental paradigms and more complex models of development. However, this conceptual virtue will be at the expense of procedural simplicity. On the other hand, if we choose one of the many shortcuts, we may be productive for the moment and thereby own more of the present but less of the future.

Acknowledgments

This contribution is based on a Division 20 (Adult Development and Aging) Presidential Address delivered at the 1977 Annual Convention of the American Psychological Association, San Francisco, August, 1977. It is dedicated to the late Klaus F. Riegel.

I would also like to acknowledge with gratitude many helpful comments on an earlier draft of this manuscript by Orville G. Brim, Jr., Steven W. Cornelius, Glen H. Elder, Jr., Marjorie Lachman, Richard M. Lerner, Vincent Morello, John R. Nesselroade, Matilda W. Riley, and Carol D. Ryff. One anonymous reviewer has also been helpful in producing a better manuscript.

References

Anastasi, A. Heredity, environment, and the question ''How.'' *Psychological Review,* 1958, **65,** 197–208.

Baltes, P. B. Longitudinal and cross-sectional sequences in the study of age and generation effects. *Human Development,* 1968, **11,** 145–171.

Baltes, P. B., Cornelius, S. W., & Nesselroade, J. R. Cohort effects in behavioral development: Theoretical and methodological perspectives. In W. A. Collins (Ed.), *Minnesota symposium on child psychology* (Vol. 11). Hillsdale, N.J.: Erlbaum, 1978.

Baltes, P. B., Cornelius, S. W., & Nesselroade, J. R. Cohort effects in developmental psychology. In J. R. Nesselroade & P. B. Baltes (Eds.), *Longitudinal research in the behavioral sciences: Design and analysis.* New York: Academic Press, 1979, in press.

Baltes, P. B., Reese, H. W., & Nesselroade, J. R. *Life-span developmental psychology: Introduction to research methods.* Monterey: Brooks/Cole, 1977.

Baltes, P. B., & Schaie, K. W. (Eds). *Life-span developmental psychology: Personality and socialization.* New York: Academic Press, 1973. (a)

Baltes, P. B., & Schaie, K. W. On life-span developmental research paradigms: Retrospects and prospects. In P. B. Baltes & K. W. Schaie (Eds.), *Life-span developmental psychology: Personality and socialization.* New York: Academic Press, 1973. (b)

Baltes, P. B., & Schaie, K. W. On the plasticity of intelligence in adulthood and old age: Where Horn and Donaldson fail. *American Psychologist,* 1976, **31,** 720–725.

Baltes, P. B., & Willis, S. L. Toward psychological theories of aging and development. In J. E. Birren & K. W. Schaie (Eds.), *Handbook of the psychology of aging.* New York: Van Nostrand-Reinhold, 1977.

Baltes, P. B., & Willis, S. L. Life-span developmental psychology, cognition, and social policy. In M. W. Riley (Ed.), *Aging from birth to death.* Washington, D.C.: American Association for the Advancement of Science, 1978.

Bayley, N. The life-span as a frame of reference in psychological research. *Vita Humana,* 1963, **6**, 125–139.

Benedict, R. Continuities and discontinuities in cultural conditioning. *Psychiatry,* 1938, **1**, 161–167.

Bengtson, V. L., & Black, K. D. Intergenerational relations in socialization. In P. B. Baltes & K. W. Schaie (Eds.), *Life-span developmental psychology: Personality and socialization.* New York: Academic Press, 1973.

Binstock, R., & E. Shanas (Eds.). *Handbook of aging and the social sciences.* New York: Van Nostrand-Reinhold, 1976.

Birren, J. E. A brief history of the psychology of aging. Part I. *Gerontologist,* 1961, **1**, 69–77. (a)

Birren, J. E. A brief history of the psychology of aging. Part II. *Gerontologist,* 1961, **1**, 127–134. (b)

Birren, J. E. (Ed.). *Relations of development and aging.* Springfield: Thomas, 1964.

Birren, J. E., & Schaie, K. W. (Eds.). *Handbook of the psychology of aging.* New York: Van Nostrand-Reinhold, 1977.

Block, J. *Lives through time.* Berkeley: Brancroft Books, 1971.

Bortner, R. W., & Hultsch, D. F. Patterns of subjective deprivation in adulthood. *Developmental Psychology,* 1974, **10**, 534–545.

Brim, O. G., Jr. *The sense of personal control over one's life.* Invited address to Divisions 7 & 8 at the 82nd Annual Convention of the American Psychological Association, New Orleans, September, 1974.

Brim, O. G., Jr. Theories of the male mid-life crisis. *Counseling Psychologist,* 1976, **6**, 2–9. (a)

Brim, O. G., Jr. Life–span development of the theory of oneself: Implications for child development. In H. W. Reese (Ed.), *Advances in child development and behavior* (Vol. 11). New York: Academic Press, 1976. (b)

Brim, O. G., Jr., & Wheeler, S. *Socialization after childhood: Two essays.* New York: John Wiley, 1966.

Bronfenbrenner, U. Toward an experimental ecology of human development. *American Psychologist,* 1977, **32**, 513–531.

Bühler, C. *Der menschliche Lebenslauf als psychologisches Problem.* Leipzig: Hirzel, 1933.

Bühler, C., & Massarik, F. (Eds.). *The course of human life.* New York: Springer, 1968.

Carus, F. A. *Psychologie. Zweiter Theil: Specialpsychologie.* Leipzig: Barth & Kummer, 1808.

Charles, D. C. Historical antecedents of life-span developmental psychology. In L. R. Goulet & P. B. Baltes (Eds.), *Life-span developmental psychology: Research and theory.* New York: Academic Press, 1970.

Charles, D. C., & Looft, W. R. (Eds.). *Readings in psychological development through life.* New York: Holt, Rinehart & Winston, 1973.

Clausen, J. A. The life course of individuals. In M. W. Riley, et al. (Eds.), *A sociology of age stratification.* New York: Russell Sage Foundation, 1972.

Clayton, V. *Wise old men—where have they all gone?* Unpublished manuscript, Gerontology Center, University of Southern California, 1975.

Communications Research Machines (Ed.). *Developmental psychology today.* Del Mar, Calif.: Communications Research Machines, 1971.

Craig, G. J. *Human development.* New York: Prentice-Hall, 1976.

Datan, N., & Ginsberg, L. H. (Eds.). *Life-span developmental psychology: Normative life crises.* New York: Academic Press, 1975.

Datan, N., & Reese, H. W. (Eds.). *Life-span developmental psychology: Dialectical perspectives on experimental research.* New York: Academic Press, 1977.

Dollard, J. *Criteria for the life history.* New York: Peter Smith, 1949.

Elder, G. H., Jr. *Children of the great depression.* Chicago: University of Chicago Press, 1974.

Elder, G. H., Jr. Age-differentiation in life course perspective. *Annual Review of Sociology,* 1975, **1,** 165–190.

Elder, G. H., Jr. Family history and the life course. *Journal of Family History,* 1977, **2,** in press.

Elder, G. H. Historical change in life patterns and personality. In P. B. Baltes & O. G. Brim, Jr. (Eds.), *Life-span development and behavior* (Vol. 2). New York: Academic Press, 1979.

Erikson, E. H. Identity and the life cycle: Selected papers. *Psychological Issues,* 1959, **1,** 50–100.

Gergen, K. J. Stability, change, and chance in understanding human development. In N. Datan & H. W. Reese (Eds.), *Life-span developmental psychology: Dialectical perspectives on experimental research.* New York: Academic Press, 1977.

Goldberg, S. R., & Deutsch, F. *Life-span individual and family development.* Monterey, CA: Brooks/Cole, 1977.

Goslin, D. A. (Ed.). *Handbook of socialization theory and research.* Chicago: Rand McNally, 1969.

Goulet, L. R., & Baltes, P. B. (Eds.). *Life-span developmental psychology: Research and theory.* New York: Academic Press, 1970.

Groffmann, K. J. Life-span developmental psychology in Europe. In L. R. Goulet & P. B. Baltes (Eds.), *Life-span developmental psychology: Research and theory.* New York: Academic Press, 1970.

Hall, G. S. *Senescence: The last half of life.* New York: Appleton, 1922.

Harris, D. B. Problems in formulating a scientific concept of development. In D. B. Harris (Ed.), *The concept of development.* Minneapolis: University of Minnesota Press, 1957.

Hartup, W. W., & Lempers, J. A problem in life-span development: The interactional analysis of family attachments. In P. B. Baltes & K. W. Schaie (Eds.), *Life-span developmental psychology: Personality and socialization.* New York: Academic Press, 1973.

Havighurst, R. J. *Developmental tasks and education.* New York: David McKay, 1948.

Hill, R., & Mattessich, P. Family development theory and life-span development. In P. B. Baltes & O. G. Brim, Jr. (Eds.), *Life-span development and behavior* (Vol. 2). New York: Academic Press, 1979.

Hill, R., & Rodgers, R. H. The developmental approach. In H. T. Christiansen (Ed.), *Handbook of marriage and the family.* Chicago: Rand McNally, 1964.

Hofstätter, P. R. Tatsachen und Probleme einer Psychologie des Lebenslaufes. *Zeitschrift für Angewandte Psychologie,* 1938, **53,** 273–333.

Hollingworth, H. L. *Mental growth and decline: A survey of developmental psychology.* New York: Appleton, 1927.

Horn, J. L., & Donaldson, G. On the myth of intellectual decline in adulthood. *American Psychologist,* 1976, **31,** 701–719.

Hultsch, D. F., & Hickey, T. External validity in the study of human development: A dialectical perspective. *Human Development,* 1978, **21,** 76–91.

Hultsch, D. F., & Plemons, J. K. Life events and life-span development. In P. B. Baltes & O. G. Brim, Jr. (Eds.), *Life-span development and behavior* (Vol. 2). New York: Academic Press, 1979.

Hurlock, E. G. *Developmental psychology.* New York: McGraw-Hill, 1959.

Huston-Stein, A., & Baltes, P. B. Theory and method in life-span developmental psychology: Implications for child development. In H. W. Reese (Ed.), *Advances in child development and behavior* (Vol. 11). New York: Academic Press, 1976.

Kaluger, G., & Kaluger, M. F. *Human development: The span of life.* St. Louis: Mosby, 1974.

Kohlberg, L. Continuities in childhood and adult moral development revisited. In P. B. Baltes & K. W. Schaie (Eds.), *Life-span developmental psychology: Personality and socialization.* New York: Academic Press, 1973.

Kohn, M. S., & Schooler, C. *The reciprocal effects of the substantive complexity of work and intellectual flexibility: A longitudinal assessment.* Unpublished manuscript, National Institute of Mental Health, Washington, D.C., 1977.

Kuhlen, R. G. Social change: A neglected factor in psychological studies of the life span. *School and Society,* 1940, **52,** 14–16.

Kuhlen, R. G. Age and intelligence: The significance of cultural change in longitudinal vs. cross-sectional findings. *Vita Humana,* 1963, **6,** 113–124.

Kuhlen, R. G., & Thompson, G. G. (Eds.). *Psychological studies of human development.* New York: Appleton-Century-Crofts, 1963.

Labouvie, E. W. Developmental causal structures of organism-environment interactions. *Human Development,* 1974, **17,** 444–452.

Labouvie-Vief, G. Adult cognitive development: In search of alternative interpretations. *Merrill Palmer Quarterly,* 1978, **23,** 227–263.

Labouvie-Vief, G., & Chandler, M. Cognitive development and life-span developmental theories: Idealistic versus contextual perspectives. In P. B. Baltes (Ed.), *Life-span development and behavior* (Vol. 1). New York: Academic Press, 1978.

Lerner, R. M. *Concepts and theories of human development.* Reading, Mass.: Addison-Wesley, 1976.

Lerner, R. M., & Ryff, C. D. Implementation of the life-span view of human development: The sample case of attachment. In P. B. Baltes (Ed.), *Life-span development and behavior* (Vol. 1). New York: Academic Press, 1978.

Löwe, H. *Einführung in die Lernpsychologie des Erwachsenenalters.* Berlin: VEB Deutscher Verlag der Wissenschaften, 1977.

Lowenthal, M. F., Thurnher, M., Chiriboga, D., and Associates. *Four stages of life: A comparative study of women and men facing transitions.* San Francisco: Jossey-Bass, 1975.

Lugo, J. O., & Hershey, G. L. *Human development.* New York: Macmillan, 1974.

Marshall, V. W. Age and awareness of finitude in developmental gerontology. *Omega,* 1975, **6,** 113–129.

McCall, R. B. Challenges to a science of developmental psychology. *Child Development,* 1977, **48,** 333–344.

Munnichs, J. M. A. A short history of psychogerontology. *Human Development,* 1966, **9,** 230–245. (a)

Munnichs, J. M. A. *Old age and finitude.* Basel: Karger, 1966. (b)

Nesselroade, J. R., & Baltes, P. B. (Eds.). *Longitudinal methodology in the study of behavior and development.* New York: Academic Press, 1979, in press.

Nesselroade, J. R., & Reese, H. W. (Eds.). *Life-span developmental psychology: Methodological issues.* New York: Academic Press, 1973.

Neugarten, B. L. *Personality in middle and late life: Empirical studies.* New York: Atherton, 1964.

Neugarten, B. L. Continuities and discontinuities of psychological issues into adult life. *Human Development,* 1969, **12,** 121–130.

Neugarten, B. L., & Datan, N. Sociological perspectives on the life cycle. In P. B. Baltes & K. W. Schaie (Eds.), *Life-span developmental psychology: Personality and socialization.* New York: Academic Press, 1973.

Newman, B. M., & Newman, P. R. *Development through life.* Homewood, Ill.: Dorsey Press, 1975.

Oerter, R. (Ed.). *Entwicklung als lebenslanger Prozess.* Hamburg: Hoffmann & Campe, 1978.

Petermann, F. *Veränderungsmessung.* Stuttgart: Kohlhammer, 1978.

Pikunas, J. *Human development: An emergent science.* New York: McGraw-Hill, 1976.

Pressey, S. L., Janney, J. E., & Kuhlen, R. G. *Life: A psychological survey.* New York: Harper, 1939.

Pressey, S. L., & Kuhlen, R. G. *Psychological development through the life-span.* New York: Harper & Row, 1957.

Quetelet, A. *Sur l'homme et le développement de ses facultés.* Paris: Bachelier, 1835.

Quetelet, A. *Über den Menschen und die Entwicklung seiner Fähigkeiten.* Stuttgart: Schweizerbart's Verlagshandlung, 1938.

Quetelet, A. *A treatise on man and the development of his faculties.* Edinburgh: William and Robert Chambers, 1842.

Rebelsky, F. (Ed.). *Life: The continuous process.* New York: Knopf, 1975.

Reese, H. W. The development of memory: Life-span perspectives. In H. W. Reese (Ed.), *Advances in child development and behavior* (Vol. 11). New York: Academic Press, 1976.

Reinert, G. Grundzüge einer Geschichte der Human-Entwicklungspsychologie. In H. Balmer (Ed.), *Die europäische Tradition: Tendenzen, Schulen, Entwicklungslinien.* Vol. 1 of: *Die Psychologie des 20. Jahrhunderts.* Zürich: Kindler, 1976.

Riegel, K. F. Developmental psychology and society: Some historical and ethical considerations. In J. R. Nesselroade & H. W. Reese (Eds.), *Life-span developmental psychology: Methodological issues.* New York: Academic Press, 1973. (a)

Riegel, K. F. Dialectic operations: The final period of cognitive development. *Human Development,* 1973, **16,** 346–370. (b)

Riegel, K. F. *Psychology of development and history.* New York: Plenum, 1976. (a)

Riegel, K. F. The dialectics of human development. *American Psychologist,* 1976, **31,** 689–700. (b)

Riegel, K. F. History of psychological gerontology. In J. E. Birren & K. W. Schaie (Eds.), *Handbook of the psychology of aging.* New York: Van Nostrand-Reinhold, 1977.

Riley, M. W. Age strata in social systems. In R. Binstock & E. Shanas (Eds.), *Handbook of aging and the social sciences.* New York: Van Nostrand-Reinhold, 1976.

Riley, M. W. (Ed.), *Aging from birth to death.* Washington, D. C.: American Association for the Advancement of Science, 1978.

Riley, M. W., Johnson, M., & Foner, A. *Aging and society.* (Vol. 3). New York: Russell Sage, 1972.

Rogosa, D. Causal models in longitudinal research. In J. R. Nesselroade & P. B. Baltes (Eds.), *Longitudinal research in the study of behavior and development: Design and analysis.* New York: Academic Press, 1979, in press.

Rosenmayr, L. (Ed.). *Die menschlichen Lebensalter.* München: Piper, 1978.

Rudinger, G. (Ed.). *Methoden der Entwicklungspsychologie.* Stuttgart: Kohlhammer, 1968.

Sanford, E. C. Mental growth and decay. *American Journal of Psychology,* 1902, **13,** 426–449.

Schaie, K. W. A general model for the study of developmental problems. *Psychological Bulletin,* 1965, **64,** 92–107.

Schaie, K. W. External validity in the assessment of intellectual performance in adulthood. *Journal of Gerontology,* 1978, **33**, 695–701.

Schaie, K. W. The primary mental abilities in adulthood: An exploration in the development of psychometric intelligence. In P. B. Baltes & O. G. Brim, Jr. (Eds.), *Life-span development and behavior* (Vol. 2). New York: Academic Press, 1979.

Schaie, K. W., & Baltes, P. B. Some faith helps to see the forest: A final comment on the Horn and Donaldson myth of the Baltes–Schaie position on adult intelligence. *American Psychologist,* 1977, **32**, 1118–1120.

Schaie, K. W., & Willis, S. L. Life-span development: Implications for education. *Review of Educational Research,* 1978, in press.

Sears, R. R. Sources of life satisfactions of the Terman gifted men. *American Psychologist,* 1977, **32**, 119–128.

Sears, P. S., & Barbee, A. H. Career and life satisfaction among Terman's gifted women. In J. Stanley, W. George, & C. Solano (Eds.), *The gifted and the creative: Fifty-year perspective.* Baltimore, Md.: Johns Hopkins University Press, in press.

Solzhenitsyn, A. I. *The gulag archipelago.* New York: Harper, 1973.

Süssmilch, J. P. *Die göttliche Ordnung in den Veränderungen des menschlichen Geschlechtes, aus der Geburt, dem Tod und der Fortpflanzung desselben erwiesen.* Berlin: Realschulbuchhandlung, 1741.

Tetens, J. N. *Philosophische Versuche über die menschliche Natur und ihre Entwicklung.* Leipzig: Weidmanns Erben. und Reich, 1777.

Thomae, H. (Ed.). *Entwicklungspsychologie.* Göttingen: Hogrefe, 1959.

Thomae, H. The concept of development and life-span developmental psychology. In P. B. Baltes & O. G. Brim (Eds.), *Life-span development and behavior* (Vol. 2). New York: Academic Press, 1979.

Thorndike, E. L., Bregman, E. O., Tiltin, J. W., Woodyard, E. *Adult learning.* New York: Macmillan, 1928.

Van Dusen, R. A., & Sheldon, E. B. The changing status of American women: A life cycle perspective. *American Psychologist,* 1976, **31**, 106–116.

Wohlwill, J. F. *The study of behavioral development.* New York: Academic Press, 1973.

The Concept of Development and Life-Span Developmental Psychology

Hans Thomae

PSYCHOLOGISCHES INSTITUT, UNIVERSITY OF BONN

BONN, WEST GERMANY

Abstract

A review of existing research data evidences behavioral changes as well as consistencies during any period of life. In addition, interindividual variability of behavior is well documented from prenatal to terminal stages. Based on this review, a conception of developmental psychology is suggested which emphasizes the consistency of "change profiles" related to certain events during the life span. Thus, the ordering of biological, social, and psychological events in a life cycle is the frame of reference for studying developmental change in psychology compared to change investigated in other behavioral sciences. This frame of reference might be conceptualized also as a complex interaction between different time trajectories (chronological, biological, social, etc.) which the individual is experiencing and behavioral change. Due to the increasing complexity of this interaction in adulthood, any developmental psychology which would exclude this stage of life from its conception would deprive itself of one of its most promising emphases and approaches.

LIFE-SPAN DEVELOPMENT
AND BEHAVIOR, VOL. 2

I. Introduction

The current flowering of the life-span view of human development may be traced to several converging roots. For example, in Europe, one of the first attempts to study the entire life course was Charlotte Bühler's (1933) extension of her developmental research on childhood and adolescence into adulthood. Her goal was to increase her understanding of the needs and tasks of youth by studying the outcomes in adulthood of developmental changes which had occurred during the first 15 years of life. It also seemed necessary to her to view the entire life span, especially the terminal stages, in order to comprehend the structure of people's basic aims.

In America, the first textbook of life-span developmental psychology goes back to Pressey, Janney, and Kuhlen's (1939) psychological survey of life. The book summarized an already substantial body of knowledge concerning changes in abilities, interests, and attitudes during the life span, and without any hesitation or doubt these changes were called "development." Other developmental psychology textbooks which covered the whole life span were written by child psychologists such as Anderson (1949, 1958) and Hurlock (1968).

In addition to these texts, an interest in change through the life span was evident in various research projects. Charles (1970) points to the impact of longitudinal studies begun during childhood which, as they continued into adulthood, could draw "researcher interests along from one age and stage to the next" (p. 25). Such studies were conducted by J. E. Anderson (1949), Jones and Conrad (1933), and Sontag, Barker, and Nelson (1958). Leaders in the field of longitudinal research were among the most active supporters of the present writer when he founded *Vita Humana,* a journal created to integrate information gathered in the study of different "stages" into a more accurate picture of the course of human life (Thomae, 1958, p. 3). Finally, in 1959, the first handbook on developmental psychology appeared (Thomae, 1959b) which defined its topic as the study of change throughout the life course (Thomae, 1959a, p. 10). This handbook was very much influenced by trends in German as well as in American psychology (Groffmann, 1970).

Together, these trends coalesced in the view that the most general characteristic of development is a series of changes that can be correlated with certain points of a temporal continuum (Thomae, 1959a). From this viewpoint it is impossible to restrict the concept of "development" to any "stage" or "period" of the temporal continuum of an individual life span. The same conclusions have been drawn by Baltes and Goulet (1970), who define the primary objective of any developmental psychology to be the study of intraindividual variability. In agreement with Fiske and Rice (1955), they believe this perspective rests on the assumption of the systematic nature of intraindividual variability and of its greater prominence compared to interindividual variability. They formulate two more assumptions for life-span developmental psychology, one related to continuous change in the human organism and the other to the age-relatedness of "a significant portion of intraindividual variability" (Baltes & Goulet, 1970, p. 13).

As one consequence of these writings, life-span developmental psychology became institutionalized in several university committees or departments (as at the University of Chicago, Pennsylvania State University, or at West Virginia University with its well-known conferences). In addition, the International Society for Study of Behavioral Development, founded in 1969, decided to define its aims through the promotion of an international exchange of information about the life-span developmental approach and the cross-cultural approach. The first two conferences of this Society (Nijmegen, 1971; Ann Arbor, Michigan, 1973) were successful in examining the entire age continuum from prenatal development to old age and death (Eisner, Siegler, & Eisele, 1974).

However, this more than 40-year history of the evolvement of a life-span view of development has progressed in the context of a somewhat contradictory trend. For several years there has existed a growing tendency to restrict developmental psychology to childhood. Recent sections on "Developmental Psychology" in the *Annual Review of Psychology* (1972–1976) report exclusively on child psychology. In addition, separate reviews on adult development and aging are published, though not as frequently. Reviewers in the area of developmental psychology, however, do not mention this latter research and, thus, appear to view developmental psychology as child psychology. At the extreme, for example, Baer and Wright (1974), while wondering if anything like developmental psychology exists at all, assert that there "certainly is a child psychology" (p. 3).

Other evidence for a prevalent non-life-span conception of development exists. For example, it is common for books of readings (Denenberg, 1972; Ewert, 1972) and textbooks on developmental psychology (Bernard, 1964; Gale, 1969) to restrict their topic to child psychology. Also, the APA journal *Developmental Psychology,* while open to life-span developmental psychology, focuses very heavily on child psychology. Finally, an important indication of the impact this child psychology view of development has had is that, at the Third Meeting of the International Society for

Study of Behavioral Development (July, 1975, Guildford, Surrey, England), the topic of life-span development was entirely excluded in favor of child psychology.*

One rationale underlying this trend to restrict the study of developmental psychology to the period of childhood may be found in several statements of Piagetians, especially those of Flavell (1970) at the first West Virginia Conference on Life-Span Developmental Psychology. In agreement with age-old viewpoints, Flavell raised serious doubts concerning the application of the term "development" to cognitive changes in adult years. These doubts were based on the comparison of intraindividual change during childhood with that during adulthood. According to Flavell, neither the criterion of a considerable magnitude of change nor that of the universal character of change can be observed during the adult years. More importantly, these changes during the adult years lack the flavor of development as "a biological growth process that lends to childhood changes their inevitability, magnitude, directionality, with species uniformity and irreversibility" (Flavell, 1970, p. 248 ff). From these criteria he further contends that "appellations like 'life-span developmental psychology' if meant to be more than metaphors, would need explicit defense" (Flavell, 1970, p. 249).

Flavell (1970) formulated explicitly much of the criticism against the life-span view of development which is usually expressed more indirectly. Thus, his arguments offer a good background against which to review existing evidence for the thesis that a study of development which excludes consideration of the entire life span is both incomplete and governed by misleading principles and hypotheses. Such evidence can be presented provided agreement can be reached regarding the fundamental role of change in defining the concept of development. Hence, any biological or social scientific bias must be renounced by participants in a discussion of the meaning of development. According to the criteria formulated by Baltes and Goulet (1970), and in response to the objections raised by Flavell (1970), this paper discusses the nature of development during childhood, adolescence, and adulthood in terms of the following propositions:

1. Change (i.e., intraindividual variability) and consistency (i.e., intraindividual invariance) can be observed from some aspects or patterns of behavior throughout the entire life span.

2. There may be differences in degree of intraindividual variability in some behavioral areas between different life periods (infancy, childhood, or adulthood). However, these differences in the degree of extant change

are not criteria for defining "developmental" and "nondevelopmental" stages of life.

3. In any period of life a considerable degree of interindividual variability regarding timing, kind, and direction of change can be observed. The degree of these interindividual differences varies for different behavior change processes and phases of the life span. However, there are indications of consistency in interindividual variability which cannot be overlooked in any conceptualization of development.

In the following sections I discuss these propositions by providing evidence for: (1) consistency in behavior change processes in periods of the life span presumed to involve considerable intraindividual variability (change); (2) change in periods presumed to be highlighted by consistency; and (3) interindividual differences in intraindividual change across the life span.

II. Consistency versus Change in Early Life

Studies on motor, perceptual, and cognitive development in infancy and childhood provide considerable evidence for change. Yet, when planning a longitudinal study of children from kindergarten age through the primary school years, we expect that they will attend all test examinations with the same degree of alertness, activity, confidence, and adjustment. Our expectations regarding progressive change in cognitive functioning might be falsified if there were no stability in these other behavioral systems during a period which is regarded by some as the prototype of development in terms of change, progress, increase of competence, etc.

Based on such experiences, researchers engaged in longitudinal studies have always been interested in both the change in behavior, in terms of progression and increasing skill, and the stability of the behavioral system. Several examples may be drawn of stability or consistency in behavior change processes within segments of the life span traditionally presumed to be periods of extensive intraindividual variation.

The stability of the behavioral system becomes evident in infancy. For example, Chess (1967) identified several temperamental patterns within the child's first 3 months of life which tended to remain stable over the course of later years. One group of children (the "easy" group) exhibited regularity of biological function, positive approach responses to new stimuli, easy adaptibility to change, a preponderance of positive mood and reactions of mild or moderate intensity. In contrast, another group showed irregularity in biological functions, predominantly negative responses to new stimuli, and slow adaptability.

Similarly, Winkelmann (1971) found highly significant correlations between rating scores for adjustment, ego control, and emotional stability at the preschool level and scores for general, as well as specific, aspects for adjustment to school after grade levels one, two, and three. Thus, consistency was found despite the fact that, on the basis of the cognitive and social changes involved in the second and third grades in Germany, one would have predicted a high degree of behavioral change. Another example of behavioral consistency across years of traditionally presumed intraindividual variability was found by Bronson (1966) in an analysis of data from the Berkeley Child Guidance Study. Bronson found highly significant correlations between scores at ages 6 and 16 years of the dimensions of "reserved vs. expressive" and "calm, ordered vs. reactive, impulsive."

Examples of consistency in cognitive processes may also be offered. Witkin and his co-workers found a "high degree of relative stability" regarding field independence (vs. dependence) from age 10 to age 14 (Witkin & Berry, 1975). Similarly, Kagan and Kogan (1970, p. 1310) point to stabilities in reflection–impulsivity scores over a period of $2\frac{1}{2}$ years. In addition, they found predictors for a reflective attitude at age 6 as early as $2\frac{1}{2}$ years (Kagan & Kogan, 1970, p. 1319). For other cognitive controls there is great evidence for cross-situational stability and stability over longer time periods.

Another aspect of consistency in behavior between ages 6 and 16 can be discussed from the findings of a German longitudinal study of children (Coerper, Hagen, & Thomae, 1954). The investigators followed 1800 children born in 1944/45 from entrance in school to 10th grade. Personality variables, such as activity, general responsiveness, emotional responsiveness, adjustment to the situation, and ego control, were assessed for each subject every year by rating scales. A factor analysis of these scales demonstrated that variance could be reduced to two factors, which were defined as "achievement related activity" and "ego control" (Essing, 1966). Two large subject groups, differing with respect to socioeconomic status (SES), showed consistently different scores on at least four of the five scales loading on the "achievement related activity" factor, with higher SES children always scoring higher. In addition, the two groups were differentiated by the patterns of consistency and change in their scores over the 10-year assessment period. Among lower SES children, the data indicated a pattern of continuously rising scores. Among higher SES children, however, there were three patterns of consistency and change, namely consistently high scores, fluctuating scores, and falling scores (Uhr, Thomae, & Becker, 1969).

Although some of the above changes may be explained by regression effects, the main findings are that stable high and low scores exist for different groups of subjects which are predictable on the basis of a subject's SES. Therefore, we can conclude that there is consistency in the period of the life cycle defined by the transition from latency to the alleged turmoil of adolescence. Accordingly, the study supports criticism against a generalized "storm and stress" model during adolescence as described by Hall (1908). Whereas this traditional model views adolescence as a transitory stage between the rapid growth of childhood, on the one hand, and the stability of adulthood, on the other, Bandura (1964), Offer (1969), Thomae (1969), Grinder (1973), and Block (1971) offer evidence for continuity rather than discontinuity of development between the ages of 10 and 16. Extreme emotional arousal and conflict characterize only a minority. Thus, the definition of adolescence as a period of extreme discontinuity of personality may be seen as an instance of overgeneralization (Bandura, 1964).

From such findings it may be possible to explain the surprising results of American longitudinal studies published since 1960. Most studies have pointed to a high degree of consistency of personality from early adolescence into adulthood, although some cases have shown a considerable degree of change (Bronson, 1967; McFarlane, 1964). An analysis of the data from the Oakland Growth Study and follow-ups of the same subjects at ages 31–38 years indicated a high degree of consistency from adolescence through a span of 15 years (McKee & Turner, 1961). This consistency referred to scores for different aspects of "drive," measured in adolescence by Murray's need-scoring system and in adulthood by the California Personality Inventory scores (McKee & Turner, 1961). Similarly, data from the Fels Longitudinal Study (Kagan & Moss, 1962) pointed to sex differences regarding consistency of certain personality dimensions in the age range from 3 to 29 years. The data for male subjects pointed to highly stable aggression scores over this age range (especially between 11–14 years and adulthood); for women, a similar degree of stability was observed regarding dependency scores. These results were interpreted by Kagan & Moss in terms of differential reinforcement contingencies for boys and girls regarding these variables in our society. The finding regarding consistency of male aggression was confirmed by Skolnik (1966) from data gathered in the Berkeley Guidance Study.

Although most of the published findings of longitudinal studies initiated between 1925 and 1930 point to consistency of behavior, there are others which stress change. For example, McFarlane and Honzik (1954) reported different frequencies of behavior problems from age 3 to 14 years. Such results may indicate considerable changes in the interactions between child and mother during this period.

However, despite such instances, there remain considerable longitudinal data supporting the idea of consistency in behavior-change processes (Bronson, 1967). For example, according to the results of repeated measures on gifted children born around 1910, the majority were close to the 99th percentile in mental ability at measurement points 1927/28, 1939/40, and 1950/52 (Terman & Oden, 1947, 1959). The evidence for consistency in mental test performance for average subjects studied in other longitudinal projects was not as conclusive as in Terman's research (Bayley, 1963; Hahn, 1972; McCall, Applebaum, & Hogarty, 1973; McCall, Hogarty, & Hurlburt, 1972; Sontag *et al.*, 1958). Some of the changes in IQ involved decreases, while others involved increases.

In sum, from all these findings and theories we can conclude that the behavioral events during infancy, childhood, and adolescence can be ordered along a dimension running from low to high change or from high to low stability. It is a matter of convenience whether we prefer ''change'' or ''stability'' as the label. The most important aspect of this dimension is the continuity of the scale; it may not be appropriately dichotomized into ''stable'' versus ''unstable'' sections. As there exist different behavior-change processes during this life period, there may exist different degrees of consistency and change in different behavioral areas such as cognition, motorperceptual skills, or emotional and social adjustment. We may even admit that during this life stage there are more behavioral elements closer to the ''high degree of change'' pole of the scale than during other life stages. Yet, despite the great extent of intraindividual variability, intraindividual consistency exists too. Now, however, let us consider the reverse of this argument.

III. Consistency versus Change in Adulthood

The stereotype of the ''changeless'' time of adulthood may have some of its roots in cultural values wherein maturity is synonymous with ''emotional stability'' and ''complete reliability.'' Yet, whatever their sources, such stereotypes have become anachronistic overgeneralizations in the face of the continuous compilation of empirical evidence pertaining to various behavior change processes.

A. CHANGES IN COGNITIVE FUNCTIONING DURING ADULT LIFE

Some basis for the "stable adulthood" stereotype is provided by studies on changes in cognitive functioning during the adult years. While the years between 25 and 60 have been found to show slow decline of mental abilities in some studies (Jones & Conrad, 1933; Miles, 1934; Wechsler, 1944), other studies have found a plateau during these years (Bayley, 1970). There is also a plateau in adulthood and a drop in performance in old age for cognitive functioning defined by Piagetian tasks (Papalia & Del Vento Bielby, 1974).

Such findings regarding the developmental course of cognitive functioning in adulthood have been questioned by many writiers, particularly those concerned with the confounding effects which results from cross-sectional designs (Baltes, 1968; Schaie, 1965, 1973). Nesselroade, Schaie, and Baltes (1972) demonstrated that cohort (generational) effects accounted for most of the variance in Primary Mental Abilities performance for a sample of subjects ranging from 21 to 71 years. A 7-year follow-up of the test scores of longitudinal subjects did not point to significant overall age changes. However, there were slight changes in a positive direction for measures of "crystallized intelligence" and minor changes in a negative direction for measures of "fluid intelligence."

According to Birren and his associates (Birren, Butler, Greenhouse, Sokoloff, & Yarrow, 1963), Labouvie (1973), Schaie (1965), Baltes and Schaie (1976), Lehr (1972), and Rudinger (1975), consistency and change during adulthood is a variable dependent on health, education, SES, and ecological and historical variables. These authors often postulate that there is no decrease in cognitive functioning provided favorable conditions exist. However, the absence of decrease is not identical with no change. There may be quantitative increases in certain functions for certain subjects (Cattell, 1971; Owens, 1966), and there may be qualitative changes, such as, for example, those mentioned by Papalia and Del Vento Bielby (1974, p. 438) concerning problem approach styles.

We might expect more information regarding qualitative change if more complex models of intellectual functioning such as Guilford's (1967) were applied. The "content" and "product" cells of Guilford's model might offer improved opportunities for studies of change in intelligence. In the future, we may, for example, be able to trace qualitative change in groups with consistent overall intelligence scores, provided research on the relationship between coping style and intellectual performance receives further clarification (Andrew, 1973). From research on learning and memory we know of the impact of different strategies for level of performance (Rowe & Schmore, 1971). These strategies may be more promising in studying change in adult behavior than using performance scores on conservation tasks or on tests which were designed originally for children but have subsequently been applied to adults (Bischof, 1969). This is also true for the study of changes in creativity during middle age (Kogan, 1973).

B. PERSONALITY CHANGES DURING ADULT LIFE

The arguments against the stereotype of low intraindividual variability in adult behavior (e.g., Friedman, 1975) are made even more convincing by research on personality variables. Charlotte Bühler's (1933) psychology of the human life course, for example, was primarily concerned with fundamental changes in personality. She postulated at least three different stages of adult life (young adulthood, maturity, and menopause or climacterium virile) and an old age period. The first stage beyond childhood and adolescence was described as one of increasing expansion and competence, the second as one of beginning restriction and internal ordering, and the third as one of transcendence or decline.

Moers (1953), Erikson (1950), and Peck (1956) formulated other hypotheses regarding psychological "stages" of adult life. All of them postulate experiences of gains and losses in social competence as a result of changing roles and changing physical conditions. From the expected sequence of these biological and/or environmental changes, these theorists predict an orderly sequence of psychological change during adulthood. Havighurst (1963), for instance, defines different developmental tasks for each of the decades throughout adult life with the implication that consistency of attitudes and expectations inhibits the adjustment of the individual to his or her changing life situation.

C. AGE ROLES AND BEHAVIORAL CHANGE

Stage theories of adult development, however, have not led to the initiation of major research projects, while approaches deriving from role theory have been more fruitful. Role theory (Havighurst, 1975; Neugarten & Moore, 1968) predicts major changes in attitude and behavior during the adult life cycle which is defined by a sequence of changing social positions and their role theoretical implications (Neugarten, 1972). This sequence has some readily generalizable aspects, as far as job entrance, beginning a family, parenting, confrontation with increasing conflict between different perceptions of the parental role, conflict between parent's dependency on parental role and offspring's attained status as young adult, moving from the status of the "young family" to the "middle-aged family" (with its fading and sometimes doubtful functions), and other changes in life situations are concerned.

Some aspects of role theory have found empirical support. For example, investigations of attitudes toward the younger, middle-aged, and older adult have reported a trend toward negative evaluation of older age groups, especially among young respondents (Aaronson, 1966; Tuckman & Lorge, 1952, 1953). This finding was supported by results reported by Schneider (1970) with a sample representative of the population of the Federal Republic of Germany. The respondents had to evaluate various activities (e.g., "looking for another job," "going for skiing on holiday," "starting to save for building or owning a house," etc.) according to which age group they could best be attributed. These items were also rated by expert and nonexpert samples along the dimensions of "social competence" and "expansion vs. restriction." An analysis of the data demonstrated the perception of a steady increase in social competence until age 49. Beginning with the early 50s the scores for expected competence and expansive activity dropped rapidly.

Parallel findings are reported by Whittington, Wilkie, and Eisdorfer (1972). College students and older adults were asked to evaluate age-related concepts using the semantic differential technique. The younger people linked the 55-year-old "active" and "strong" man with attributes like "bad" and "untrustworthy." These findings lend support to the hypothesis that age norms and age expectations constitute a system of social control (Neugarten, 1972, p. 14). For middle-aged men these age expectations have detrimental consequences related to employment or reemployment chances. Following untrained youth and married females, men older than 45 run the next greatest risk of losing their jobs and/or being unable to find new ones, especially in an era of recession (Sobel, 1970; Thomae & Lehr, 1973).

The psychological problem inherent in this situation is related to the dissonance between the middle-aged worker's ability to perform at a competent level, even in highly complicated production systems (Schmidt, 1972), and the prejudice against this age group as one being unable to compete with younger workers. Even if a person remains employed, he faces a situation requiring him to implement more effective or new techniques in order to overcome pejorative expectations. The situation of the aging employee is one example of the impact of the age-grading system, which defines adult life as a sequence of challenges and risks which require adjustment, including changes in behavior, attitude, and expectation. If people were as stable and rigid during adulthood as predicted by child psychologists, they could not meet the developmental tasks defined by the age norms and age constraints of our society. Therefore, change is programmed into the individual's life course during adulthood by social as well as (presumably) biological conditions (Jarvik, 1962).

1. Life Review and Perceived Change

If "cognitive representations of the situation" are seen as those variables which mediate between stimulus and response (Baldwin, 1969), then perceived changes in a person's own life situations may be cues for behavioral change. From this point of view, life histories gathered by interview procedures can be important. In 1954, Thomae, Lehr, Koch and others began to study on the life histories of young and middle-aged white collar employees (Lehr & Thomae, 1958), which was extended later to a study of the life histories of a low-middle class sample of 741 women and 570 men born between 1890 and 1939. (Lehr, 1969a; Lehr & Thomae, 1965; Scheffler, 1970).

A content analysis of these life histories showed that there was an average of 17.5 "turning points" or major changes in each of these biographies. The majority of these changes were reported for the years between adolescence and old age. The greatest percentage of the changes (38.5%) was related to personal problems and experiences, such as getting acquainted with a person or with attaining or losing some special skill. Almost the same percentage (36.4%) consisted of changes related to the age-grading system in society, mainly in terms of changes in family structure (e.g., birth of a sibling, beginning or end of father absence, engagement, marriage, birth of own children, growing up, death of children, empty nest transition, death of parents, or death of a spouse). These family-centered changes were reported more often by women than by men ($p < .01$). Moreover, the age-grading system with regard to occupational life contributed 15.4% of reported change (e.g., entrance into a career, promotion, changing of job and/or occupation, intermission of occupational career due to marriage or children, or reentrance into labor force). The remaining reports of changes (17.8%) were related to historical–political events (World War I or II, occupation of Germany, being a prisoner of war, the economic crisis of 1930, the economic inflation of 1923, and/or 1946–1948, a loss of home due to air raids, Hitler's seizure of power, or political persecution).

Lehr (1976) emphasizes the variety of personal events which are perceived as instigators of change. Therefore we have to expect a high interindividual variability, at least for those reports which relate change to personal encounters or experiences. However, for 61.5% of the reports, the decisive events are related to the order in which biological or social changes appear in the life cycle, or to the manner in which historical events interfere with the life histories of these individuals. Therefore, we can regard these reports as evidence for an orderly sequence of changes in a majority of the life histories, especially during the years of young adulthood to old age.

2. Conflicts During Adult Life

A random selection of the life histories used for the analysis of perceived change was also evaluated in terms of reported conflicts, stresses, or problem situations (Lehr, 1976). These life histories came from the interviews of 320 men and women from the 1890–1930 cohorts. While the greatest number of conflicts was reported by the whole sample for the 15–19 year age group, the younger male respondents experienced the highest rate of conflict in the third decade. In addition, for women and for other age groups, the difference in the rate of reported conflict for the periods 15–19 and 20–29 years did not differ as markedly as one might expect from the "storm and stress model" of adolescence. While there was a drop in reported conflicts for the age period 20–24 years, the rate increased substantially for the age period 25–29 years, especially for men.

The older respondents reported even more conflicts for the 40–45 age group and a decrease for the years after 55. One of the most decisive sources of this tendency of rising, decreasing, and increasing number of conflicts was the military–political history experienced by this German sample. For the older cohorts, World War I interfered with their life plans and expectations; for the younger cohorts this interference was due to World War II. However, many of the older subjects got involved in the turmoils of political life after 1933.

Therefore, there will probably be cohort differences when the younger age group moves into their 40s; during this time they may experience peace and democracy compared to the catastrophes experienced by the older individuals at the same ages. However, among reference ages for which comparisons are possible, for those born before and after 1910, the analogies in history between 1910 and 1930 and between 1930 and 1948 are reflected in a similar sequence of reported conflicts by these cohorts for their lives between 20–25 and 40. It may be due to these cohort equivalences, in the representation of certain conflict areas in the total pool of 13,316 reported conflicts analyzed by us, that we found a considerable degree of consistency in the rank order of these areas for different reference ages, i.e., the age to which the conflict refers (i.e., age 15–19, 20–24, 25–29, or 30–34).

However, despite the confounding cohort effects one can observe changes in the relevance of certain conflict areas with different reference ages. This is true for both sexes in their relationship with their children. Conflicts in this area showed a steady increase with increasing reference age. One reason for the increase may be the empty nest reaction. However, for most of our subjects, the main problem was not separation from their children but, instead, stemmed from the older generation's high degree of identification with the aims, successes, and failures of their children, and even their grandchildren.

From what we know about this reaction tendency (Thomae, 1976), it very often seems to have compensatory effects. If the children or grandchildren have success and appear to be well off, the parents' own failure or bad luck is perceived as less frustrating or depressing. On the other hand, if the offspring's situation is less favorable, the old parent holds himself responsible. Therefore, while a higher percentage of child-centered problems in the older reference ages may point to generational conflicts or to empty nest reactions, it may more frequently mean a high degree of involvement in the ambitions and frustrations of the younger generation. The most important aspect of these findings for our discussion is the increasing involvement of the elderly in the affairs of the young. This finding does not fit into relevant role expectations, or to the stereotype of the stable, unchanging adult personality which is preferred by some child psychologists (Friedman, 1975).

Further evidence for change (intraindividual variability) in behavior during adulthood is provided by our findings among women concerning the rank order of conflicts or problems regarding parents. After a decrease to 6% of all reported conflicts between 30 and 34 years, we found an increased percentage of parent-related conflicts or problems in women for reference ages past 35. This tendency is very often referred to as the parent–spouse conflict in wives, which is explained by the increasing demands of sick and/or dependent parents on their daughter. These demands very often interfere with the interests of her own family. Therefore, new decisions and new changes in behavior are programmed into the lives of middle-aged women (Lehr, 1961). This programming is provided by societies which foster ideologies of equalitarian rights for men and women, yet whose cultural traditions assign any solution of family problems to the female role (Lehr, 1969a).

The studies summarized represent only some examples of changes due to problem areas which are programmed into the lives of adult persons according to their social roles. The "mature" person who remains changeless and motionless in the face of the different challenges, threats, and increasing opportunities of the adult years is a stereotype, having no psychological reality.

3. Reaction to Problem Situations

In the Bonn Longitudinal Study of Aging, we followed approximately 180 men and women of the 1890–1895 and 1900–1905 cohorts from 1965 to 1972 (Thomae, 1976). In the first year we interviewed our subjects about how they coped with problems and stress situations in three reference times: from the end of World War II through the currency reform in 1948, in the year 1955, and at the present time (1965). Interviews centered around the subjects' socioeconomic, occupational, familial, and housing situations. As most of the respondents had faced many problems, especially during the 1945–1948 period, there existed good opportunities for eliciting memories of past problems and the ways in which they were met. The information on problem situations existing immediately after the war and the concomitant patterns of adjustment became the basis for classification of adjustment patterns. These adjustment patterns were rated on nine-point scales by trained raters. The rank order of adjustment patterns in the reports of men (born 1900–1905) in the area of occupational problems in 1948 and 1956 is given in Table I (from Thomae & Simons, 1967).

The rank order correlation between the adjustment patterns reported for 1948 and 1965 is not significant. The difference in the structure of overall adjustment to the situation is explained primarily by differences in the rating scores for four adjustment patterns. "Adjustment to the institutional aspects of the situation," i.e., adjustment by applying to the employment office, the former employer, the trade union, or local authorities, was most important for getting or keeping a job in 1948. It was less important in 1965 when half of these men were retired, and problems in this area usually had to do with getting the highest possible pension or finding a postretirement job. Another major pattern of adjustment to poor occupational opportunities (and a high degree of economic disorder) was accepting whatever job opportunities appeared by chance. This involved looking around for jobs, keeping good contacts with informed people, maintaining motivation, and maintaining flexibility in accepting whatever was offered. It is understandable that this adjustment pattern was not relevant in occupational situations for men around or past retirement age in an affluent society with (relatively) high pensions. On the other hand, in 1948 these men (about 45 years of age) did not react in an evasive manner to the occupational situation, and they could not solve the problem by identifying with the aims and successes of their children or grandchildren.

It should be emphasized that the reaction patterns of people in the age group 45–65 were sufficiently flexible to adjust to the changing demands of social, political, and economic situations. There remain consistent hierarchical preference patterns, e.g., achievement-related behavior.

TABLE I

**Rank Order of Adjustment Patterns to Occupational Problems
as Reported by Men (Age 60–75) for 1948 and 1965[a]**

Adjustment pattern (1948)	Adjustment pattern (1965)
1 Achievement-oriented behavior	1 Achievement-oriented behavior
2 Adjustment of the institutional aspects of the situation[b]	2 Identification with the aims and/or successes (eventually failures) of children and grandchildren
3 Adjustment to the habits and/or needs of others	3 Seeking and/or cultivating social contacts
4 Establishing and/or cultivating social contacts	4 Accepting situation as it is
5 Using chance opportunities[b]	5 Adjustment to the habits and/or needs of others
6 Active resistance to obstacles	6 Evasive reactions
7 Accepting situation as it is	7 Adjustment to the institutional aspects of the situation
8 Hope for help from others	8 Hope for help from others
9 To rely on others	9 Active resistance to obstacles
10 Aggressive reaction	10 Depressive reaction
11 Asking others for help	11 Aggressive reaction
12 Depressive reaction	12 To rely on others
13 Resignation in favor of others	13 To disengage from situation
14 Identification with the aims and/or successes (eventually failures) of children[b]	14 Resignation in favor of others
15 Evasive reaction[b]	15 Using chance opportunities

[a] After Thomae and Simons (1967).
[b] Tau (Kendall II) = .276, $p > 5\%$. Significant cohort changes occurred primarily for items (1948 ranks) 2 (to 7), 5 (to 15), 14 (to 2), and 15 (to 6).

However, some reaction styles which were useful after the World War II currency reform period were no longer meaningful in 1965. On the other hand, growth of one's own family and the careers of offspring provided new instruments for compensating for deficits in life satisfaction. If personality is defined as a pattern of reaction tendencies, we can conclude from these findings that change in personality during middle age is not only possible, but it may be required in order to survive.

This conclusion, at first, may sound contradictory to the work of Maas and Kuypers (1974). These investigators found highly consistent personality scores in the parents of the Child Guidance Study. Comparing the interview data from these parents when they were in their early 30s and when they were age 70 indicated that interindividual variability prevailed.

Thus, Maas and Kuypers (1974) emphasized the interindividual aspect in their evaluation of the data. However, they also found very clear intraindividual changes, especially in the group of men. The greater degree of consistency demonstrated in the Berkeley Sample, as compared to our findings, may be explained by differences in the history of Germany and the United States. German men and women of the cohorts 1890–1905 were more involved in the turmoils of Hitler's dictatorship and World War II, whereas most of the American fathers and mothers suffered more from World War I and the depression. Therefore Maas and Kuypers' (1974) and our own studies demonstrate clearly the social and historical dependency of continuity and change in adulthood. They complement each other in that they study the conditions under which change vs. consistency or constancy prevail.

In sum, we may conclude this section on intraindividual variability in adulthood by a citation from Bayley: "In general change is most rapid and most obvious at the two ends of the life span, in infancy–childhood and in old age senility. However, even though it tends to be forgotten and even though the various behavioral functions of the young adult are often treated as stable, change is continuous right through the mature adult periods" (1963, p. 127). Indeed, it does not appear justifiable to assume as a general proposition that the period of adulthood is one of stability and no change.

IV. Interindividual Variability Across the Life Span: Overview

There is a tradition of conceptualizing development by the prevailing role of intraindividual vs. interindividual variability (Gardner, 1964; Gesell, 1945; Olson, 1957; Piaget, 1972; Werner, 1957). Flavell (1970), whom we have chosen as a representative of the child-centered type of developmental theorizing, followed this tradition by rejecting the idea of a life-span developmental psychology on the basis of the high amount of interindividual variability of behavior beyond adolescence. Therefore, our emphasis in this section is on the demonstration of interindividual differences in the first 18 years and in old age. These periods have been chosen because it is intraindividual variability which is regarded by many writers as the most striking trend during these segments of the life span.

A. INTERINDIVIDUAL DIFFERENCES IN INFANCY AND CHILDHOOD

At least since Gesell's (1948) longitudinal studies, interindividual variation in infant and child development has been observed by many writers. Birns (1965) pointed to interindividual differences in human neonates' responses to stimulation. Studies on individual records of neonates' spontaneous movements (such as startles, smiles, erections, and reflex sucks) revealed interesting and often self-consistent sequences in these behavioral classes (Korner, 1969). A considerable body of research has indicated, too, that consistent interindividual differences can be observed from the first days of life (Kessen, Williams, & Williams, 1961) and during the months up to more than 1 year (Chess, Thomas, & Birch, 1959; Thomas, Chess, Birch, Hertzig, & Korm, 1963).

In a cross-national longitudinal study of children, Hindley and his associates (Hindley, Filliozat, Klackenberg, Nicolet-Meister, & Sand, 1966) found significant differences in the age of walking among the various samples in this project (Brussels, London, Paris, Stockholm, and Zurich). Sex or social class differences were not related to age of walking. Tischler (1957) pointed to individual differences in early vocal expressions and Graefe (1963) to individual differences in early form perceptions (age of infants: 10–13 weeks). Corah and Gospodinoff (1966) studied color–form preferences in preschoolers, third graders, and adults. They found a developmental trend toward increase in form perception; however, interindividual differences of scores for color–form preferences (ranging theoretically from 0 to 18) varied from 0 to 18 in preschoolers, 0 to 17 in third graders, and 0 to 17 in adults.

As one additional example, Schaffer (1966) found a wide scatter of individual differences in response to hospitalization among 22 infants (prior to 30 weeks of age, after the infants' return home). The developmental quotient rose by 31 points in one case and dropped in another case to the other extreme by 6 points. The general deprivation syndrome described by Spitz (1945) could not be observed in this study. The vulnerability to deprivation was associated with activity level. Activity level is regarded by Scarr (1966) as constitutional determinant of development which results in many interindividual differences in response.

A great variety of sequences of increase, consistency, and decrease was also found by Hahn (1972) in a German longitudinal study of children (Coerper, Hagen, & Thomae, 1954; Hagen & Thomae, 1962). Mental development between 6 and 14 years as defined by Wechsler intelligence scores was represented for this sample of approximately 1200 boys and girls by many variations in continuity of increase, plateaus, and accelerated increase and decrease of performance. Predictability of later achievement often was very low.

Another approach to the study of interindividual variation is concerned with the study of cognitive styles (e.g., differentiated, impulsive, reflective, analytical, etc.). Mussen (1970) concluded from the research trends between 1945 and 1970 that Carmichael's *Manual of Child Psychology* should include a chapter on individual variation in cognitive development. Kagan and Kogan (1970) reviewed the large body of related research. The variation indicated in this and previously cited papers demonstrates that the developmental psychology of infancy and childhood must include the important topic of individual differences and that these differences between individuals cannot be defined only in terms of slower or faster speeds of development. There are qualitative differences suggestive of the view that all children characteristically reach many cross-points during their development and at each point, development may proceed in one of several different directions. Further research on early determinants of cognitive style or of different response patterns should stress the relevance of qualitative interindividual differences in childhood development, rather than differences regarding speed in attaining certain skills or "structures."

As for the explanation of large interindividual differences, differences in cognitive and personality development in children beyond infancy are often correlated with environmental data. It is not possible to discuss the great amount of data on correlations between mental and personality development and, for example, SES, parental attitudes, sibling position, and home vs. institutional care (e.g., Hanson, 1975; Holtzman & Diaz-Guerrero, 1976; Honzik, 1967). Just one example of environmental correlates of interindividual differences in child development may be noted. McCall, Appelbaum, and Hogarty (1973) studied five groups of children from the Fels Longitudinal Study, each group representing different patterns of change in IQ from $2\frac{1}{2}$ to 17 years. The largest group did not show change. However, two groups showed an increasing pattern, and two a decreasing one. Education of parents and parental behavior were correlated with the patterns of change.

B. ADOLESCENCE AND THE PROBLEM OF GENERALIZATION IN DEVELOPMENTAL PSYCHOLOGY

Adolescence as conceived by G. Stanley Hall (1908) is the prototype of radical change, from gradual physical and mental growth during latency, through the storms and stresses of puberty, to postadolescence and maturity. This "storm and stress model" influenced textbooks of developmental psychology for a long time. Another universal sequence of development during the teen-age years was postulated by Eduard Spranger (1926, 1966), whose book influenced generations of psychologists and educators in Middle Europe and Japan. According to this theory, preadolescence is a time of increasing psychological distance from the family and other former social ties. Introversive tendencies combined with social distance aid in the search for a life plan, which should be adapted to reality in late adolescence.

According to many psychologists, cognitive development in preadolescence and adolescence is influenced by the physical changes going on during this time. One group believes that physical maturation will impair mental development, especially if it starts very early; others predict an acceleration of mental development in the case of early maturers. This opinion is connected with theories of mental "spurt" during adolescence, a view generally questioned (Wall, 1975). The spurt was first found by Ljung (1965), but only for girls in the age range of 10–12 years. In boys, there was a tendency toward steady increase. Studies on psychophysiological relationships of early and late maturers point to different developmental styles which represent outcomes of the reaction of the social environment toward physical acceleration vs. retardation. As early maturation in boys is more accepted, these boys will have a more positive self-concept and more hope for success and will be more efficient in achievement tasks (Mussen & Jones, 1957).

According to Mussen and Bonterline-Young (1964), these differences will vary from culture to culture. Some of the differences between early and late maturers can be explained by differences in SES and parental attitudes (Lehr, 1969b). Interindividual differences in development during adolescence are also to be expected from Witkin's theory concerning the socializing effects of such variables as child-care practices and father absence on degree of differentiation. Cross-cultural research points to many varieties of development during this stage (Witkin & Berry, 1975), and it should be remembered that criticism of the "storm and stress model" of adolescence began some time ago with Mead's (1928) cross-cultural research in Samoa and New Guinea.

In addition to cross-cultural research, intracultural and even intraclass variations of personality development during adolescence have become so evident (Abe, 1974; Campbell, 1969; Coleman, 1961; Comer, 1975; Rosenmayr, 1972) that more and more writers on this topic no longer try to describe a universal model of development during this stage. Jaide (1964) analyzed the social and political attitudes of German adolescents and defined four to five "types" of social and political behavior. In a study on the impact of "youth culture" on Swedish adolescence, Andersson (1969) summarized his findings by emphasizing group and individual differences. Furthermore, Nesselroade and Baltes (1974) found that the contextual change provided by a given cultural movement in the United States (1970–1972) was of greater importance in adolescent personality development than chronological age. In fact, in the Nesselroade and Baltes study, large interindividual differences in trends existed which made the normative role of age sequences less than powerful.

Another approach toward a differential psychology of adolescence came from the analysis of the data of 126 subjects in the German Longitudinal Study of children (Coerper, Hagen, & Thomae, 1954) who were followed up to their 21st to 22nd year. Uhr (1968) found three consistent styles which could be differentiated in terms of problem centeredness. Those who showed the most critical and realistic view of past and future situations were "problem-centered" youth; those who were optimistic or without any worries about present or future situations or did not show a differentiated future time perspective were called "problem-free"; and a third group scored intermediate between these two extremes.

The psychological meanings and ecological implications of social class were studied by Lehr and Bonn (1974) among 600 adolescents in 1971–1972. Interviews provided information on the real and the perceived life space of the subjects. The authors found that in an affluent society, such as Western Germany, the lower middle-class adolescent's life space is defined as a limited one, but one of social stability and emotional balance. The life space of upper middle-class adolescents is open in reality but is at least partially influenced by the demands of an achieving society and, as such, has less social stability and more emotional disturbances. This finding has some similarities with that of Cesa-Bianchi and Callgari (1974), who found in lower class Milanese adolescents "a more remarkable maturity" regarding coping styles than in upper and upper middle-class adolescents. These results may be valid only for industrialized cities and for adolescents not living in poverty. Such studies as those mentioned here indicate the difficulty in generalizing from studies of adolescents. The development of the psychology of adolescence is in great danger if it does not focus on differential aspects, as general trends cannot be confirmed by studies which cover the whole range of adolescent groups (Nesselroade & Baltes, 1974).

C. INTERINDIVIDUAL DIFFERENCES IN AGING

While interindividual variability generally is expected for the adult years between 20 and 55, many writers predict a distinct increase in intraindividual variability accompanied by a decrease of interindividual variation in old age. Generally speaking this intraindividual variability is supposed to be identical with declining abilities, activities, and social ties.

Gerontological research of the last 20 years has contributed to revision of this deficit model of aging and has demonstrated increasing interindividual variability in old age (Birren, Woodruff, & Bergman, 1972, p. 72). Evidence for this increasing interindividual variability comes also from biology and medicine. Variance in scores for blood pressure and glucose among members of the same cohort increase with increasing age (Koller, 1972). From a geriatric point of view, Schubert (1969) stressed the indicators for great interindividual variability of the aging process. There are also contributions from psychiatry which point to many varieties in the aging process in the area between "normal" and "psychopathological" aging (Böcher, Heemskerk, & Marx, 1973).

In addition to research on cohort effects (Baltes, 1968; Baltes & Schaie, 1976; Schaie, 1965), a major contribution to the revision of the former view of a general mental decline was made by cross-sectional research which controlled for education of subjects (Granick & Friedman, 1967; Green, 1969; Rudinger, 1974). In some of these studies, decline in the older cohorts decreased, while in others it disappeared, when subjects with the same educational background were compared. The important contributions of education and occupational situation to psychological differences between members of the same cohort are related to socioeconomic status. Thus, Britton, Bergmann, and Savage (1967) and Rudinger (1974) demonstrated that SES explains the variance in WAIS performance to a greater degree than age.

Of the other variables which are closely related to differences in cognitive functioning and adjustment, physical health may be the most decisive. The Bethesda Study on aged men (Birren *et al.*, 1963) demonstrated this, as did Klonoff and Kennedy (1966), Spieth (1964), Hulicka (1967), Lehr (1972), and Rudinger (1974). All of these studies support Spieth's (1964) thesis that mental decline is a variable more dependent on increasing health problems than on increasing age. Furthermore, we may mention those findings which are related to the stimulating effects of the environment on the cognitive and emotional–affective status of the ill and/or handicapped aged persons (Gottesman, 1973; Weinstock & Benett, 1969). As the environments of aged persons differ in degree of stimulation, interindividual variability is also to be expected as a result of this ecological factor.

Also, contrary to the belief of age-related increases in homogeneity are the findings in studies on personality and adjustment of a higher degree of interindividual variability in psychological functioning in older age groups. Aside from those reported by Reichard, Livson, and Petterson (1962) and Williams and Wirths (1965), many other variables have been found to correlate with life satisfaction in old age (Adams, 1973; Thomae, 1974). Such findings demonstrate the high degree of differences in this global measure for persons of the same age. Finally, we may refer to

discussions of disengagement theory which point to the impact of biological and social conditions on the degree of social interaction reported by
elderly people and their degree of satisfaction with this state of social
interaction (Neugarten & Havighurst, 1969, p. 145). Neugarten and
Havighurst (1969) question whether variation in social conditions solves
the problem of individual variation, i.e., why are some individuals living
in the same general setting more content than others? In this connection,
they point to personality as a common denominator for the crucial moderator variables (also see Maas & Kuypers, 1974).

Important evidence for interindividual variability in aging comes also
from American logitudinal studies. Birren *et al.* (1963) summarized their
findings on the personalities of healthy elderly men by stating that the
usual stereotypes of universal rigidity among this age group were unsup-
ported by the data which, instead, showed a high degree of interindividual
variability in performance and behavior among persons belonging to the
same age group. Furthermore, although the interests of the workers of the
Duke Gerontological Study on Aging were more focused on "normal
aging" (Palmore, 1970, 1974), one of the main findings of this large
interdisciplinary project pointed to the "wide variation in aging patterns"
(Palmore, 1974, p. 290). The assessment of this interindividual variation in
both biological and psychological domains became, therefore, one of the
most relevant topics in the second progress report of the study (Palmore,
1974). Similarly, the Bonn Longitudinal Study of Aging gave evidence of
great interindividual variability in the aging process (Thomae, 1976).

The findings summarized above are just a selection of the research
outcomes which brought a new orientation in psychological research on
aging: Instead of defining general norms for consistency and change of
cognitive functioning and personality and adjustment for middle to old
age, gerontologists are beginning to predict which patterns of aging will
result from the particular biological, psychological, and social conditions
of earlier periods in the transition into and during old age. The focus has
become the study of the conditions under which both change and consistency result without assuming that one or the other is necessarily the
dominant theme.

V. Conclusions

This chapter has presented an evaluative review of findings in distinct
age groups and for specific behaviors through the life-span. This overview
of data regarding behavioral consistency and change may be summarized
by the following statements:

1. Every age period in human life evidences behavioral changes.

2. There is evidence that in any period of life consistency of behavior can be observed.

3. Interindividual variability of behavior is well documented from pre-natal to terminal stages.

Findings relating to the first two points can be integrated by reference to the postulated scale of low–high change or high–low consistency as one of the fundamental dimensions of development. Although we stressed the presence of "consistencies" across the life span, the essential component of a concept of development refers to changes of different degrees. Therefore, we are in agreement with those writers who consider low to high change as the more relevant label. The majority of the findings from empirical research point to gradual change. We expect, therefore, a continuous sequence of gradual changes as the normal pattern of development throughout the life span. This position is in direct contrast to those (e.g., Flavell, 1970) that view one period of the life span as being more appropriate to the study of development than another.

On the other hand, there exists a high degree of interindividual variability regarding not only degree of change, but also onset, direction, and quality of change. The most important aspect of these interindividual differences refers to patterns of changes, i.e., different combinations of change scores within different behavioral processes. The first pioneers of child psychology, such as Preyer, Shinn, and Stern, reported these patterns of change in their diaries on their own children. Between 1930 and 1950, a search for the patterning was one of the ideas in the minds of the leaders of longitudinal research with children (see also McCall, 1977).

At the present time, the study of patterns of change has been successful within more restricted age ranges, such as infancy, adolescence, or old age. The evaluation of the Berkeley Child Guidance Study, as done by Block (1971), demonstrates opportunities for following interindividual variations in the combination of low and high change across longer segments of the life cycle. Such studies as this and others might result in a conception of developmental psychology which emphasizes the consistency of "change profiles" related to certain events during the life span. Chronological age per se does not appear to be sufficient for organizing research and theory in the field. Event-focused research would enable us to differentiate developmental change from other types of behavioral change in such a way as to make it clear why objections to the use of the concept of development for other periods of the life span are neither cogent nor persuasive.

One scientific position which illustrates, from another vantage point, the shortcomings of the chronological age concept as the primary criterion for defining development is the evolution of distinct concepts of time. With the extension of time, we are facing the problem of the different meanings of time (Baltes & Goulet, 1971). Whenever we try to explain changes related to more extended parts of the life cycle, chronological time is just one type of time we may consider. From basic research in physics and biology we know of many aspects of time (Fraser, Haber, & Müller, 1972). Furthermore, there exists "social time" in terms of rather well-ordered sequences of different status systems according to culturally defined age norms (Neugarten & Datan, 1973), and there are quite a few conceptualizations of psychological time (Aaronson, 1972; Baltes & Goulet, 1971; Buss, 1973; Cohen, 1967; Fraisse, 1963; Munnichs, 1977; Nuttin, 1964).

We suggest, then, that rather than defining development as the study of age-change relationships, it is necessary to conceive of this complex process using as a frame of reference the different times or aspects of time the individual is faced with in proceeding from conception to death. From this viewpoint, the life span of an individual might be defined as a sequence of interactions between different aspects of time and behavioral change. Comparing the criteria offered so far to discriminating the study of change in any of the behavioral sciences from the study of developmental change, there is no alternative to this interactionist definition of development. As pointed out by Landsberg (1970) and by Dobbs (1971), any process of change has the quality of unidirectedness (irreversibility) and ordered structure. In this sense, it is perfectly appropriate to apply a developmental conception to all periods of the life span, and not only to the periods of childhood and adolescence.

In sum, objections to the use of the concept of development beyond childhood (e.g., Flavell, 1970) are based on wrong suppositions. The way to discriminate developmental changes in behavior from other types of behavioral changes is to consider the complex meanings of time to which developmental psychologists have to relate changes of behavior. As the complexity of the interaction between different dimensions of time and different behavioral changes is becoming increasingly relevant, we may even say that life-span developmental psychology is the only approach which focuses on developmental change. From this viewpoint, we might reformulate the comment of Baer and Wright (1974) in the following way: From many studies using only very limited time ranges we may wonder if the psychology of childhood or adolescence is related at all to developmental change. However there certainly is a life-span developmental psychology which, due to the complexity of the change phenomena involved, is less likely to focus on changes which are judged to be irrelevant or trivial if strict criteria of a concept of development are applied.

Acknowledgment

The author is indebted to Richard M. Lerner, Judy K. Plemons, Jackie Unch, and Vincent Morello for their valuable contributions to the content and style of this chapter.

References

Aaronson, B. S. Personality stereotypes of aging. *Journal of Gerontology,* 1966, **21,** 458–462.

Aaronson, B. S. Time, time stance, and existence. In J. T. Fraser, F. C. Haber, & G. H. Müller (Eds.), *The study of time.* Heidelberg: Springer, 1972, 293–311.

Abe, J. Rural-urban differences in the behavior of adolescents in present day Japan. In H. Thomae & T. Endo (Eds.), *The adolescent and his environment: Contribution to human development* (Vol. 1). Basel, New York: Karger, 1974.

Adams, D. L. Correlates of satisfaction among the elderly. *Gerontologist,* 1973, **13,** 58–61.

Anderson, J. E. *Psychology of development and personal adjustment.* New York: Holt, 1949.

Anderson, J. E. A developmental model for aging. *Vita Humana,* 1958, **1,** 5–18.

Andersson, B. E. *Studies in adolescent behavior.* Stockholm: Almqvist & Wiksell, 1969.

Andrew, J. M. Coping style and declining verbal abilities. *Journal of Gerontology,* 1973, **28,** 179–183.

Baer, D. M., & Wright, J. C. Developmental psychology. *Annual Review of Psychology,* 1974, **25,** 1–82.

Baldwin, A. L. A cognitive theory of socialization. In D. Goslin (Ed.), *Handbook of socialization theory and research.* Chicago: Rand McNally, 1969.

Baltes, P. B. Longitudinal and cross-sectional sequences in the study of age and generation effects. *Human Development,* 1968, **11,** 145–151.

Baltes, P. B., & Goulet, L. R. Status and issues of a life-span developmental psychology. In L. R. Goulet & P. B. Baltes (Eds.), *Life-span developmental psychology.* New York, London: Academic Press, 1970.

Baltes, P. B., & Goulet, L. R. Exploration of developmental variables by manipulation and simulation of age differences. *Human Development,* 1971, **14,** 149–170.

Baltes, P. B., & Schaie, K. W. On the plasticity of intelligence in adulthood and old age. *American Psychologist,* 1976, **31,** 720–725.

Bandura, A. The stormy decade: Fact or fiction. *Psychology in the Schools,* 1964, **1,** 224–231.

Bayley, N. The life span as a frame of reference in psychological research. *Vita Humana,* 1963, **6,** 125–139.

Bayley, N. Development of mental abilities. In P. H. Mussen (Ed.), *Carmichael's manual of child psychology.* New York, London: Wiley, 1970.

Bernard, H. W. *Human development in Western culture* (2nd ed.). Boston: Allyn & Bacon, 1964.

Birns, B. Individual differences in human neonates responses to stimulation. *Child Development,* 1965, **36,** 249–256.

Birren, J. E., Butler, R. N., Greenhouse, S. W., Sokoloff, L., & Yarrow, M. F. *Human aging: A biological and behavioral study.* Bethesda, Md.. National Institute of Health, 1963.

Birren, J., Woodruff, D., & Bergman, S. Research, demonstration, and training: Issues in methodology in social gerontology. *The Gerontologist,* 1972, **12,** 49–83.

Bischof, L. B. *Adult psychology.* New York: Harper & Row, 1969.

Block, J. *Lives through time.* Berkeley: Bancroft, 1971.

Böcher, W. E., Heemskerk, J. J., & Marx, M. W. *Rehabilitationsmöglichkeiten alternder Menschen.* Bonn: Schriftenreihe des Bundesministers für Jugend, Familie and Gesundheit, 1973.

Britton, P. G., Bergmann, K., Day, D. W., & Savage, R. Mental state, cognitive functioning, physical health, and social class in the community aged. *Journal of Gerontology,* 1967, **22,** 517–522.

Bronson, W. C. Central orientations: A study of behavior organization from childhood to adolescence. *Child Development,* 1966, **37,** 793–810.

Bronson, W. C. Adult derivates of emotional expressiveness and reactivity-control; developmental continuities from childhood to adulthood. *Child Development,* 1967, **38,** 801–817.

Bühler, C. *Der menschliche Lebenslauf als psychologisches Problem.* Leipzig: Hirzel, 1933.

Buss, A. R. A conceptual framework for learning effecting the development of ability factors. *Human Development,* 1973, **16,** 273–292.

Campbell, E. Q. Adolescent socialization. In D. A. Goslin (Ed.), *Handbook of socialization theory and research.* Chicago: Rand McNally, 1969, 821–859.

Cattell, R. B. *Abilities: Their structure, growth, and action.* Boston: Houghton, 1971.

Cesa-Bianchi, M., & Callgari, P. Differences in the behavior of Milanese adolescents belonging to opposite socio-economic status. In H. Thomae & T. Endo (Eds.), *The adolescent and his environment.* New York: Basel, 1974.

Charles, D. C. Historical antecedents of life-span developmental psychology. In L. R. Goulet & P. B. Baltes (Eds.), *Life-span developmental psychology: Research and theory.* New York, London: Academic Press, 1970.

Chess, S. Temperament in the normal infant. In J. Hellmuth (Ed.), *Exceptional infant* (Vol. I). New York: Brunner-Mazel, 1967.

Chess, S., Thomas, A., & Birch, H. G. Characteristics of the individual child's behavioral response to the environment. *American Journal of Orthopsychiatry,* 1959, **29,** 791–802.

Coerper, C., Hagen, W., & Thomae, H. (Eds.), *Deutsche Nachkriegskinder.* Stuttgart: Thieme, 1954.

Cohen, J. *Psychological time in health and disease.* Springfield, Ill.: Thomas, 1967.

Coleman, J. S. *The adolescent society.* New York: The Free Press of Glencoe, 1961.

Comer, J. P. Manhood at puberty; the dilemma of disadvantaged males in this technological age. In S. R. Berenberg (Ed.), *Puberty.* Leiden: H. E. Stenfurt Kroese, 1975.

Corah, N. L., & Gospodinoff, E. J. Color-form and whole part perception in children. *Child Development,* 1966, **37,** 837–842.

Denenberg, V. H. (Ed.), *The development of behavior.* Stamford, Conn.: Sinnauer, 1972.

Dobbs, H. A. The dimensions of the sensible present. *Studium Generale,* 1971, **24,** 369–387.

Eisner, H. C., Siegler, I. C., & Eisele, F. R. Contemporary views on behavioral development: A review. *Human Development,* 1974, **17,** 231–234.

Erikson, H. E. Growth and crises of the healthy personality. In M. Senn (Ed.), *Symposium on the healthy personality.* New York: J. Macy Foundation, 1950.

Essing, W. Untersuchungen zu einem Beurteilungssystem der Persönlichkeit. *Archiv für die gesamte Psychologie,* 1966, **118,** 73–85.

Ewert, O. *Entwicklungspsychologie.* Köln: Kiepenheuer, 1972.

Fiske, S. W., & Rice, L. Intraindividual response variability. *Psychological Bulletin,* 1955, **52,** 217–250.

Flavell, J. H. Cognitive changes in adulthood. In L. R. Goulet & P. B. Baltes, (Eds.), *Life-span developmental psychology: Research and theory.* New York, London: Academic Press, 1970.

Fraisse, P. *The psychology of time.* New York: Harper & Row, 1963.

Fraser, I. T., Haber, F. C., & Müller, G. H. *The study of time.* Berlin, Heidelberg: Springer, 1972.

Friedman, S. B. Emotional maturation and behavior. In S. R. Berenberg (Ed.), *Puberty.* New York: J. Macy Foundation, 1975.

Gale, R. F. *Developmental behavior.* London: Macmillan, 1969.

Gardner, D. B. *Development in early childhood.* New York: Harper & Row, 1964.

Gesell, A. *The embryology of behavior.* New York, London: Harper, 1945.

Gesell, A. *Studies in child development.* New York, London: Harper, 1948.

Gottesman, L. E. Milieu treatment of the aged in institutions. *Gerontologist* 1973, **13,** No. 1, 23–27.

Graefe, O. Versuche über visuelle Formwahrnehmung im Säuglingsalter. *Psychologische Forschung,* 1963, **27,** 177–224.

Granick, S., & Friedmann, A. S. The effect of education in the decline of test performance with age. *Journal of Gerontology,* 1967, **22,** 191–195.

Green, R. F. Age-intelligence relationships between ages sixteen and sixty-four: A rising trend. *Developmental Psychology, 1969,* **1,** 618–627.

Grinder, R. E. *Adolescence.* New York, London: Wiley, 1973.

Groffmann, K. J. Life-span developmental psychology in Europe: Past and present. In L. R. Goulet & P. B. Baltes (Eds.), *Life-span developmental psychology: Research and theory.* New York, London: Academic Press, 1970.

Guilford, J. P. *The nature of human intelligence.* New York: McGraw-Hill, 1967.

Hagen, W., & Thomae, H. *Deutsche Nachkriegskinder 1952-1961.* München: Barth, 1962.

Hahn, M. *Einige Veränderungen von Intelligenzleistungen im Kindes- und Jugendalter.* Unpublished doctoral dissertation, Bonn, 1972.

Hall, G. S. *Adolescence* (2 vols.). New York: Appleton, 1908.

Hanson, R. A. Consistency and stability of home environmental measures related to IQ. *Child Development,* 1975, **46,** 470–480.

Havighurst, R. J. Dominant concerns in life. In L. Schenk-Danzinger & H. Thomae (Eds.), *Gegenwartsprobleme der Entwicklungspsychologie.* Göttingen: Verlag für Psychologie Hogrefe, 1963.

Havighurst, R. J. Life style transitions related to personality after age fifty. In J. Shanan (Ed.), *Proceedings of the 2nd Symposium of the International Society for Study of Behavioral Development.* Kibbutz Aravim, Israel: 1975.

Hindley, C. B., Filliozat, A. M., Klackenberg, G., Nicolet-Meister, D., & Sand, E. A. Differences in age of walking in five European longitudinal samples. *Human Biology,* 1966, **38,** 364–374.

Holtzman, W., & Diaz-Guerrero, R. *Personality development in two cultures.* Austin: University of Texas Press, 1976.

Honzik, M. P. Environmental correlates of mental growth: Prediction from the family setting at 21 months. *Child Development,* 1967, **38,** 337–364.

Hulicka, I. M. Short term learning and retention efficiency as a function of age and health. *Journal of the American Geriatric Society,* 1967, **15,** 285–294.

Hurlock, E. B. *Developmental psychology.* New York: McGraw-Hill, 1968.

Jaide, W. *Das Verhältnis der Jugend zur Politik.* Neuwied: Luchterhand, 1964.

Jarvik, L. F. Biological differences in intellectual functioning. *Vita Humana,* 1962, **5,** 195–203.

Jones, H. E., & Conrad, H. S. The growth and decline of intelligence: A study of a homogenous group between the ages ten and sixty. *Genetic Psychological Monographs,* 1933, **33,** 223–298.

Kagan, J., & Kogan, N. Individual variation in cognitive functioning. In P. H. Mussen (Ed.), *Carmichael's manual of child psychology* (Vol. I). New York, London: Wiley, 1970.

Kagan, J., & Moss, H. A. *Birth to maturity: A study in psychological development.* New York: Wiley, 1962.

Kessen, W., Williams, E. J., & Williams, J. P. Selection and test of response measures in the study of the human newborn. *Child Development,* 1961, **32,** 7–24.

Klonoff, H., & Kennedy, M. A comparative study of cognitive functioning in old age. *Journal of Gerontology,* 1966, **21,** 288–303.

Kogan, N. Creativity and cognitive style: A life span perspective. In P. B. Baltes & K. W. Schaie (Eds.), *Life-span developmental psychology: Personality and socialization.* New York, London: Academic Press, 1973.

Koller, S. Normalwerte im Alter. *Zeitschrift für Gerontologie,* 1972, **5,** 362–370.

Korner, A. F. Neonatal startles, smiles, erections, and reflex sucks as related to state, sex, and individuality. *Child Development,* 1969, **40,** 1039–1053.

Labouvie, G. V. Implications of geropsychological theories for intervention: The challenge of the seventies. *Gerontologist,* 1973, **13,** 10–14.

Landsberg, P. T. Time in statistical physics and special relativity. *Studium Generale,* 1970, **23,** 1108–1158.

Lehr, U. Veränderungen der Daseinsthematik der Frau im Erwachsenenalter. *Vita Humana,* 1961, **2,** 193–228.

Lehr, U. *Frau und Beruf: Eine psychologische Analyse der weiblichen Berufsrolle.* Frankfurt: Athenaeum, 1969. (a)

Lehr, U. Die Acceleration der Entwicklung als biologisches und sozialpsychologisches Problem. *Zeitschrift für Entwicklungspsychologie und Pädagogische Psychologie,* 1969, **1,** 55–70. (b)

Lehr, U. *Psychologie des Alterns.* Heidelberg: Quelle & Meyer, 1972.

Lehr, U. Die Frage der Gliederung des menschlichen Lebenslaufes. *Actuelle Gerontologie,* 1976, **6,** 337–345.

Lehr, U., & Bonn, R. Ecology of adolescents as assessed by the daily round method in an affluent society. In H. Thomae & T. Endo (Eds.), *The adolescent and his environment.* Basel, New York: Karger, 1974.

Lehr, U., & Thomae, H. Eine Längsschnittuntersuchung bei 30–50 jährigen Angestellten. *Vita Humana,* 1958, **1,** 100–110.

Lehr, U., & Thomae, H. Konflikt, seelische Belastung und Lebensalter. *Forschungsberichte des Landes Nordrhein-Westfalen Nr.* 1455. Köln-Opladen: Westdeutscher Verlag, 1965.

Ljung, B. O. *The adolescent spurt in mental growth. Stockholm studies in educational psychology,* **8,** Stockholm: Almqvist & Wiksell, 1965.

Maas, H. S., & Kuypers, J. A. *From thirty to seventy.* San Francisco, London: Jossey-Bass, 1974.

McCall, R. B. Challenges to a science of developmental psychology. *Child Development,* 1977, **48**, 333–344.

McCall, R., Appelbaum, M. I., & Hogarty, P. S. Developmental changes in mental performance. *Monographs of the Society for Research in Child Development,* 1973, **38** (3, Serial No. 150).

McCall, R., Hogarty, P. S., & Hurlburt, N. Transitions in infant sensorimotor development and the prediction of childhood IQ. *American Psychologist,* 1972, **27**, 728–748.

McFarlane, J. W. Perspectives on personality consistency and change from the Guidance Study. *Vita Humana,* 1964, **7**, 115–126.

McFarlane, J. W., Allen, L., & Honzik, M. *A developmental study of the behavior problems of normal children.* Berkeley: University of California Press, 1954.

McKee, J. P., & Turner, W. S. The relation of 'drive' ratings in adolescence to CPI and EPPS scores in adulthood, *Vita Humana,* 1961, **4**, 1–14.

Mead, M. *Growing up in New Guinea.* New York: Norton, 1928.

Miles, C. C. The influence of speed and age on intelligence scores of adults. *Journal of Genetic Psychology,* 1934, **10**, 208–210.

Moers, U. *Die Entwicklungsphasen des menschlichen Lebens.* Ratingen: Henn, 1953.

Munnichs, J. M. *Chronological, social, and psychological time.* Paper presented at the World Conference on "Old age: A challenge for science and social policy." Vichy, France, April 1977.

Mussen, P. *Carmichael's handbook of child psychology.* New York, London: Wiley, 1970.

Mussen, P., & Bonterline-Young, H. Relationships between rate of physical maturing and personality among boys of Italian descent. *Vita Humana,* 1964, **7**, 186–200.

Mussen, P. H., & Jones, M. C. Self-conceptions, motivations, and interpersonal attitudes of late- and early-maturing boys. *Child Development,* 1957, **28**, 243–256.

Nesselroade, J. R., & Baltes, P. B. Adolescent personality development and historical change: 1970-1972. *Monographs of the Society for Research in Child Development,* 1974, **39** (Serial no. 154).

Nesselroade, J. R., Schaie, K. W., & Baltes, P. B. Ontogenetic and generational components of structural and quantitative change in adult cognitive behavior. *Journal of Genetic Psychology,* 1972, **27**, 222–228.

Neugarten, B. L. Personality and the aging processes. *The Gerontologist,* 1972, **12**, 9–15.

Neugarten, B. L., & Datan, N. Sociological perspectives of the life cycle. In P. B. Baltes & K. W. Schaie (Eds.), *Life-span developmental psychology: Personality and socialization.* New York: Academic Press, 1973.

Neugarten, B. L., & Havighurst, R. J. Disengagement reconsidered in a cross-national context. In R. J. Havighurst, J. M. Munnichs, B. L. Neugarten, & H. Thomae (Eds.), *Adjustment to retirement.* Assen: Van Gorcum, 1969.

Neugarten, B. L., & Moore, J. W. The changing age-status system. In B. L. Neugarten (Ed.), *Middle age and aging.* Chicago: Univ. of Chicago Press, 1968.

Nuttin, J. *Motivation und Zeitperspektive.* Bonn: Vortrag, 1967.

Offer, D. *The psychological world of the teen-ager: A study of normal adolescent boys.* New York: Basic Books, 1969.

Olson, W. C. Developmental theory in education. In D. B. Harris (Ed.), *The concept of development.* Minneapolis: University of Minnesota Press, 1957.

Owens, W. A. Age and mental abilities: A second follow up. *Journal of Educational Psychology,* 1966, **57**, 311–325.

Palmore, E. *Normal aging* (Vol. I). Durham: Duke University Press, 1970.

Palmore, E. *Normal aging* (Vol. II). Durham: Duke University Press, 1974.

Papalia, D. E., & Del Vento Bielby, D. Cognitive functioning in middle and old age adults. *Human Development*, 1974, **17**, 397–472.

Peck, R. Psychological developments in the second half of life. In J. E. Anderson (Ed.), *Psychological aspects of aging*. Washington, D.C.: American Psychological Association, 1956.

Piaget, J. Intellectual evolution from adolescence to adulthood. *Human Development*, 1972, **15**, 1–2.

Pressey, S. L., Janney, J. E., & Kuhlen, J. R. *Life: A psychological survey*. New York: Harper, 1939.

Preyer, W. *The mind of the child*. New York: Appleton-Century, 1908.

Reichard, S., Livson, F., & Petterson, P. G. *Aging and personality*. New York: Wiley, 1962.

Rosenmayr, L. New theoretical approaches to the sociological study of young people. *International Social Sciences Journal*, 1972, **24**, 216–256.

Rowe, E. M., & Schmore, M. M. Item concreteness and reported strategies in paired-associate learning as functions of age. *Journal of Gerontology*, 1971, **26**, 470–475.

Rudinger, G. Eine Querschnittuntersuchung im Altersbereich 20-90 Jahre. *Zeitschrift für Gerontologie*, 1974, **7**, 323–333.

Scarr, S. Genetic factors in activity formation. *Child Development*, 1966, **37**, 663–673.

Schaffer, H. R. Activity level as a constitutional determinant of infantile reaction to deprivation. *Child Development*, 1966, **37**, 595–602.

Schaie, K. W. A general model for the study of developmental problems. *Psychological Bulletin*, 1965, **64**, 92–107.

Schaie, K. W. Methodological problems in the descriptive developmental research on adulthood and aging. In J. R. Nesselroade & H. W. Reese (Eds.), *Life-span developmental psychology: Methodological issues*. New York, London: Academic Press, 1973.

Scheffler, S. *Wiederaufnahme einer Berufstätigkeit bei Frauen*. Unpublished doctoral dissertation, Bonn, 1970.

Schmidt, H. *Ältere Arbeitnehmer im technischen Wandel*. Unpublished doctoral dissertation, Bonn, 1972.

Schneider, H. D. *Soziale Rollen im Erwachsenenalter*. Frankfurt: Thesen Verlag, 1970.

Schubert, R. Verschiedene Formen des Alterns. In R. Schubert (Ed.), *Flexibilität der Altersgrenze*. Darmstadt: Steinkopff, 1969. Pp. 1–3.

Shinn, M. W. *The biography of a baby*. New York: Houghton Mifflin, 1900.

Skolnik, A. Stability and interrelations of thematic test imagery over 20 years. *Child Development* 1966, **37**, 389–396.

Sobel, I. Economic changes and older workers utilization patterns. *Interdisciplinary topics in gerontology, (Karger Verlag No. 6)*, 1970, **43**, 64.

Sontag, L. W., Barker, C. I., & Nelson, V. L. Mental growth and personality development: A longitudinal study. *Monographs of the Society for Research in Child Development*, 1958, **23** (2, Whole No. 68).

Speith, W. Cardiovascular health status, age, and psychological performance. *Journal of Gerontology*, 1964, **19**, No. 3, 277–284.

Spitz, R. A. Hospitalism: An inquiry into the genesis of psychiatric conditions in early childhood. *Psychoanalytical study of children*, 1945, **1**, 55–74.

Spranger, E. *Psychologie des Jugendalters* (25th ed.). Heidelberg: Quelle & Meyer, 1966. (Originally published, 1926.)

Stern, W. *Psychologie der frühen Kindheit bis zum sechsten Lebensjahr*. Leipzig: Quelle & Meyer, 1914.

Terman, L. M., & Oden, M. H. *Genetic studies of genius: The gifted child grows up* (Vol. 4). Stanford: Stanford Univ. Press, 1947.

Terman, L. M., & Oden, M. H. *The gifted group at mid-life.* Stanford: Stanford University Press, 1959.

Thomae, H. Foreword. *Vita Humana,* 1958, **1**, 2–3.

Thomae, H. Entwicklungsbegriff und Entwicklungstheorie. In H. Thomae (Ed.), *Handbuch der Psychologie, Vol. 3,* 2nd ed. Goettingen: Verlag für Psychologie Hogrefe, 1959. Pp. 3–20. (a)

Thomae, H. (Ed.), *Handbuch der Psychologie, Vol. 3: Entwicklungspsychologie* (2nd ed.). Goettingen: Verlag für Psychologie Hogrefe, 1959. (b)

Thomae, H. *Vita Humana. Beiträge zu einer genetischen Anthropologie.* Frankfurt: Athenaeum, 1969.

Thomae, H. Anpassungsprobleme im höheren Alter aus psychologischer Sicht. *Actuelle Gerontologie,* 1974, **4**, 647–656.

Thomae, H. (Ed.). Patterns of aging. Findings from the Bonn longitudinal study of aging. *Contributions to Human Development,* 1976, **3**. Basel: Karger Verlag.

Thomae, H., & Lehr, U. *Berufliche Leistungsfähigkeit im mittleren und höheren Erwachsenenalter.* Goettingen: O. Schwartz, 1973.

Thomae, H., & Simons, H. Reaktionen auf Belastungssituationen im höheren Alter. *Zeitschrift für experimentelle und angewandte Psychologie,* 1967, **14**, 290–312.

Thomas, A., Chess, S., Birch, H. C., Hertzig, M. E., & Korn, S. *Behavioral individuality in early childhood.* New York: New York University Press, 1963.

Tischler, H. Schreien, Lallen und erstes Sprechen im der Entwicklung des Säuglings. *Zeitschrift fur Psychologie,* 1957, **160**, 210–263.

Tuckman, J., & Lorge, I. Attitudes toward older workers. *Journal of Social Psychology,* 1952, **36**, 149–153.

Tuckman, J., & Lorge, I. Attitudes toward old people. *Journal of Social Psychology,* 1953, **37**, 249–260.

Uhr, R. *Persönlichkeitsentwicklung im frühen Erwachsenenalter.* Unpublished research report. Department of Psychology, University of Bonn, 1968.

Uhr, R., Thomae, H., & Becker, J. Entwicklungsverläufe im Kindes und Jugendalter. *Zeitschrift fur Entwicklungspsychologie und Pädagogische Psychologie,* 1969, **1**, 151–164.

Wall, W. D. Intelligence and cognition. In S. R. Berenberg (Ed.), *Puberty.* Leiden: Stenfert Kroese, 1975.

Wechsler, D. *The measurement of adult intelligence* (3rd ed.). Baltimore: Williams & Wilkins, 1944.

Weinstock, C., & Benett, R. The relation between social isolation and related cognitive skills of a Catholic and Jewish home for the aged. *Proceedings of the International Congress on Gerontology, Washington,* 1969, **2**, 98.

Werner, H. The concept of development from a comparative and organismic point of view. In D. B. Harris, (Ed.), *The concept of development.* Minneapolis: University of Minnesota Press, 1957.

Whittington, S., Wilkie, F., & Eisdorfer, C. Attitudes of young adults and older people toward concepts related to old age. *The Gerontologist,* 1972, **12**, Part II, 55.

Williams, R. H., & Wirths, C. G. *Lives through the years.* New York: Wiley, 1965.

Winkelmann, W. *Persönlichkeit und Schulanpassung bei Grundschulkindern.* Bonn: Bouvier, 1971.

Witkin, H. A., & Berry, J. W. Psychological differentiation in cross-cultural perspective. *Journal of Cross-cultural Psychology,* 1975, **6**, 4–87.

Zazzo, B. *Psychologie differentielle d'adolescence.* Paris: Presses Universitaires, 1965.

Dialectics, History, and Development: The Historical Roots of the Individual–Society Dialectic

Allan R. Buss

DEPARTMENT OF PSYCHOLOGY, UNIVERSITY OF CALGARY
CALGARY, CANADA

Abstract

The individual–society relationship is an idea that has a history. Unfortunately, its history has been largely forgotten by those who should be remembering it. Thus, the recent concern within life-span developmental psychology for what has come to be called the individual–society "dialectic" suffers from a lack of a historical appreciation of the issues. This chapter traces the idea of the individual–society dialectic back to two theoretical failures: that of orthodox Marxism and that of orthodox psychoanalysis. The ideas of Reich, Fromm, and Erikson are considered insofar as these individuals attempted to accommodate the new historical realities confronting them by expanding on the idea of an individual–society dialectic. Finally, a fundamental paradox is noted concerning the individual–society relationship—a paradox that would appear to make that relationship unmistakably a dialectical one.

I. Introduction

Dialectical concepts and thinking have a long history. Like many ideas, dialectical ones can be traced back to the early Greeks. Recently there has

LIFE-SPAN DEVELOPMENT
AND BEHAVIOR, VOL. 2

been an attempt within North America to incorporate dialectics into psychology. The prime movers of this recent interest in psychology and dialectics have been Joseph F. Rychlak and the late Klaus F. Riegel. Rychlak's (1968) book, *A Philosophy of Science for Personality Theory,* first introduced psychologists to the intellectual history of dialectics and its relevance to understanding the works of Freud and Jung. Riegel, beginning with a series of articles and chapters in the early 1970s (e.g., 1972a, 1972b, 1973, 1975), emphasized the value of dialectics for developmental psychology, including the idea of a dialectic between the changing or developing individual and the changing or evolving society. It is the latter idea that constitutes the subject matter of the present chapter.

In spite of the recent concern for the individual–society dialectic within developmental psychology, it would appear that there has been little conceptual progress beyond earlier efforts to deal with this issue. Part of the explanation for the apparent lack of significant theoretical and conceptual advancement concerning the issue of the individual–society dialectic is the inherent difficulty of the task. However, I believe that an additional factor is that important past efforts have been forgotten. There has generally been no historical appreciation of the idea of an individual–society dialectic as constituting a real problem in recent psychological treatments. That is to say, there is a history to the idea of the individual–society dialectic, and to make theoretical progress on this issue requires one to take cognizance of its history.

The history that we are alluding to is itself part of an ongoing social, as well as intellectual, dialectical process. The changes and transformations that the idea of an individual–society dialectic has undergone are based upon concrete sociopolitical events, and the failure of previous theoretical efforts to accommodate the new social realities.

It is not the purpose of this chapter to review recent contributions to a dialectical psychology. Rather, my intent is to try and recover a bit of recent history for those life-span developmental psychologists interested in the idea of the individual–society dialectic. In so doing, we may at least clear the way for moving beyond past and present theoretical efforts to deal with the individual–society dialectic. Thus, the present chapter is propaedeutic to a major coup in this area—nothing more, but certainly nothing less.

II. The Historical Problem

A. THE FAILURE OF ORTHODOX MARXISM

Historically speaking, it was Marx who gave modern expression to the dialectical nature of the relationship between the individual and society:

Men make their own history, but do not make it just as they please; they do not make it under circumstances chosen by themselves, but under circumstances directly encountered, given and transmitted from the past. (Marx, quoted in McLennan, 1971, p. 125)

However, Marx did not supply the needed social-psychological theory to explain the individual–society dialectic. The pressure for a more analytic treatment of the idea of a changing or developing individual, in a changing or evolving society, goes back to the failure of social revolution in the West just after World War I. The proletariat's refusal to rise up against the bourgeoisie and seize control over its own destiny in post-World War I Europe was contradictory to Marx's prediction of the collapse of capitalism due to its inherent contradictions. The revolution that did materialize in 1917 occurred in what was really a feudalistic rather than a capitalistic society, and it did not produce the democratic and emancipatory social order that Marx had envisioned as arising out of the ashes of bourgeois capitalism. Orthodox Marxism had failed, and during the aftermath of the Great War and the Russian Revolution, there were three major attempts to supplement and rework its core in order to make the theory at least compatible with recent sociohistorical events, and, it was hoped, thereby to transform it into a more valid theory of social and historical change.

One attempt to revise Marx was Marxism–Leninism (also known as "vulgar Marxism" by its critics—see below). This solution to the failure of orthodox Marxism was based upon Lenin's theory of the party. According to Lenin, the revolution should be directed from the top by a small revolutionary elite, rather than emerging spontaneously from the rank and file, or bottom. Lenin was quite successful in bringing into being a new social order based upon the power of the party. That society, however, did not conform to Marx's emphasis upon emancipation, democracy, and freedom (e.g., see Buss, 1977). Lenin emphasized a hierarchical, one-way bossing relation in both the political and the scientific arenas. Marxism–Leninism, and dialectical materialism, were based upon an authoritarian, unidirectional view of the relationship between the party and the masses, and between nature and ideas, respectively.

A second attempt to "update" Marx became known as "Revisionism." Revisionists sacrificed the iron cage of economic determinism, and thus dialectical materialism, for a more subjective, idealistic, or free will approach to achieving the socialist state based upon ethical considerations. Led by Bernstein, the revisionists formed the Social Democratic Party and advocated democratic and peaceful means for transforming society into a socialist state.

A third group steered a dialectical course by bringing the materialist and idealist dimensions of Marxism together. The major figures in this neo-Marxist group included the Hungarian Georg Lukacs, the Italian Antonio

Gramsci, and the German Karl Korsch. Although different in many respects, all three attempted to emphasize the Hegelian foundations of
Marxism during the 1920s. They thus stressed the active subject within
the context of a concrete or objective historical reality before discovery
and publication of Marx's *Economic and Philosophic Manuscripts* of
1844. The latter works actually confirmed the various Hegelian interpretations of Marx's thinking and supported neither the objective one-way
economic determinism of dialectical materialism, nor the subjective
one-way determinism of Bernstein's revisionism, but rather a truly dialectical conception of base and superstructure, social structure and cognitive
structure, sociology and psychology, society and the individual.

Lukacs, Gramsci, and Korsch (1970) all emphasized the view that
consciousness and ideology were not merely the "reflection" of social
and economic relations of production but, rather, constituted separate
and independent forces of history. Of course ideas, the collective consciousness, or ideologies, were still seen as connected to the material
base, but they also had a life over and above that base. In other words,
they were dialectically connected to the material base.

In spite of the important insights of the early Hegelian interpreters of
Marx, none of them produced a social-psychological theory that accounted for the mediation between the objective material base and the
subjective psychological superstructure. More specifically, the early
Hegelian Marxists did not explain the concrete or specific form of
bourgeois ideology that served to prevent the postwar proletariat from
seizing their historical opportunity for successful revolution. According to
all objective measures, the moment was ripe, yet they failed to keep their
appointment with destiny named social, political, and economic emancipation. Korsch (1970) was at least aware of the need for such a social
psychological theory during the period (1918–1922) when he was interpreting the failure of socialist revolution as being due to psychological or
ideological factors:

> In the fateful months after November 1918, when the organized political power of the
> bourgeoisie was smashed and outwardly there was was nothing else in the way of the
> transition from capitalism to socialism, the great chance was never seized because
> the *socio-psychological* preconditions for its seizure were lacking. For there was
> nowhere to be found any decisive *belief* in the immediate realizability of a socialist
> economic system which could have swept the masses along with it and provided a clear
> knowledge of the nature of the first steps to be taken. (Korsch, 1970, p. 10; original
> emphasis)

Thus the failure of orthodox Marxism was due to its ignoring the
psychological importance of bourgeois ideology in reducing the revolutionary potential of the proletariat. What was now needed was a social

psychological theory that explained the hidden, covert, or subjective forms of domination that had now emerged. In other words, overt repression and exploitation had now become replaced by more subtle mechanisms of psychological control brought about by the internalization of capitalist irrationality. The exploited now accepted the exploiters and their own exploitation! What was now required was theoretical analysis and an even more powerful and radical critique of class consciousness than Marxism was able to provide.

Thus Western neo-Marxists increasingly turned to a study of psychoanalysis during the 1920s and 1930s in the hope of flushing out in a more concrete fashion the individual side of the individual–society dialectic. In this way they sought to achieve theoretical understanding of the psychological mechanisms that served to reproduce and support social reality—however alienating that social reality might be. Consistent with the emphasis upon the dialectic between theory and practice, such theoretical effort was considered to be prerequisite to undermining false consciousness, and to negating the integration of the individual into an irrational society.

B. THE FAILURE OF ORTHODOX PSYCHOANALYSIS

While neo-Marxists were scurrying around looking for a powerful psychological theory, there was also pressure to provide a more adequate analysis of the individual–society relationship from the other side. That is to say, post-Freudians were attempting to supplement psychoanalysis with social, cultural, and historical considerations.

The importance of Freud and psychoanalysis within the history of ideas has been well documented by others, and thus there is no intent to repeat here that intellectual groundwork. Rather, I wish to very briefly focus upon some aspects of psychoanalysis that are most relevant to the idea of the individual–society dialectic. In this way we will be in a position to appreciate just what post-Freudians were reacting to *vis-à-vis* the idea of the individual–society dialectic.

While the conceptual shortcomings of orthodox Marxism were related to its not taking into sufficient account the psychological side of the individual–society dialectic, that of orthodox psychoanalysis was the converse: it ignored the social, cultural, and historical side. Those who were to later attempt a synthesis of Marxism and psychoanalysis had an important insight: Each alone was reductionistic in so far as it committed the error of sociologism and psychologism, respectively, yet together their individual truths could flourish by complementing one another.

The criticism that Freud ignored the role of social and cultural factors in affecting the psyche is a well-worn saw. In Freud's view, there was an endless repetition from generation to generation of the same developmental sequence. While it is true that Freud advanced a theory of psychological development that he believed to be universal, it is also true that his theory contained some important ideas *vis-à-vis* the individual–society dialectic. For one thing, the individual–society relationship in psychoanalysis was considered to be one fraught with conflict. Society, or civilization, was a mixed blessing, since it is achieved at the unavoidable price of harnessing, inhibiting, and repressing many of the individual's most basic and powerful life-drives and instincts. Thus the achievement of civilization cripples and scars the individual, psychologically speaking.

A second idea of Freud's that is relevant to the idea of the relationship between individual and society concerns his theory of the origin of society, and its symbolic repetition within each family. Very briefly, Freud adopted Darwin's theory of the Primal Horde, which was really a sort of myth as to how society began. According to that myth, the primal father of the clan threatened all other males with castration if they had sexual contact with any of the women in the clan. Eventually the primal father was killed by the other males of the clan, and the idea of the nuclear family became established to avoid such problems in the future. Freud supplemented this theory with some ideas from Greek mythology and thereby advanced his notions concerning the Oedipus conflict and the development of the superego. While there is no need to become tangled in the details of this rich theory, the important point for our present purpose relates to the structure of Freud's developmental theory and its relationship to history. That is to say, in Freud's view individual development within the family was a reenactment, in symbolic form, of the history of the species. In other words, Freud subscribed to the notion that individual development repeated species development, or that ontogeny recapitulated phylogeny.

Post-Freudians were to expand and modify the idea of ontogeny recapitulating phylogeny, as well as Freud's view that the unavoidable conflict characteristic of the individual–society relationship was one that was rooted in the unchanging, essential, universal human psyche. Freud's pessimistic, deterministic, ahistorical theory of the individual and society was an expression of an age that had seen the end of the high tide of the optimism so characteristic of much of the 19th century. Freud's time was one that held out little hope. The evidence was mounting against the historical idea of continual progress in the human condition. In a sense, Freud arrived at a similar conclusion for the development of the human psyche as had Hegel for history in general: Human development (or history) had reached the end of the line. However, it is also true that post-Freudians were to become sensitive to the rapidly changing world around them and to the growing interest in cross-cultural questions. To them and to their generation, history was very much on the move and, along with it, were new possibilities for the changing, developing individual psyche.

In summary, then, the theoretical failure of both classical Marxism and psychoanalysis can be seen as due to a model of the individual–society relationship that was inadequate in light of the new social realities. Marxism was heavy on the side of society and short on the individual, while psychoanalysis had the opposite emphasis. Some attempts were made to salvage the truth content of both Marxism and psychoanalysis by bringing them together (e.g., Reich, Horkheimer, Fromm—see Section III, B). Such attempts can be contrasted with those post-Freudians with a sociohistorical approach that was not Marxist inspired (e.g., Erikson—see Section III, C). In both cases, however, the overriding concern was with formulating a model or theory that provided a more valid interpretation of the individual–society relationship in light of new sociohistorical realities. Let us now examine these various theoretical attempts to avoid the errors of both sociologism and psychologism.

III. Proposed Solutions

A. REICH

In looking back at the various attempts to achieve greater theoretical understanding of the individual–society dialectic, one cannot help but be struck by the developmental orientation. This developmental orientation stems from a major underlying theme of the various attempts to synthesize individual and social development that concerned most, if not all of the various attempts to synthesize Marx and Freud—the role of the family in reproducing an alienating and irrational society through its child-rearing habits. Thus, according to several neo-Marxists of the 1930s, the new enemy of exploitation and domination lay in the patterns of psychological development that the family executed with great efficiency, rather than the individual capitalists per se. It was the deep structure of society, the family, that produced a character structure that was susceptible to manipulation and submission.

In Wilhelm Reich's book of 1933, *The Mass Psychology of Fascism*, we find a bold attempt to account for the mass movement of fascism in terms of the family—the chief social agent responsible for the creation of the authoritarian personality. In his words:

> The authoritarian state gains an enormous interest in the authoritarian family: *It becomes the factory in which the state's structure and ideology are molded.* (Reich, 1970, p. 3; original emphasis)

Most important for our present purposes is to note Reich's appreciation of the dialectic between the individual and society within the context of the role of the family in reproducing a conservative, traditional, or, more accurately, outdated character structure—a character structure that comes into conflict with changed socioeconomic relations:

> The basic traits of the character structures corresponding to a definite historical situation are formed in early childhood, and are far more conservative than the forces of technical production. It results from this that, as time goes on, *the psychic structures lag behind the rapid changes of social conditions from which they derive, and later come into conflict with new forms of life.* This is the basic trait of the nature of so-called tradition, i.e., of the contradiction between the old and the new social situation. (Reich, 1970, pp. 18–19; original emphasis)

In the above passage we see that, in contrast to an orthodox Marxist view, the motor of history was not merely changes in the means and relations of production. The latter was certainly an important and necessary factor, but it comprised only one side of the dialectic. The internalization of social structure into character structure, the transformation of social categories into psychological categories, the conversion of social relations into ideology—in short, the subjective or psychological element—comprised the other side of the dialectic of history.

In common with Freud, then, Reich stressed the conflict between the individual and society, although he added the important historical dimension to this process. For Reich, the individual–society conflict had its basis in the contradiction between an older sociohistorical reality, as represented in the character structure of the adult, and the newer sociohistorical reality in which the adult functioned. The development of character structure in childhood was thereby seen to be a process that was historical to its very core. This very important insight of Reich's set him apart from Freud. For Freud, the invariant nature of humanity from generation to generation carried with it no provision for any changes or transformations in the basic rhythm of the developmental process. Reich's emphasis of over 40 years ago on the historicity of childhood implies that the very concepts we use to describe development are historical, and that therefore one cannot understand the developing individual divorced from its sociohistorical context. Thus Reich's approach may be seen as an important precursor of the current fervor with which the childhood–history dialectic is studied (e.g., de Mause, 1976; Gillis, 1974).

B. FROMM AND THE FRANKFURT SCHOOL

Perhaps the most systematic and concentrated onslaught at trying to better understand the failure of revolution in the West—of providing a social psychology that mediated between base and superstructure, society and the individual—was that of the Frankfurt School. The Frankfurt Institute for Social Research was established in 1923 and was committed to a critical social theory of society and the individual based upon an interest in human emancipation. During the 1930s under its most eminent director, Max Horkheimer, the Institute flourished and produced some of its more important critical studies of Marxism and psychoanalysis. Characteristic of the contributions of its illustrious membership at this time—Horkheimer, Fromm, Marcuse, and Adorno—was the union of Freud and Marx for better understanding the new internalized forms of dominance and repression. In the 5-year project *Studies on Authority and Family* (published in 1936), the Institute's members explored, as did Reich at that time, the role of the family in the service of producing an authoritarian character structure.

In the theoretical section of the some 900-page *Studien,* Fromm developed the thesis that Freud's strictly biological and psychological account of authority had to be supplemented, perhaps even replaced, by a historical approach that emphasized socioeconomic factors. Fromm later developed this idea in a more systematic and comprehensive way in the English language book of 1941, *Escape from Freedom.* In this book, Fromm echoed many of the same concerns and impressions as did Reich concerning the family, society, and authority. *Escape from Freedom* was premised upon the importance of ideas and ideologies as independent forces in history. In addition, of course, there was the specific socioeconomic context in which such ideas arise. The link—the cement holding society together at any particular historical moment—was thought to be psychological.

Adopting Reich's term of "character structure", Fromm (1941) rejected Freud's ahistorical view of human nature and placed the nature of humanity, the "*social* character structure," squarely in history: "We look upon human nature as essentially historically conditioned" (p. 290). Thus, according to Fromm, needs arise and form a unique social character structure in the context of new socioeconomic conditions. In fulfilling those needs, individuals satisfy their individual or psychological requirements but, in addition, serve the interests of that society. In Fromm's words, "The social character internalizes necessities and thus harnesses human energy for the task of a given economic and social system" (p. 284). Critical in this whole process is the family, which is "considered to be the psychological agent of society'' (p. 284). And it is in the structure and dynamics of the family where the contradictions, conflicts, and crises between the individual and society are manufactured.

Thus, the social character structure inculcated in childhood by the parents represents the internalization of a historically unique set of social and economic relations. When the child becomes an adult, then that adult's character structure may be inconsistent with the new social and economic realities that may have arisen since childhood. Conflict thus develops between psychological interests and social interests. According to Fromm, the mismatch between current character or psychological structure (past social structure that has been internalized), and current social structure is the breeding ground for aberrant ways of satisfying psychological needs. It is within this theoretical context that Fromm explains the authoritarian personality, the sadomasochistic character structure, and the rise of Naziism and Fascism as mass movements.

Fromm's attempt to integrate history, sociology, and psychology may be viewed as lying within the tradition of a Hegelianized Marxism, with the important addition, however, of a social psychology that mediated between base and superstructure. The locus for that social psychology, which was the glue that bonded together psychological and social interests under conditions of little socioeconomic change, was the interdevelopment of ideas, psychological structure, and social structure within a dialectical unity. This important methodological commitment can be especially appreciated in the following statement:

> Economic forces are effective, but they must be understood not as psychological motivations but as objective conditions: psychological forces are effective, but they must be understood as historically conditioned in themselves; ideas are effective, but they must be understood as being rooted in the whole of the character structure of members of a social group. In spite of this interdependence of economic, psychological, and ideological forces, however, each of them has also a certain independence. (Fromm, 1941, p. 298)

In addition to historicizing Freud's idea of an individual–society conflict, Fromm also went beyond Freud in another important aspect of the individual–society dialectic. Fromm adopted the structural model of ontogeny recapitulating phylogeny but grafted new ideational meat upon those bones. For Fromm, the important story to be told about humanity's past concerned the rise of the idea of the individual, and the accompanying gains of greater self-consciousness and freedom. That is to say, the history of humanity has been one of breaking the ''primary ties,'' mastering nature, and achieving a sense of separateness and greater self-consciousness. ''Freedom from'' the primary ties prepares society for the next important stage—"freedom to" actualize the human possibilities, and to chart a course of social development that is consistent with the values of reason and liberty.

Now, the important point to note in the present context is that, in Fromm's view, individual development involved the same pattern as historical or species development. That is to say, the breaking of the primary ties (the family), the mastery of nature, the sense of separateness, the achievement of self-consciousness, and the growth of reason and freedom—all of these were characteristic of both history and ontogeny. Moreover, the same hurdles and setbacks that may plague social development can also occur at the individual level. That is to say, one can choose to escape the burdens and responsibilities that accompany freedom by giving up critical reason and individuality—thereby achieving a state of false security. The latter involves uncritically committing oneself to an idea, ideology, or group that is irrational yet nonetheless relieves one of the pain of choice, freedom, and individuality.

Horkheimer's opening theoretical essay of *Studies on Authority and Family* contained many of the major methodological points that Fromm later employed in *Escape from Freedom*. Horkheimer's essay has been translated into English and appears in his 1972 book *Critical Theory*. In the section dealing with the family, Horkheimer weaves back and forth from the critical and negative view of the family that Marx developed and the more positive interpretation that Hegel provided. Horkheimer pointed out in a dialectical way that the importance of the family in the new age was precisely due to its decline in importance as an agent of society. The previously positive aspects of the authority structure of the family for socializing the young was now no more—due to certain social forces that have led to the usurping of the father's authority by extrafamilial institutions. In other words, the previously rational authority structure of the family (for that historical point in time) had been undermined and the void was filled by the sometimes irrational authoritarian figures within society. Here Horkheimer was relying upon the theoretical argument previously discussed in connection with Reich and Fromm—the mismatch between the current character structure (based upon the internalization of outdated socioeconomic relations) and the new historical realities.

A more thorough treatment of the contributions of the Frankfurt School in relation to the idea of a changing individual in a changing society is beyond the scope of this chapter. Most important for our present purposes is to note that they wrestled with the historical failure of Marxism in the West after World War I and, in the process, transformed both classical psychoanalysis and classical Marxism. In so doing, they carved out the beginnings of a social-developmental psychology. That social-developmental psychology was certainly not similar to what may go under that banner today. It was really a thoroughly dialectical, historical, and critical development social psychology. Thus, for example, the role of the family in the misdevelopmental process *vis-à-vis* current social reality, was a function of the rapidity of socioeconomic change. Authority within the family was increasingly becoming irrational due to certain social structural changes. Future recovery of the positive function of the family lay in social transformation.

C. ERIKSON

There were some post-Freudians that considerd themselves faithful to the essential ideas of Freud, although they stressed the ego rather than the unconscious, as well as sociocultural considerations. Neo-Freudians, such as Horney, Sullivan, Erikson, and others, attempted to correct the ahistorical view of human nature within classical psychoanalysis by emphasizing the social and cultural determinants of personality development. Their concern for social factors affecting individual development was part of a more general Zeitgeist that was tied in to the rapid development of the disciplines of sociology and anthropology during the 1920s and 1930s. However the neo-Freudian concern for society, culture, and history did not stem directly from an interest in Marxism and its failure. Rather, in contrast to post-Freudian neo-Marxists, such as Reich and Fromm, the neo-Freudians approached the individual–society dialectic from an initial position that emphasizes the individual, or psychology. Their reworking of that dialectic did not, in general, contain the radical social critical dimension that was characteristic of the neo-Marxists.

A partial exception to the latter observation is Erik H. Erikson. Erikson's psychosocial therapy of ego development did contain some social criticism. Erikson, more than any of the other neo-Freudians, was also genuinely interested in historical and sociocultural issues for their own sake, rather than simply regarding them as subordinate to the concerns of psychology. His treatment of the individual–society dialectic was much more analytic and substantial than other neo-Freudian efforts. It is for these reasons that Erikson is singled out here for consideration in terms of his treatment of the individual–society dialectic.

Erikson's appreciation for the interpenetration of psychology and history is evident by his placing of Freud's theory, as well as his own, within a historical context. Thus, in Erikson's view, Freud's psychosexual developmental theory cannot be understood unless one appreciates the Victorian society from which it sprang. From a society in which there was real sexual repression there arose psychoanalysis which was to provide the appropriate antedote. It was through a psychoanalytic understanding of the sexual repression, inhibition, and conflict that critical self-consciousness, or emancipation, was to be won.

However, the society in which Erikson developed his developmental theory was quite different from Freud's. Erikson, the very successfully converted American, was struggling with the unique sociohistorical realities that demanded significant revision of psychoanalysis. Erikson desexualized psychoanalysis and replaced Freud's emphasis on the unconscious with a concern for the ego. The new historical problem to be explained for a developmental psychology in the postindustrial, technologically advanced Unites States was ego diffusion and the loss of ego identity. Thus in contrasting his own patients with Freud's, Erikson (1963) states:

> The patient of today suffers most under the problem of what he should believe in and who he should—or, indeed, might—be or become; while the patient of early psychoanalysis suffered most under inhibitions which prevent him from being what and who he thought he knew he was. (p. 279)

Erikson developed his psychosocial theory of ego development and ego identity in response to the new historical realities confronting the developing individual: "We begin to conceptualize matters of identity at the very time in history when they become a problem" (p. 282). Ego identity for Erikson was a lifelong process, and thus he proposed a life-span developmental theory consisting of eight distinct ego stages. First set out in *Childhood and Society* in 1950, and later elaborated in *Identity and the Life Cycle* in 1959, Erikson viewed development as two-dimensional. Parallelling, yet also interpenetrating, each other were the development of the individual (ontogeny) and the social evolution of society (history). Corresponding to the eight stages of individual development were eight stages of social development. For Erikson, ontogeny also recapitulated history.

Figure 1 represents Erikson's psychosocial stage theory of ego development. At each of the biological stage divisions there is a psychological crisis that is resolved in one of two ways, and that outcome is carried forth, for better or for worse, into the next stage. Not indicated in Fig. 1 are the corresponding social stages of development. Thus the social counterpart of the individual's sense of trust is the institution of religion; of autonomy and self-control is the institution of law and order; of initiative is economics; of industry is a culture's technology; of identity is some kind of ideology; of intimacy is ethics; of generativity is education, art, and sciences; and finally, of integrity are all the great cultural institutions, including economics, politics, philosophy, and religion. It is in this last stage that the beginning and end of the life-cycle come together, insofar as

	1	2	3	4	5	6	7	8
VIII MATURITY								EGO INTEGRITY VERSUS DESPAIR
VII ADULTHOOD							GENERATIVITY VERSUS STAGNATION	
VI YOUNG ADULTHOOD						INTIMACY VERSUS ISOLATION		
V PUBERTY AND ADOLESCENCE					IDENTITY VERSUS ROLE CONFUSION			
IV LATENCY				INDUSTRY VERSUS INFERIORITY				
III LOCOMOTOR- GENITAL			INITIATIVE VERSUS GUILT					
II MUSCULAR- ANAL		AUTONOMY VERSUS SHAME, DOUBT						
I ORAL SENSORY	BASIC TRUST VERSUS MISTRUST							

Fig. 1. Erikson's psychosocial stage model of ego development. (From Erikson, 1963.) Not indicated are the corresponding social stages of development (see text).

the development of trust in the young child depends upon the integrity of their parents.

Admittedly Erikson did not develop the sociohistorical stages as well as his psychological stages. One is never certain of the exact relationship between the two developmental processes, except that society plays a crucial role in the individual outcome of the various stages. In contrast to Freud, who viewed the relationship of the individual and society to be fundamentally one of conflict, Erikson saw society in mainly a supportive role. Individual development was facilitated by society's institutions, and in achieving individual goals one was simultaneously advancing society, and vice versa. Thus the interface of the individual and society, of psychology and history, was generally one of compatibility, nonconflict, integration. The noncritical interpretation of the role of society *vis-à-vis* individual development has led some (e.g., Jacoby, 1975; Roazen, 1976) to charge Erikson with having supplied us with a bourgeois theory that is conformist in nature and supportive of the status quo. However, no simple judgment can be made on this issue, since Erikson has certainly been critical of much of society. His theory must be viewed as containing both conformist and critical dimensions. The critical content of Erikson's theory is present even in 1950, when he lashed out at the adverse effects of industrialization and technology upon development:

This idea of a self-made ego was . . . reinforced and yet modified by industrialization and by class stratification. Industrialization, for example, brought with it mechanical child training. It was as if this new man-made world of machines . . . offered its mastery only to those who would become like it. . . . Thus, a movement in child training began which tended to adjust the human organism from the very start to clocklike punctuality in order to make it a standardized appendix of the industrial world. (pp. 294–295)

In the above passage we get a strong impression of a psychologist looking at development in its historical context for purposes of criticizing alienating and repressive social forces. The above passage is not an isolated one, and in several places Erikson is critical of social institutions and structures that hinder ego development and the achievement of freedom..At the same time, Erikson's ambivalence toward American society is revealed in his sometimes naive and accepting attitude toward the family. In much contrast to Reich, Fromm, and Horkheimer, Erikson (1950, 1963) considered the family to be the breeding ground for the democratic rather than the authoritarian personality! Consider the following:

The American family . . . tends to guard the right of the individual member—parents included—not to be dominated. . . . [there is a] give-and-take [that] cuts down . . . the division of the family into unequal partners. . . . The family becomes a training ground in tolerance of different *interests*—not of different *beings* . . . [there is] an automatic prevention of autocracy and inequality. (pp. 316–318)

Admittedly Erikson's model was the American rather than the European family, yet such a positive, uncritical description is suspicious from a dialectical–critical standpoint. The family, for Erikson, represents all that is good in the American political system, where "The analogy . . . to the two-party system is clear" with its "checks and balances" (p. 318). The problem of authority and the family does not exist in the American family according to Erikson: "The adolescent swings of the American youth do not overtly concern the father, nor the matter of authority, but focus rather on his peers" (p. 318). Thus, it is one's peers rather than the structure of the family that is the source of youth's conflict and rebellion.

It would appear that, for Erikson, the family belongs in the same category as apple pie and motherhood. Or does it? In marked contrast to some of his positive musings on the American family, we can find the counter view in Erikson as well. Consider:

This long childhood exposes adults to the temptations of thoughtlessly and often cruelly exploiting the child's dependence by making him pay for the psychological debts owed to us by others . . . . We have learned not to stunt a child's growing body with child labor, we must now learn not to break his growing spirit by making him the victim of our anxieties. (p. 100)

Characteristically, Erikson the radical critic of the family betrays that position in the very next sentence, when he states that "If we will only learn to let live, the plan for growth is all there" (p. 100). The position expressed here is conformist and capitulatory. Unfortunately the critique is defused as soon as it is made.

Yet, in a noncritical sense (assuming that that makes sense!), Erikson does view the family dialectically. Thus the developing child within the family is only one side of a more complex process. In Erikson's (1959) words:

> It is as true to say that babies control and bring up their families as it is to say the converse. A family can bring up a baby only by being brought up by him. His growth consists of a series of challenges to them to serve his newly developing potentialities for social interaction. (p. 55)

Thus the relationship between children and parents is reciprocal and dialectical—each changes and is changed by the other through time.

Erikson's psychosocial theory of ego development is concerned with conflict, crises, and their successful resolution. The problem for each individual is to preserve a thread of continuity in the context of change and growth. Ego identity is achieved by the ego functions that integrate, synthesize, and resolve contradictions. However, maintaining a sense of continuity and sameness through time requires that the individual's development be consistent with the major trends of history. For Erikson, psychological growth and health is possible only to the extent that the individual is not out of step with society. At times integration of the individual and society seems for Erikson to supercede justified confrontation, conflict, and alienation. The price of continuity, synthesis, and integration may be the achieving of false continuities, syntheses, and integrations.

We may reach the above conclusion in yet another way. Mastery of one's environment and of one's experience is a theme that appears often in Erikson's writings. While Erikson is concerned with individual mastery through development, he would seem to be satisfied with a sense of mastery rather than real mastery. Erikson is too much the subjectivist—being too satisfied with a sense of mastery, continuity, and identity rather than critically examining the objective situation. Such a position once again leads him to conformist conclusions, as when he states:

> The growing child must, at every step, derive a vitalizing sense of reality from the awareness that his individual way of mastering experience is a successful variant of the way others around him master experience and recognize such mastery. (1959, p. 89)

Another aspect of Erikson's theory that potentially leads to false continuities, resolutions, and integrations concerns the outcome of each of the eight developmental stages. Thus I can imagine a society where the more valid reaction is shame and doubt rather than autonomy, guilt rather than initiative, identity diffusion rather than identity. The conflict and confusion that an individual experiences may represent a healthy response to a social reality that is psychologically (not to mention physically) repressive, alienating, and constricting. Integration of the individual into society is not an absolute to be unquestioningly sought after. Thus I disagree with Erikson's view that the healthy individual in the eighth and final stage of life chooses integrity versus despair and disgust, where integrity is defined as follows:

> It is the acceptance of one's own and only life cycle and of the people who have become significant to it as something that *had to be* and that, by necessity, permitted of no substitutions. (1959, p. 98; emphasis added)

Unqualified acceptance of one's total life history, and by implication of the external forces that have helped shape that life, is too heavy a price to pay for the comfort of integration.

In summary, then, Erikson's theory, like others previously discussed, was an attempt to look at the individual–society dialectic in its sociohistorical context. The conflict in that dialectic is historical, rather than absolute, and is based upon a mismatch between social structure and psychological structure. Resolving that conflict can involve altering the individual (capitulation to social reality), or altering that social reality (critique of social structure). Erikson is ambiguous as to which solution is most desirable.

Finally, we can note that Erikson's model of individual development paralleling sociohistorical development was a closed rather than an open one. For Erikson, the structure of ego development was universal (his stage theory), although the psychological content of the various stage solutions was cultural and historical. Thus in a real sense, Erikson's attempt to historicize psychoanalysis fell somewhat short of the mark. The structure of his developmental theory was as absolute and rigid as was Freud's, although that rigidity is not as apparent.

IV. Conclusion: Rethinking the Individual–Society Dialectic

So far I have attempted to reveal some of the twists, turns, and developments that the idea of the individual–society dialectic has taken through history. The transformations and modifications of that idea were a response to certain sociopolitical events, and to the conceptual limitations of both classical Marxism and psychoanalysis for accommodating the new social reality. A key idea to emerge in those later refinements of the individual–society dialectic was that individual development repeated the basic themes and stages of the species' history. The implications of that idea for greater theoretical understanding of the individual–society dialectic have yet to be explored. Let us end by hinting toward the beginning of such an exposition.

There has been a lot of loose talk within the life-span developmental literature about the individual–society dialectic as involving mutual or reciprocal determination—each influences and is influenced by the other. Yet such a conception provides no rationale for understanding the concrete direction of both individual and historical development. That is to say, does the hypothesized mutual determination between the individual and society simply involve a random tradeoff of pushes and pulls? Or is it more than that? I believe that the way toward making sense out of the individual–society dialectic, and to inject some intellectual power into that idea as well, is to frame it in the context of ontogeny recapitulating phylogeny.

Freud's basic insight that individual psychological development repeats the themes and crises (in symbolic form) of the social history of the species is, I believe, an extremely valuable one. We can historicize the model and provide for the changing nature of psychological development by noting that the history of the species continually unfolds. Freud's paradigm (as well as Erikson's) dealt with a history that was prematurely cut off and dead, rather than one that was open and alive. If we view development as fundamentally a teleological process, where the telos is ever more progress or advancement in terms of such things as reason, the mastery of nature, and the humanization of social relations, then we can begin to make sense out of both historical and individual development in terms of each other. One can read history through ontogeny, since ontogeny contains, in code form, the history of the species. Indeed, that is what Piaget has done insofar as he has attempted to identify the historical counterpart of his individual developmental stages (preoperational, concrete operations, formal operations) in such areas as the history of mathematical thinking. The important point, then, is that ontogeny and history are structurally part of the same developmental process. They belong to a single developmental totality. Each informs and is informed by the other. The structure of each is contained within the other.

While the above model is appealing to the extent that it suggests various kinds of developmental structure analyses, it is necessary to push onward if one is to grasp the truly dialectical aspect of the individual–society dialectic. Consider the following final thought.

The social development of a property of an entire culture (e.g., reason, freedom from the primary ties, formal operations, individuation, self-consciousness) is dependent upon, or conditional upon, like development at the individual level (i.e., reason, freedom from the primary ties, formal operations, individuation, or self-consciousness, respectively). Similarily, individual development and the achievement of some more advanced state is conditional upon the existence of a like developmental state at the social level. In other words, one cannot have reached a given developmental level at the social level before that same developmental level has been reached by the majority of individual menbers of that society, and vice versa.

The individual–society dialectic is not such because of such matters as reciprocal causation, simultaneous antecedent–consequent status, and the like. The latter attributes do not make the individual–society relationship distinctly dialectical (though they might in fact be valid attributes of that relationship). What makes the individual–society dialectic a dialectic is that a given level of development on one side of the relationship is dependent upon, while at the same time is a condition for, that same level of development on the other side of the relationship. This fundamental paradox needs further analysis. Hopefully the reader may be one who can push this idea further than I have been able to do.

V. Summary

The individual–society relationship is a key idea for a life-span developmental psychology. An adequate conception of the changing or developing individual, in a changing or evolving society, must involve dialectical thinking. Part of such dialectical thinking is a historical appreciation of the origin of this idea and of the reality that nurtured it into being. The recent history of the idea of an individual–society dialectic is rooted in two theoretical failures—failures in the sense of not adequately accommodating the then current sociopolitical reality as experienced. One of these was the failure of orthodox Marxism to account for the lack of social revolution in the West just after World War I. Neo-Marxist thinkers at this time began to feel the need for a social-developmental theory to explain the psychologizing, or internalization, of various social forces of irrationality, repression, and alienation. Orthodox Marxism had not anticipated the latter phenomenon and thus provided no social-developmental theory to explain it.

The second theoretical failure that contributed to a concern for the individual–society dialectic was that of psychoanalysis. Neo-Freudians attempted to supplement Freud's exclusively biological theory of personality and personality development with sociocultural factors. Erikson was probably the most successful revisionist in offering a psychosocial theory of development that partially accommodated the historical dimension in the individual–society relationship. The post-Freudian era was one that supported such ideas as cross-cultural differences, historical change, the resurgence of a belief in the possibility of progress, and, in general, a renewed optimism that was now founded upon the notion of controlling and manipulating the human environment. These new social experiences could not be integrated within orthodox psychoanalysis.

Finally, a brief reconceptualization of the idea of an individual–society dialectic was undertaken—more as a challenge to the reader than as a closed and finished model. There it was proposed that the idea of an individual–society dialectic contains a contradiction—a puzzle that cannot be solved through clever mental gymnastics. It is this contradiction that makes the individual–society relationship a dialectical one.

Acknowledgment

This chapter was written under the partial support of Social Sciences and Humanities Research Council of Canada Grant 410-78-0006-X1.

References

Buss, A. R. Marx and the Russian Revolution: Betrayal of the promise. *Humanist in Canada*, 1977, **10** (4), 2–5.

de Mause, L. The evolution of childhood. In G. M. Kren & L. H. Rappoport (Eds.), *Varieties of psychohistory*. New York: Springer, 1976.

Erikson, E. H. *Identity and the life cycle*. New York: International University Press, 1959.

Erikson, E. H. *Childhood and society*. New York: Norton, 1963. (First published in 1950.)

Fromm, E. *Escape from freedom*. New York: Holt, Rinehart & Winston, 1941.

Gillis, J. R. *Youth and history*. New York: Academic Press, 1974.

Gramsci, A. *The modern prince*. New York: International Publishers, 1957.

Horkheimer, M. *Critical theory*. New York: Herder & Herder, 1972.

Jacoby, R. *Social amnesia*. Boston: Beacon, 1975.

Korsch, K. *Marxism and philosophy*. New York: Modern Reader, 1970.

Lukacs, G. *History and class consciousness*. Cambridge, Mass.: MIT Press, 1971.

McLellan, D. *The thought of Karl Marx*. London: Macmillan, 1971.

Reich, W. *The mass psychology of fascism*. New York: Farrar, Straus & Giroux, 1970.

Riegel, K. F. Influence of economic and political ideologies on the development of developmental psychology. *Psychological Bulletin*, 1972, **78**, 129–141. (a)

Riegel, K. F. Time and change in the development of the individual and society. In H. W.

Reese (Ed.), *Advances in child development and behavior* (Vol. 7). New York: Academic Press, 1972. (b)

Riegel, K. F. Developmental psychology: Some historical and ethical considerations. In J. R. Nesselroade & H. W. Reese (Eds.), *Life-span developmental psychology: Methodological issues.* New York: Academic Press, 1973.

Riegel, K. F. Adult life crises: Toward a dialectic theory of development. In N. Datan & L. H. Ginsberg (Eds.), *Life-span developmental psychology: Normative life crises.* New York: Academic Press, 1975.

Rychlak, J. F. *A philosophy of science for personality theory.* Boston: Houghton Mifflin, 1968.

Roazen, P. *Erik H. Erikson.* New York: Free Press, 1976.

Author Index

Numbers in italics refer to the pages on which the complete references are listed.

Subject Index

A

Adolescents
  depression hardship and personality of, 127
  family relations and, 128–133
  pre-depression relationship of parents and, 133–140
  intercohort comparisons of, 140–145
  interindividual differences in, 299–301
Adulthood, *see also* Later adulthood
  consistency versus change in, 288
  age roles and behavioral change, 290–297
  cognitive functioning, 289–290
  personality, 290
  intelligence in, study of, 69–73
  primary mental abilities in
    generational versus ontogenetic differences in, 84–92
    health and environmental factors related to, 97–101
    magnitude of differences across ages and cohorts, 93–97
    description of variables, 73–75
    sequential studies of, 78–84
    research in, 101–110
Age differences, in primary mental abilities, 76–78
Age roles, behavioral change and, 290–297

C

Change, *see also* Historical change
  consistency versus
    in adulthood, 288–297
    in early life, 285–288
  ontogenetic and biocultural, 269–271
Childhood, interindividual differences in, 297–299
Cognitive development, in adulthood, 107–110

Cognitive functioning, adult changes in, 289–290
  training research in, 45–53
Competence, performance versus, in problem solving, 57–59

D

Demographic factors, primary mental abilities and, 97–98
Development, *see also* Family development; Life-span development
  concept of, 262–268
  metamodels of, 3–4
    mechanism, 4
    organicism, 5
  nature of
    assumptions concerning human nature and personality development, 171–172
    definitions of, 172–175
    scope of, 268–269
Dialectics, history and, *see* History

E

Early life, consistency versus change in, 285–288
Education, depression hardship and, 145–149
Environmental factors, primary mental abilities and, 99–101
Erikson, Erik, 324–329

F

Family development
  implications of age stratification and life-course literatures for, 189–190, 196–197
  cohort differences and, 191–196